The Rise and Fall of Patrice Lumumba

THOMAS KANZA

The Rise and Fall of Patrice Lumumba

Conflict in the Congo

THOMAS KANZA

G.K.HALL&CO.

70 LINCOLN STREET, BOSTON, MASS.

SCHENKMAN PUBLISHING COMPANY, INC.
Cambridge, Mass.

This is an expanded version of the *Conflict in the Congo* first
published by Penguin Books in 1972. It contains three new chapters:
Nasser and Lumumba, Who was Responsible for the Murder and *From
Lumumba to Mobutu.*

First published by
Penguin Books Ltd, Harmondsworth,
Middlesex, England in 1972.

Library of Congress Cataloging in Publication Data

Kanza, Thomas R
   The rise and fall of Patrice Lumumba.

   Expanded version of Conflict in the Congo published
in 1972 by Penguin Books, Harmondsworth.
   Includes index.
   1. Lumumba, Patrice, 1925 - 1961. 2. Zaire — Politics
and government — 1908 - 1960. 3. Zaire — History — Civil
War, 1960 - 1965. 4. Prime ministers — Zaire — Biography.
I. Title.
DT658.2.L85K36 1979   967.5′103′0924   79-10426
ISBN 0-8161-9015-1

This publication is printed on permanent/durable acid-free paper
MANUFACTURED IN THE UNITED STATES OF AMERICA

Contents

Introduction

In a sense history has been very kind to me. As a representative of my country and its people, I have had the privilege of getting to know a great number of the major figures from other countries who had any part to play in Congolese affairs before and since independence: figures whose actions and decisions have influenced the course of events not only in the Congo itself but all over Africa.

I undoubtedly gained the admiration and esteem and indeed the friendship of some, the disappointment and dislike of others. But all of us, whether actors or observers, leaders or led, will need the detachment that only comes with time, before we can realize fully how disappointing and discouraging were those first years of official 'independence' in Africa.

In a European context there would be nothing special about my life. But as a Congolese and an African I can only be grateful for being so privileged. Privileged, yes; but lonely too.

In 1952, aged nineteen, I left the Congo to go to university in Belgium. At twenty-five I began an international life as an official of the EEC in Brussels. At twenty-seven, by then a minister in Lumumba's government and my country's ambassador to the UN, I spent two years in New York. At twenty-nine I was in New Delhi as the Congo's special envoy, before spending two years in charge of the Congo's first embassy in London. At thirty-one I returned to Africa, where I travelled extensively, visiting the capitals of all the independent African countries as the minister for foreign affairs in the revolutionary Congolese government in opposition to Moïse Tshombe and his white mercenaries. At thirty-three I decided to withdraw from political life.

Thus, between twenty-three and thirty-three I was involved

in the kind of active public life which most people do not experience until they reach forty or fifty, and many never experience at all. I visited most of the countries of Europe and Africa, the USA, and several South American and Asian countries.

In writing this, my first book, about my Congolese and African experiences, my intention is to share with the coming generation in the Congo some of what I learnt through my involvement in the political life of Patrice Emery Lumumba.

I write without bitterness to anyone – white or black. My name is one that has been linked with many different Congolese and foreign persons, groups and political régimes. And in due course public opinion tends to associate a name with what it has stood for, even if only for a short while.

When I talk of Kasavubu, Lumumba, Tshombe, Mobutu, Bomboko, Kalonji, Nendaka, Munongo, Gizenga, Mulele, Kamitatu, Gbenye, Soumialot, Kashamura, and the rest, I shall be talking of them as I knew them – not as they may be known to the world through the mass media. All these, and many other names both in the Congo and elsewhere, will occur in relation to contacts which I had personally with the people concerned. To pronounce final judgement on the influence they exercised, or the part they played in the tragi-comedy of the Congo, will be for the next generation.

Much that is incredible, extravagant, ambiguous and unjust has been written about Patrice Lumumba. What has been said of him includes pretty well everything that can be said of a truly outstanding man, or a genius. Such men always have exceptional qualities, which make them famous and set them apart, but they also have failings in proportion to these, which may destroy them, and will certainly make them hated, even sometimes by their closest friends.

Patrice Lumumba was without question an extraordinary man, and perhaps also a genius. But he was first and foremost an African nationalist, a young politician who managed to work effectively in the blazing inferno of the Congo. This was how I knew him: as a man, a politician, a leader and a friend.

It is not humanly possible to write the whole story of Lumumba and the Congo. Even in a hundred years' time there will still remain unsolved questions, especially relating to the period just before independence and the tragedy which followed it. Any interpretation of the drama must remain incomplete: for it is in general impossible to know either *exactly* what happened or *exactly* what was said. The dead cannot speak, and there are many secrets buried forever with them; just as they have had attributed to them much that they did not in fact ever think or intend.

Lumumba was a man born to lead others. Very early on in his political life he evinced the characteristics of such a man. He was to be subjected to grave injustices, but he always fought against them, either by charm or by force.

In 1960 the Congo was led by Lumumba. This was almost an accident, for the colonial administration could have rigged the elections in order to produce a very different result. His rise to power was quite incredible and his enjoyment of it all too short – but meteoric, exciting, historic, unique.

Brought to power legally in June 1960, Lumumba was, by January 1961, simply the dust of history – having known glory, received honours, savoured the joy of being his people's chosen leader, and also known humiliations, calumnies, and a veritable way of the cross to his Golgotha in Katanga.

Let it be said from the start that I have no family or tribal ties with Lumumba. The first time I heard of him was in 1954, and I first met and talked with him in Belgium in 1955. But I realized even then that this man, whom we looked on as a simple provincial *évolué*, would sooner or later become a historical figure.

Lenin was the father of Soviet revolutionary strategy. For the Chinese the equivalent position is held by Mao Tse-tung. In the Egyptian revolution Nasser was both the brains and the moving power. His personality embodied a movement far wider than the borders of his own country. Despite the (often unjustified) attacks upon him both as a leader and a man, Kwame Nkrumah remains one of the fathers of the revolution in Africa south of the Sahara; for, whatever else may be said, Ghana's independence was certainly the starting point for all black Africa's independence

9

movements. The influence of Fidel Castro is quite out of proportion to the size of his little country: he symbolizes liberation for the peoples of central and south America.

Despite his brief political career and tragic death – or perhaps because of them – Lumumba entered history through the front door: he became both a flag and a symbol. He lived as a free man, and an independent thinker. Everything he wrote, said and did was the product of someone who knew his vocation to be that of a liberator, and he represents for the Congo what Castro does for Cuba, Nasser for Egypt, Nkrumah for Ghana, Mao Tse-tung for China, and Lenin for Russia.

His death completely altered the course of events in the Congo. It divided the whole country and its people. Indeed Lumumba was argued about in Africa, in Europe, in America and in Asia. He made himself hated and feared; but he also made himself loved. And this was more for what he said as a statesman than for what he achieved as a politician. As a statesman he spoke a great deal – too much in fact – both in public and in private. As a politician he worked fantastically hard; he manoeuvred cleverly to attain his objectives, and achieve the first stage in his ambitions. His enemies became afraid – indeed panic-stricken. His friends misinterpreted what he said: they exaggerated his words, giving what he said and did the meaning they wished rather than the meaning he intended.

Now, dead, Lumumba is more of a force than he was in his lifetime. History has already shown us that Lumumba is a time-bomb.

1 The Congolese in Belgium

In 1956 Belgium had only some thirty students – both priests and laymen – from the Congo, Rwanda and Burundi.

Prince Joseph Baranyanka-Biroli was the first to arrive at Louvain university from Burundi, and I was the first man from the Congo. In 1956 I was in my fourth and final year of reading psychology, and Paul Mushiete was in his third year in the same subject. He and I saw each other daily, since we lived in the same house in the rue de Tirlemont. Mario Cardoso lived a few blocks away. During the previous three years I had stayed with the Lecointre family in Chaussée de Wavre, at near-by Heverlée; Aimé Lecointre had acquired an interest in the Congo and Africa in general from Professor Guy Malengreau, one of the sponsors of the Congolese university of Lovanium and director of the Institut Africain at Louvain. Marcel Lihau was staying with the Theunissen family (Theunissen was the former director of Léopoldville radio), who had adopted a young Congolese girl, Adèle Blackson, then attending secondary school at Louvain. Two Congolese medical auxiliaries, Martin Ngwete and Jean Nkondi, were on a training course at Louvain. André Boboliko, Paul Muhona, César Kakemba, Albert Atundu, Theodore Tshiswata, Fidèle Nkundabangenzi and others were attending a course for trade union leaders at the École Sociale at Heverlée. The Jesuits Henri Matota and Joseph Manvwela, and one Dominican priest, all from the Congo, were students at Louvain university. Princes Louis Rwagasore and Joseph Biroli were staying at the Home Colonial.[1] Bruno Monteiro, an African from Dahomey, who was studying medicine, often joined our group. Justin Bomboko and André Mandi from the Congo and Isidore Rwubusisi from

1. A hostel for Belgian students whose families lived in the Congo, but in which no Congolese had stayed up to that time.

Rwanda were students at the Université libre in Brussels. All of these were later to play a significant rôle in Congolese politics or academic circles.

The colonial administration had never encouraged Congolese to visit Belgium; and until the Brussels World Fair in 1958 very few of us had been given an opportunity to meet Belgians in their own country. We were a privileged few, and throughout our stay had to consider ourselves ambassadors of our country, knowing that a great many Belgians would base their opinion of the Congolese people on the impression we made. A small number of older Congolese had preceded us and settled in Belgium. They worked either in the Musée Colonial at Tervueren, near Brussels, or as messengers wearing decorative uniforms in the large colonial enterprises. A few Congolese seamen occasionally came ashore in the port of Antwerp; and those of them who chose to settle sought refuge in a sailors' home there, run by missionary priests.

The Socialist–Liberal coalition government which came to power in Belgium after the 1954 elections, however, began encouraging Congolese to visit the metropolis and initiated a system of annual study tours for *évolués*,[2] notables and traditional chiefs selected by the administration according to some mysterious criteria. The selected groups included natives from each of the six provinces in the colony, with representatives from particular groups such as teachers, administration employees, social workers and traders.

Following the government's example the trade unions, Catholic and Protestant missions, and the large colonial enterprises competed with one another to send faithful servants on short visits to Belgium, in order that these might see at first hand the economic and social developments there. This enabled some ten or more Congolese, who later played an active rôle in politics, business or the trade unions, to visit Belgium and see some of the sights of Europe.

Most Congolese students in Belgium were detribalized and strongly favoured national unity. Belgians regarded them as being

2. Initially, a term used to describe educated Congolese who adopted European dress and customs; but which Belgians came to use as a word for any Congolese whom they deemed to have ideas above his station.

12

radical and even extremist, and found it easier to talk patronizingly to notables and other visitors as these seemed more moderate, in their speech at any rate, than the students.

Among the Congolese students themselves, distinctions were already being drawn. Congolese visitors believed that students at the Catholic university of Louvain were protégés of the colonial administration and the missionaries. They were always on their guard in the discussions they had with us on the struggle against colonialism, and felt more at ease with students at Brussels university.

At first sight Brussels university does appear more liberal and progressive than Louvain. It has an easy-going atmosphere and its students enjoy greater freedom of action, speech and social activity. Most of the teaching staff are anti-clerical, and missionaries are distinctly unpopular. The students, none of them priests, openly declare their Marxist or liberal sympathies. Louvain, on the other hand, is a small, mainly Flemish provincial town; and at the university the emphasis is on the humanities, Christianity and scientific subjects. It is one of the oldest Catholic European universities; priests and nuns are numerous among its students; and it is virtually impossible for a non-Catholic to hold a teaching post there – whereas all the teaching staff at Brussels are laymen, and many secularists.

The Catholic religion is not imposed on students at Louvain university; and it is not even a prerequisite for admission. Nevertheless, lectures there are delivered in terms which would scarcely recommend themselves to agnostics or anti-Catholics.

Another category of Congolese students emerged in the Congo itself, when Lovanium university was opened at Léopoldville in October 1954. Set up by the Catholic university of Louvain, of which it is a subsidiary, it produced its first graduates in 1958. Although its academic standards are undoubtedly equal to those of a great many European universities, it cannot provide that broadening of knowledge and outlook which is not learned from books and is acquired only from contact with people of other countries and cultures. Nevertheless, the first Lovanium graduates were undoubtedly very valuable material. They included Albert Ndele, Joseph Mbeka, Marcel Tshibamba, André Ilunga,

Pierre Lebeughe, Henri Takizala and Auguste Mabika-Kalanda.

Most of the lecturers at Lovanium were young compared with their counterparts in Europe. Although eminently qualified, they had been only assistant-lecturers before coming to the Congo; and this sudden promotion gave them a certain sense of superiority, which made them treat the students with undue severity. Certainly this was the view of some distinguished former teachers of mine when I saw them on their return from Lovanium, after they had spent some time there as visiting professors. On the other hand the same professors expressed amazement at the results achieved at Lovanium, considering the climatic conditions and study facilities there. Indeed, these results were often superior to those achieved by many students under far better conditions in Europe.

The Rev. Luc Gillon was the rector of Lovanium university. He was under forty at the time of his appointment, and was made a Monsignor soon afterwards. His family is one with connections outside Belgium and its university circles, and has included some very distinguished scientists. He is himself a physicist of repute, and is also an outstanding planner and administrator. I first met him at Louvain in 1952 when he was a reader at the university and chaplain of the Home Colonial. Having little knowledge of the Congo he approached the task of developing the first Congolese university with an entirely open mind.

Abbé Gillon's appointment put an end to bitter disagreements between Louvain university on the one hand and the colonial administration and the Jesuits on the other. At first the Centre Universitaire Lovanium, as it was then called, was run by Jesuit Fathers, on the basis of an agreement between their order and Louvain university. I had met its first rector, the Jesuit Father Jacques Schurmans, in the Congo and later in Belgium, and had great respect for him. But the Jesuit presence at the university had created a number of delicate and complex problems. A monopoly of education in the Congo had been granted to missionary orders according to an agreement based on the division of the colony into spheres of influence for each order. There were over ten such orders operating in the Congo, and these were further divided into Flemish- and French-speaking missions. That Catholic university

14

education in the Congo should be entrusted to Jesuits alone was wholly unacceptable to the other missionary orders. Father Schurmans's replacement by Abbé Gillon, a secular priest, was therefore welcomed by the missionaries and academics in Belgium.

My arrival at Louvain in 1952 followed a great many bitter discussions and required some high-level intervention. Father de la Kethulle de Ryhove, founder and principal of the Institut St Joseph, where I had done my schooling, brought much pressure to bear on the colonial administration. With the strong recommendations from Professor Guy Malengreau and the written approval of Monsignor van Waeyenbergh, rector of Louvain university, my admission to the Institut de Psychologie et de Pédagogie was finally secured.

To keep me in funds an arrangement was worked out between my family (my father and two elder brothers) and Romain Nélissen, a Belgian businessman in the Congo and the owner of *L'Avenir*, a local paper, who was also a friend of Father de la Kethulle de Ryhove.

As the first Congolese university student in Europe I had to face many difficulties and prejudices which future generations of students will never know. On the other hand I was granted various privileges, and was able to form friendships in circumstances which they are not likely to experience.

Someone had to be the first to knock on the door and to open it to others. I have never regretted being the guinea-pig in an experiment which most Belgian colonialists regarded as dangerous if not impossible for any Congolese at the time.

2 Paul-Henri Spaak and the Congo

While at Louvain in 1956 I was invited to the Ministry of Foreign Affairs to meet Paul-Henri Spaak, the Belgian minister for foreign affairs. R. Rothschild, a career diplomat who was the minister's principal private secretary, had arranged the interview, through the kind offices of Joseph Biroli-Baranyanka.

Spaak was on the point of visiting the Congo to attend the fiftieth anniversary celebration of the Union Minière du Haut-Katanga, the major mining enterprise in the Congo; and since he had very little knowledge of the colony he had wisely decided to talk to some Congolese in Brussels before his departure.

Jean Bolikango, who was then teaching in Léopoldville, had arrived in Brussels a few days previously; and as he was better acquainted than I was with the situation in the Congo, I suggested to Rothschild that the minister might learn a great deal from him, so Bolikango duly accompanied me to the interview, which took place at five o'clock one afternoon in the reception room of the Ministry in the rue de la Loi. Bolikango and I were delighted to have this opportunity of a frank talk with the world-famous statesman.

In view of Spaak's prestige in Europe and his brilliant performance in national politics we were appalled by what seemed to us his ignorance of the Belgian Congo and its native population. He was shocked and affronted to learn that some of his countrymen in the Congo were not behaving as well as they should. For him the Congo was a gem in the Belgian showcase, and an instrument in the country's foreign policy and military alliances. He appeared never to have given a thought to the welfare of the Congolese people, but to share the belief held by many of his countrymen that Belgium had accomplished a miracle on the African continent and had nothing to learn from anyone.

He had of course met some Africans, mainly intellectuals and diplomats, in his travels around world capitals, but knew hardly any Congolese. And yet, as foreign minister of Belgium, it was he who represented the Congo's interests in world affairs.

The talks with him and his private secretary were satisfactory, however, to the degree that agreement was reached on two points. First, Bolikango was to be responsible for part of the minister's programme in Léopoldville. He was to arrange for *évolués* and other Congolese to meet the minister; and these were to be allowed to express their views quite openly. Instructions to that effect were to be sent to the governor-general through the Colonial Ministry. Secondly, Spaak was to receive me again on his return to Brussels.

The minister left for Katanga a few days later, to join the group of high-ranking persons on the free trip provided by that state within a state, the Union Minière.

Bolikango and I then went to Paris, where my friend Dr Louis-Paul Aujoulat, the French deputy for Cameroun, arranged meetings with African deputies at the Palais Bourbon, the French Chamber of Deputies. Bolikango thus had the unexpected opportunity to meet Félix Houphouet-Boigny, Léopold Senghor, Sedar Modibo-Keita, Hilaire Aubame, Ahmadou Ahidjo and others. He returned to Brussels and thence to the Congo, delighted with his visit to Europe and in particular with having made what promised to be such fruitful contact with the Belgian foreign minister.

Alas, the well-laid plans went awry. Spaak was suddenly recalled to Belgium because of a mining disaster and never got to Léopoldville where Bolikango awaited him. All he saw of the Congo were the achievements of the Union Minière and the rich plantations of Belgian settlers in Kivu province. As a spokesman for the Congo on other matters he would presumably continue to rely on reports of the colonial minister, the big industrial enterprises, and the self-avowed experts in the Belgian socialist party.

3 The Homecoming – October 1956

In 1952, when I first left the Congo, progressive Europeans and Congolese in Léopoldville all seemed to be living in fear – the fear of meeting outsiders or visitors who might give them cause to think, and aggravate their frustration at learning to endure the bitterness of the colonial situation that they could do nothing to change.

There had been few such people then; but now, four years later, when I returned home, they were increasing both in numbers and unobtrusive activity. Their activity and dynamism may have appeared somewhat greater than they were because everyone around them displayed such incredible resignation and inertia in face of the situation. Progressive Europeans formed a class apart within white society; and as for blacks suspected of being trouble-makers, their privilege was to have their dossiers in the Sûreté grow inexorably thicker.

Outwardly nothing had changed. The white man and his laws still ruled, and the Congolese continued to bear their lot stoically. But many Europeans were already afraid. Most Congolese hoped for a non-violent change that would give them independence; and some of them found the courage to express such thoughts, in speeches or in the press. Although these men were more inclined towards reform than to revolution, the colonial administration regarded them as little better than criminals.

After my stay in Europe, where most thinking people had become aware of the need for change, I was more of a revolutionary than a reformist. It seemed to me that my countrymen on the spot were unduly preoccupied with day-to-day problems, and had no more than a worm's-eye view of the sinister implications of colonialism. But I couldn't altogether detach myself from them, and largely conformed with the prevailing mood.

Actualités Africaines, a weekly supplement to *L'Avenir*, invited me to give a lecture to a group of Congolese and Europeans on 11 November 1956. I was bold enough to entitle it 'The Congo, a country of two *évolués*'. I concluded the lecture with a quotation from an article written by a Belgian: 'revolutionaries may not all be embittered men, but every embittered man advances the revolution.'

Making such a statement in public was at that time playing with fire, and it did indeed cause alarm in colonial circles, where it was regarded as a deliberate act of subversion. But many of my countrymen were overjoyed, for I had openly declared what they had long believed in their hearts.

On my return home I had been engaged by the Pères de Scheut missionaries and was in charge of the three-year teacher-training programme of secondary education at the Institut Saint Joseph. I also taught at the Institut Supérieur des Sciences Sociales and at the Institut d'Education Physique. My appointments themselves had raised no problems; but my receipt of a salary equal to that of Europeans in similar positions, a matter in which I was setting a precedent, was the subject of a controversy between the colonial administration and the Congolese, which was extensively discussed in the local press.

The issue was discreetly resolved, by presenting me with a *carte d'immatriculation*. At that time only holders of this card were allowed to move towards integration in European circles without fear of insult; in short, they were a new class of Congolese allowed to live as the Europeans did. They were permitted to buy alcohol, sit in European restaurants and nightclubs, see uncensored films at European cinemas, and send their children to European schools.

The *carte de mérite civique* was available, on application, to any Congolese who considered himself sufficiently detribalized. Those who wanted additional privileges, among them to come within the provisions of Belgian civil jurisdiction, applied for the *carte d'immatriculation*. The Magistrature would then order a thorough investigation of the applicant's private life and personal habits. Very few fulfilled the requirements. In 1956 only 120 Congolese, from a population of thirteen million, were holders of the *carte d'immatriculation*; and fewer than 900 held the *carte de mérite civique*.

The colonial administration well knew that though I would never apply for the card, my being without one would not deter me from moving freely in European society. To avoid possible unpleasant incidents the governor-general instructed the district commissioner of Léopoldville to issue a card to me as a special courtesy. There was also some talk of my being allocated an apartment in the European district but I declined the privilege, preferring to live at my parents' house in the district then referred to as the *Cité indigène*, or native quarter.

4 Congo

On 30 March 1957 my brother Philippe, Mathieu Ekatou and I launched *Congo*, a weekly publication and the first independent newspaper to be published entirely by Congolese. Though we were joint owner-editors, I myself decided to stay in the background.

The colonial authorities firmly believed that the venture had been master-minded by European advisers and was financed from communist sources. A senior official of the colonial Sûreté was assigned to keep a close watch on our movements and on what went on in the paper's offices. In fact, as the administration discovered to their disappointment, there were no European conspirators, and no communist funds behind the scheme. It had been made possible by an arrangement with Romain Nélissen, who leased to us the printing press of *L'Avenir*, which he owned. Jean-Jacques Kandé, one of the most competent Congolese journalists of that time, was editor-in-chief. My brother Philippe, Ekatou and Kandé had previously been on the staff of *Actualités Africaines*, then edited by a young Belgian journalist, Pierre Davister. Contributors to *Actualités Africaines* included Joseph Mobutu, André Ngenge, Oscar Moningi and Adrien Mokese.

My teaching assignments prevented me from taking an active part in the paper; but my brother and Ekatou kept me constantly informed, and we all met together whenever an important decision was required.

The governor-general, Léon Pétillon, nevertheless believed that I was solely responsible for the tone and contents of *Congo*, and I was frequently summoned to Kalina, the part of Léopoldville where the administrative offices were situated, to be unjustly reprimanded. Pétillon refused to see either my brother or Ekatou. 'Without your help, Philippe Kanza and Mathieu

Ekatou couldn't possibly be so well informed and so arrogant,' he said. This view was typical of the administration's failure to recognize the level of maturity and knowledge which many Congolese had attained.

Clearly, *Congo* and the obstinate governor-general were on a collision course. We felt sure that our temerity would not long be tolerated and that sooner or later some excuse would be found to suppress our paper. It lasted, in fact, for exactly five months. It was seized on 24 August 1957 and banned from publication five days later. No reason was given; nor was there any need to give any. The law simply did not provide for any freedom of the press in the Congo.

5 Return to Europe

Shortly after the seizure of *Congo* I resigned my three teaching posts and prepared to return to Europe for further university education, this time in Paris.

The vice-governor-general, Lafontaine, a former colonial attorney-general, tried to prevent my departure with the help of his friend and subordinate Sergoygne, the acting attorney-general. But the governor-general intervened and I was allowed to leave: though on condition that I gave up the idea of Paris, and studied in Belgium.

On 11 November 1957, exactly one year after giving my lecture 'The Congo, a country of two *évolués*', I parted from my family and my country, once again to go abroad for an indefinite period.

I was now better able to understand the real situation in the Congo, and knew that colonialism could not last for very much longer. *Ata Ndele*, as they say in Lingala – 'sooner or later' – those Congolese who now demanded reform would be demanding revolution.

Before I left I received an unexpected and encouraging message from a Belgian Jesuit bishop whom I knew only by name: Joseph Guffens. He had once been a missionary in the Kwango-Kwilu province; but he had been relieved of his post because his ideas were altogether too liberal for a bishop, and recalled to Belgium.

I was on friendly terms with Father Cardol, the Jesuit Rector of the school for European children at Léopoldville, and it was he who gave me the message – a truly providential one. It seemed that Bishop Guffens, who was aware of my unhappy press venture, was determined to help me to the fullest extent permitted by the discipline of his order, although he had never met me. He wanted me to get in touch with him in Brussels as soon as possible.

I travelled to Paris on 11 November and from there telephoned

Bishop Guffens to express my appreciation and announce my arrival. Meeting him was a turning-point in my life. He was able to appreciate my bitterness and dejection. He suggested that I register at the Collège d'Europe, a post-graduate institution at Bruges, rather than at Brussels University or again at Louvain. I readily agreed, whereupon he began pulling strings – the powerful ones of a Catholic bishop in Belgium – in order to arrange my admission and obtain a student's grant for me.

Within four weeks I was once again a student. Courses at the Collège d'Europe (a post-graduate school) last only one academic year, so that by the summer of 1958 I had obtained a diploma in advanced international studies and submitted a thesis on 'The conflict of classes in a colonial and multi-racial society'.

I was very happy at Bruges. Frequent conversations with Guffens and with Henri Brugmans, the rector of the College, did much to rehabilitate me after my unfortunate experiences in the Congo. Guffens restored my self-confidence. He taught me a lesson which applied to both of us: that it is not always advisable to be in the right too soon. He painstakingly explained to me the complex and interrelated rôles played by the Church, big business and the colonial administration in the Congo. My conversations with him and our many discussions at the college enabled me to see the Congo as part of a vast structure which was more complex than I had realized.

Brugmans, who is of Dutch origin, is a passionate believer in international cooperation and has devoted most of his life to the concept of European unity: gaining acceptance for it, first among the general public and then at the institutional level.

Events on the African continent had not yet reached their subsequent gale force, but I was beginning to look beyond national aspirations and to see the need for African unity. I came to realize that regional and ultimately international cooperation depend to a large extent on scientific and technological progress, the development of ideas and an increase of unity among peoples.

Living in common with some forty students of various nationalities also taught me a lot about human nature. The Collège d'Europe 'decolonized' my thinking. I was now involved in European problems, which up to then had baffled me or simply failed to excite any interest. I now knew that these problems would arise at some time or other in Africa, perhaps in a more violent form, and that effective means for solving them would not be easy to find.

6 General de Gaulle

I was at the Collège d'Europe when General de Gaulle was returned to power in May 1958. The dramatic event was closely followed by everyone at the college, and I was no exception. I felt that it would herald a new era, which would either advance or delay European unity. It was also bound to have a considerable impact on the African continent, where de Gaulle was sometimes referred to as 'the man from Brazzaville', because the French Congo had rallied to his cause during the war. Decolonization would surely, I thought, become part of his official policy.

The General and Félix Eboué, the former governor of the French Congo,[1] had for many years enjoyed a popularity among the Congolese of Léopoldville such as no Belgian public figure had ever achieved. I was only ten years old when Eboué and his family had made an official visit to Léopoldville; but I vividly remember everyone's pride at seeing a black man treated with such respect by those very same Belgians who wanted us to believe that we could never attain the same level of development ourselves. And we believed that de Gaulle had come to teach the Belgians a lesson in the political freedom which they deliberately withheld from us.

After the Second World War de Gaulle had given to the people of the French colonies in Africa the pride of citizenship in a great nation – a privilege the Belgians persistently refused to extend to us. The people of Brazzaville, only just across the river from Léopoldville, had for some time considered themselves superior to us because they were citizens of *L'Union française*, whereas we were mere colonial subjects, with no right even to Belgian nationality. The Belgians referred to us as *indigènes* or *autochtones* (natives) and believed that this would always be an adequate

1. Félix Eboué was of West Indian (French Guyanan) origin.

description, except for those of us who were sufficiently european-
ized to earn the title of *évolués*.

'The defenders of Belgian paternalism considered that the
Congolese were better fed and had better housing and medical
care than all other Africans. Every village of any size had a dis-
pensary, a school and a church.'[2]

What more could anyone want ? Such was the Belgian attitude
in May 1958.

2. Verbeek, Roger: *Le Congo en Question*, Presse Africaine, Paris, 1965, p. 36.

7   Introducing Lumumba

I first met Lumumba in 1955 when he visited Belgium for the first time with a group of other *évolués*, on a government-sponsored tour. He was then regarded as a 'provincial *évolué*' since he came from Stanleyville, the capital of Orientale province, and people in Léopoldville tended to regard people from the provinces as slightly less '*évolué*' than themselves. He spent a month touring Belgium; and he more than other members of his group showed a keen interest in all he saw and easily made social contacts.

In Stanleyville Lumumba was much in the public eye and was chairman or secretary of no fewer than seven associations. In particular he was chairman there of the Association des Évolués. The colonial authorities regarded him as somewhat dangerous and kept a close watch on him. His European friends tended to be those considered to be liberals, and he himself was an active member of the Cercle libéral de Stanleyville. Indeed most of his Belgian friends were anti-communist: some of them had influential connections in the Belgian Socialist–Liberal coalition government which had come to power after the 1954 elections; and they had commended him to the attention of Auguste Buisseret, the minister for the Congo. Buisseret himself, a Liberal, had very progressive ideas, at least compared with his predecessors in the post. In the colonial sphere this meant that he fought against the influence of Catholicism and its missionaries. In 1954 he had appointed a special group of experts to examine education in the Congo and was determined to implement its recommendations, some of which had severely criticized mission performance. His principal private secretary, Breuls de Tiecken, a former senior official in the colonial administration, was equally anti-clerical and highly unpopular with the missionaries in the Congo.

Lumumba, who was tall, slim, always well-dressed and sociable, made an instant impression. He appeared to me as the living symbol of mankind's struggle for emancipation. His powers of observation and oratory impressed all his friends and aroused fear in his critics. He had an astonishing ability to cope with difficult situations and was often able to impress people whom one would have thought better informed and educated than himself. His thirst for knowledge was insatiable; he was a voracious reader and to a large extent self-taught. In this he was helped by European friends who obtained books and periodicals for him from abroad. He realized at an early stage, during his visit to Belgium especially, that he would have to overcome a great many obstacles if he was to achieve his ambitions. The next time I saw him was in the Congo in 1957, and he was in a very unhappy situation.

After Lumumba's return from Belgium Buisseret had decided to appoint him to his staff at the Ministry, which Lumumba would have been the first Congolese to join. But the appointment never materialized, probably because it displeased the authorities at Stanleyville. Lumumba, then employed at the Post Office, was arrested, charged with embezzling Post Office funds and sentenced to two years' imprisonment by a district court. The Belgian and colonial press seized upon the incident as a way of discrediting him. Many colonial Belgians were very eager to prevent his rise to popularity and power: prevention, they thought, was better than cure. He appealed, and was transferred to Léopoldville; and it was there in 1957 that I saw him for the second time, in the prisoner's dock at the Tribunal de première instance. He was neatly dressed and had a dignified look about him.

The avocat général, de Warseghere, addressed the court for the prosecution. In his statement he extolled Belgian colonization for all the benefits of civilization that it had brought to the Congo. He denigrated the black race and pointed to Lumumba as a typical example of those Congolese who nursed the illusion of being equal to the white man and capable of taking his place in certain fields.

Maître Jabon, a member of the Cercle libéral in Léopoldville, was Counsel for the Defence, but Lumumba seemed not to want his services. After Maître Jabon had made a brief statement on the prisoner's behalf, Lumumba spoke in his own defence at some length. I was covering the trial for *Congo* and felt sorely tempted to write that I saw in Lumumba a man who would sooner or later become a great Congolese leader; but this would undoubtedly have exasperated the colonial authorities and would not have helped him. I was seated next to A. J. Hubert, the assistant district commissioner, who had told the clerk of the court that he was prepared to speak in favour of Lumumba. Hubert was witty, jovial and fond of the good life. He was also a Liberal and therefore anti-clerical.

Meanwhile, in Belgium, supporters of colonial reform and members of the Liberal party in particular had started a campaign for Lumumba's release. Catholics and socialists also brought some pressure to bear. Lumumba's best defenders, as it turned out, were in Belgium and not in the Congo. There were few communists among them; all were simply Belgians with a sense of justice. In addition, some Belgian journalists and politicians found the affair an ideal opportunity for discrediting the colonial administration. The minister for the Congo himself was understandably resolved to secure the release of a Congolese whom he had selected to join his staff. From Brussels came the order that the trial must on no account be allowed to develop into a political or racial scandal. The court reduced Lumumba's two-year sentence to six months, which he had already served. He was, however, kept in custody a few more weeks to allow the dust to settle.

After his release, he thought it unwise to return to Stanleyville, where people who had failed to discredit him might seek revenge in some other form. Belgian friends in Léopoldville found him a job as sales manager of the Bracongo Brewery, better known by the brand name of its beer, 'Polar'. Its competitor was the Bralima Brewery, also known by the name of its beer, 'Primus'. I and the other editors of *Congo* knew the local managers of both breweries and benefited from their commercial rivalry through the advertising that they both placed with us. I had also, while in Brussels, met some of the management in the head offices of both breweries.

Lumumba was a great success in this job, for he was a born leader and had amazing organizational ability. I believe that he would have emerged as a leader whatever his occupation, even if he had started as a house-servant or taxi-driver; but the Polar job provided him with a long-sought chance to practise the various skills required of a politician, although he had to proceed with caution, since the colonized had no political rights at the time.

Lumumba's job was to be Polar's public relations man: to get the beer well publicized among the mass of the Congolese, and win over some of the market from its rival, which had become so popular that for months Polar's sales had been going down. Primus was waging a clever publicity campaign against Polar, and Lumumba had to contend with this, as well as simply working to promote his own product.

It was a good testing ground: if Lumumba were to do well in this new job, he would have benefited from an experience of great value to his political future. His own career was not dissimilar to that of Polar beer: only a few days before, he had been denigrated, described as a dangerous element, as dishonest, unscrupulous, and worse still perhaps, as a foreigner – an immigrant to Léopoldville in search of popularity and influence there. The methods he used in winning a market for Polar were the same as those he used in achieving his own political victory.

Each of us, it is said, has the defects of his abilities; but most of the Western press in general, and the Belgian in particular, saw only defects in this man whom they so detested. Very few papers made any attempt to indicate the abilities of one whose life was an unending struggle, and ultimately a tragedy. Lumumba was cast as a demagogue; and in effect did have, to the highest degree, the abilities needed to carry a crowd along with him: he could adapt what he said to suit his audience, and knew very well when, where and how to use his personality. Few professional journalists, either Congolese or European, realized the almost superhuman efforts and methodical planning that Lumumba used as a business-man to get Polar back on its feet. In quite a short time Lumumba, the foreigner from Stanleyville who could barely speak Lingala, became one of the most popular and sought-after figures in the capital.

He wanted continually to re-model, re-think and re-organize; in other words, he wanted to revolutionize, which would often call for new and sometimes quite unpredictable methods. As part of his job, he spent half his time in the cafés, bars and dance halls of the African quarter, and he would fall into conversation with customers having drinks other than the one he was promoting. With the help of his Congolese friends he had got to know Léopoldville well within only a few days. Of his opponents he was not afraid – which was both a strength and a weakness. His European employers introduced him around in colonial circles and he became a focus of interest for various business circles in Léopoldville.

In order to get at the men, Lumumba started first on the women. This strategy yielded rich results; for once a woman was persuaded, it was not hard for her to get her husband to change to Polar as well. Lumumba made himself well liked among the women in the city by regularly giving them free vouchers for beer. Through them, and especially by dealing with certain women's groups, Lumumba managed to make Polar the town's favourite drink. A demagogue, yes, and not too scrupulous, perhaps; but above all, Lumumba had a nose for business, a flair: he could win new sympathies without forgetting to make careful use of older friendships as well.

1. (*Overleaf*) King Baudouin I arriving at Léopoldville on 29 June 1960 for Independence Day celebrations. With him are (l.-r.) Joseph Ileo, president of the Congolese Senate, Joseph Kasavubu, President, and Patrice Lumumba, Prime Minister.

Belga

2. (*overleaf*) Commander of the UN forces in the Congo, Swedish General Carl von Horn and assistant Secretary-General of the UN, Ralph Bunche, followed by General Alexander of Ghana Armed Forces arrive with the author for a meeting with Patrice Lumumba, July 1960.

Pressens Bild AB

3. (*above*) Patrice Lumumba arriving at the UN Headquarters in New York, July 1960. With him are (l.-r.) André Mandi, the author, C. Weregemere, and the UN chief of protocol.

Leo Rosenthal

4. (*opposite*) Patrice Lumumba and Dag Hammarskjöld at their first meeting at the UN Headquarters, July 1960. On the right is Joseph Okito, vice-president of the Congolese Senate.

Leo Rosenthal

5. (*opposite*) The author, Dag Hammarskjöld, André Mandi, and André Matubanzulu at the UN Headquarters, July 1960.

United Nations

6. Patrice Lumumba with Andrew Cordier.

Leo Rosenthal

7. The author at a UN Security Council session on the Congo crisis, July 1960.

Leo Rosenthal

8 Lumumba as the Third Man

When Lumumba founded the *Mouvement National Congolais* (MNC) in Léopoldville in 1958, he was conscious of introducing new ideas in a community which would not be receptive to them. The Congolese in Léopoldville had long been dominated by the Bakongo tribe, which was fiercely proud of its traditions and language and wanted the country to be divided into tribal regions. The *Abako (Association pour la Sauvegarde de la Culture et des Intérêts des Bakongo)* was formed in 1950, originally to safeguard these traditions. Joseph Kasavubu assumed its leadership in 1954, and it became a political movement in 1956. My father, Daniel Kanza, became its vice-president.

In 1958 foreign observers in Léopoldville assessed the Congolese political climate mainly by the policies and statements emanating from the central committee of *Abako*. The movement had launched a platform for immediate, total and unconditional independence, because its conception of the nation was limited to the area of the Lower Congo; and the very presence of the Belgians in this was considered an affront to the dignity and traditions of the tribe. Kasavubu and many of his followers dreamed, indeed, of reuniting the Bakongo areas in the French and Belgian Congo and in Angola, to restore the ancient Kongo Kingdom. This idea, though archaic, nevertheless acted as a catalyst in precipitating the political consciousness of other groups and tribes in the Congo.

Jean Bolikango of the Bangala tribe, then teaching in a Catholic mission school, had strong tribal convictions as well, and he and Kasavubu became implacable enemies. A few years previously they had been close friends, both serving on the central committee of the alumni association, the *Adapes (Association des Anciens Elèves des Pères de Scheut)*, Bolikango as president, and Kasavubu

33

as secretary-general. But by 1958 the articulate Congolese population seemed divided into pro-Kasavubu and pro-Bolikango groups with the divisions entrenched in tribal rivalries. The administration at times openly supported Bolikango and his followers, regarding them as more tractable since they had not demanded immediate independence. On the other hand, it accused the Bakongo of separatist and communist tendencies. Externally, Bolikango was popular with the Belgians and the Church, whereas Kasavubu and his extremist central committee appealed to the leaders of the more militant African states, although few of these knew Kasavubu himself except by name. Some *Abako* members had, in fact, sent their children secretly via Brazzaville to be educated in eastern European countries.

Lumumba himself was the embodiment of that different, dynamic nationalism which was gradually spreading over the whole country. He demanded that the Congo be given its freedom as a national entity, as indeed should all peoples of Africa. There was a generation gap in both the Bakongo and Bangala tribes. The younger men in both abandoned tribalist ideals in favour of a national and pan-African view, and in this they were closer in their aspirations to Lumumba – the third man – than to either Bolikango or Kasavubu.

The popularity of Lumumba caused the rise of a fourth man, Albert Kalonji, seemingly loyal to national and nationalist ideals, but passionately devoted to his tribe, and making use of its animosities to other tribes to carve out his own political ambitions, as the leader of the Baluba in Kasai. For some months he was a declared supporter of Lumumba, and then suddenly left him to rejoin the band of moderate pro-western and pro-clerical politicians. At that point Kasai province split into two: with one tribe, the Lulua, favouring Lumumba, and the other, the Baluba, favouring Kalonji.

In Katanga the Union Minière and some rich and powerful Belgian settlers took under their wings the two major political parties of the province – Sendwe's BALUBAKAT and Tshombe's CONAKAT. The presidents of both parties were supported at the time by local financial interests. But Tshombe differed from Sendwe (whose popularity depended on the Baluba of northern

Katanga) in being highly corruptible. Elected president of the
CONAKAT, he could only build up his political influence with the
help of Belgian and foreign business interests. Having squandered
the family fortune he was at the mercy of these new creditors, who
knew how to keep him permanently in their debt. Sendwe on the
other hand, a practising Protestant and fine family man, led the
BALUBAKAT in the old paternalist ways of the traditional chiefs.

The first MNC committee, set up in 1958, gave a fair indication
of the movement's national aims and its rejection of tribalist
ideas. Most of those elected to it had already expressed their
nationalist views publicly or in written articles. Albert Nkuli was
assistant secretary general, and Joseph Mbungu the treasurer.
Members included Joseph Ileo, Joseph Ngalula, Alphonse
Nguvulu, Gabriel Makoso, Maximilien Liongo, Arthur Pinzi and
Albert Kalonji.

A split then occurred in the movement. And this, in July 1959,
was in my view a typical example of the way in which the Belgian
Trinity (the Church, Big Business and the Administration) tried
to influence the course of Congolese politics, with the Church in
this instance operating through Belgian professors at Lovanium
University. On 16 July the Central Committee published a
letter from Albert Kalonji, president of the Kasai provincial
branch, which he was increasingly turning into a Baluba tribal
association contrary to the unitarian aims of the movement. He
demanded that the leadership of the movement should be
changed, as it was increasingly becoming a one-man show. The
Central Committee decided, without consulting Lumumba, to
remove him as president and establish a collective leadership
instead. It was a move largely conducted by men who enjoyed the
protection of the Church: Joseph Ileo, Joseph Ngalula, Martin
Ngwete, Albert Kalonji, Joseph Mbungu, Gabriel Makoso and
Abbé Joseph Malula (who later became Archbishop of Léopoldville, and then a Cardinal). Cyrille Adoula, who professed to be a
socialist, kept his distance from this group, although connected
with it.

Lumumba reacted with all the energy of a rejected prophet. In a
series of statements to the press and in written articles, he un-

35

veiled the machinations behind the plot to unseat him. In time, the movement was divided into two separate wings known as the MNC–Lumumba and the MNC–Kalonji.

I often saw Lumumba in those days, rushing about to deliver articles or conduct interviews. He appeared to me to be fighting a very lonely battle. When all went well, he would be surrounded by friends and fulsome admirers, some of them false and even actively conspiring against him; but at the first sign of trouble he would find himself alone and fighting single-handed. He had long ago learned that 'God helps those who help themselves', and he looked upon every friend as a potential enemy.

Working methodically, making the utmost capital out of his political intuition and his gift of persuasion, he formed the plan of drawing together the genuinely nationalist parties and thus putting an end to coalition-groups working under the guidance of the Belgians or the clergy. Political divorces began to take place everywhere: the tribalist parties were beaten to the draw by Lumumba. In Léopoldville province the PSA returned to its nationalist ideal. In Kasai the Lulua tribe declared itself for Lumumba; in Katanga the Union Minière found Sendwe and the northern Baluba less cooperative; in Kivu, the European settlers found that they could no longer lay down the law, since the CEREA of Kashamura and his friends was now fiercely nationalist; and Orientale province was in no doubt, since it had sworn fidelity to its prophet Lumumba. In Equateur province the very inter-tribal antagonisms, together with the multiplicity of tribes, combined to favour national aspirations and stifle tribal passions; Antoine-Roger Bolamba, Mathieu Ekatou and other 'Lumumbists' were active there. Maurice Mpolo assured Lumumba of the support of the area round Lake Léopold II.

Given these certainties, these alliances he could trust, Lumumba could go forward against all opposition as the champion of national unity and territorial integrity. Forced to support their tribalist claims, his political opponents were revealed as possible separatists and secessionists.

Lumumba envisaged a dynamic unity, which would not prevent considerable decentralization in administration and even in economic affairs; his tribalist opponents envisaged vague forms of federation or confederation, with provincial secession bringing autonomy or semi-autonomy. Their ill-defined terms were based on tribal aspirations which could ultimately lead only to a complete fragmentation of the Congo. The hopes and wishes of certain Belgians were set on the Congo's finally becoming some six different states, nominally independent, with the periodic bonus of major or minor tribal conflict ending in fratricide. This could only be the ultimate goal of all the efforts to effect division being systematically undertaken by the colonial administration – efforts made in obedience to the concerted orders of the real rulers of the Belgian colony. In the Congo the crown and the cross of Christ have always gone forward hand in hand with money.

Having brought about a split in the M N C the anti-Lumumbist forces went on to create a new movement, bringing together in a kind of federation a number of political groups whose bases were tribalist but whose declared sympathies were for Christianity, federalism, and anti-communism.

Steps were taken at once to get together such political leaders as Kasavubu, Ileo, Bomboko, Kalonji, Tshombe, and Munongo. And at last a new grouping emerged: the *Parti solidaire africain,* or P S A. Made up of an amalgam of tribes, the group had determined to combat the political influence of the Bakongo in Léopoldville province, and led by Jesuit-trained Congolese it was not one that could be readily entrapped by the larger alliance of Belgian financial circles and Catholic missionaries. Antoine Gizenga was president of the P S A and Pierre Mulele and Cleophas Kamitatu respectively its secretary general and provincial president.

The influence both of colonial financial interests and the Catholic church made itself felt within the various Congolese party committees themselves. Mgr Kimbondo of Kisantu and Abbé Jean Loya both acted as important advisers in Kasavubu's *Abako.* Mgr Joseph Malula of Léopoldville was in constant contact with the leaders of Kalonji's M N C. The Jesuits gave unobtrusive advice to Gizenga's P S A; while the leaders of Tshombe's CONAKAT were being openly directed by the Union Minière in Katanga – which also kept a close watch on Sendwe's BALUBAKAT with its relatively progressive views.

37

Lumumba kept watch on the activities and movements of tribalists and nationalists more carefully than ever, clericals and anti-clericals alike. He did not take long in rallying the PSA, whose leaders were well aware of the power wielded by the Church in affairs of state.

9 Political Awakening in the Congo: 1958–9

When the Brussels World Fair opened its doors in April 1958 the city was in its Sunday best. It was inundated with tourists as never before; it was a meeting-place for the whole world. Travel agents from every continent were selling plane, train and boat tickets to passengers for Belgium. Americans mingled with Russians without being frightened of catching communism from them, and the communist tourists were astounded by the opulence of capitalism. South African racialists chatted as man to man with African and American Negroes, apparently unconcerned that they were doing something they would never think of doing in their own country. The Vatican gave freely of its bells and carillons to everyone. The Arab states reminded westerners and easterners alike that it was their lands which had been the cradle ⸃of civilization. And amidst all this, Belgium was offering the world its proverbial hospitality, and showing off the Congo with all its wealth and its happy colonized people: some in clerical dress, some in suits or military uniform, others in African costume.

During the World Fair Belgium lifted its colonial barriers to let through a few hundred of its colonized, and so gave them a chance to become mentally decolonized through contact with the outside world. The number of Congolese who visited Europe for the World Fair was about a hundred times as great as the total number which had come to Belgium during the whole eighty years of Belgian colonialization, and the influence that this experience had would be hard to overestimate. In Brussels the Congolese visitors discovered that a human being is the same wherever he is, and that no one people or race has the monopoly of any virtue or vice. They came in contact with men and women of all nations and races. And even the Congolese clergy felt that

the moment had come to make a serious effort to draw the attention of the administration to the irrepressible tide of history.

In the lecture he gave in May 1958 on 'The Black Soul in
Contact with the West' to the Congress of Christian Humanism
(held in Brussels as part of the World Fair), Abbé Joseph Malula
reminded the Belgians that

throughout the world a reasonable desire for freedom is held to be
legitimate. Why should the Congo be an exception? The Congolese
have no wish for fanatical nationalism; the nationalism they want is a
result of irritations, injustices, unsatisfied claims, and a resentment that
has built up over the years and is now reaching a crisis.

Mgr Joseph Guffens was in charge of a large and magnificent
Congolese pavilion, and asked me to join my fellow-countrymen
in taking an active part in making this a success. Regretfully I had
to refuse, as I was about to leave for the United States.

In October the World Fair closed, but the Congolese centre
remained open. This centre was nicknamed 'La Belgique
Coloniale' or 'Colonial Belgium'; it was situated in Tervueren
Park, slightly outside the centre of the city. The Congolese who
had been invited to the Fair fell into two groups: those who went
home afterwards; and those who stayed in Europe. The former
group assessed the value of their visit; it included quite a number
of those who were to be politically influential in the future, and
who during their seven months' trip had met people from almost
every country on earth. Which of these contacts should be maintained? What conclusions had they drawn; and what resolutions
seemed to suggest themselves for the future?

Their return home could not fail to have an effect either on their
own fellow-countrymen, or on the European settlers. For the
first time they had spoken on an equal footing with Europeans,
Americans, Russians, Chinese, Arabs, Japanese, Indians. For
them, Belgium was to be from then on just one country like any
other, with good and bad aspects, and its people just like any other
people in the world, with their own particular history, their joys
and sorrows, their problems and prejudices.

As opposed to the group which returned home, another group

of Congolese sought refuge in various Belgian towns, or in the many educational establishments in Brussels. Both groups had achieved a mental decolonization during the Fair which would make it hard for them ever to accept the colonial yoke again.

10 The United States

As a boy I had peculiar ideas about Americans in general and black Americans in particular. During the war some American servicemen had been stationed near Ndolo Airport at Léopoldville, and to me and my contemporaries these men behaved as if they owned the world. They certainly commanded the respect of our Belgian masters who, for one thing, did nothing to stop coloured Americans from entering European restaurants and nightclubs from which the Congolese were debarred at the time. This made a tremendous impression on us and we used to think that Americans, especially black Americans, would some day help us in our struggle for freedom. Some of us used to worship black American celebrities, and photographs of black American sports champions or show-business personalities are to this day kept as precious mementoes in some Congolese households. Every time an American Negro scored a victory in some sport or another, we regarded this not as an American citizen's achievement, but as one black man's personal victory over the whites. Despite our expectations, however, the American servicemen eventually left the Congo without having changed the status of the Congolese in any appreciable way.

As a student in Europe I began to look at black Americans in a more objective way. I went to see several black sports aces and musicians perform; but found it difficult to form an opinion because these somewhat commercialized personalities differ little from their white counterparts in the entertainment industry. I was in touch with some coloured American students in Europe and there was always instant sympathy between us, but most of them came from northern states and had suffered rather less from racial discrimination. Whenever a racial incident in America was reported in the European press, these students would say that such reports were probably exaggerated and in any case confined to a specific locality. On such occasions, too, the European press would seize the opportunity to point out that the USA would do well to concentrate on its own Negro problem instead of interfering in the affairs of 'their' blacks in Africa. Discussions between Europeans and Americans on this subject always seem to me a dialogue between two deaf people. Each, though aware of the injustice suffered by the black man in his own territory, proclaims that the other's problem is far more urgent and crucial.

The black American outside the USA often seems to me to have a split personality. If a celebrity, he enjoys the respect and courtesies to which this entitles him, and is aware that he would not enjoy similar treatment in the USA. On the other hand he rarely loses sight of the advantages of his US citizenship. Once, when the subject of American Negroes came up in an inter-racial gathering, one of them declared, 'I'm not a Negro, I'm an American.' Some time before I myself went to the USA, I had come to regard black Americans simply as Americans with similar physical traits to ours, but who might, as often as not, be as patriotic as any white American. I also thought that we shared these traits not only because of our common ancestry but also because the economic and social conditions of black Americans were probably similar to ours.

Many Africans at the time looked to the USA as the leading power in the Western world, able to dictate its policies to all the countries within this bloc. Because the United Nations had sponsored many improvements in the condition of colonial subjects, and many Africans believed the United Nations to be predominantly an instrument of American policy, admission to the United Nations was always given top priority by newly independent African states.

An opportunity to visit the United States was therefore the dream of many Congolese, and I was no exception. I longed to acquire first-hand knowledge of the most powerful capitalist nation, to find out how people of my own race lived in it and to see at first hand the functioning of the UN.

For me the dream became a reality in 1958, when I was invited to participate in the International Seminar at Harvard University

43

summer school, which was then organized by Professor Henry A. Kissinger. Some forty-five people from more than fifteen countries were taking part, among them members of parliament, journalists, trade unionists and teachers. I was the youngest of them all. We spent a few weeks at Harvard, followed by a tour of various American cities. The discussions and everything we saw proved to be an invaluable experience, and I shall record some of my impressions here.

Outside America the term 'Negro' means a black man. American racism, however, classifies as 'Negro' or 'coloured' anyone with the faintest trace of Negro blood. In my part of Africa we talk of whites, mulattos and blacks, but in America the human race is divided into 'whites' and 'Negroes'. This creates problems for the unwary, because many who might be suspected of being coloured are white, while other people who might be taken for white are classified as coloured. I was to learn that black Americans have evolved various strata of society among themselves according to the shading of colour.

Another surprise for me was the distinction made between 'American' and 'non-American' Negroes, and I soon discovered how this distinction affected me. I spoke little English at the time and, since I could not be mistaken for 'one of ours', was no doubt spared many an indignity.

One thing I didn't like about many American Negroes was their fondness for hair-straighteners and other cosmetic aids to disguise the physical traits of the black race, as though they were ashamed to belong to it.

An American friend invited me to spend a weekend at his apartment in Harlem. Kwame Nkrumah was expected on a visit to New York a few days later, and everyone was very excited; people who were on speaking terms with him or had known him all their lives were somehow cropping up everywhere!

One evening my friend took me to a smart restaurant in Harlem popular with the local intelligentsia. The décor was lush, the food expensive and the customers, most of them in liberal professions, looked very distinguished indeed. Everybody seemed to know everybody else, and my friend introduced me around. All were Negroes, though in another country I might have taken some of them for white. The manager's wife told me that white people were welcome to come, but felt uncomfortable in the place and rarely did so.

I asked my friend whether the sporting and musical celebrities I had heard about in the Congo ever ate in his restaurant, and gathered from his reply that there was not 'one' Harlem but many different communities there.

The conversation turned to Nkrumah's expected visit.

'There's a black man who's shaking up Africa,' someone said.

'We taught him how to do it,' said another; 'it was his eight years over here that taught him what to do.'

I agreed that this might be so.

'When are you Congolese going to have your Ghana?'

This was said by a portly and comfortably seated customer who was obviously an armchair revolutionary. I just smiled and concentrated on my chicken dinner.

A man of around forty who talked incessantly joined our table. I was told that he was the editor of a New York magazine for Negro readers. He announced in a loud voice that he was putting out a special issue on 'that great Negro', Nkrumah. I was introduced to him.

'My, am I glad to meet you!' he exclaimed, and then asked, with some sarcasm, 'What hole did you get through out of your Congolese paradise to fetch up in lousy Harlem?' I replied that my escape had been through the usual hole, for study abroad. Everybody laughed at this, and the magazine editor pulled up a chair and sat beside me. He said he wanted to do a feature on the Congo which would include an interview with me.

'Very little is known about that paradise of yours over here,' he said. 'Why don't more of you come abroad? How many doctors, lawyers and engineers in your country are black? Are any newspapers published by Congolese, and if so why don't they stir the people up? How long do you think the Congo will remain in Belgian hands? Is there a national movement? Do the Congolese ever wonder what the Belgians do with Congolese copper, gold, diamonds and uranium? How many Africans have shares in the Union Minière? How do a black man's earnings compare with a white's?'

I gave him some evasive replies. I was by then becoming the centre of attraction; a small crowd had gathered around our table, and a number of them expressed their views on the Congo and colonialism. I then decided to ask a few questions myself.

'What do you all think of Governor Faubus of Arkansas?'

'Oh, he's just a desperate character who's living in the past,' someone answered.

'He goes on barking because he's lost his bite,' the magazine editor said.

I asked whether anyone present had thought of returning to the South to help the oppressed coloured there.

'We help them more by staying in the North,' he said.

I then asked whether many Negro intellectuals made mixed marriages in the US. He replied that most American marriages were mixed anyway, since the country was a melting pot for all races, and a lot of so-called whites had Negro blood.

'We have so many nice black girls to choose from,' he said. 'I can't think why some guys ask for trouble by marrying white girls.'

I asked a young man, a dentist and a bachelor, whether he'd think of marrying an African girl.

'Sure, but she'd have to become American,' he replied.

'Even if she were the heiress to some throne in Africa?' someone asked.

'In that case I might consider giving up my American citizenship to be an African prince consort,' the dentist said.

Among American Negroes in more modest circumstances I found a touching sincerity, and their pride in belonging to the black race reminded me of tribal elders in Africa. With those who did not pretend to be anything but what they were, especially those who had suffered from racial persecution, there was instant understanding and similarity of ideas which at times made me feel as though I were talking to Africans of the older generation. In fact many of these people prefer to call themselves 'Afro-Americans' rather than just Americans.

Together with other members of my group I left New York for Washington where we stayed in an international students' hostel, two or three to a room. I learned that racial discrimination was still strong in Washington and that even non-American Negroes such as West Indian, Latin-American and African diplomats had a hard time finding a place to live.

The programme on the first day was a visit to Howard University where the great majority of students were Negroes. First, however, I made a courtesy call at the Belgian embassy, having been urged to do so by the seminar organizers. I was very courteously received by Baron Dhanis, secretary for Congolese affairs. Some of the earliest Belgian colonizers in the Congo were called Dhanis, and I presumed that he belonged to the same family. Information about the Congo was at the time obtainable only through the Belgian information service and, in Washington, from Baron Dhanis's office. Naturally this information was designed to paint a rosy picture of colonialism.

11   Europe Again

After Harvard I returned to Europe to begin my career as a staff
member of the European Economic Community in Brussels, a
post in which I was to spend some two years. I was in the Community's overseas department, whose aim was to achieve economic
integration in Europe as a step towards European political unity.
People of the various European countries all have differences in
temperament, background, traditions and outlook which Africans
often fail to appreciate. They may be prepared to defend their
common European interests when threatened from without, but
remain very different from one another. Their efforts to overcome
their cultural and traditional differences set an example which
people of other continents and the developing countries in
particular would do well to follow. As an African I observed from
a detached position the inter-office struggles for power between
various nationalities and the Community's policy with regard
to developing countries. Joseph Baranyanka-Biroli of Burundi,
Mamadou Traoré of Mauritania and I were the first Africans to
join the staff of the Community. Apedo-Amah of Togo and
Adama Cissoko of Mali joined it later in 1960.

12 December 1958 – Lumumba in Ghana

When Kwame Nkrumah convened the first All-African People's Conference in Accra on 5 December 1958 several Congolese political leaders were invited to participate, but the Belgian colonial administration hesitated to issue the necessary passports. At the last moment, however, it allowed three members of the MNC – Lumumba (its president), Gaston Diomi and Joseph Ngalula – to make the trip. Another Congolese, Jean-Pierre Dericoyard, a businessman who spoke English, accompanied them. He was ostensibly travelling for reasons of his own but was probably at the same time acting as watchdog for the administration, whose policies he approved of. Kasavubu himself never made the trip because his inoculation certificates were not in order – or so the administration declared.

The three MNC men showed astonishing solidarity, although their political ideas had begun to differ. Lumumba's were nationalist, socialist and pan-African, Diomi's were similar to those of the *Abako* and Kasavubu, and Ngalula's were wholeheartedly pro-West and pro-clerical.

Participants in the Conference knew little about politics and tribal conflicts in the Congo; they believed Kasavubu and his *Abako* to be the pre-eminent spokesmen for the Congolese people in their struggle for freedom, and therefore assumed that Lumumba was one of Kasavubu's young lieutenants. Nkrumah had never met Kasavubu, but his government had given considerable assistance, both financial and advisory, to the *Abako*. This had been done mainly through Ghanaians long resident in the Congo who had kept in touch with the Bureau of African Affairs at Accra, itself headed by a West Indian, George Padmore, and responsible only to Nkrumah. Lumumba behaved with great tact and for the sake of Congolese unity refrained from mentioning that he was Kasavubu's rival for political leadership. In a statement to the Conference he said:

The Congolese people are aware of the winds of freedom blowing over the African continent. Their long-dormant political consciousness is beginning to assert itself and will do so even more in the next few months. The people are solidly behind us in our struggle.

Lumumba met many leaders from other African countries at the Conference. He was able to have long conversations in Swahili, which he spoke fluently, with Tom Mboya of Kenya who was the chairman. Observers and agents from Eastern and Western countries were also present, and some of them made offers of various kinds to Lumumba. An American who spoke very good French offered his services as an interpreter to Lumumba, who knew no English, and the offer was accepted. Nkrumah later discovered, however, that this 'interpreter' was, in fact, a CIA agent; and Lumumba may well have told him more than was advisable. To people from Western and Eastern countries alike Lumumba vented his anti-colonialist and anti-Belgian feelings in a way he had never been able to express to his Belgian friends, however militantly anti-colonialist these had been. Diomi and Ngalula were not present at these talks, which Lumumba held in private.

All participants, and Nkrumah in particular, were plainly impressed by Lumumba's oratory, energy and faith in the pan-African ideal. He constantly stressed that because of the Congo's central position on the African continent its struggle for freedom was not the struggle of just one country but of the whole continent. None of the participants had believed that any Congolese existed who were aware of this important fact, and many of them began to wonder whether Lumumba might not be far more dynamic and nationalistic than the man whose lieutenant they supposed him to be. As a tribute to his personality, Lumumba was appointed Congolese representative on the steering committee of the Conference. And later, in the early months of 1959, he strengthened his African contacts by attending a meeting of that committee in Guinea and a seminar in Nigeria.

On their return to Léopoldville, Lumumba, Diomi and

Ngalula held delirious meetings to report on the Accra Conference. Some foreign press correspondents put the attendance at one of them at some 7,000. At a meeting on 29 December 1958, Lumumba announced a new programme for the MNC, based on the Accra resolutions. He also declared that independence was not to be regarded as a gift from Belgium but as a fundamental right of the Congolese people.

Three days later, New Year's Eve was celebrated by the colonial Belgians with their usual opulence. For the Congolese, however, it marked a turning-point. They had become aware of their status in relation to that of other peoples in Africa.

13 The January 1959 Riots

On 4 January 1959, a week after Lumumba's public meeting, Léopoldville was torn by violent riots which had the appearance of a mass uprising. Over fifty people were killed and more than 200 injured. Léopoldville had long been a powder keg, and it exploded when the central committee of the *Abako* defied some colonial officials. As a result the movement was proscribed and its leaders arrested. Lumumba was at the time working hard to strengthen his own movement – he was still sales manager for Bracongo – and no action was taken against the MNC.

I was in Brussels at the time and my brother André joined me there on the day after the riots. He had come to Belgium to pursue his studies as an accountant and was working at the Banque Lambert. He told me that all had been quiet in Léopoldville when he had left early in the afternoon of 4 January, but that *Abako* followers were in a state of agitation while awaiting the announcements which members of the central committee were to make at a public meeting. Kasavubu had crossed the river that morning to consult Abbé Fulbert Youlou – who was then prime minister of the Congo – in Brazzaville.

My father remained in Léopoldville. He was regarded as even more extremist than Kasavubu by the authorities and was in particular resented by Jean Tordeur, mayor of Léopoldville, in whose administration he worked. He had often been upbraided by Tordeur for his political activities. Employees of public bodies were not supposed to take part in any political activity at the time but my father openly ignored this regulation. In this he behaved no differently from other *évolués* who were in the public service and remained in politics. But Tordeur was especially incensed by my father's activities and determined to teach him a lesson at the first opportunity.

52

A meeting of the local branch of the *Abako* in the Kalamu district, at which members of the central committee were to speak, was due to be held in the Y M C A building there on Sunday 4 January. On 3 January Tordeur sent a letter to the local president banning the meeting, and since Kasavubu was absent the branch president called on my father as vice-president for advice. He advised the branch president to call on Tordeur at his house on Sunday morning, to explain the impossibility of telling members at so late an hour to keep away, and to warn him that there might be trouble as a result. If Tordeur remained adamant, my father said, some ten men would have to be posted at the entrance of the building to prevent members from entering it. On Sunday morning the branch president telephoned my father to say that he had not been able to see Tordeur who was not expected home before one o'clock. My father told him that there was no alternative but to post men at the entrance and, confident that all would be well, went to attend a Protestant service.[1] After this he went to visit friends in the suburb of Binza, returning late in the afternoon. He first heard about the riots while on his way back. People had been killed and wounded; shops had been looted; cars had been burnt, and some streets barricaded – all because of the ban on the *Abako* meeting. At nightfall, order had still not been restored.

At four-thirty the following morning a Belgian adjutant and three armed Congolese from the Force Publique came to arrest my father with a warrant to compel his attendance at court. He was taken to the police station in Avenue Lippers and after being searched was thrown into a cell. At seven-thirty a.m. he was brought before a Belgian examining magistrate, Dubuisson, a *Substitut* of the Procurcur du Roi. Other members of the *Abako* central committee were arrested in the course of the day. A warrant had been issued for Kasavubu's arrest but he was nowhere to be found. He had returned to Léopoldville but was in hiding. He gave himself up to the police a week later. All members of the central committee had been arrested on the charge of 'inciting racial hatred' under Article 75*b* of the Congolese penal code.

1. Although my father had brought up all his children in the Catholic religion because of the educational advantages, he was himself a staunch Protestant.

14 The *Déclaration Gouvernementale*

The entire colonial edifice had been so shaken by the January 4 riots that the Belgian government announced on 13 January 1959 its proposals for a decolonization policy. This was known as the *Déclaration Gouvernementale* and was approved in both Chambers by senators and deputies who had suddenly become alive to the Congolese problem. The *Déclaration* stated that the Congolese people would be led towards independence *graduellement et progressivement*. These words gave rise to serious misunderstandings between Belgians and Congolese, because to the latter they clearly implied that it was to be the colonizers rather than the colonized who were to set the pace.

To the Belgians, 13 January 1959 was a historic and painful day, marking their capitulation; the day on which they gave up hope of keeping the Congo indefinitely under Belgian colonial rule. For the Congolese however, few of whom knew anything about Belgian constitutional procedures, it was a day like any other.

The P S C (*Parti Social Chrétien*) Liberal coalition government, in power since the 1958 elections, and all parties in the Opposition voted in favour of the *Déclaration*. During the debate in the Lower Chamber the only Communist deputy called attention to the fact that a great many ministers, for all their declared interest in de-colonization, sat on the boards of various colonial corporations. In so saying, this deputy rendered a distinct service to those Congolese who might have considered exploiting the differences between Belgian political parties.

In Brussels the general impression was that the *Déclaration Gouvernementale* had been personally suggested and recommended by the young King of the Belgians. The large mining houses and other influential colonial companies who had hesitated formerly to accept the principle of de-colonization had to

accept the evidence. We had the impression that they were reassured by those two words *graduellement* and *progressivement*. In
fact, in a speech made on the same day, King Baudouin proclaimed: 'We are resolved to lead the Congolese people, without
fatal delays but also without precipitate haste, to independence
in prosperity and peace.' These companies were convinced that
they would be given the time necessary to adapt, without serious
loss, to the political changes which would be taking place between
Belgium and the Congo.

15 Congolese Reactions

A week or so after the *Déclaration* had been approved, Belgian information media spread the hopeful news that 'the number of Congolese who accept and agree with the *Déclaration Gouvernementale* is increasing daily.' They expected this report to be accepted without question throughout the world. But the imprisoned *Abako* leaders knew nothing of what was going on; they had not been informed of the *Déclaration*.

Lumumba declined to comment on the *Déclaration*, pending the views which these leaders might express. He realized that the *Déclaration* was largely the outcome of *Abako* activities; that its imprisoned leaders were therefore the heroes of the moment, and that it would be impolitic for him to reveal his opposition to the movement at this time. Indeed, he took up the cudgels on their behalf and became one of their most vigorous defenders. He visited Belgium and travelled all over the country; speaking at universities, giving press conferences, and being interviewed on both radio and television. He showed himself to be a brilliant tactician, and though this impressed many Belgians, it alarmed a few others, the colonially rich in particular. He preached anti-colonialism to such well-informed audiences as those at the universities of Brussels, Louvain, Liège and Antwerp, stressing that his views wholly reflected those of the imprisoned *Abako* leaders and in fact of all Congolese not in the pay of Belgians. When taxed privately about his extremist attitude he replied: 'I am only saying out loud what every Congolese thinks. You may believe what you please, but I know that sooner or later I shall be proved right.'

I saw much of Lumumba during his visits to Belgium. I arranged his meeting with the heads of the overseas department of the Common Market, where I was working. On this occasion Lumumba was able to inquire into the Common Market intentions in Africa and put forward his point of view as a politician and a nationalist. And I arranged certain meetings between Lumumba and Belgian businessmen, as well as meetings with Belgian politicians who were not necessarily progressive. I did so not only to give Lumumba the opportunity to meet these Belgians, but also to give the Belgians their first opportunity of hearing the views of a Congolese nationalist.

I respected him for defending the cause of the *Abako* leaders and admired the way that he fearlessly pitted his wits against those of more experienced and cynical people than himself. He had, however, one indubitable advantage over them: his boundless faith in the ultimate victory of the Congolese people.

I believe that there was a sincere friendship between Lumumba and myself, and I felt that he trusted me. I had proof of this when he let the Common Market officials know that he would not hesitate to call on me to join the first Congolese government, should he be fortunate enough to be its leader. His statement was afterwards confirmed, because as soon as he was requested to form the first Congolese government, a year later, he immediately telephoned me to ask me to hand in my resignation and join him in the Congo.

16 The *Abako* Leaders' Ordeal

The colonial administration knew that it could not detain the *Abako* leaders without trial indefinitely. They were, however, kept in prison for two months, during which they were brought at regular intervals before the Parquet,[1] presided over by a senior colonial magistrate, and told that they were to remain in custody 'pending investigation'. The Prosecution was conducted by Sergoyne, a *Substitut* of the Procureur du Roi, who was no friend of my family since the time when he had failed to have me arrested and prevent my return to Europe in 1957.

Abbé Youlou used his influence to engage a Paris lawyer, Maître Jacques Croquez, to act for the defendants before the Parquet. Youlou's dubious rôle in the direction of the *Abako* party was not yet apparent; but I had reason to believe that Youlou was concerned only about the fate of Kasavubu and had no intention of helping my father. This was not altogether surprising in view of my father's own attitude towards him. Some months previously, members of the *Abako* central committee and of the PSA had held a secret meeting at Youlou's residence in Brazzaville, at which my father, Kasavubu, Kamitatu and Mulele had been present. My father had walked out of the meeting, saying that he could no longer tolerate Youlou's control of *Abako* activities through his influence over Kasavubu. He vowed never to return to Brazzaville so long as Youlou was in power. My father suspected at the time that Youlou was trying to extend his

1. In the colonial judicial system at the time (it was reformed in 1958 but the reforms were not applied until 1960) the Parquet selected the level (i.e. territory, district, court or Tribunal de première instance) at which to prosecute; depending on the maximum penalties permitted by the law violated, and upon whether the sentence which could be given at that level appeared appropriate to the prosecution if conviction was obtained. (Footnote provided by the translator.)

authority to a part of the Belgian Congo, and was perhaps in this acting on orders from Paris.

After this incident I was the only member of my family to keep in touch with Youlou. I saw him several times in Brazzaville and also visited him in his luxurious Paris residence. Our relations were cordial, but I was extremely suspicious of his motives in engaging Maître Croquez.

This lawyer was not known to any member of the *Abako*. It became evident to me that Youlou's French advisers had good reasons for asking Croquez to take up the case: they wanted to acquire useful contacts, through him, in order to influence political circles in Léopoldville. That Youlou never chose to inform me of his choice led me to institute further steps. Thus I decided on a plan of my own to ensure that my father and the other *Abako* leaders besides Kasavubu should be adequately defended. I approached the minister for the Congo, Maurice van Hemelrijck; Nyssens, president of the Belgian Bar Association; and the Belgian Human Rights Committee. I was convinced that the fate of the *Abako* leaders would ultimately be decided in Belgium and not in the Congo. Pressure would, therefore, be needed both within the Congo and at an international level. Maître Nyssens, no doubt with the backing of the courageous minister, left for Léopoldville to ensure that legal formalities were properly observed. Some of the prisoners held the *carte du mérite civique* or the *carte d'immatriculation*, and the latter brought them within Belgian jurisdiction. Nyssens also undertook to ensure that the prisoners were properly treated. Kasavubu and my father were detained in a military camp, and the remaining committee members were in the Ndolo civil prison. Nyssens visited them all.

Nyssens's intervention and the engagement of Croquez aroused considerable curiosity in Belgium. The affair involved most of those who would sooner or later emerge as important spokesmen of the Congo.

The whole Kanza family rallied to help my father. My brother André, who was with me in Brussels, accompanied me in all my interviews with Nyssens. In Léopoldville, my brother Philippe

and my sister Madeleine-Sophie were very active. A rumour
arose that my father, who was in poor health, had died in prison;
and this caused such a public outcry that the authorities were
obliged to allow Philippe to visit my father and see for himself.
Madeleine-Sophie had previously called on Sergoyne at his office,
and had made a scene which had considerably shaken him.
Philippe, when visiting my father, told him about the arrangements I had made for a Belgian lawyer to defend him.

My suspicions about Croquez were later confirmed when he
became special adviser to Kasavubu while remaining in close
contact with Youlou and with Paris. Nevertheless, Croquez's
brilliant defence before the Parquet impressed the Belgian magistrates, and he acquired fame in both Belgium and the Congo.
Abako followers referred to him as their 'saviour'.

Maître Robert Goffin, secretary general of the Belgian
Human Rights Committee, agreed to act for my father. I was
informed that Youlou was gravely displeased about this. But I
arranged for a friend in Brazzaville to tell him and his advisers
that since Croquez had not been chosen by any of the *Abako*
leaders and we did not even know the names of those who had
sent him to Léopoldville, and since I had been given no assurance
that my father's interests would be properly defended, I had every
intention of seeing to this myself.

It was generally acknowledged that Belgium and the Congo
would sooner or later go their separate ways. The January riots
were a real psychological shock to the millions of Belgians at home
who had no material interests in the Congo, and caused among
them considerable heart searching.

In Léopoldville, however, many Belgians were unable to face
up to the facts. The *Abako* prisoners were shouted at by the
Belgian magistrates but talked back in no uncertain terms. In the
cité africaine of Léopoldville several Congolese were arrested
and some were killed by stray bullets from the guns of
Congolese soldiers and police firing at the orders of their white
officers.

In an interview for the paper *La Libre Belgique* I said:

The Belgians have committed one of the most serious of all errors –
an unfortunately common one among colonizers. Prison, as everyone

knows, is the waiting room where the political man sits until he receives his popular mandate. The time will inevitably come when Belgians will have to deal on an equal footing with the men who are at present in prison.

The popularity of the *Abako* leaders was indeed increasing enormously, while this period also allowed a free Lumumba to further his own cause. The *Abako* central committee had time to get used to prison life. They appeared twice before the tribunal to hear their detention being prolonged from one month to another, 'for the needs of the judicial inquiry'.

I was summoned to the minister's office two days before he was due to travel to the Congo. Van Hemelrijck was showing great boldness at the time. He was no doubt inspired by and sought to emulate the decolonization policies adopted in France by de Gaulle's government. I told him that if the *Abako* leaders were not released at an early date, I would have grave doubts about the future of Belgian-Congolese relations. He thought about this for a moment and then said: 'Before I get back from the Congo you will get a pleasant surprise.'

He was as good as his word. At five a.m. on 13 March, three *Abako* leaders were removed from their prisons and flown to Belgium in a military aircraft, while their colleagues were discreetly returned to their homes. The governor-general, Henri Cornélis, and his staff breathed freely again, believing their reputations to be unharmed by the affair. My brother Philippe phoned me the news soon after the plane took off. A colonial official had called on him the previous day to tell him that all prisoners were to be released, but that Kasavubu, Daniel Kanza and Simon Nzeza would be leaving the country.

I was anxious to know whether the three men were technically still in custody or whether they had been released like the others. The minister's secretary, presumably on the minister's instructions, briefed me on the situation, and I immediately informed my brother André, Faustin Nzeza who was a student at Liège, and the Jesuit father Henri Matota. The official explanation was that the three leaders had been released but 'deported, with their consent' for consultations with the Belgian government. My predictions to *La Libre Belgique* were thus proved correct earlier than I had supposed: people who had once been branded as 'trouble-makers' were now to be consulted.

Van Hemelrijck clearly lacked neither imagination nor courage, but this made him very unpopular with those other influential and important Belgians who persisted in ignoring the wishes of the Congolese people.

17 Kasavubu and Lumumba in Belgium

Lumumba had campaigned actively for the leaders' release and stood out as the paramount champion of Congolese unity. He was determined to talk to them privately before they made any public statement and begged me to arrange this.

The ministry for the Congo, however, though besieged by people of all political tendencies eager to interview them, was equally determined that no one should see them for the time being and had taken strict precautions to ensure this. I was one of a very small circle in constant touch with the leaders, and the ministry consulted me about all these requests; but the three men had specifically asked me to ensure that they be left in peace for a few days. Kasavubu was in a suspicious and uncommunicative mood. My father was unwell. All three wanted to rest after the hardships of prison and take time to consider carefully the *Déclaration Gouvernementale*.

The hotel where they stayed was kept secret for three days during which only the minister's attaché, my brother André, Faustin Nzeza and I were in touch with them. In the Congo it was rumoured that the three *Abako* leaders had been deported to some unknown destination and that they were still prisoners. To allay such fears the three jointly signed a document stating that they had arrived safely, were free men in the eyes of the law, and were being well treated. They stated further that they intended to make the most of their stay in Belgium, which they were visiting for the first time, to learn about the country's institutions; and they appealed to the population of the Congo to remain calm until their return home.

During these three days I was pestered not only by journalists wanting to interview the three men, but also by Lumumba. I had to respect the leaders' wishes and turned down these requests.

Only a few persons, such as the Jesuit Father Henri Matota and two Ghanaian diplomats, special envoys of Kwame Nkrumah, were allowed to meet the leaders at their own desire, and they did so in my apartment.

After the release of the *Abako* leaders Lumumba felt compelled to alter the tone of his press conferences, in particular his references to the Belgian authorities and to van Hemelrijck, who had after all seriously endangered his own political career by releasing men who were regarded as criminals and trouble-makers in important business and political circles. Lumumba had at last realized that the Belgians would use the *Abako* leaders as a means of checking his own growing popularity and possibly of discrediting him in national and international opinion.

I saw a great deal of Lumumba, and also of Kasavubu during this time, and so had ample opportunity to form an opinion of their characters and ideas. The two men were very different both in temperament and in ideals. Lumumba gave the impression of being prepared to sacrifice his life if need be to the cause of Congolese unity. The Accra conference had made him aware of the importance of a strong and prosperous Congo and the need for national unity to override tribal and personal differences. To him power was merely a means of achieving this aim. Kasavubu, on the other hand, enjoyed the trappings of power and regarded it as an achievement in itself. He shared with Abbé Youlou, who disliked both Lumumba and my father intensely, a mystical belief in the superiority of the Bakongo tribe. He also believed that he had few serious rivals in his claim to tribal leadership. He merely tolerated the presence of my father as a means of exerting his authority over some sub-tribes of the Lower Congo who disputed his leadership. In fact, these sub-tribes were prepared to accept his leadership only if he consulted a representative from each one, such as my father was.

Kasavubu and my father were very different in personality and temperament, and I always knew that it was only a matter of time before they would clash. My father was frank and outspoken and had democratic ideas about leadership, while Kasavubu had a passion for secrecy and intrigue. Kasavubu also feared Lumumba to such an extent that he emphatically refused to meet him while in Brussels. I acted as go-between and was in a difficult position because I could not betray Kasavubu's wishes on the one hand, and knew, on the other, that under these circumstances a meeting would annoy Kasavubu and only do Lumumba an ill-service. The more Lumumba insisted on meeting Kasavubu the more adamant the latter became, and the two men eventually left Belgium without having exchanged viewpoints or eliminated misunderstandings. If they had done so, Congolese unity and a plan for decolonization by peaceful methods might well have emerged. Both were exceedingly anxious to know the other's reaction to the *Déclaration*, and used me as a communication link for this purpose.

One Saturday afternoon I met Lumumba and gave him an outline of the *Abako*'s views. He was about to give a lecture at the club called Les amis de la Présence Africaine. In my student days I had been a founder member of that club together with two Belgian friends, Jean van Lierde and Pierre Houart, and other Congolese students. Lumumba undertook to endorse the *Abako*'s views, with which he agreed, in his lecture, but said that he would wait to read the official text, due to be published two days later, before stating his position publicly.

Later on the same day the three *Abako* leaders met van Hemelrijck secretly at a religious institution in the centre of Brussels. My friend Bishop Guffens, who had the highest regard for the minister, had helped to arrange this meeting place, and I drove the three men there in my car, making all sorts of detours to dodge pursuing journalists. This was the first opportunity the minister had to meet the men whose release from detention he had arranged against the opposition of the colonial magistrature.

I was present at this meeting which, although outspoken, proceeded amicably. Although Kasavubu and his lieutenants were personally grateful to van Hemelrijck, they could not lose sight of the fact that they represented the Congolese people, and that van Hemelrijck spoke on behalf of the imperial power. The minister stressed how he had risked his career by releasing them and expressed the hope that his gamble would pay off politically. Kasavubu spoke in vague and elusive terms. My father was frank and to the point. Simon Nzeza kept silent and took notes. I joined in occasionally to clear up some misunderstanding or other. I had the impression that the Minister had the backing of the King, who attached importance to the aspect of human relations in the situation. The meeting ended on a friendly note and another was arranged, to take place after the leaders had publicly stated their reactions to the *Déclaration*.

They had gone over the *Déclaration* carefully in their comfortable quarters at the Park Hotel. I had made Lumumba's own reactions known to them and told them that he was anxious to align them with those of the *Abako*. The three leaders were now able to see that Belgium was at last prepared to grant independence, at any rate in principle. But they considered that the *Déclaration* had been made deliberately obscure, and contained too many loopholes; so they decided to outdo Belgian evasiveness in their reply. It was drafted in my apartment with the help of Father Matota, Faustin Nzeza and myself, and we spent an entire night over the task. Kasavubu on that occasion appeared to agree with the views which Lumumba had expressed, except for a few very minor details. Both of them wanted a single nation; but Kasavubu favoured a federation of several states, whereas Lumumba, deeply concerned with the international rôle the Congo ought to play, saw unity as having priority over internal reorganization.

The three leaders delivered their carefully drafted reply to the minister on 16 March. It safeguarded the minister's prestige but at the same time avoided any compromise of political capital by the Congolese. One sentence read:

> If public opinion should wish to know our views on the *Déclaration Gouvernementale* of 13 January and how it can be put into effect, we can but quote a Kikongo proverb: *Mbisi ka kitesakana mu ntinu ko* [even a skilful hunter can miss his prey in a moment of panic].

This was later misinterpreted and misconstrued by a number of European observers. The *Abako* leaders just meant that they needed time to think and to weigh the *Déclaration Gouvernementale* before committing themselves.

The statement continued:

> Since the King of the Belgians has solemnly undertaken to grant independence, and in view of the good will shown by the authors of

the *Déclaration*, we would be prepared, at some later stage, to discuss its implementation. The impact of conflicting ideas can often throw light on a subject.

This last sentence was found offensive by Belgians who did not understand how the Congolese could possibly doubt Belgium's sincerity. Parliamentarians regarded it as a deliberate insult, and most Belgian papers expressed their indignation. The authorities in Brussels and Léopoldville could ill conceal their disappointment that in spite of all their efforts and patience some Congolese should still be impervious to the counsel of their tutors. Van Hemelrijck, for his pains, was severely criticized in parliament.

18   18 March 1959

The Belgian lower chamber was packed when van Hemelrijck faced his critics after the publication of the *Abako* statement. Whatever their political colour or ideology, deputies were all agreed on the need to settle the fate of Belgium's black subjects with or without the latter's consent.

Van Hemelrijck, somewhat like a prisoner in the dock bravely conducting his own defence, spoke in Flemish, Belgium's other official language. Among other things, he said:

The release of Kasavubu, and of Daniel Kanza in particular, might have given rise to all sorts of rumours if they had remained in Léopoldville. They now agree, we have been told, to discuss the implementation of the new decolonization policy, and this has given rise to a lot of misunderstanding. I should stress that there will be no further discussions or negotiations except within the legal framework to be set up in the Congo, in consultation with all political parties and through existing institutions. The *Déclaration* makes it clear that no measures are to be taken concerning the future of the Congo without consulting Congolese political parties. We are constantly reminded that Léopoldville is not representative of the Congo as a whole. Nor is the Lower Congo for that matter. Nevertheless, recent events in Léopoldville have had highly disturbing effects on the atmosphere and on the Congo's standing abroad, on its entire economy and on the outlook of all those who live there.

Belgian financial groups endorsed the *Déclaration* but were offended by the 'insolence' of the *Abako* statement and deeply disturbed that Lumumba had endorsed it. As always, the colonial administration could be counted upon to follow their directives. On the other hand it seemed that the Crown and the Church had faith in van Hemelrijck, who kept them regularly informed of his decisions. The *Abako* statement had however raised such a storm

68

of protest that van Hemelrijck's supporters felt they could no longer back him up in the face of opposition from the financial consortia and the colonial administrators who followed the line dictated by big business. He probably guessed at this stage that his days as minister were numbered.

The *Abako* statement landed like a bomb in the Congo; to the dismay of the colonial authorities who promptly decided to send to Brussels some members of the Interfédérale, a pro-Belgian movement, in the hope that these men by spreading rumours that neither Lumumba nor the *Abako* enjoyed any prestige in the Congo would check the nationalist leaders' growing popularity. I was warned about this in a letter from a friend in Léopoldville. Without being either of the Bakongo tribe or an admirer of Lumumba, he was a respected journalist and well-informed about the intentions of the local authorities and Catholic hierarchy. He wrote:

I am sending you one of the local papers with its article on the impending departure of Interfédérale men to Brussels as guests of the Minister. What it says about reactions here and in the Upper Congo area in particular is utter nonsense. These so-called Interfédérale leaders have no following whatsoever over here, least of all in the Upper Congo. They will be leaving on 24 March. Their secret adviser, Robert van Hecke, burgomaster of the Léopoldville commune, will be leaving on the same date or the day before, supposedly on a private trip; but you may rest assured that it is to shepherd his protégés. I'd be glad if you would keep an eye on them and let me know what they get up to in Brussels and who their contacts are. You really must let it be known in Belgium that there is no truth at all in the rumour that the *Abako* statement has not been well received here, although it is being widely discussed, both favourably and unfavourably. I rely on you to warn other Congolese in Brussels.

After the parliamentary debate, I and some Belgian friends arranged for the *Abako* leaders to meet various editors-in-chief of the Belgian press, in order to enlarge on their statement. The meeting took place in the apartment of Raymond Scheyven, a P S C deputy. Ten or more Belgians were present. Scheyven, intelligent, rich, and of considerable charm, was one of the directors of the Société Générale de Belgique, known as 'la

Générale', a giant holding company with a controlling interest in the Union Minière du Haut Katanga. My father was unable to attend, because of his health, but I accompanied Kasavubu there. On this occasion, Kasavubu was unusually articulate. He put across the Congolese point of view admirably, and skilfully fielded some tricky questions put to him.

Although the storm raised by their statement had not yet died down, the three leaders carefully prepared a second statement setting out Congolese aspirations in greater detail. Later that evening they had a further (and secret) meeting with van Hemelrijck, though without reaching any further agreement.

Considering their work in Belgium to be at an end they spent a few more days visiting industrial plants and business firms, and then prepared to leave. Arrangements for their return journey were made in secret; as had been the case with their arrival. They left Brussels at the crack of dawn on 11 May by car, accompanied by the minister's attaché, for Geneva, where anonymous reservations had been made on a flight to Léopoldville. I flew to Geneva via Paris later that morning, and we all met in Sabena's Geneva office at noon. I gave the leaders the day's Belgian papers commenting on their second statement. After a quick tour of the city we had some ice-cream in a lakeside café, and then made for the airport.

As the plane taxied off and I waved good-bye for the last time from the terrace, the attaché heaved a sigh of relief. 'Mission completed, thank God,' he said.

'For you, perhaps,' I remarked. 'For them it's only just beginning.'

Four weeks later van Hemelrijck, together with members of his staff, was in Léopoldville on a tour of the Congo. I was also there on a brief visit. Five months had gone by since 13 January, the date of the *Déclaration Gouvernementale*, but Léopoldville was still very much a colonial city, with a European and a 'native' quarter. The Congolese were in a highly excited state, to be expected of a people engaged in struggle. The Belgians, on the other hand, lived in fear, tempered by attempts at forced politeness. Giant posters reminding us that 'Belgium keeps its promises' had been put up in all the main thoroughfares.

Relations between Brussels and Léopoldville had cooled considerably since the January 4 riots. The two capitals were separated by a wide abyss, and van Hemelrijck had worn himself out
acting as a bridge over it, rather than attempting to construct one.
He genuinely liked Africans and was liked by them in return. In
fact the Congolese referred to him as the 'minister of independence' at the time. Colonial Europeans, on the other hand,
loathed him, labelling him as a 'nigger-lover'.

19 The Crown, the Financial Consortia and the Administration

Three months before the elections to the communal and territorial councils were due to take place, and at a time when his presence in the colony was essential, Governor-General Henri Cornélis took two months' leave.

I wonder whether Congolese politicians were aware at the time of the memorandum which the vice-governor-general, André Schoeller, sent to van Hemelrijck on 2 September 1959. Schoeller, of little reputation in the Congo, was highly esteemed in Belgium, for he was later appointed governor of Katanga while remaining vice-governor-general of the Congo. In his memorandum Schoeller stressed the following five points:

(1) the need for a strong centralized state which could, however, have a federal structure;
(2) with regard to a constituent assembly, it was essential that once national chambers had been set up, these should organize the country's primary level institutions;
(3) apart from drafting a constitution, the national assemblies should have full legislative powers in all internal affairs except those which would come within the competence of the Belgian-Congolese community;
(4) these procedures were the only hope of creating the community. The chances of its success would be weakened considerably if the colony were divided into autonomous provinces;
(5) he was strongly opposed to a provisional government being set up before the elections. Although there was a strong demand for this in some quarters, government should be deferred till after the assemblies were constituted.[1]

1. Dumont, G. H.: *La Table Ronde Belgo-Congolaise, Editions Universitaires*, Paris, 1961.

These proposals were undoubtedly transmitted to the royal palace, as the memorandum was sent after Schoeller had consulted Count d'Aspremont-Linden, assistant private secretary to the prime minister, Gaston Eyskens. The Count was a nephew of the grand marshal of the royal court, was closely associated with the royal family, and also had connections with the Société Générale and the Union Minière. He had been designated by the prime minister to undertake a secret fact-finding mission in the Congo. Van Hemelrijck had not been informed, and he resigned on the day that the memorandum was received in Brussels.

Van Hemelrijck was replaced by two men, both of the PSC; Auguste de Schrijver for Congolese political and administrative affairs; and Raymond Scheyven for economic affairs. This division of power was a compromise imposed by the powerful groups which effectively governed the Congo. Van Hemelrijck, who had been appointed minister for the Congo and Ruanda–Burundi in November 1958, had thus been in office for less than a year. He was one of the very few Belgian politicians able to keep a balance, at any rate temporarily, between the aspirations of the Congolese people and the financial interests of those who lived off the riches of the colony. Few Congolese were aware of the reasons for his resignation. De Schrijver was promptly named the 'Minister of Autonomy'.

While in office van Hemelrijck had a fair amount of time in which to carry out his programme, but by September 1959 this was fast running out and de Schrijver was faced with a telescoped timetable. In the Congo, van Hemelrijck's resignation was regarded as a capitulation to the powerful interests which ruled the country. Once again the financial consortia had gained the upper hand, with Scheyven looking after their interests, and Cornélis, who should have resigned after the January riots, remaining governor-general.

20 Before the Round Table – December 1959

In December 1959, a decisive month in the history of the Congo, I was still working with the European Economic Community in Brussels, but was closely involved in the preparations for the Belgian–Congolese Round Table Conference.

Although I was, of course, no longer a student, the Association of Congolese Students in Belgium had elected me vice-chairman of the committee and entrusted me with its public relations. Marcel Lihau, then at Louvain University, was chairman; and Albert Ndele, second vice-chairman.

Congolese delegations were arriving at Brussels in quick succession. Most of them, especially those calling themselves nationalist, contacted me immediately. And though some were to remain steadfastly loyal to their party's policy, others allowed themselves to be influenced by ideological and financial pressures. My apartment was the scene of many private meetings between Congolese politicians and students. I recall in particular one evening when Kasavubu, Gizenga, Kalonji, Ileo, Munongo, Adoula, Lihau, Ndele, Loliki, Mpase, Bolela, Mushiete, Cardoso and Bololiko were all present.

We spent the whole of that evening exchanging views on the various problems concerning the internal situation in the Congo, as well as the present and future relations between the Congo and Belgium.

At the beginning of the evening, the atmosphere was calm and friendly; but as we gradually came to certain delicate problems, the tone of the discussion progressively grew sharper. I can remember, for instance, that a very bitter exchange of views took place between Godefroid Munongo from Katanga and Albert Kalonji from South Kasai. They were on the point of coming to blows, and we all had to intervene to calm them down.

The different new political options which had come to exist for the Congolese politicians could be sighted during the course of the discussion. The student representatives present that evening tried their best to lessen partisan tendencies by insisting on the necessity of national unity and mutual understanding between the political leaders, regardless of their region or their tribe of origin.

Territorial and communal elections were to be held in the Congo later that month. The nationalist parties – the *Abako*, the PSA, MNC–Lumumba and MNC–Kalonji – had decided to boycott them. Those parties supporting the elections were 'pro-Belgians'.

The Brussels police kept a close watch on the hotels where the Congolese stayed, taking note of all visitors, Belgian or others, who called on them. The Congolese were also quite blatantly trailed wherever they went.

When making their courtesy calls on Scheyven, the Congolese politely made it clear that they had come to Brussels for the sole purpose of discussing politics and were not concerned with financial matters for the present. Scheyven was quick to realize that obtaining political freedom was foremost in their minds. Members of the Belgian Socialist Party, then in opposition, warmly welcomed the Congolese and gave the impression that they would support the Congolese viewpoint rather than that of the Belgian government. This was especially evident in the case of Léo Collard, president of the party; Jos van Eynde, the vice-chairman; and Louis Major, the Syndicaliste deputy. King Baudouin followed the situation closely and frequently summoned Scheyven and de Schrijver and other Belgian officials concerned, in order to discover what they were thinking.

The Association of Congolese Students, which had some eighty members at the time, took this opportunity to bring itself up to date on the situation at home. It called the attention of the delegates to their grave responsibilities, urging on them the advantages of a united front.

Names of candidates for the elections were to be submitted by eight p.m. on 4 December. Scheyven and de Schrijver confronted the nationalist leaders on that day. Two minutes before the deadline Maurice Willaert, de Schrijver's principal private secretary, consulted his watch. The two ministers did likewise. And de Schrijver, staring at Kasavubu in a professorial and paternalist manner, said: 'It will soon be eight o'clock, Mr President. You would be doing the Congo a service by asking your followers to submit their lists of candidates.'

Kasavubu adjusted his spectacles, watched by all Congolese present with bated breath. Would he give in at this stage ? Calmly, in his rather high voice, Kasavubu once and for all destroyed the last illusion of the two ministers. He replied: 'If we were to accept your proposals we would be doing my people a grave disservice.' This was the start of a race against time by the Belgian government and a frantic round of meetings, lobbying and travelling.

Interviewed by the Socialist paper *Le Peuple* on 8 December Kasavubu said: 'This is all a put-up job. Political parties, none of them with any following among the Congolese people, are being manufactured by the dozen at the drop of a bank-note.' This statement caused embarrassment to the Belgian government, since it echoed the views of the socialist and communist press. It also gave credence to the view that Kasavubu and Lumumba were drawing closer together.

Belgian public opinion was gravely concerned about what the Congolese might do on their return home if their demands were not met. The Belgian government was aware of this and willing to make serious concessions. De Schrijver became physically exhausted and gave up insisting on juridical formalities. Scheyven was anxious that political questions should be settled with all possible speed, so that when it came to economic affairs he would emerge as *the* minister, with de Schrijver in the rôle of a brilliant second-in-command.

On 15 December, a few weeks before the anniversary of the January riots, de Schrijver told parliament that 'it would be in the interests of all concerned to speed up the proceedings'. His predecessor, van Hemelrijck, had fallen by the wayside in attempting to do just that in July 1959; and how de Schrijver proposed to go about it now was a highly debatable question.

The dèlegations willing to participate in the elections wanted assurances that these would be properly conducted, while the militant nationalist wing considered that elections supervised by the colonial authorities could not but be improper. The Belgian Catholic Conservatives had frequently called attention to the invalidity of electoral processes in the socialist states; yet arrangements for elections in the Congo differed little from those under totalitarian régimes, since they were directed towards the success of 'stooge' leaders acceptable to the administration. The Congolese were convinced that the results would be rigged.

Like all colonial administrations, that of the Belgians had a long record of arbitrary rule and other malpractices. Van Hemelrijck had made an honest attempt at checking such abuses, but this would have exposed the administration's dependence on the interlocking network of financial interests, and would have met stiff opposition from the right-wing lobby in the government. Inevitably, van Hemelrijck had to go.

The Congolese discovered that, unlike van Hemelrijck, de Schrijver re-asserted the old colonial hard-line, even though he belonged to the party supposedly based on Christian principles. Moreover the Belgian press, which supported the minister, undermined relations by publishing misleading information. For example, it alleged that only eight per cent of the Congolese population were in favour of the *Abako*/MNC/PSA parties, while ninety per cent backed the *Parti National du Progrès* – a party which had been formed only two weeks before and which was openly supported by the colonial administration and Belgian financial groups. The two ministers, by defending the interests of these groups, further increased mutual mistrust.

The Congolese question had by now become a Belgian political issue. Public opinion in Belgium was well-intentioned, but had been exposed far too long to falsified reports from the only source of information about the colony – the propaganda service known as *Inforcongo* – to know enough about the background of the situation. The PSC was more closely associated with the financial groups than was the Socialist Party; but the conduct of Socialists in Congolese affairs had been scarcely more commendable. Their anti-clerical views clouded objectivity; and in the period from 1954 to 1958 when the Liberal–Socialist coalition was in power they had done little more than pay lip-service to the principles of socialism where these applied to the Congo. Since the Congo was in fact ruled by the financial groups and the colonial administration, ministerial changes produced few if any significant changes in the *status quo*.

Lumumba was at this time in prison. He had been arrested in Stanleyville on 1 November, charged with having provoked the riots which followed a rally of unitarian parties, and sentenced to six months' imprisonment.

On 15 December de Schrijver announced in parliament that a conference, which would be called the Round Table, would meet in mid-January 1960, to set up political structures in the Congo. At the same time the King, deeply disturbed by worsening Belgian–Congolese relations, unexpectedly decided to make a quick tour of the major cities in the colony. He took off in a military aircraft later on the same day, accompanied by the minister, and was already airborne when the news was announced. He wanted to see for himself the changes which had taken place there since his successful visit in 1955, when the Congolese had hailed him as *Mwana Kitoko* and *Bwana Kitoko* (the handsome boy or the handsome chief).

The King must have found the picture a very dismal one, if he looked at the Congo objectively. The *Abako* had all but taken over law and order in Léopoldville and the Bakongo area; and the MNC had won over public opinion in the Orientale province. In Katanga the King stifled a scheme, launched by the business community with the help of the Union Katangaise and CONAKAT parties, to announce immediate secession. In the Kivu, settlers appeared to want annexation by the Katanga. In the mineral-rich Kasai fighting had broken out between the Lulua and Baluba tribes. Albert Kalonji, the Baluba leader, had been arrested in August, put under house arrest at Kole but released in September. The secessionists hoped that he might bring South Kasai into their scheme. With the exception of the northern regions, which were not economically self-supporting, the colonial structure was falling apart.

On the other hand freedom of the press had at last been instituted, and in December 1959 my brother Philippe and Mathieu Ekatou were able to resume publication of *Congo*, which became even more successful than during its brief period of existence in 1957. I represented the weekly in Europe, supervised its Brussels office, and contributed to some of its features: notably those entitled 'Azanga-Nzungu has seen . . .'; 'Some impartial advice'; and the 'Saturday Mwanbe'.

2l The Round Table Conference

It would appear that the conclusion which King Baudouin drew from his lightning visit to the Congo confirmed Schoeller's suggestions – which also, of course, happened to coincide with the ideas of the financial groups. The King attributed opinions very like Schoeller's to the hundreds of Congolese he had met: 'I heard their accounts, and received their opinions. All they said seemed to indicate a general wish to organize the future state on the basis of a considerable autonomy for the provinces, with limitations and statutes in accord with their varying regional characteristics.'

This statement from the King was seen as an order to be carried out by the Belgian plenipotentiaries, for the preservation of Belgian interests in the Congo. If the Congo became an independent but more or less federated state, Belgium would still possess all the means of pressure and persuasion she needed to continue to act there, whether directly or indirectly, and to safeguard her financial, economic, missionary and humanitarian undertakings in the Congo.

The Congolese politicians did not appear to understand that Belgium was intending to make their country independent in name only. Their immediate concern was to choose those who were to visit Brussels as the Congo's representatives; and the colonial administration worked hard to get the delegation packed with a fair number of moderate, federalist leaders, so much preferable to the 'Lumumbists' and other supporters of a unitary state.

On Wednesday, 20 January 1960 the historic Belgian–Congolese conference known as the Table Ronde Politique opened in Brussels. It brought face to face the representatives of the various

Congolese political parties – of whom all the major ones were represented – and the members of the Belgian parliament and government.

The Belgian prime minister, Gaston Eyskens, professor of political economy in the Flemish section of the Faculty of Law and Economic Sciences in Louvain University, gave the opening speech. Albert Lilar, the Belgian deputy prime minister, was appointed president of the conference; while my father from *Abako* and Paul Bolya, president of the PNP, were chosen to be its vice-presidents. The members of the *Bureau de la Conférence* were Joseph Kasongo, Moïse Tshombe, François Kupa and Jean Bolikango for the Congo; and the Socialist Henri Rolin, and the Christian Socialist, André Dequae, former minister for the colonies, for Belgium.

On Saturday, 20 February it was Eyskens again who delivered the closing speech. Those representing the two countries had spent a month discussing the problems involved in the birth and life of an independent state. In effect nearly all the problems were touched on except those of really vital importance to any state's survival – the economic, financial, military and diplomatic ones. In this the Belgians systematically betrayed the good faith of the Congolese.

The matters of money, defence, security and foreign relations were all purposely put off for discussion at a later date. In their innocence most of the Congolese delegates were quite satisfied and some were positively jubilant: they were convinced that they had won independence for the Congo. Each was preparing to give his own version of what had happened at the Round Table to his political or tribal supporters. For most of them the most important objective appeared to be the fixing of a definite date for the proclamation of independence.

The deliberations of the Brussels Round Table covered sixteen points, each forming the subject of a resolution; and those sixteen resolutions formed the provisional Constitution, officially entitled *La Loi Fondamentale*, on which future Congolese government was to be based. These were the sixteen points:

1. Date for the proclamation of independence
2. The structure of the state
3. Constitution of the first central government
4. Powers of the first government
5. The head of state
6. The structure of the Congolese parliament
7. How it should be constituted
8. Constitution and legislation in the future state
9. Division of powers between the central and provincial authorities
10. Structure of the provincial institutions
11. Organizing of elections
12. The exercise of executive power up to 30 June
13. Future relations between Belgium and the Congo
14. Economic and financial problems
15. The status of Belgian colonial officials
16. The exercise of judicial power.

On the Belgian side, the Round Table seemed the dawn of a new day. Both the rulers and those with interests of any kind in the Congo – bankers, politicians, missionaries, businessmen – now felt themselves in a position to sum up the abilities of those who were to lead the Congo.

Ever since the bloody events of January 1959 in Léopoldville, and also those of the following October in Stanleyville, Belgium had officially accepted that the Congo should be given internal self-rule. However, once Belgium realized that Congolese public opinion was immovable on the point, the idea of self-government was displaced by that of independence, with full collaboration between the Congo and Belgium. The Congolese were to have nominal power, but Belgium would continue to rule her former colony by having effective control of all its military, economic, financial and diplomatic arrangements.

With this in mind, public opinion in Belgium and the West was relieved to find that resolution no. 14, relating to economic and financial questions, was approved. It read:

1. The Congolese delegations:
   – aware of their immense responsibilities towards their Congolese fellow-citizens,

– determined at all costs to avoid the Congo's accession to independence resulting in any economic and social regression, or any form of disturbance or disorder,

– anxious, on the contrary, for their country's independence to go hand in hand with rapid economic expansion, an increase in industrialization, and a rising standard of living for all in peace and public order,

– anxious, too, to preserve a well-balanced economy in order to preserve the purchasing power of Congolese currency and confidence in the Congo's future in the worldwide arena:

2. Realize the value of securing the inflow of investment and technologists, both from Belgium and elsewhere, who will contribute, within the context of Congolese law, to increasing the economic importance of the Congo, and an improved standard of living for her people:

3. Entrust to the Conference on economic, financial and social problems, the task of preparing the text for the conventions relating to technical aid and economic cooperation to be established between Belgium and the Congo.

This resolution was unanimously and unreservedly approved,[1] indicating a total failure in watchfulness on the part of the Congolese. Though representatives from both countries had discussed the future of our country for an entire month, the real fate of the future Congolese state was to be determined by decisions and commitments to be made at a second Round Table, described as Economic and Financial.

Given the short time that the Congolese politicians had in which to go through the various stages preceding the proclamation of independence, the Belgians were certain of being able to impose their opinions and plans without any real difficulty.

The electoral campaign, the parliamentary elections, the formation of the first Congolese government, the election of the first head of state, and preparations for the independence celebrations were all so many major reasons why the politicians representing the Congo could not spend time in Brussels disputing the thorny economic and financial issues that had to be settled between the two countries. This second crucial conference was held from 26 April to 16 May. The Belgian experts involved in financial dis-

1. Dumont, Georges H., *La Table Ronde Belgo-Congolaise*, Paris, 1961, pp. 193–4.

cussions and negotiations gave the appearance of taking quite seriously the talks that they had with the young students who made up the Congolese delegation, talks which covered the complex of technical problems which formed the real substance of Congolese independence. The basis for their talks was a collection of working papers prepared by Belgian experts. The Congolese had not the experience to recognize the glaring omissions in them, the absence of certain vital information, just as they had no way of knowing the various secret financial and other agreements which had been made between the Belgian government and some of its allies, and between Belgian financial bodies and other European and American business concerns.

From the Congolese point of view the January–February Round Table did have two beneficial effects. It had made possible the first meeting in the flesh of various politicians from all over the country, each of whom was looked on as a god by his own party, region or tribe. It also made each of them aware of the difficulty – if not the impossibility – of anyone's hoping to wield total power in so enormous and variegated a country as the Congo. Not one of them possessed a truly national popularity. The extent of prestige varied with the person; this was clear from the importance and publicity given by the international press to the statements and views expressed by the different politicians from the Congo. Certainly some names stood out, but their importance abroad was strictly in relation to their popularity either in their place of origin, or their political party, or – at least for some foreign circles – to the support that they enjoyed among influential people in Belgium.

On the other hand, the disadvantages of the Round Table were many. Whereas the Belgian delegates were a homogeneous group, skilled at concealing their internal political disagreements for the sake of Belgian prestige and advantage, the Congolese constituted a disparate delegation, disunited, and little aware, even perhaps at times totally unaware, of the real problems at issue.

Anxious to get publicity and often quite ignorant of the unorthodox procedures indulged in by colonial power on such occasions, the Congolese delegates almost all fell into the traps set for them, both in the conference hall and its corridors, and in their various hotels. As ever, the colonial power was adept at following the maxim, 'Divide and conquer'. Overwhelmed by the apparent understanding and fatherly trust that they received from the Belgians; thrilled by the atmosphere of artificial equality so sedulously created; and dazzled by the glories of freedom from colonial rule flashed before their eyes in one solemn and meaningless speech after another: the Congolese representatives lost all sense of proportion and all idea of time, realism and objectivity. They were all newcomers to Brussels, and felt their foreignness keenly.

What would have happened at the political Round Table if it had taken place on Congolese soil and not in the unfamiliar and insulated atmosphere of Brussels ? In the metropolis the Belgian participants were quite at home, whereas the Congolese were fish out of water – indeed, they looked to some observers more like vicious crocodiles – who could only get back to their native element after ending their negotiations on the beach. The dissensions, mutual jealousy and mistrust existing among the Congolese helped to blind them to the practical difficulties of setting 30 June 1960 as the date for independence. To get the new national institutions set up and working would take far longer than four months if it were to be achieved in peace, order and confidence.

This atmosphere of rivalry and competition among the Congolese was the reason for the incident deliberately provoked by Kasavubu, when, on the advice of his foreign friends, he left the conference to make an unofficial tour of Europe before coming back to take his place among his compatriots at the discussions. There was in fact a struggle for power going on under the surface among the groups. Up to that time Kasavubu, Bolikango and Tshombe were all fighting to become top dog – in prestige, in popularity and in international reputation.

Patrice Lumumba, uncontested leader of the nationalists, was in prison in the Congo, after his condemnation to six months' penal servitude by the Stanleyville Court on 21 January. On the day following, or two days after the opening of the Round Table, he was transferred from Stanleyville to Jadotville prison. His then supporters and collaborators – Joseph Mbuyi, Victor Nendaka,

Joseph Kasongo, and Jean-Pierre Finant – threatened to boycott the conference if Lumumba were not present there. They declared: 'If Lumumba does not come to Brussels the MNC delegation will regretfully be obliged to stay away from the Round Table.' On Monday 25 January de Schrijver was warmly applauded as he informed the conference that he had 'pleaded with the procurator-general in the case to set Patrice Lumumba free for long enough to enable him to take part in the work of the conference.' Lumumba was to leave Elisabethville that day.[2]

The release of Lumumba, his impending arrival in Brussels, and his triumphal appearance in the Palais de Congrès where the conference was being held suddenly hit the headlines in both Belgian and Congolese newspapers. For a time these events totally eclipsed the news of what was actually taking place at the talks.

The general impression was that the conference only really began its work after the arrival of Lumumba, leader of the MNC delegation and spokesman for a 'united, independent and neutralist Congo'. On 26 January he landed at Brussels airport where he was met by a crowd of admirers and 'friends'.[3]

All of a sudden his statements became more important than those of any other Congolese delegate; and other delegates, especially those who were locked in a behind-the-scenes struggle for power, had to alter their tactics accordingly.

Kasavubu, Bolikango and Tshombe felt it necessary to draw attention to themselves, so as not to look like minor national leaders. Bolikango got advice from colonial officials and Catholic missionaries; Tshombe received assurances from someone high in the financial world; Kasavubu received guidance, through discreet and effective intermediaries, from influential groups with which he did not himself have any contact. By-passing the tacit agreements existing among the various Congolese delegates, Kasavubu provoked an incident which his secret advisers thought would bring him a good deal of attention. The object was to make him appear the only immovable, farsighted and truly nationalist of all the Congolese. At the opening of the session at which

2. Dumont, Georges, op. cit., p. 39.
3. Notable among them were Wetor Nendaka, Joseph Mobutu, Albert Kalonji, Joseph Mbuyi and Jean-Pierre Finant.

Lumumba put in his first appearance, Kasavubu declared:

As president of the *Abako*, and spokesman for all my friends, I think I may say that this *is* a genuinely constituent assembly. It is time that we all shouldered our responsibilities. The delegates present genuinely represent the Congolese people. There need be no question of trying to find anyone better qualified to do so. There is therefore no point in waiting for elections before forming a constituent assembly. If Belgium thinks otherwise, there is no point in continuing these discussions . . .

After which he left the hall, followed by his colleagues Edmond Nzeza-Nlandu, founder of the *Abako* but long since a docile follower of its now president, and Philibert Luyeye, his private secretary. This seemingly spur-of-the-moment departure, taken together with Kasavubu's attitude from the start of the Round Table, had at least three separate motives:

First, he wanted to face Lumumba with a *fait accompli*, and force him to become either a disciple or a rival.

Second, he wanted a good excuse to leave the conference and the surveillance of his colleagues, so as to be free to have secret dealings with various eminent middle men who did not want to emerge from the shadows. Since they could not call on him, he must go to call on them.

Third, he meant to put his vice-president Daniel Kanza, who was also vice-president of the conference, in an awkward position: he must either align himself with Kasavubu, or dissociate himself from him publicly.

In effect what Kasavubu was saying fitted in very well with the ideas of all the other Congolese nationalists present. But he had not discussed it with them beforehand since he wanted to act alone and win distinction for himself at their expense. Indeed history might have taken a very different course had the conference stuck to three points: fixing the date for independence; setting up a provisional or temporary government; and arranging the hand-over of power. Kasavubu could have put just such a proposal forward after consulting his colleagues. The politicians who had come to Brussels were for the most part representative of the Congolese people and well fitted to discuss and determine the future of their country. What was needed was a little more care, a little more realism and less of mistrust and mystery, to save the future of what was then still a Belgian colony, but was gradually, as it turned out, being prepared to become an 'international colony' of the West.

Acting as he did at the suggestion of his foreign advisers Kasavubu was assuming a terrible responsibility for the history of our own country for generations to come. I myself had often been consulted by Kasavubu in the days when, as president of *Abako*, he wanted to take a public position on any matter involving international affairs. He obviously mistrusted my father, whose temperament was entirely different from his own, and their political opinions became more and more divergent. But he continued to evince great esteem for me, and asked my advice whenever possible. He valued my objectivity, I think.

I was, as I have said, involved in the preparations and talks which resulted in the decision to organize this Round Table conference on the future of the Congo. Before, during and after the conference, my apartment was the scene of innumerable discussions and deliberations among Congolese politicians, exchanges of opinion between Congolese students and leaders, meetings between Congolese and Europeans. I was also Kasavubu's intermediary with various African nationalist leaders, including Nkrumah.

But Kasavubu and his European personal advisers did not bother to consult me about this new tactic of his. Beforehand, I had done everything possible to present him as a man of integrity, totally incorruptible; but I felt obliged to suggest a more reserved approach towards him by those Congolese leaders and journalists of every nationality who came to ask what I thought after the session. Kasavubu was well aware that the Congolese delegates would be watching his contacts outside the conference and outside Brussels, and this caused him some anxiety. When Lumumba asked my advice as to what attitude to adopt, I suggested that he go ahead and for the present pay no attention to Kasavubu. I was sure that the man could not afford the luxury of leaving the conference altogether; he *must* come back. And so, a few days later, he did.

The Belgians, having done nothing to promote among the Congolese any exercise of national responsibility, suddenly found that they had to achieve in four months what they had refused to do for the past fifty years.

In effect, what they had decided to concede was an independence rotten at the roots. The Congolese were drunk on the notion of independence, which they equated with becoming free from the white man's yoke. Belgium knew quite well what kind of problems and disappointments they would face after 30 June, yet Belgian officials did nothing to help obviate any of them.

At the Round Table the Belgians succeeded in getting the Congolese representatives to accept formulae whereby their democracy would be totally patterned on the Belgian model. The *Loi Fondamentale* had juridical implications exactly like those of the Belgian monarchical constitution: a head of state who 'rules' but does not govern; a government supervised and able to be dismissed by the head of state; an over-large and relatively powerless parliament consisting of a chamber of representatives and a senate. There was furthermore a colonial *Force Publique* more in the nature of an expeditionary force than the basis for a real national army; and a carefully worked out limitation to the powers of the central government, which would enable the provincial authorities to make decisions against the national interest, but to the advantage of foreign big business.

When the Round Table ended on 20 February, the Congolese spokesmen acclaimed Belgian–Congolese friendship, and Belgium's understanding as shown towards 'her' Congo in a series of fine promises, full of sentiment but wholly devoid of content. To the Congolese, the ending of the Round Table meant the beginning of a series of experiments which were for the most part anything but happy. They believed that all misunderstandings with Belgium had been cleared up; henceforth, they thought, there would be no more dishonest dealings of any kind between the two countries and their peoples. They felt proud of having won independence. Indeed, so ingenuous were they that they really believed in a 'Belgian miracle'.

Their closing speeches were highly emotional, a veritable

competition in eloquence. As for the Belgians, they showed that they were aware of the difficulties lying ahead, full knowing the poison injected into the so-called independence they were granting – indeed Eyskens made no pretence to conceal the fact in his closing speech:

In the financial sphere, Belgium is also fully conscious of her obligations: she has planned for substantial aid to deal with the problems of the budget, and intends to do everything to foster investment, both public and private. A healthy growth in the economy, investment, a balanced budget – these are indispensable conditions for the economic expansion which must take place, and which must be the basis for any kind of social progress. . . . Never forget that there may be those outside your country who covet your riches, and will make capital out of the slightest sign of weakness or dissension on your part . . .

The next day, at eleven a.m., King Baudouin received the Congolese delegates and their Belgian opposite numbers in the gallery of his palace in Brussels. In his speech he gave some moral advice to the colonized, and drew particular attention to the advantages of good behaviour after independence, since Baudouin would never let the work of his great-great-uncle be dishonoured and destroyed.

Our thoughts turn once again to King Leopold II, who founded the state of the Congo eighty years ago. In a territory wholly unexplored, almost unknown to the rest of the world, peoples and tribes, often hostile to one another, a prey to slavery and sickness, were brought together into a splendid empire. What was so exceptional and admirable is that my great-great-uncle achieved this union not by conquest, but essentially through a series of treaties signed in harmony between the King and the traditional chiefs, treaties enabling the Belgians to bring security, peace, and all the elements of prosperity to the very heart of Africa. Those who succeed us at the head of the Congolese government will see how vast, bold, and, I do not hesitate to say, generous, has been Belgium's work in the Congo. We came there when everything was still to be done. This Congo we now hand back to you with an established administration, large towns, railways, roads, airports, hospitals, schools, an intellectual élite, a monetary system, industries, well-developed agriculture, and a standard of living and economic activity that many new countries will envy you . . .

Cyrille Adoula, as Congolese spokesman, made a polite reply.

Kasavubu was not present at this audience with the king. He had slipped away from Brussels the previous evening, together with his private secretary, Luyeye. My father was not there either; at my suggestion he had gone on the same plane as Kasavubu. I had indirectly learnt of Kasavubu's intention to reach Léopoldville before any of the others and get my father dismissed by the *Abako* central committee as soon as possible. Since my father had disapproved of Kasavubu's attitude during the Round Table – which was ambiguous and dictatorial, to say the least – he had already been labelled a traitor by the more fanatical members of the party. To them my father, though vice-president of the conference and of the party, should unhesitatingly have followed Kasavubu out of the conference hall, without questioning his party president's intentions and motives.

My father was trusted by most of the Congolese delegates, to whom he was an elder statesman: he could not have left the Round Table without giving a reasonable and serious excuse. Then, too, as vice-president of his party he wanted to be kept informed of the party's position – and not just turned into a yes-man. Keenly aware of the dilemma in which they would place him, Kasavubu and his advisers had been fairly well able to predict how he would react. To this extent their little *coup* was well calculated to make public the conflict between *Abako*'s president and vice-president. But I could not bear knowingly to let them trap my father this way, and that was why I made such a point of getting him on to Kasavubu's plane. Kasavubu was furious at seeing us come into the air terminal together; he certainly had not expected such company on the trip home. The plane was an hour late. I sat with my father at a table not far from Kasavubu, Luyeye and their Belgian adviser. We exchanged frozen smiles. When they finally left, I shook Kasavubu's hand politely at the foot of the gangway, wishing him good luck and a pleasant journey, before bidding a somewhat warmer farewell to my father.

In Léopoldville, the fact that my father arrived with Kasavubu made it impossible for 'King Kasa' and his supporters to develop the rumour of treason which they had been spreading about him. But it was only a matter of time. Kasavubu was determined to get rid of the vice-president whose presence made it impossible for him to carry out in the party the commitments he had made as an individual, or which had been made for him by his friends outside the country. Indeed, increasingly his mistrust of my father was fortified by fear, since through me my father was better informed than anyone else in the party about Kasavubu's foreign friends. Youlou, whom Kasavubu regularly consulted; Croquez, the lawyer, with whom Kasavubu stayed in Paris on his way to Brussels – these were only the middle-men. The president of the *Abako* was not yet aware of all the political and financial connections of his friend Youlou; similarly, he had unlimited confidence in certain special envoys from Europe and America without having any notion of their involvements or ulterior motives.

Anicet Kashamura, who went to Paris with Kasavubu, gives this account:

A month after the establishment of the *Collège*,[4] we were invited to Belgium. The object of the trip was to give our assent to the labours of the Economic Round Table. Lumumba was the first to refuse to go: he went to Stanleyville, where he concentrated on the electoral campaign. When we got to Brussels with Kasavubu, we refused to approve the conference's conclusions. We took the opportunity of going to Paris to see Maître Croquez, in the rue de Varenne. He revealed to us the economic means by which Belgian interests intended to undermine the independence of the Congo. It was a matter of selling the shares of the Union Miniére and other large Congolese firms. Kasavubu told his secretary Philibert Luyeye to take the file with him. He intended to table an action against Belgium at the international court in the Hague.[5]

Yet somehow Kasavubu had managed to make himself appear a kind of infallible god in the eyes of the Bakongo peoples; he could do what he liked, for they would never see through him. But history will.

Before independence, all the Congolese politicians visiting Belgium knew how and where to find me in Brussels. To many of them, especially those who thought themselves nationalists, my

4. *Collège Exécutif Général*, the interior governing body of the Congo, between the Round Table and Independence.

5. Kashamura, A., *De Lumumba aux Colonels*, Paris, 1966, p. 23.

father was their brother in the struggle, their ally in battle. But, given the years I had spent in Europe and my links with the outside world and though I represented therefore a kind of symbol they could boast of, something precious, whose help and advice, moreover, they sought whenever they needed it, they never associated me with the political race in their discussions.

More than one well-known politician talked to me in confidence, and some even entrusted me with secret and delicate missions. They looked upon me as a man apart, unattached to any one tribe, any one political party. My attitude made them recognize that I was a sincere nationalist, but I was clearly not one of those who intended to make politics their career. I had carried out my fight against Belgian colonialism on a completely different level from theirs. I had never known the thrill of an election campaign, with all the political and financial compromises it entailed. I had never spent long nights in bargaining for votes, in secret agreements to be financed by liberal and progressive Europeans, or by opportunists who stood to gain by the activities and expenditure of political parties – as for instance the extravagances into which their new status led the poorer politicians, who were ambitious but inexperienced.

My fight against Belgian colonialism had been a subtle, bitter, and merciless torture. Since 1952 I had been completely alone, and understood by none of my compatriots: there were some who respected and admired me, others who envied or perhaps pitied me, and still others who stood in a judgement which excluded pity. I was mistrusted by some highly placed Europeans who continually reminded me that I was just another black man. I was valued by others; but though these did not belong to the group who insulted me, nor did they ever dare openly to defend me.

This sense of isolation and solitude was something I continued to feel even after independence. I was to be a minister, but also an ambassador. In fact, my country and my fellow-countrymen succeeded in turning me into a politician-diplomat – which was a bizarre novelty to some, and a highly dubious combination to others. Yet I was still a Congolese citizen, and, even more, an African citizen; privileged, but alone.

I had no choice. Would I ever have?

22 Lumumba: *Formateur* of the Government

As I have said, I had been in Brussels working for the Common Market since 1958. After the Round Table Lumumba asked me how I would feel about giving up my job there shortly before independence, and becoming the Congo's ambassador to Belgium, Holland and Luxembourg, and also permanent representative of the Congo to the EEC. I agreed to this suggestion, and held myself in readiness to resign when he gave the word. The legislative elections in the Congo took place in April and May; and the nationalist parties had a large enough majority to give Lumumba the opportunity of becoming either prime minister or head of state. He thereupon confirmed his request that I resign and come back to Léopoldville. I had no hesitation over doing so, but I did have some regrets. My superiors and colleagues in the overseas department were astonished, as I had given them no hint of my plans. They told me that I was being very imprudent to give up a well-paid job for this shaky proposition; however they gave a small cocktail party at practically no notice, to wish me good luck in the very uncertain future of the Congo. Then I came home.

At twenty-six I became one of my country's first heads of diplomatic mission. I still felt confident of the Congo's future, which promised to be more dignified, better organized, more honourable and more African under a nationalist régime. My diplomatic career began on the very day of my leaving the EEC. Yet up to then there had been nothing to suggest any affinity between Lumumba, the politician, and myself, the international official.

A few weeks earlier Lumumba had had the opportunity to see for himself the workings of the politico-economic labyrinth which helped to create the solidarity of the Belgian–Congolese community.

94

The Political Round Table had been misleading. But the Economic Round Table was sheer trickery on Belgium's part; its results stand as a monument to Belgium's shame, in her determination to give the Congo an independence poisoned and truncated from the first. Our children and grandchildren will perhaps be able to tell the whole story and be believed.

After the Political Round Table, the volcano, which had been smouldering for some months within the *Abako,* began to erupt. The unspoken opposition between the president and vice-president came into the open and reached a point of no return. There was a joke headline in the Belgian socialist daily, *Le Peuple*: 'When the Kanzas dance, Kasa gets out!' Now the Kasas began to dance, but the Kanzas did not get out! In my own opinion the lamentable dissension between Kasavubu and my father was one of those politico-religious events typical of the whole jungle of the colonial situation in the Congo.

Lumumba and most other politicians and people of influence in the country attached great importance to the fact that I was the first Congolese layman in history to get a university degree. During their short visits to Brussels and Paris, people like Kasavubu, Bolikango, Tshombe and Lumumba became aware of the fact that I could command an international audience, and that I had most useful connections, both in Europe and Africa. I was not a political leader, but I had travelled a lot in Europe during my studies, and made friends in many different places. However, the fact that I was a Kanza, and that there was dissension within the *Abako*, made it generally supposed in the Congo that I was an opponent of Kasavubu, and similarly that I must be a serious rival to Justin Bomboko.

For Bomboko, Lumumba felt an almost pathological mistrust.

After my resignation from the European Common Market, then, I went back to the Congo. I stayed with my parents in Léopoldville, and twice Lumumba came to see me there. My father was present each time. During his first visit, Lumumba declared that he wished 'Papa Kanza', though not elected as a member of parliament, would be a member of his government if he himself became prime minister. 'I know,' he said, 'that the Belgians will do their best to get Kasavubu or Kalonji made head of government. They may even succeed, who knows? After all, they are still the masters here.'

Lumumba promised that he would manage somehow or other to get my father into his government. Almost jokingly, he told us that his chance of becoming prime minister was dependent on his accepting Kasavubu as president of the republic. He also confirmed the proposal that he had made in Brussels, of sending me as ambassador to Benelux and the Common Market.

'But,' he added, 'the Belgians are doing all they can to get Justin Bomboko into the Ministry of Foreign Affairs. They must have some reason. If they won't accept "Papa Kanza" as minister, I am disposed to put your name forward for the job.' This I unhesitatingly rejected. I told him that he absolutely must not put forward my name for Foreign Affairs: I was not a member of parliament nor of any political party.

Lumumba was convinced that the Belgians wanted to get their pawns into all the top jobs in the independent Congo. In Katanga, the Belgian government had had the provisional constitution amended so as to allow the appointment of Moïse Tshombe as president of the province, with its wealth of mines: an amendment voted in the Belgian parliament on 16 June, only a fortnight before independence. Had not articles 110 and 114 of the *Loi Fondamentale* been altered, Tshombe might never have become president of the province at all, and would never have been in a position to proclaim the secession of Katanga. The amendment was more or less demanded by Schoeller, whose last act as governor of Katanga was to hand over his seat to Tshombe. Later, by way of thanks for services rendered, Schoeller was named *Grand Maréchal de la Cour*. He had certainly done wonders for the interests of Belgium and the Crown in Katanga. Of such coincidences – and well-planned moves – is history composed.

Six weeks before independence, Ganshof van der Meersch was appointed Minister of African Affairs, living in Léopoldville. The Congo was thus to be ruled by a resident Belgian minister and Governor-General Cornélis.

At van der Meersch's suggestion, the king made an attempt to get rid of Lumumba by officially naming Kasavubu *formateur* of the government. Kasavubu immediately set about finding a candidate for prime minister. Interestingly, he did not set about forming a governing team with himself as prime minister, but assumed that his mandate was to be president. The names he put forward as possibilities for the head of government were not chance choices, but friends of his with the same support as he himself had outside the Congo. Among the candidates he suggested were Albert Kalonji, Joseph Ileo, Cyrille Adoula and Justin Bomboko.

But quickness of decision was not one of Kasavubu's strong points. This enabled Lumumba to achieve a political move which brought the scales down on his side, and gave pause to those who thought that they could get rid of him without taking local realities into account. For the first time the Chamber of Deputies was to elect its own president. Joseph Kasongo was the name put forward. Supported by Lumumba and his political allies he was elected by a majority, for Lumumba virtually controlled parliament. From then on, it was clear, any candidate for the post of prime minister would have to be put forward and supported by Lumumba himself in order to be constitutionally appointed by parliament before 30 June.

Belgium was committed in the eyes of the world to granting independence to the Congo on that date, so that there could be no question of delay for further manoeuvres. At the same time she could not hold to her commitment without the country's having a national government. The Belgian authorities had no love for Lumumba but they had to bow before the evidence and accept him as a necessary evil. The word accordingly went round among the various Belgian and other interested parties. After the president of the Chamber of Deputies had been elected Kasavubu was dismissed as *formateur* – indeed there had been no proper reason why he should ever have been given the job.

On the advice of van der Meersch Baudouin appealed once again to Lumumba. He named him official *formateur* of the first Congolese government. Lumumba came back to see us at my father's house. He now told us: 'I have been accepted as prime

97

minister because it looks as though we shall be forced to have Kasavubu as head of state.' My father and I both got the impression that he had – perhaps against his will – been made to accept this compromise by various foreign powers, to whom he had 'temporarily' decided to submit so as to achieve the first stage in the fulfilment of his ambitions.

Lumumba's submission to the will of Belgium and equally Belgium's acceptance of him as prime minister, were both purely tactical steps. The atmosphere was one of mutual mistrust, misunderstanding, and denigration. Any important suggestion from the Belgian side would be ill-received *a priori* by Lumumba; and similarly, any move, any word from Lumumba would automatically be seen in the worst possible light by influential Belgians.

That second time he came to see us, Lumumba was obviously nervous. He was in a hurry, which was natural: time was working against him and he knew it. He told us with complete frankness that, since Kasavubu was to be president, he could not include my father in his government. Politically, Lumumba needed an influential Mukongo ally; but for the moment he dared not choose my father, for his own position was not yet sufficiently secure. 'It may be possible to save "Papa Kanza" one of the responsible posts in the administration,' he said, 'for instance, though I can promise nothing, perhaps the job of mayor of the capital, and the title of Governor of the city of Léopoldville.'

Having thus dealt with my father, he asked me for my final decision on the ministry of foreign affairs (Jason Sendwe was also there, having come along with Lumumba). 'If you go back to Belgium as ambassador', he said to me, 'and Bomboko becomes minister of foreign affairs, I warn you that you'll regret it. Bomboko doesn't like you. He'll do everything he can to discredit you, and Kasavubu will support him because he hates your father. It is absolutely vital for me to create a balance between the pair of you; I must work out some kind of compromise so that you won't be under his orders.' He added: 'There was a time when I thought of giving the job to André Mandi, because he knows Bomboko very well, but he doesn't carry the same weight as you do internationally.'

'There must be some other compromise to be found,' I said;

'for instance, I could be a member of the government and ambassador to the United Nations in New York – those two jobs would not be incompatible.' In all justice, I could not stand as a rival to Bomboko: he was a member of parliament, and I was not; he had a political party, and I had not.

I had known we should face difficulties after independence: on many occasions I had expressed my fears over the problems we should have, with Belgium in particular, owing to our being given independence without any of the preparation we needed for it. During my visit to the United States in 1958, I had done what I could to sound out the views in influential circles there on the colonial problem in general, and that of the Congo in particular. I came to have good reason to think that the US, through the intermediary of the United Nations, would play a decisive part in the independent Congo.

Lumumba, too, was well aware that the great powers envied Belgium, and coveted the wealth to be got from the soil and the mines of the Congo. He shared some of my own fears, and immediately accepted my suggestion that he send me to New York; but *not* under the control of Bomboko and his ministry of foreign affairs (to which he decided to appoint Mandi secretary of state). His intention was that I should deal not only with the United Nations, but also, as a stop-gap, with the United States and Canada, where we would not at first have ambassadors.

23 Lumumba's Government – its Formal Investiture

On 23 June 1960 at 10.40 p.m. in the Palais de la Nation, with independence seven days away, Joseph Kasongo, president of the Chamber of Deputies, declared open the session which was to approve Lumumba's government. Lumumba was given the floor immediately, and announced the composition of his government. He then made his first main speech of the evening.

This speech was warmly applauded by most deputies, and by all the observers and invited guests present. It was followed by a heated debate in spite of the late hour. The remarks made by most of the speakers indicated the jealousy and ambition of the Congolese politicians who were personally opposed to Lumumba. From that moment on, it was possible to discern the intrigues developing behind the scenes against Lumumba's government. I will quote some interventions from the supporters of Kasavubu, Kalonji and Tshombe which, even at that early date, indicate the beginnings of a secessionist alliance among the provinces of the Lower Congo, Kasai and Katanga.

Samalenge (Katanga) considered that amalgamating the posts of prime minister and minister of defence was contrary to the principles of democracy.

Nyembo (Katanga), although included in the government, thought that more ministerial posts should have been given to his party, CONAKAT. This party would not accept the government as constituted, and its members were ready to declare Katanga's independence in agreement with the provincial assembly.

Mopipi (Maniema) said that the six deputies from his region were moved by the interests of the country as a whole, and were neither selfish nor separatists. Nevertheless, he resented the fact that no one from Maniema had been included in the government. If this situation were not remedied, he could envisage the formation of an autonomous Maniema government. Only Bashis from South Kivu were, it seemed, represented in the government.

Nzeza-Nlandu (Bakongo) recalled that the *Abako* had laid down a number of conditions for participating in the present government. None of these conditions had been met. He was not opposed to the present government, but regretted that the *Abako* had not been consulted on its composition.

Albert Kalonji (South Kasai – of which he was later to declare himself the 'emperor') said that he had found Lumumba's speech 'melodious', but considered that it did not satisfy the needs of the people. He deplored that his party had not been consulted, since it had given of its best in the struggle for independence. He added truculently that he had obtained the highest number of local votes of any of the deputies, and that he was proud not to have been included in a government which was anti-Baluba and anti-Batshoke and had shown such lofty disregard for the wishes of the people in the Kasai, who constituted a large section of the population. He would urge members of those tribes not to serve the government in any way, and would take steps to create a sovereign state with Bakwanga as its capital.

Referring to Lumumba's pan-African tendencies, he said that Africa consisted of regions very different from one another, and that the Congo's wealth of resources was coveted by many of its neighbours. Trailing behind the pan-African waggon was therefore a doubtful venture, unless it could be proved that it would be in the Congo's interests to do so.

Dericoyard (Azande) expressed displeasure that no one from Azande, which had a population of some 1,200,000, had been included in the government. Azande had once been a vast empire, with a high degree of civilization. If Azande interests were not more adequately represented in the government, he would reserve the right to revive this empire.

Lumwanza (Oubangui) deplored the fact that both his party and his district had been overlooked, especially since the present government would be unable to operate without the revenues of that district. Unless the matter were put right, he would form an autonomous government in the region.

Monote (Equateur) expressed misgivings over the intentions of the government, which was suspected of having ties with communist countries. In his view, the government was a house built on sand.

Muteba (Katanga) thought that the country would be unable to support the cost of so many ministers, and also felt that the Ministry of Defence should have been given to someone from Katanga. Since it had not, there was a danger that this province might secede.

Peti-Peti (an influential member of the PNP) said that the Lumumba team was wholly unacceptable to his party, and that if a vote were called for, he would ask all members of his party to leave the Chamber.

Lumumba was then given the floor to answer his critics. They had called attention, he said, to the lack of a definite programme and to an inequitable distribution of seats. His team would draw up this programme as soon as possible, and the Chamber would then be free to approve or reject it. He urged the deputies to bear in mind that they represented a nation and not a region. Independence was only a few days away; representatives of other countries had already arrived in Léopoldville, and it was essential for the country to have a government.

Replying to Nzeza-Nlandu, he said that he had indeed consulted the *Abako*, both verbally and in writing through Kasavubu, who was present in the Chamber. On appointments from CONAKAT, he had consulted Tshombe and the CONAKAT parliamentary delegations on several occasions. In reply to Kalonji, he said that he had repeatedly endeavoured to get in touch with him through his cousin Tshimbalanga, but that Kalonji had always refused to see him. He suspected Kalonji of having wanted deliberately to sabotage the constitution of his government. With regard to PNP allegations of his having ties with communists, he said that everything which was 'progressive' was liable to be labelled 'communist'.

In conclusion, he urged the Chamber to think of the country's future and reminded the deputies of the heroic sacrifices made by those who had been killed in the riots at Léopoldville on 4 January and at Stanleyville on 30 October 1959. He much regretted, now independence had at last been won, that anyone should be spoiling the country's chances by thinking only of party interests.

When a vote was taken, 80 members out of the 137 were present. Of these, 74 voted for, 1 against, and 5 abstained. The Chamber rose at 2.05 a.m.

On the next day, in the Senate, Lumumba won a more substantial vote after a heated debate. His government was approved by 60 votes to 12, with 8 abstentions. Joseph Ileo, the president of the Senate, was not a Lumumba partisan and had in fact opposed his appointment as prime minister. Cyrille Adoula, who was a Senator at the time, had also strongly objected to the composition of Lumumba's team. He had been offered – but refused – a ministerial job. He was well informed on Belgian and Western intentions concerning the Congo, and probably wanted to see which way the cat would jump before committing himself.

He was one of the few Congolese politicians to tell Lumumba, frankly and amicably, that the latter had made a mistake in agreeing to be head of a government which was being attacked from all sides. Lumumba should have waited till the people were more mature and the politicians more experienced.

After these two votes of confidence, I found myself officially a member of a government for the first time. I had to wait, however, until after independence before receiving my credentials as Ambassador Extraordinary and Plenipotentiary to the United Nations.

Looking over the government list afterwards, I realized what a veritable agony the whole thing must have been for Lumumba. I thought of the negotiations and bargainings, the intrigues and the pressures he had had to deal with before arriving at his final choice. I was not surprised that he had chosen to be himself both prime minister and minister of defence, since he had told us that he intended to do so on his second visit to my father. I was for the same reason prepared for Bomboko to have foreign affairs. But what did surprise me enormously was the absence of such names as Adoula, Bolikango, Kalonji, Maonda and Pinzi. Though everyone knew that none of them had a very high opinion of Lumumba, I had thought that they would agree to become ministers in the hope that they would, at least to some extent, get their point of view across and their ideas accepted. The thirty-six ministers amounted to a team of fantastically varied individuals, of different classes, different tribes, and different political leanings. It was all too likely that their separate ambitions would dangerously conflict.

Lumumba was apparently accepted as leader by them all. He had the qualities of which leaders are made, the skills of a commander; but to command, coordinate and lead a group as ill-assorted as it was hastily created, would not be an easy job. Lumumba was a leader of men and behaved as such – whereas in fact he should have behaved more like a teacher with schoolboys. All of us were ministers for the first time in our lives; and for the majority this involved a fundamental and instantaneous change from being vote-catching demagogues to being responsible and thoughtful statesmen.

Lumumba could be aggressive, astute, sentimental, courteous, charming and tactful. One of his political opponents admits that it was easy to discredit him only as long as one did not know him personally. From a distance, Lumumba looked like an enemy who had to be overcome by anyone envying his position. But people who were with him a great deal found him the personification of dynamism, watchfulness and insight. His look was so penetrating that it could be an almost tangible reproach to some; whereas to others it expressed a real sense of understanding.

Lumumba trusted no one but himself: rightly or wrongly, or perhaps both to some extent. It was wrong in that he turned good friends into implacable enemies by his attitude of suspicion, which inevitably looked like arrogance, vanity and overriding ambition. One simply has to make allowances for him, people said. Lumumba was a very special kind of man: he achieved success through the strengths of his nature, but could not hold on to it because of the weaknesses. As prime minister those weaknesses were far more obvious than the strengths, and he gave his enemies cause to fear him where he might have made use of them. He could not, and did not keep his power. Could he have acted in any different way? God alone knows.

More than once before independence, Lumumba's most fanatical supporters offered simply to liquidate his enemies for him; but to this he would never agree, for he preferred a political, democratic victory over living opponents to an easy and dramatic victory over dead ones.

I will say something now about each of the major members of his team as I then found them.

The deputy prime minister, **Antoine Gizenga,** I knew quite well. He was president of the PSA, and had for some months worked in collaboration with *Abako*, during the time when my father had been its vice-president and Kasavubu its president. He was born in 1925, in the Gungu territory, in the Léopoldville province district of Kwilu. His primary schooling was in the Catholic mission of Muhaku, and his secondary (six years of Latin-orientated humanities) in the Minor Seminary of Kinzambi. He had done three years of philosophy in the Major Seminary of Mayidi, and then spent a year in charge of the Catholic mission of Mbeno.

After his studies, he worked first in the office of the Banque du Congo Belge in Kitwit, and later in the colonial administration in Léopoldville. He went on to become a teacher in a Catholic primary school. His great relaxation was playing the guitar. I knew him to be taciturn, but determined and indeed at times obstinate; he was also a romantic, and basically sentimental.

Before independence, and during the time of the Round Table, he did some travelling in eastern Europe. He went to Berlin – both East and West – and Prague, and may even have got as far as Moscow. Such a journey was not unusual during our fight for national liberation; he was not going there for any kind of indoctrination, but to make contacts, and to let the socialist world know something of the Congolese people, their aspirations, and the means they were using to rid themselves of the Belgian yoke. He also went to Guinea, and met Sékou Touré, for whom he had a great admiration. And he brought back with him the incomparable Madame Andrée Blouin. On his return to the Congo, he was automatically labelled a communist by the Sûreté Coloniale, and put on the black list of people who were dangerous and must be watched.

Gizenga certainly had great qualities: he was a thoughtful man, who acted carefully, and whose silence and determination won him respect on all sides. His firmness in decision was invaluable. Though he made a splendid second-in-command, I never felt that he would have made a good prime minister.

Justin Bomboko, Lumumba's minister of foreign affairs, was one of the most ambiguous and interesting figures of the whole post-independence period. He was the great balancing artist, the trapeze-man, so to speak, of the Congo. Though older than myself, he started at university while I was in my third (next to last) year in 1955. His supporters and patrons were the powers of the Socialist–Liberal régime which governed Belgium from 1954 to 1958. Professor Arthur Doucy, director of the Solvay Institute of Sociology, took Bomboko totally under his wing, and appointed himself his academic adviser, director of conscience and political godfather. Indeed, Bomboko's electoral campaign was methodically worked out and organized in 1960 by male and female experts specially sent to Equateur province by the Solvay Institute – with the result that he was elected a deputy there while sauntering round Brussels.

I was partly aware of his ambitions, and the rôle that certain important people in Brussels wanted him to play in Belgian–Congolese relations. I was never opposed to him politically; in fact we felt a certain comradeship during our stay in Belgium. But there were many Congolese politicians and students who were convinced that there was an unspoken rivalry between us, and said so on every occasion. Bomboko was the first Congolese to be admitted to the Université libre in Brussels, three years after I had been accepted at Louvain. The antagonism that existed between the Belgian students in the two universities came to extend also to the Congolese.

In January 1960 I came to realize the bitterness that Kasavubu felt towards my father. I did not know what his feelings were to myself, but our relations remained friendly, polite and relaxed, in spite of the battles going on within *Abako*. Lumumba did not trust Bomboko, as the latter was aware. Thus, there was a certain parallel between him and me: Kasavubu appeared to favour him, while Lumumba showed a certain consideration towards me. We were both determined to do our best for our country and for our fellow-countrymen, and to do it in what seemed to us the best way.

Bomboko cherished political ambitions, whereas I felt myself drawn to diplomacy. There were rumours flying round about the pair of us and our relationship, some of which were fantastic in the extreme. It may well be that we were being considered by different Belgian interests as future leaders whom they might do well to cultivate. As a student at Louvain I was liked and trusted in Catholic and clerical circles. As the favourite of the anti-clerical socialist government, Bomboko was looked upon as the future spokesman for the socialists of the Congo. I myself left Belgium without having committed myself politically, ideologic-ally, financially, or in any other way to any group in Belgium. Whether the same was true of Bomboko I do not know.

Marcel Bisukiro, a native of Kivu and now minister for international commerce, was a man I did not know; I met him for the first time in the corridors of parliament just before the government was sworn in.

Albert Delvaux, resident minister in Belgium, lived in Léopoldville, and I knew him well by hearsay. His mother was Congolese, his father probably a Belgian. He himself was a businessman, well and successfully established in Léopoldville. Before independence he passed as a European rather than an African, which gave him certain social and economic advantages. But as independence and the elections drew near, Delvaux recalled that his mother was Congolese, and got himself made a candidate in the Kwango, an area where there were at the time very few educated men to choose from. There he worked hard, and without much difficulty was elected deputy as a member of LUKA, a tribal political party affiliated to the PNP, the pro-Belgian party ironically nicknamed by most people *Le Parti des Nègres Payés* (instead of *Le Parti National du Progrès*).

The nomination of Delvaux to this particular job in Belgium was far from displeasing to our former colonizers, who knew and thought highly of him. They did not need to fear any anti-Belgian extremism from him.

Rémy Mwamba, the minister of justice, had had a certain amount of legal experience, for he had been working for a long time in various tribunals in Katanga. He belonged to a group of Katanga-born Congolese who considered themselves more politically mature than 'the Congolese'. He was a friend and confidant of Jason Sendwe, leader of the BALUBAKAT, but also claimed to be a cousin of Tshombe, who led CONAKAT. It looked as though, since these two men hated each other, he himself might later emerge as a third force capable of commanding Katanga.

Christophe Gbenye, minister for home affairs, was a man I did not know personally until I met him at the prime minister's house. I did, however, know that he was the assistant to the mayor of Stanleyville, and one of Lumumba's most loyal lieutenants. I had also been told that he came from the same tribe and village as Victor Nendaka, who had once been a Lumumba supporter, but was now his personal enemy.

Pascal Nkayi, minister of finance, and a member of *Abako*, was one of Kasavubu's trusted men. I had known him when he was a post office employee. Prior to his appointment he had evinced no special skill or experience in financial matters. I was astounded to find him in the job. It seemed a crazy choice in a country like ours, which still had to fight to win its economic and financial independence; but there it was. Kasavubu had insisted that this ministry be given to one of his men; and it was thought that since the minister would be surrounded by foreign experts, his own competence would not matter very much. Long before independence, Kasavubu himself had been an official in the finance department of the colonial administration, so he knew something of it. His contacts in Brazzaville, Paris, Brussels and Geneva were always kept quiet, but there were foreign technicians and experts only waiting for the word to come and look after his protégé in the Ministry of Finance. The choice of Nkayi was a soothing one to Belgian and other Western financial interests.

Alois Kabangi, minister for economic coordination and planning, a native of Kasai, impressed me as being an intellectual, self-made, who was able to express himself clearly and thoughtfully, and with definite ideas about his work. He showed method in discussion, and I valued him greatly for so obviously knowing what he was doing.

Alphonse Ilunga, minister of public works, seemed to like pomp, and gave an impression of being both impulsive and vain.

A native of Luluabourg, he only supported Lumumba because he was an opponent of Kalonji, and he seemed to me totally unfitted for the job he had been given.

Joseph Lutula and **Alphonse Songolo,** ministers respectively of agriculture and communications, were both strangers to me. Both came from Stanleyville, and it appeared that their loyalty to Lumumba was rewarded by their being given places in his government.

Joseph Yav, minister for economic affairs, I knew well. Since we had first met in Brussels, we had been in fairly regular contact. We were often involved together in various private talks with European financiers interested in the Congo. But his part in such talks was always that of Tshombe's lieutenant. I realized before I left Brussels that he was quite sure of getting this portfolio, and that he was committed to the people who gave the money to support Tshombe's CONAKAT. While the government was being formed, Yav had seen no need to come back to the Congo; he was comfortably settled in Brussels where, to judge from his contacts and his activities, he was working out (on behalf of CONAKAT) details of the plan for Katanga's secession. His presence in this particular ministry was demanded by the Belgians, who held the monopoly of imports and exports and were determined, whatever happened, to keep a check on every licence issued by the ministry.

Joseph Masena, minister of labour, was a member of Gizenga's PSA, and completely loyal to his leader. He impressed me as being sincere, courageous and consistent.

Joseph Mbuyi, minister for the middle classes, had a strong and delightful personality. Elegant, dignified, never expressing empty emotion, he was a fine example of the pride of his Maluba tribe; and from the Round Table Conference, I got the impression that he was one of the brains in Lumumba's MNC – of which he was secretary general.

Grégoire Kamanga, minister of health, was a splendid medical assistant, who had been a quite outstanding student. His teachers lamented the fact that he had not continued on to the university and become a doctor. I gathered that his shortness of stature gave him some sort of complex; but as a skilled medical assistant he would make, I was convinced, an excellent minister of health. Here was clearly one minister who had been given a job for which he was fitted.

Edmond Rudahindwa, minister of mines and power, was a mystery man, a native of Kivu, very silent in any group. I knew nothing of his earlier connections with the Kivu settlers and the financial interests in the eastern Congo, but came later to realize that he was no innocent. The rich European planters in Kivu valued him and considered him a useful choice as far as their rights and interests were concerned. The Belgian mining companies had probably given their blessing to his nomination; and Lumumba was apparently pleased to have this ministry responsible to a Kivu man rather than to a fanatical supporter of Tshombe. I wonder whether he knew what he was doing.

Antoine Ngwenza, minister for social affairs, was an old friend of mine. He had been my scout-leader! I was sure he would make a good minister, especially in this particular post. He had always been interested in problems relating to education and welfare. He had had a good secondary education, and plenty of experience in the field. He was not a member of parliament, but warmly supported Bolikango; indeed it was probably not only his ability, but also his membership of Bolikango's party that got him his job in the government.

I was surprised to find **Pierre Mulele** in the ministry of education and the fine arts; though he was undoubtedly one of the best minds in the PSA, of which he was secretary general. Born in 1929 at Isulu-Matende, in Léopoldville province, he had his first schooling in the Catholic missions of Totsi and Kitwit; after two years in the Minor Seminary of Kinzambi, he went on to continue his secondary schooling in Leverville (Kwilu district). He also took some courses at the school of agriculture in Yaseke, in the Bumba territory of Equateur province. In 1950 he was drafted into the *Force Publique*, in which he served for two years, stationed in turn at Coquilhatville, Thysville and Léopoldville. And during his military service he was in the same battalion as Joseph Mobutu and Antoine Mandungu. In September 1952 he was demobilized, and entered the colonial administrative service, in which he remained until November 1959. He was among a group of *Abako* politicians who went abroad before independence.

He seemed to have been struck by certain socialist ideas which he had seen in action in Guinea and elsewhere. It was his ambition to reorganize and unify the various nationalist parties into one immense popular party, with a programme similar to that of Guinea's Parti Démocratique. The Ministry of Education certainly provided him with a handy instrument for revolutionizing the minds of the younger generation of the Congo: he could revise the syllabuses, and review the authoritarian methods employed in Congolese schools. For that reason alone, Mulele was feared in advance by the missionaries – particularly the Catholics – as having communist notions. He lived by the strictest self-discipline, and had the will of a soldier; indeed his determination at times verged on parody. Like Gizenga he was absolutely obstinate, deeply sincere, and intensely anti-colonialist.

Anicet Kashamura, minister of information, seemed to me a man of intelligence. I chanced to be present at a lecture he gave in Belgium at a meeting of the Belgian Young Socialists in the Université libre. Though perhaps somewhat carefree and disorganized professionally, he had a philosophical conception of power which was far from the obvious realities of democratic life. He would find it hard to be a success in this new job, and it was a key post in any young government trying to get itself established. Lumumba was extremely fond of him, and believed him to be incorruptible – in the sense that the Belgians hated Kashamura and would hesitate to ask him to betray his prime minister. Kashamura seemed embittered and acid; his socialism was the simplest anti-clericalism; that is, he was only a socialist to the extent that his ideas were the opposite of those held by the missionaries and the European settlers. Having come from Kivu, he was in a good position to understand the mentality and behaviour of the established European settlers who lived there in so princely a style.

Maurice Mpolo, minister of youth and sport, was a childhood friend of mine. We had been at school together, but he had had to leave rather early for personal and family reasons. He was quick-tempered and daring, and his character gave the appearance of being hard. His youth had been very turbulent, and he had had much to suffer; among the young men of Léopoldville, he was considered one of the tough ones. Shortly after leaving school, he had become a policeman, and was feared for the reputation he had then achieved as an intractable and merciless man to cross swords with. But the young people of the city were proud to see him become a politician, a respected member of parliament, and a man with a voice in the MNC. His local popularity made him one of the party's major assets in the area round Lake Léopold II.

Joseph Mobutu was private secretary to the prime minister. Together with Jacques Lumbala, the second private secretary to the prime minister, he was the closest official collaborator that Lumumba had. He could see him often; and Lumumba, for his part, could appeal to Mobuto or Lumbala at any time to be an intermediary between himself and other members of the government. Both private secretaries had access to all the information, public or confidential, official or personal, that Lumumba was given. I met Mobutu in 1957 when I came back to Léopoldville after my studies in Louvain. My brother Philippe was working as a journalist with Jean-Jacques Kandé and Mathieu Ekatou on Romain Nélissen's anti-clerical daily, *L'Avenir*. Pierre Davister, a young Belgian journalist who had just left the clerical daily, *Courrier d'Afrique*, was also now working for *L'Avenir*. Nélissen had set up two leaflets to slip into the copies that went to the Congo, containing articles by African commentators, journalists and reporters. At that time Mobutu was a sergeant in the *Force Publique*. He was also one of the most regular contributors to *Actualités Africaines*. I had occasion to have several talks with him over the editing of *Actualités* when he brought in his articles (under the pseudonym of José de Banzy). To him, journalism was a means of perfecting his intellectual education; but also, in view of the low pay that soldiers got, his articles were useful in earning for him a few hundred extra francs a month. A native of Banzyville (Oubangui), he used his birthplace along with his own name to produce his pseudonym: hence José, for Joseph; and 'Banzy' for Banzyville. A few months later he was demobilized. I next saw him in Belgium, where he was doing a course in current affairs and journalism. In Brussels, Mobutu lived discreetly. He was Lumumba's guardian angel on all his trips to Belgium. They often worked together on the vast piles of mail that Lumumba had to answer. Paul Fabo, an African from Dahomey, and editor of the weekly, *L'Afrique et le Monde,* gave Lumumba the use of an office in rue de Ruysbroeck, where he could work in peace.

Mobutu succeeded in winning Lumumba's confidence to such a degree that Lumumba considered him his go-between in finding the support he would need from all parts of Europe when he became prime minister. I chanced to find out that Mobutu and I had been born on the same date, 14 October, two years apart. Lumumba was amused to hear this, and said, 'Well Thomas, I always trust Libra people because they are thoughtful; they never decide anything without considering it carefully first. They are sincere in their friendships, determined in their decisions, and stable in personality and character. Generally they are pleasant to deal with.' It sounded as though he knew the Libra horoscope by heart!

I was by no means surprised to find Joseph Mobutu next in the presidency of the council, a key position in the government. This position put him just where he needed to be so as to observe, coordinate and check everything connected with the prime minister's office and the government in general; according to reliable information, the two future private secretaries to the prime minister (he and Lumbala) had virtually been the final arbiters in the composition of Lumumba's team.

Jacques Lumbala was a brilliant Katangese, and presented himself as a lawyer. In fact he had done some legal study by correspondence course, before becoming a defence counsel in the native courts in Elisabethville. He knew a lot about what was going on in the political and financial world of Katanga, and was a fine speaker and full of self-confidence. But it could scarcely be said that he was a convinced supporter of Lumumba. His political opinions were close to those of the pro-Belgian Congolese and the members of the PNP. His nearness to Lumumba would be hard to explain simply in terms of political ideas. But though an influential member of a reactionary party created and financed by the Belgian administration, he was a friend and confidant of Mobutu's; and this doubtless played an important part in getting him the similar post of private secretary to the prime minister. He was dominated by a desire for power and honour.

The secretary of state for foreign affairs, **André Mandi,** whom I had known in Belgium, was a student at the Free University in Brussels at the same time as Bomboko, whose colleague he had previously been since their administrative studies in Kisantu. He knew far more than we did of the various problems and difficulties that Bomboko had had to contend with there. Before his arrival in Belgium, Mandi had been distinguished in the Congo for the socialist ideas he put forward in the trade unions. He was a civil servant, and one of the group of officials in the Congolese union, APIC,[1] which was recognized by the colonial administration as having 'socialist' tendencies.

Articulate, and good at making an impression, Mandi had become a supporter of Lumumba's while still a student. He was also a friend of Mobutu's, and probably made use of the fact to get close to Lumumba, who included him among his technical advisers. As secretary to the foreign minister, Mandi was given the job of checking on Bomboko, whom Lumumba did not trust. Like myself, Mandi was not a member of parliament; had he been, he would probably have been foreign minister in Bomboko's place. For the present, Mandi was merely the eyes and ears of Lumumba in the foreign affairs department.

Antoine Kiwewa was secretary of state for commerce. A native of Kwilu province, like Gizenga, Kamitatu and Mulele, he had spent most of his life in Orientale province, in Stanleyville, and it was there that he had known Lumumba. He seemed to have fairly progressive commercial ideas, and was a real businessman, with a good head for bargaining and a fondness for intrigue.

André Tshibangu, a young Congolese intellectual, was well placed in the Secretariat of State for Finance. With a minister of finance who knew very little about financial matters, it was comforting to have Tshibangu working with him and providing a useful counterbalance. He was one of the first university students to have been educated in the Congo itself, having studied at Lovanium.

The secretary of state for justice was a former official, **Maxmilien Liongo;** he had worked in the department of justice in the colonial administration for a long time. Serious, conscientious,

1. APIC = Association pour le Personnel Indigène de la Colonie.

and highly thought of, Liongo was a leading member in the officials' trade union, APIC.

Raphael Batshikama, a great fan of Kasavubu's, was the secretary of state for home affairs. Before independence he had worked in the finger-print department of the Office for Native Affairs. And he had been in a position to help procure the identity documents needed to get *Abako* and PSA nationalists secretly out of the country when they wished to go abroad.

Christophe Gbenye, minister for home affairs, was a supporter of Lumumba, and political director of the MNC. And doubtless that was why Kasavubu had been so keen on getting one of his own protégés into the same ministry. For this ministry was seen as being of the utmost importance, given the coercion that the police had used during the rule of the Belgians. Rightly or wrongly, Congolese politicians were convinced that real power could only lie in the hands of whoever controlled the police, since the police were in possession of information about everyone; about the past and present activities of nearly every citizen of prominence, black or white; and particularly about all the Congolese who had become ministers, members of parliament, holders of high office, and wealthy businessmen.

Albert Nyembo, secretary of state for defence, was a fervent supporter of Tshombe. Since Lumumba himself was in charge of national defence, Tshombe and his friends had to make sure that they got one of their men into his department. They feared military action after the proclamation of the secession of Katanga. Nyembo's mission, therefore, was to discover Lumumba's intentions, and in particular what use he was going to make of the national army.

Antoine-Roger Bolamba, secretary of state for information, was well known as a Congolese poet and writer. Formerly editor of *La Voix du Congolais,* and a protégé of those who favoured the Liberal Party in Belgium, Bolamba was made attaché to the office of the Belgian minister Buisseret in 1956. Buisseret had hoped to give the job to Lumumba, but the latter had been arrested in Stanleyville by the colonial administration only a few days before the appointment was to have been officially announced.

A member of the same tribe as Bomboko, Bolamba remained in

touch with him during his period in Buisseret's office. In the political area, his ideas were different from Lumumba's. Indeed, he was long thought of as one of the favoured sons of the Belgian administration. From *La Voix du Congolais* the Belgians were able to follow and discover the viewpoint of the educated Congolese. This review was printed at the expense of the administration, and supervised by important Belgian functionaries, but it was read throughout the country by the Congolese *évolués* and intellectuals of the time.

Alphonse Nguvulu was secretary of state for economic planning and coordination. He was a left-wing trade unionist whom the Belgian socialists wanted to promote. His were the socialist ideas from the turn of the century; but, never having made any methodical study of the socialist theories to which he continually referred, his ideas were somewhat confused. In his party he was surrounded by a group of young Congolese who were trying to learn from him what they could of Marxist ideology and methods. They had followed individual courses given in Léopold-ville by Marxist Europeans – in secret, so as not to attract the attention and annoyance of the colonial administration. These young intellectuals edited *L'Emancipation*, a paper indirectly financed by Lumumba himself.

Georges Grenfell, minister of state, had been one of the first MNC members in Stanleyville. A former fighter in the Force Publique, he was one of Lumumba's most trusted men when it came to any delicate job that needed to be done at a national level. His loyalty was beyond question, and his feelings for Lumumba were those of fatherly watchfulness and sincere admiration.

Paul Bolya, minister of state, was president of PNP, and though from the same tribe as Bomboko and Bolamba, does not seem to have shared their point of view. He was a medical assistant, and very well known in Léopoldville, where he held a responsible post in the school for training medical assistants. He had had contacts among the Belgian Liberal Party through the good offices of Dr Lewillon, who had long been his immediate boss and pro-tector. He was never a tribal extremist. His friendship for Joseph Diangenda, a son of Simon Kimbangu, the prophet, made him a supporter of the significant 'Kimbanguist' movement.

Charles Kisolokele, minister of state, and a native of the Lower Congo, was the eldest son of Simon Kimbangu, and was able, with his brother Joseph Dianganda as intermediary, to make use of a large number of the Bakongo for whom 'Kimbanguism' was a religion. His presence in the government provided something of a counterbalance, therefore, since the followers of Simon Kimbangu were a group apart, a homogeneous group within *Abako*. They were more ready to follow the instructions of their religious leader Dianganda than those of the *Abako* committee. And Lumumba clearly hoped to divide the Bakongo by exploiting the contradictions and varying tendencies among the tribes to the advantage of his government.

Politically, *Abako* had two wings – Kasavubu's and my father's; but among the people of the Lower Congo there were several internal movements related to the various Bakongo sub-tribes and their religious affiliations – Protestant or Catholic. The Kimbanguists supported *Abako* in the hope that the party would make their belief one of the official religions of the Congo. For its followers, Kimbanguism was an independent African religion, unconnected with any of the religions brought in from outside. A revelation had been made direct to Simon Kimbangu, they believed, and during his lifetime he had worked miracles. The Belgians had responded by imprisoning him and keeping him exiled in Katanga, far away from his home in the Lower Congo, for thirty years (from 1921 to 1951). He died in 1951; and though the Catholics claimed to have converted him before his death, no one believed them.

André Ngenge, minister of state, was linked with Bolikango and Ngwanza both tribally and politically. He had worked as private secretary to a Belgian lawyer in Léopoldville, Maître Delattre. Everything he did was sincere and straightforward; he lived honourably, avoiding problems and hating any form of intrigue. He was a man of intelligent awareness, and a declared supporter of the left. But really his political ideas were more or less the same as those of most of the Congolese who had grievances against the missionaries. They often called themselves 'socialist', when in point of fact they were a combination of nationalist, anti-clerical and Marxist elements.

24 Towards Independence: The Illusion of Power

The politicians of the Congo believed that they were now in a position to determine their fate and the fate of their country. But in practice the true fate of that country was still being played out thousands of miles from Léopoldville and Elisabethville. The Congolese had become useful tools and highly vulnerable pawns. Most of those in politics had been to Belgium at least once since the Round Table conference in January. A good deal of fuss was made of them; there was no lack of interested groups to fawn upon them, making them offers and proposals, and trying to discover their intentions, their personal ambitions and their financial needs.

Since the revolt of January 1959 the people of the Congo had consisted of two major groups: on the one hand politicians of great determination and greater or lesser conviction; and on the other the mass of the people who looked forward to freedom, unity, harmony and prosperity for their homeland.

Politics is the art of compromise but the Belgians had never taught the Congolese this. Indeed, forgetting that men come and go whereas peoples remain, most Congolese politicians had developed a notion of power which was restricted to the one idea of eliminating opponents by any possible means, rather than reaching some accord with them. This fact was already evident within the parliament and the government.

The presence of foreign representatives in Léopoldville for the independence celebrations brought out into the open the existence within the government itself of small cliques pursuing their own interests. Ministers and members of parliament were much in demand, with invitations to cocktail parties, luncheons, dinners, receptions, conferences, pouring through their letter-boxes.

Certain of the ministers received special attention from the delegations of socialist countries, and of those who saw themselves as the progressives of Africa or Asia. Others only met one another in the company of Westerners, or of Africans and Asians known to favour the West.

The splits which were invisible when the government was first constituted now steadily grew. We no longer hesitated to describe this or that colleague as a reactionary or a pro-Belgian; while others were labelled anti-colonialist, socialist, progressive or anti-imperialist – for they were almost always to be seen in company with Guineans, Ghanaians, Egyptians, Czechoslovakians or Russians.

To belong to this or that political party once again became important. In every issue of the government list, the names were now followed by initials indicating which political party the minister belonged to. This, of course, encouraged interested foreigners to pigeonhole the ministers by their parties, either nationalist or moderate – with nationalist implying progressive and socialist-tending; while moderate implied pro-Western and conservative.

The first meetings of our Council of Ministers were unforgettable. Our discussions were of the most desultory kind. All of us were happy, or at least cheerful and satisfied, at being ministers. It was play-acting; some of it pure comedy, some nearer to tragedy. We were ministers; we, the colonized, now had titles and dignity; but we had no power at all over any of the instruments we needed to carry out the functions expected of us. We argued about offices, about suitable and available sites for them, and how they should be shared among us. We discussed the allocation of ministerial cars; the choosing and allotting of ministerial residences; arrangements for our families and their travel – some from the country into the capital; others, from the African part of Léopoldville to what had been the European part. In short, we talked endlessly, laughed ourselves silly, and concluded by generally agreeing that the Belgian colonizers were to blame for all our troubles.

Those among us who took ourselves seriously in the rôle of 'distinguished men', addressed each other as 'Your Excellency';

while those with socialist leanings called each other 'Comrade'. And for the moment our most pressing problem seemed to be that of settling the precedence of ministers and others in authority, so as to prevent disputes, traffic jams and general confusion whenever there was an official and public celebration of an Independence event. The government appealed to the chief of protocol in the Belgian Ministry for Foreign Affairs to help us work out an order of precedence; and the result was a near-perfect copy of that used in Belgium.

The group chosen by the Congolese parliament to govern presented a somewhat jumbled picture, with Lumumba in charge.

Each time the Council of Ministers met I was amazed at how people so different, so opposed in their ideas, with such complex personalities and such diverse and divergent ambitions could hope to form a homogeneous group for effective and coherent administration.

For what was involved was the work of governing, of preserving the sovereignty and integrity, of a country eighty times the size of Belgium, three times that of France, ten times that of Great Britain.

The new Congo was fertile with intrigue: its wealth coveted by other countries, African and non-African, Eastern and Western alike. Lumumba wanted to see the Congo become a kind of centre of gravity, a focal point of African independence; and the African peoples who were not yet free were pinning great hopes on Lumumba and his government.

I could not help remembering all those pointless discussions we used to have as students in Europe. We talked in theory of colonialism, neo-colonialism, paternalism, imperialism, independence and emancipation. But they were all abstractions, notions, pious utopian hopes and wishes. Now here was I, a member of the team entrusted with the crushing job of actually winning that emancipation for the Congolese people; achieving in reality that long-dreamt-of independence. It was up to us to give the people of the Congo the happiness that they had so long hoped and waited for.

Within that team I felt an outsider; I did not really feel that I was one of the government – I still seemed to be in my old ambiguous situation of a privileged but solitary Congolese. I was a minister of no political party; and though certainly a friend of Lumumba's, not one of those completely in his confidence.

I had only to look through the list of ministers to be quite certain that Lumumba would generally dispense with the advice of the majority, and act rather on that of his more intimate friends.

I could feel no special honour in being always one of that little group which met chiefly at night, with him and a few foreigners, both African and others. For various reasons, he set store by my point of view, but he never associated me in the secret dealings that went on among the politicians of the Congo. I was most often consulted when the situation was one that extended beyond the context of inter-Congolese intrigue.

25 Lumumba – Caught in a Trap

When the Lumumba government was formed, the Congo was still a Belgian colony: ruled according to a provisional constitution voted by the Belgian parliament and based on the resolutions of the Belgian–Congolese Round Table Conference. According to that provisional constitution (*La Loi Fondamentale*), the election of the Congolese head of state had to take place 'within forty-eight hours of the appointment of the president of the Senate and swearing-in of a speaker'.

Kasavubu was the happy man elected, and his election was the result of intrigues, bargaining, various compromises, and pressures from both within and without the country. Bolikango was the only candidate in opposition to Kasavubu. Neither could have been elected without the approval of Lumumba and the parliamentary group of Congolese nationalists, and of this both were aware. The pressure groups knew it too.

Lumumba had promised Bolikango the votes of his party, the MNC, which, in conjunction with the other nationalist parties, held the majority of votes in both houses. But Bolikango discovered to his cost that this was the promise of a political tactician and did not in fact bind Lumumba to anything. Lumumba was acting at all times in his own interests and those of his party.

It had always been Lumumba's ambition to become prime minister. A thorough study of the *Loi Fondamentale* convinced him that the function of head of state was a nominal one, like that of a constitutional monarch. What he wanted was the power to act. Such an ambition could never have been fulfilled, it seemed, without certain concessions and compromises. He may well have committed himself out of tactical necessity.

His enemies were more numerous than he ever realized. Chief among them were those who were jealous, ambitious like himself, and vengeful. What he had seen as a right to be earned by the democratic means of parliamentary elections, suddenly became a favour to be won from Belgium by means of concessions and deals.

Ultimately, Lumumba only became prime minister on condition that he would do all he could to get Kasavubu elected as head of state. This agreement was made without the public or even most of those in the government knowing anything about it, and to the fury of Bolikango. There were certain people outside the Congo who, though favourable to Lumumba, had high hopes of Kasavubu at that time. Their special envoys in Léopoldville had been ordered to do everything they could to achieve a compromise between Kasavubu and Lumumba. Though friends and indeed admirers of Lumumba, they were deeply concerned over the *Abako*'s threat to bring about the secession of the Lower Congo if Kasavubu were not elected president. The pressure groups that distrusted Lumumba saw Kasavubu as a delaying agent, a shrewd politician, a lazy but ambitious man who would have the courage to get rid of Lumumba should the need arise.

On 24 June 1960, the day when the head of state was to be elected, I was present in parliament. In the chamber, the members of the government sat in the first three rows on the president's left. Before the session began, Bolikango had asked me to find out from Lumumba which candidate the nationalist parties were going to support. The results of the presidential election would depend on Lumumba's decision, and, at Bolikango's insistence, I asked him. I immediately sensed that Lumumba, as a politician and supremely a tactician, had made Bolikango a promise he was not going to keep. He had needed Bolikango's supporters to vote for him in the government elections; but when it came to the point, had said nothing to influence the nationalist deputies and senators into formal support for Bolikango. I had to go back and say *something* to this man, for whom I had always felt respect and esteem. 'If I were you,' I said, 'I should abandon this candidature; it will probably end in humiliation. Why not withdraw gracefully just before the votes are cast? If you do, history will remember you as the man who forgot self-interest in favour of peace in the Congo and happiness for our people, and withdrew from a contest to prevent its becoming a brawl.'

We all knew that outside parliament there was a tense situation that might explode into violence at any minute. There could easily be a civil war between the Bangala, originally from the Upper Congo, and the Bakongo, from the Lower Congo – a civil war that would essentially be a battle between Bolikango's supporters and Kasavubu's. But Bolikango replied that he trusted Lumumba, and was sure he would keep his word. It appeared that Lumumba had actually put the promise in writing.

Bolikango was one of those Congolese politicians who believed that honesty and keeping one's word were the most important characteristics of political men. He could not conceive of anyone's using deceit, still less violence or brutality, as a tactic for success.

Mpolo had told me that he intended to intervene during the session of parliament in the hope of getting the presidential election adjourned. His idea was an excellent one: he wanted to give Lumumba time to reconsider his position, and thus, if possible, prevent the election of Kasavubu as head of state. Mpolo determined to do this after Lumumba had given the word to vote for Kasavubu.

Joseph Kasongo, the president of the Congress (the combined lower and upper chambers) was not, however, very astute. He was afraid of Lumumba and what he might do. Mpolo took the floor and made his unexpected intervention. It was possible and, indeed, legal – he argued – to delay the presidential elections. The Congolese representatives would still have forty-eight hours in which to consider the matter, without any breach of the *Loi Fondamentale*. They must put the interests of the Congo first, and not those of Belgium. Considering the tension outside parliament itself, and indeed all over the country, as well as the pitch of excitement among the deputies and senators, he suggested to the president of the Congress that the session be adjourned, to allow further consultations among the various political parties.

Mpolo's parliamentary colleagues simply did not understand what he was saying. A great many of them were not really aware of how serious the situation was; of the national and international implications in the election of the Congolese president. Even though the *Loi Fondamentale* apparently only gave prerogatives of honour to the head of state, as in Belgium, the personality of whoever was chosen would still be of enormous importance. So often a man creates or alters a function, just as sometimes a function may change the man who fulfils it.

Kasongo made the historic error of publicly and inopportunely asking the advice of the prime minister and the assembled representatives, instead of simply using his authority to adjourn the session. Lumumba was obviously displeased by Mpolo's proposal. And the assembly was altogether too excited to make a rational decision.

The Congolese parliamentary annals record the following exchange:

THE PRESIDENT: I ask the honourable assembly to proceed directly to the work of designating the head of state.

MPOLO: In a short time, as the president has just said, we shall be voting for the head of state. You know how the situation is at present in this town of Léopoldville; you know as I do that there are two candidates for the position of head of state. I consider that we are moving too fast to get our government well established, given the rumours that are rife. Every one of you is aware of what is going on at present in the African part of town. That is all I will say now, and I leave it to someone else to make a proposal.

[*Sounds of protest.*]

THE PRESIDENT: I ask the prime minister whether this request is being made in the name of the government.

[LUMUMBA *shook his head in answer to* KASONGO's *question.*] Mr Minister, you have just asked that this session be adjourned; do you want a vote taken on that?

[THE SECRETARY *read the following passage from the* Loi Fondamentale]:

SECRETARY: Within forty-eight hours of the appointment of the president of the Senate and the speaker, the two chambers will . assemble together under the chairmanship of the senior of their two presidents. Having finally determined the formalities, that assembly will pronounce its choice for the head of state.

Article Twelve – The appointment of the head of state must

be approved by a two-thirds majority of all members of both houses gathered together.

Article Thirteen – If, within eight days of the meeting of both chambers together the majority demanded in Article Twelve has not been achieved, the function of head of state is to be temporarily assumed by the president of the Senate.

THE PRESIDENT: Mr Minister, a request for adjournment must come not from the cabinet, but from the members of the assembly: if the members of the assembly ask for an adjournment, then it shall be granted.

PINZI: Since the provisional *Loi Fondamentale* has not yet been altered by the two chambers, we should stick strictly to it. We must apply it now. I consider that the proposal of our honourable colleague Mpolo is simply another manoeuvre.

KALONJI: On the first occasion of our parliament's meeting together with the government elected by both chambers, it hardly makes sense for the first act of the Congolese parliament to be a derogation of the *Loi Fondamentale*, on which our democracy is founded. I think it is simply logical, civic and patriotic to refuse our friend Mpolo's request. Once a minister starts to undermine the *Law*, what will become of our country? We must hold fast to the *Loi Fondamentale* until it is changed, as our friend Pinzi has so wisely remarked.

SAMALENGE: . . . There is talk of postponing the appointment of the head of state. Yesterday *we* urged the postponement of any vote of confidence in the government and everyone resisted. It was said that we have, after all, only a few days until the proclamation of independence. Today, Mpolo talks of troubles and tensions. But we were not concerned by those troubles and tensions yesterday!

Yesterday we formed our government and voted our confidence in it. Today, because the election of a head of state is involved, we start to talk about something else. These are tricks, gentlemen.

We are here today to vote for the head of state: we must do it.

All three speakers were supporters of Kasavubu. They knew that Lumumba was committed to getting him elected, despite his promise to Bolikango. The election of Kasavubu was a political victory over Lumumba. Pinzi, a member of the *Abako*; Kalonji, a personal enemy of Lumumba's; and Samalenge, a member of Tshombe's party, were afraid that if the election were not held directly, Kasavubu would not win it. So the assembly rejected the suggestion of adjournment. It was a significant moment, for the three deputies who spoke against the suggestion represented the three political movements which were in league against Lumumba, even though certain of their leaders actually belonged to his government.

The Mpolo incident was closed. The assembly applauded automatically, and they passed on to the identification of the candidates before voting for the president.

My father was present, in the visitor's gallery. More than once he had drawn Lumumba's attention to evident weaknesses in Kasavubu's character. He was anxious to do so yet again before the presidential election. He called me out of the chamber, and asked me to beg Lumumba to come out for a few moments and speak to him on a matter of great importance. Lumumba agreed, for he respected my father enormously – like most Congolese, he used to call him 'Papa Kanza'. The three of us stood talking in a corner of one of the corridors of the building. Conversations of this kind always attracted attention, for Lumumba was the key figure in the history then being made in the Congo.

My father said these prophetic words to Lumumba: 'My dear boy, it is not too late to change your decision. I have just heard that at your request the nationalist parties are going to vote for Kasavubu – so in a few moments he will be president of the Congo. I am afraid you will have cause to regret this later on. I know Joseph Kasavubu well – far better than you do – and I can only say that independence without a president would be better than having Kasavubu as head of state. If you let him become president, he will behave to you exactly as he has behaved to me. For a time he will appear to collaborate with you, and later he will betray you – cruelly and cynically. You will be publicly humiliated, and God alone knows what will happen afterwards.'

I was moved to tears. Lumumba was polite but evidently impatient. He wanted to get back into the chamber, yet was impressed by my father's seriousness, and his anxious and fatherly tone.

I, too, tried to persuade Lumumba in the presence of Mpolo, who had just been defeated in the assembly: 'Prime Minister, you may think that I am simply supporting my father, but it is not just that. I recall that you gave your promise to vote for Bolikango. I don't know what you may have promised Kasavubu. Could you not get this election postponed? Then you, as well as the other members, would have time to consider objectively and calmly. Possibly a third candidate might come forward who would be more readily acceptable to everyone, and not arouse such controversy and animosity.'

But Lumumba was immovable. His decision, he said, was irrevocable. We must all try to forget the misunderstandings and injustices of the past. He was convinced that Kasavubu would make an excellent president: better than Bolikango who was, in Lumumba's view, merely a pawn of Belgium and protégé of the Catholics.

I was surprised to hear Lumumba so ready to pronounce judgement on Bolikango in this way, seeming not to appreciate his qualities. He went on to say, 'If Kasavubu is not elected, the Bakongo will revolt, and we all know what disturbances will occur before and after June the 30th. They may even secede to Congo–Brazzaville, and that would mark the beginning of the end for our hard-won independence.'

He left us no further chance to disagree with him. Indeed his appearance and his speech that day were so assured that clearly no one could have made him change his mind. Was he then so totally committed to Kasavubu?

Mpolo rejoined us just in time to say: 'Patrice, you are wrong to pay no attention to such advice from friends who have nothing to gain by deceiving you. You'll regret it one day, always thinking you know best.'

Mpolo knew Lumumba well enough to call him *tu*, but still could not convince him. The die was cast. Only Lumumba himself knew in his heart why it was so essential to elect the Congolese head of state at once, that very day, and why it must be Joseph Kasavubu, whom he did not admire or even trust.

At this point we separated. Lumumba, Mpolo and I returned to our seats in the chamber, and my father, disappointed and sadly discouraged, went back up to the visitors' gallery. The presidential election took place with a certain dignity, despite the tension and anxiety. The result gave Kasavubu the necessary majority of votes: to the jubilation of the Bakongo, and consternation of all the Bangala peoples. The very first scrutiny showed Kasavubu to have 159 votes against forty-three for Bolikango, with eleven abstentions. The chosen candidate had a certain protocol established in advance. He said a few words of thanks to his former parliamentary colleagues, made some promises he could never keep, declared his delight in the most moving terms, and withdrew, escorted and protected as befitted his status.

The session rose at 7.50 p.m. The night of 24 June was noisy all over the capital and indeed throughout the Congo, as the people tried to see the event in its proper perspective: Kasavubu was the 'new Baudouin of the Congo', said the masses.

Intending to offer my sympathy to Bolikango, I went to his home that same evening. He lived in the Commune of Limete, on the road out to Njili airport. I found his house crowded with members of his tribe, and political supporters. Some of them refused to let me in, on the grounds that my family were Bakongo: to them, all Bakongo were supporters of Kasavubu and of the *Abako* party. But others recognized me, among them Cyrille Adoula, Antoine Ngwanza and André Ngenge. They were aware of my sincere feelings for 'Monsieur Jean', and insisted that I be allowed in.

That evening, the Bangala took stock rather belatedly of their failure in judgement, and their lack of political organization. Kasavubu had in fact been elected by the Congolese parliament as a whole. Yet the Bangala had an absolute majority in parliament; they could have abstained *en bloc* and by so doing prevented the election of a Mukongo for whom they had little love. Instead they had preferred to elect Kasavubu, as directed by Lumumba, who was not from the Lower Congo at all. Not one of all the Bangala in parliament had dared to give public support to Mpolo's proposal to adjourn the session.

As soon as he heard that I was there, Bolikango admitted me. His wife, 'Mama Claire', was nervous at seeing me, but Bolikango hastened to reassure her, and thanked me for coming. He had by now realized his mistake, and knew that he should have accepted my suggestion that he withdraw his candidature before the voting began. I did the best I could to console him, and other friends went on doing so all night and for days afterwards. For him it was the most bitter failure in his entire career.

It now remained only for Kasavubu to be sworn in constitutionally, which was done on 26 June. So, four days before independence, the Congo had a national government, and an elected head of state, who was to take the place of Baudouin I, King of the Belgians, on 30 June 1960.

With our national institutions thus established, the Belgian colony was soon to become the Republic of the Congo. The Congolese themselves were already celebrating independence, known variously as *Dipanda* in Lingala, *Kimpwanza* in Kikongo, and *Uhuru* in Swahili. They drowned all their colonial neuroses in drink, music and dancing, and tried to bury all memories of the colonial past.

26 Katanga before Independence

In October 1958 political life in Léopoldville was organized around the conflict of three movements, centring on the personalities of three local politicians: Joseph Kasavubu, leader of the Bakongo tribes; Jean Bolikango, leader of the Bangala tribes; and Patrice Lumumba, a leader who declared himself above all tribal rivalries.

The *évolués* in the province of Katanga were equally aware of the political forces they represented. The Confederation of Tribal Associations of Katanga, known as CONAKAT, really dates back to 4 October 1958. Its first president, Godefroid Munongo, was an ex-seminarian working in the colonial administration. His family name was a well-known one in the history of the Bayeke tribe of Katanga. His brother was the traditional high chief of the Bayeke in Bunkeya; and Godefroid, at that time aged thirty-three, was in fact a descendant of the old dictator Msiri.

A week after his election as president of CONAKAT, Munongo contacted the colonial authorities in Katanga and found them favourably disposed to support the new political group. At first, CONAKAT never envisaged the political emancipation of the Congo as a nation. Its real objective was restricted to defending the interest of those considered to be 'genuine Katangans'.

There were many Congolese living in Katanga who belonged to tribes from outside the province. The rapid industrialization and urbanization of Katanga had attracted thousands of people who belonged to the neighbouring provinces of Kasai and Kivu, and even such neighbouring countries as Ruanda, Burundi, Tanganyika, Northern Rhodesia[1] and Angola.

Before the creation of CONAKAT, there had been another

1. Northern Rhodesia later became Zambia, and Tanganyika is now Tanzania (from Tanganyika and Zanzibar).

political group, the Congolese Union, which received its inspiration and support from the Catholic missions. The Congolese who lived in Katanga but originated from Kasai had formed themselves from 1955 onwards into a cultural and ethnic federation which was called the Association of the Central Kasai Baluba in Katanga, and became in 1957, *Fegerbaceka*. This association seemed opposed to taking part in any collaboration with the colonial and missionary groups in Katanga. It was thought too extremist, and dissolved on 10 November 1958, a month after the formation of CONAKAT. The European groups in Katanga, the colonists, the workers in the mining industry and the missionaries, were delighted to see *Fegerbaceka* go, since it had seemed to be introducing into Katanga the nationalism then burgeoning in Léopoldville.

These Katangese Europeans were mainly Belgians, united in the UCOL-KATANGA and the FEDACOL (Congolese Federation of the Middle Classes). They made no secret of the fact that they had taken CONAKAT under their wing. The threat of Katanga's secession regularly made by these Europeans was a form of pressure – indeed blackmail – used against the Belgian colonial authorities who ruled Katanga from afar, either from Brussels or Léopoldville. The notion of 'genuine Katangans' was extended to include those European colonists, and most of the other foreigners who followed a policy of trying to install a large European population in the provinces of Katanga, Kasai and Kivu.

Two Congolese, Isaac Kalonji, originally from Kasai, and Moïse Tshombe, both businessmen and leaders of *Acmaf-Katanga*, were held in considerable respect among the colonists and other Europeans in Katanga.

In May 1958 a Belgian colonist, Achille Gavage, founded the Union Katangaise: he was aiming at the formation of a single party open to the settlers and also to all those Europeans working in both the colonial administration and private companies in Katanga. This Union Katangaise envisaged the division of the Congo into large autonomous regions; the federation of those regions with Belgium; and the encouragement of immigration from Belgium and other Western countries. Those who hoped for this intended the huge area of Katanga to absorb the diamond-fields of Kasai, and wanted a Belgian military presence to preserve it against 'communist' infiltration and any other possible subversive movements.

Such an idea was not one to displease the whites in Rhodesia, South Africa or Angola, whose views on the future of this part of Africa and the emancipation of Africans were almost identical. It was a notion which made possible, in response, a vague cohesion among all the manifold tribal associations of Katanga. Jason Sendwe, a Muluba from Katanga, and a member of the Protestant Council of the Congo, who presided over the Baluba Association of Katanga, approached Tshombe, and his association became a member of CONAKAT. The Baluba Association of Katanga, or BALUBAKAT, dated from 1957 (Rémy Mwamba was its vice-president). It consisted of the reorganized associations of the major Baluba chiefdoms, and was intended to promote mutual help among the Baluba themselves, as well as their harmony with other peoples. Those who had been Sendwe's rivals for the position of president, Evariste Kimba and Bonaventure Makonga, had joined CONAKAT before as a form of vengeance.

In the middle of 1959 Munongo handed over his position as president of CONAKAT to Tshombe. Around the same time the Union Katangaise (comprising the settlers and the 'Katangan separatist' Europeans) joined up with CONAKAT, thus supposedly turning it into a group which represented the undivided interests of everyone living in Katanga, and could speak in the name of all its citizens, whether black or white. But this marriage at once led to a political divorce; for the entry of the Union Katangaise into CONAKAT alienated the BALUBAKAT of Jason Sendwe and Rémy Mwamba.

The elections in the communes and territories at the end of 1959 made clear how effective the influence of the Europeans was over Tshombe's CONAKAT: 'In October, November and December 1959 the links between the leaders of the Union Katangaise and CONAKAT were strengthened, with the former providing "technical and material assistance" to the president, Tshombe, from money directly supplied from the local Europeans.'[2]

2. Libois, Jean-Gérard: *Sécession du Katanga*, Ed. Crisp, Brussels, 1963, p. 27.

CONAKAT stood for an 'autonomous and federated Katanga'. Sendwe and his BALUBAKAT were totally opposed to separatism, and had reason to believe that the Europeans in Katanga wanted to prevent any alliance between the Baluba in Katanga and those in Kasai. Once out of Tshombe's CONAKAT, Sendwe negotiated alliances with *Actar* (the social and cultural association of the Tshokwe) whose leader was Ambroise Muhunge, and *Fedeka* (the federation of associations of people of Kasai origin) which was made up of the Lulua, Luba and Basonge tribes and had been founded after the dissolution of *Fegerbaceka*.

Isaac Kalonji, the provincial president of *Acmaf*, was elected vice-president of *Fedeka*. Victor Lundula, who was at that time in Jadotville, formed a group of *évolués* from the Kasai in sympathy with Sendwe and in opposition to Tshombe.

In Katanga the Belgians were delighted by the enormous understanding and friendship that they received from the leaders of CONAKAT who – with only the most minute differences – behaved exactly like their counterparts in the National Progress Party (PNP), the party of black workers inspired, supported and financed by the colonial administration.

In point of fact, through the PNP, the colonial administration managed to preserve the unity of the five provinces of the Congo excluding only Katanga; at the same time, through CONAKAT, the same administration was encouraging the federal, if not confederate, system which was to turn Katanga into an autonomous state. In December 1959 Tshombe declared 'that a federal Congo including a Katangese state might or might not be possible, but that in either case Katanga would work for real community with Belgium'.

Meanwhile Lumumba had been in prison in Stanleyville since November. *Abako* was politically out-manoeuvred. There was a rumour that the Lower Congo would eventually secede from the rest of the Congo and become the Republic of the Central Congo from 1 January 1960.

A semi-official list of the 'Mukongo government' had been handed out to press agencies and local papers in Léopoldville. The attitude of Fulbert Youlou and the encouragement he gave to the Bakongo separatists gave cause to wonder whether the priest-president and his French assistants in Congo-Brazzaville were not conspiring with CONAKAT and the *Union Katangaise.* Certainly, this rumour of a (totally imaginary) planned *coup d'état* by the Bakongo was deliberately spread and exploited by the European separatist groups in Katanga and their supporters in Belgium.

Such a rumour was in fact just what they needed, since it helped to provide the necessary justification for Katanga itself to secede, taking with it parts of Kasai and Kivu. A manifesto put out by the European settlers in the *Union Katangaise* foretold in so many words the 'proclamation of an independent Katanga, unless the formula of a Federal Congolese State were preserved'.

27 The Fatal Triumvirate: Lumumba, Kasavubu, Tshombe

In effect, at the end of 1959 and the beginning of 1960 the political situation in Katanga was nothing like as confused as it was made out to be. Positions were clear: the Congolese nationalists in Katanga favoured a united Congo, and were fighting to escape the domination of the settlers and enslavement to the mining companies which caused the rain to fall and the sun to shine in the province. Under the leadership of Sendwe, these people aligned their ideas with those of Lumumba and his supporters.

The Congolese separatists in Katanga were dependent, ideologically and financially, on the mining companies. Their political moves were dictated by the Europeans who made common cause with them, and the colonial officials who simply obeyed whatever directives came from Brussels. Tshcmbe was their apparent leader; but from behind the scenes he was closely watched by Godefroid Munongo, Jean-Baptiste Kibwe, Evariste Kimba and a number of traditional chiefs who enjoyed some importance in their tribes.

The ambiguous position of Kasavubu, the uncontested leader of the whole Lower Congo – who was a nationalist with some people, a tribalist and secessionist with others – was a great encouragement to Tshombe and his friends. From now on, the opposition between Congolese politicians was basically an opposition between centralism and federalism: between nationalists on one side, and tribalists and secessionists on the other.

Shortly before the Round Table Conference in Brussels, the federalists became divided amongst themselves. Those who believed in Kasavubu spoke in defence of unity within federation; those who hated Lumumba and wanted to see the Congo disunited, but effectively led by Tshombe's Katanga, were aiming for a Belgo–Congolese confederation. Abroad, the centralists had some strong support in Belgium, especially among socialist groups; and they were counting on finding friends in the USA, at least as long as an independent and stable Congo would not be so independent as to become openly anti-imperialist and pro-communist. Individual progressive Americans who had met Lumumba in Accra in 1958, and followed his political career since then, were already comparing him with Nkrumah, Sékou Touré and Nasser. They approved enormously of his anti-Belgian and pan-African views; they also knew that Lumumba had never visited any of the communist countries. Some even hoped to see Lumumba in opposition to Nkrumah; and the centre of the African liberation movement shift from Accra to Léopoldville. In their view, Ghana was too small, and not well enough placed geographically, to be the key point of Africa. In addition, Nkrumah was altogether too ambitious to be liked, and too subtle to be really understood by the Americans.

The socialist states found it opportune to offer Lumumba and his centralist supporters in the Congo the most fulsome praise, and to assure him of their support and their solidarity with him in his struggle against the balkanization of the Congo.

But the fact was that the Congolese federalists had firmer, safer and more realistic support than did the centralists.

In his brief stay in the USA, Professor A. A. J. van Bilsen, adviser to *Abako*, had had meetings with American and international groups to discuss technical aid to the independent Congo. In Washington in particular, he met officials in the State Department. He also went to Boston – the Kennedys' political fiefdom – and made contact with people at Harvard who were specially concerned with African emancipation.

To the correspondent of the *Belga* agency in New York, van Bilsen stated that he had found all over the US a lively interest in the new state, and a wish to help it, indeed to give it priority of importance. He made it clear that his mission had not been undertaken on behalf of *Abako* alone, but of all the nationalist parties allied with it. According to van Bilsen, the International Cooperation Administration was prepared to send a fact-finding mission to the Congo with the object of working out a programme of technical aid for the new state. He had also had contacts with

World Bank officials, with members of the social department of the UN, and with the Carnegie Foundation. In all this he was accompanied by Joseph Yumbu, a member of the *Abako* central committee. Kasavubu was assured of France's support to the extent that he worked for the division of the Congo into a number of autonomous states, as desired by Tshombe. The same was true of Britain, whose outlook on matters Congolese depended on the danger or safety they might represent to its own financial interests south and east of the Congo. The USA, on the other hand, saw Kasavubu simply as the leader who was to keep the Congo – whether united or federalized – within the western sphere of influence. With his proverbial calm and his discretion, he seemed to inspire more confidence than the fiery, excitable Lumumba.

This American attitude was to some extent determined by the official Belgian position: Lumumba was popular and dynamic, but uncontrollable; Kasavubu was respected, sensible, even a little timid, but lazy; Tshombe was servile, a trickster, ambitious, and lacking in will-power.

On the eve of independence, the stability, peace and prosperity of the Belgian Congo depended on the harmony, the give-and-take, the cooperation of these three men. They were, in short, politically fated either to reach an understanding in order to govern, to remain in power and to survive; or to fight one another in order to perish individually, and as a result reduce the Congo to chaos. Without wanting to, and perhaps without even realizing it, they formed a disastrous triumvirate.

Only in this light can we look at the success or failure of one or more of the Congo provinces' attempts at secession. For this was the political situation that prevailed in the Congo in June 1960.

The men concerned – Lumumba, Kasavubu and Tshombe – did not recognize this. Each mistrusted the other two, and each cherished the ambition of being the one to govern the Republic alone, whether as a centralized state or a federal one.

Their ambition was to remain a chimera; for despite the fact that in most of the developing countries the two functions were combined in one man, it never became possible for any one of them to become both prime minister *and* president of the Republic.

28   East and West in the Congo; Ralph Bunche Arrives

What Washington knew of Lumumba came through information provided by Brussels, official reports from the American consulate in Léopoldville, and American secret agents working in the Congo. Even before they knew anything at all about him, there were influential American groups which had already written him off as a dangerous character, probably a socialist, but certainly a friend of Nkrumah, and an admirer of men like Sékou Touré, Modibo Keita, Nasser and Castro.

American officials considered that Belgium, by granting independence in a moment of panic to a country which lacked experienced and effective leaders, had created a situation favourable to communist infiltration. The American embassy in Brussels showed a discreet interest in the Congolese politicians who visited Belgium; but to prevent the Belgians from suspecting any attempt to show sympathy to the colonized, it courteously informed the Belgian Ministry of Foreign Affairs of such encounters with the Congolese.

In Léopoldville the American consulate had kept up secret but regular contacts with Kasavubu's *Abako*. I myself was aware of this before independence; I had even taken part in certain discussions between *Abako* leaders and officials from the American consulate. From those discussions – carefully planned in advance and arranged through trustworthy intermediaries – it had emerged that the American government was not opposed to African nationalism, provided that it did not do anything to counter American capitalist interests. Washington would tolerate nationalism that was neutralist, but fight against any nationalism with communist leanings.

With this discreet assurance and concealed encouragement from the Americans, Kasavubu had never himself given signs of going too far. The positions he took were firm, but never extreme. Abbé Youlou and his French assistants supported *Abako* and were generous in giving far from disinterested advice to its leaders. The fervent nationalism expressed by some members and the committee of *Abako* was in complete contrast with Kasavubu's own moderation and prudence.

Lumumba, on the other hand, had never had American contacts. He set great store by his Belgian friends, whose outlook was somewhat narrow; they had no influential connections with America, and did not think it opportune to look for secret contacts there. They were individually admirable Belgians – liberals or socialists – but had no international breadth of vision.

Since January 1960 three Congolese parties had managed to keep in secret contact with the Americans: Kasavubu's *Abako*, Tshombe's CONAKAT, and the section of the MNC led by Albert Kalonji, Joseph Ileo, Joseph Ngalula and Cyrille Adoula. These contacts were at various different levels, according to the interests of different groups. For Kasavubu's *Abako* the contact was mainly political and diplomatic; one American objective was to prevent the French from annexing the Lower Congo with the connivance of Abbé Youlou. With Tshombe's CONAKAT, the contact was in the financial sphere, and also concerned with preventing communist infiltration into that part of the Congo so rich in mines and minerals. Albert Kalonji interested only those American financial groups which wanted to control the Congolese diamond market. Tshombe and Kalonji had been to the USA two months before independence. Cyrille Adoula was approached directly by the central office of the ICFTU (International Confederation of Free Trade Unions) in Brussels, an international organization under American control. Adoula was the secretary general of the Congolese trade union allied with the General Federation of Workers in Belgium (FGTB), a union affiliated to the ICFTU.

As to the socialist states, all they had to go on was guesswork. Their diplomats and agents in Belgium and the Congo were collecting information about every Congolese of influence. As independence drew near, their representatives tried to get in touch with those Congolese whose nationalism was anti-capitalist, anti-western, and above all, anti-American. But when it came to financial aid, they were not very generous; they were quite willing to abandon financial corruption for the corruption of minds. The few Congolese in whom they were interested were paid; but the payments were chicken feed, except to one or two – and these only got more as a result of fierce bargaining. The Belgian communist party acted as a liaison between the communist world and the Congolese nationalists; this was a grave mistake on our part, for the Belgian communist party was larded with double agents, and was in any case far more Belgian than it was communist. Some of its leaders differed from the leaders of other Belgian parties only in the rhetoric with which they denounced Belgian colonialism.

On 28 June, two days before independence, all the foreign government delegations were in Léopoldville. Some among them had special problems to which, from our Congolese point of view, they accorded an importance out of all proportion.

The American delegation, for instance, had a most vital problem to resolve. Bomboko, Mwamba and I had gone to greet them the day before at Njili airport. They were led by Robert Murphy, President Eisenhower's personal representative. Among the group there was a certain Clare Timberlake; they had barely disembarked before Murphy introduced him to us as the ambassador designate to the Congo. The American senate was due to start its summer recess almost at once, and every ambassador's nomination must be approved by the senate. It was thus vital that the Congolese government's acceptance of Timberlake be passed on to the senate before it broke up for the summer. The American delegation really worked to achieve this. The staff of their consulate had not waited for Robert Murphy's arrival to start things moving. Eisenhower's personal representative could not possibly be allowed to fail in his mission. He held all the trump cards, in this vastly rich country preparing to throw off the yoke of Belgium – only to fall imperceptibly under another yoke of a more subtle, impersonal and international nature.

On 26 June, the date on which the Congolese head of state was sworn in, I made contact with the UN through the intermediary

141

of Dr Ralph Bunche. He had come to the Congo as under-secretary of the UN to represent the secretary general at the independence celebrations. From the moment of his arrival he had been received by the Congolese with the greatest sympathy and the most profound respect. He was one of the few coloured Americans to have earned an undisputed reputation on the international level; and in his dealings with the new government of the Congo, the fraternity of race played a part that must not be underestimated. I did not know what the Belgian colonial authorities thought of him. He must have met them, since he had arrived in Léopoldville before the first Congolese government took office.

But despite all our esteem for him, Bunche had three major obstacles to contend with. First, he did not speak French, which made it impossible for him to have any confidential talks with the Congolese in the absence of an interpreter. To minimize this dis-advantage he had brought with him a UN official of Chinese (Formosan) origin, Fou Chin-Liu, who spoke faultless French and for that reason had a certain advantage over Bunche and to some extent dominated him. The presence of the interpreter was needed at every important interview – whether official or private – between Bunche and the Congolese or any other French-speaking foreigners. Liu, intelligent, diplomatic, learned and charming though inscrutable, soon won the friendship of the Congolese officials, who finally came to deal directly with him whenever they wanted to have any contact with Bunche.

As an American born and bred, Ralph Bunche could never get away from the all-pervasive watchfulness of American agents, whether official or merely officious. He was always conscious of this, and his whole attitude was affected by their supervision. He could not meet the Congolese authorities without a witness; nor, in consequence, could he expect them to be totally frank with him. He continued, however, to show himself a most discreet diplomat, totally faithful to the instructions of his chief, the secretary general, and a most skilled official: he collected informa-tion and requests, which he passed on to New York, and then waited patiently for his superior's instructions before committing either himself or the secretary general and the UN. But the

American check on his activities became virtually complete; for, having no office of his own in which to work as he would have wanted, he was always forced to ask for assistance from the Diplomatic Mission in Léopoldville. Though the latter was still only a consulate, it was already doing the work of an embassy. And after 30 June 1960, the American consulate became one of the largest embassies in the Congo. It was fully staffed, and supplied with the most up-to-date equipment.

Furthermore, however great his competence, his diplomacy, his strong personality, the Belgian colonial authorities – who were in power until 30 June 1960 – still saw him as just another coloured man. His position was thus extremely delicate, in that he could never take any position or express any view about the relations between the white colonizers and the black colonized without being misinterpreted and suspected by either or both. That was his third handicap.

My first meeting with Ralph Bunche took place after the head of state had been sworn in. It was a meeting that could hardly be other than pleasant, being straightforward and friendly. It was a courtesy meeting, involving an exchange of diplomatic politenesses. Liu, the interpreter, was present, and the interview took place in the Hotel Stanley where Bunche was staying. I felt that he was doing his best to become free of his linguistic dependence on Liu. Whenever he was with a Congolese and not involved in official exchanges, he would try from time to time to interject a few French sentences.

The admission of the Congo to the UN was one of the points I wished to discuss with him. In the minds of colonized peoples, the admission of the new state to membership of the UN was a kind of seal set on their independence, and Lumumba had commissioned me to undertake the customary formalities for our achieving this.

When I met Bunche I took the opportunity to discuss the letter requesting admission which the Congolese government must submit to the secretary general. To save time, it was decided to make the application by means of an official telegram from the prime minister to the secretary general. Lumumba signed the text we had worked out, and gave it to Bunche to send to the secretary general the day after independence was proclaimed.

On 1 July it went off; twenty-four hours later Hammarskjöld acknowledged receipt of the telegram, and replied that the security council would meet to discuss it on 7 July.

Having once met Bunche, I did my best to maintain contact with him, so as to facilitate collaboration Letween the Congolese government and the UN. Bunche's meetings with the Congolese authorities were regular and direct: Bunche always knew whom to consult for every bit of information needed, every decision we asked for. Our meetings became more and more frequent. From exchanging ideas that extended beyond the limitations of the official and diplomatic sphere, we gradually grew to be friends, on Christian-name terms. Bunche's task was also made easier by the fact that I could speak English. If the need arose, he could telephone me without having to use his interpreter.

29   29 June 1960

During a brief talk we had with Lumumba on 29 June, we discovered his personal reaction to the presence of the King of the Belgians in the Congo on Independence Day. 'We' were a group of five friends and colleagues of his.

He had, he told us, hoped that Prince Albert, King Baudouin's brother, would be delegated by the royal family to be its representative. He thought the King should have waited to visit the Republic of the Congo later on, at the official invitation of the new government. Lumumba would then have been able to offer Baudouin the privilege and honour of being the first foreign head of state to visit the Republic. But this was not to be, for Kasavubu had already confirmed the invitation to the King, and the King had agreed to come; indeed, he had already left Brussels for the Congo.

In the course of the same conversation Lumumba commented that the Belgians wanted to humiliate him, and only trusted Kasavubu. 'The Belgians want to humiliate the Congolese people by humiliating me,' he said.

He seemed to know what he was talking about. His sources of information were many and varied. He was very wary of false rumours, and had learnt to mistrust the many rumour-mongers who swarmed around him, but he was under no illusion as to the intentions of Belgium towards himself. The influential Belgians he numbered among his friends had told him of secret talks in Brussels, Léopoldville and Elisabethville, at which he had been discussed, and means had been examined for dealing with him 'temporarily' until he could finally be got rid of. 'The Belgians', he added, 'have managed to get Kasavubu made president; they have now decided to give the Congo its independence, but with strings attached. I have reason to believe that they have received some kind of promises – that Kasavubu is ready to accept those strings, in view of his silence and the whole attitude he seems to be adopting.'

Van Bilsen spent a lot of time with Kasavubu, and Lumumba was very distrustful of him. He knew things about him that I did not, although van Bilsen was one of my oldest Belgian friends: his progressive ideas as put forward before independence pleased the Congolese, and his influence with Kasavubu had, as time went on, grown considerably. But Lumumba tried to convince us that van Bilsen was playing a two-faced rôle in Congolese politics. I was puzzled: I believed that van Bilsen was sincere in his beliefs and opinions; but I also realized that for the past few months he had been influential in Belgian Catholic political groups, and had the ear of those close to Baudouin. How far could he remain a sincere friend of the Congo without betraying both Belgium and his Catholic contacts?

On the eve of independence Lumumba decided that he would not let himself be humiliated, and told us what he had determined. He refused to have any part in the diplomatic events that were to take place the next day. Kasavubu was to make a speech, the contents of which he, the prime minister, knew nothing. This in itself was unconstitutional.

'I am quite sure', he said, 'that the Belgian prime minister would not put up with such an action on the part of King Baudouin. If the Belgian government can begin by going over our heads and dealing directly with Kasavubu, what price the *Loi Fondamentale*?' 'My government', he continued, 'is popular, legal and constitutional, and I shall make sure that all foreign governments treat it with respect – including the Belgians. They are trying to create a precedent – a dangerous precedent – and we must not submit to it. King Baudouin will also make a speech. We do not know what he is going to say. In all courtesy the Belgian prime minister could, and should, let me know the main points in his king's speech. But I am quite sure that Eyskens, Wigny and the other Belgian ministers will do no such thing.'

I was astonished to hear Lumumba talking like this, and the four other people there were equally so. We were all disturbed at the failure of tact and consideration shown by the Belgian govern-

146

ment towards the new young government of the Congo; that the Belgians should still be so narrow-minded, contemptuous and paternalistic towards these former citizens of their colony who were now ministers of state. It seemed to me to be purely and simply meanness (in the sense in which children use the word). That very morning a treaty of friendship, help and cooperation had been signed between the two governments.* And yet, so soon, the Congolese prime minister was feeling himself insulted and humiliated by the Belgian government. Pierry Wigny, the Belgian foreign minister, was hypocritically putting out a communiqué that proclaimed the bonds of friendship and solidarity, the mutual respect for the sovereignty of two independent states, and how the two governments would be holding consultations on an equal footing over all matters of common interest. Now it seemed that the treaty was simply an international legal smokescreen for the Belgian government. There may perhaps have been some intention of friendship and cooperation, but there was certainly none of acting on an equal footing. Had there been, then Lumumba's fears would have been unfounded. In effect, the group of Belgian and Congolese ministers who had formally signed the Belgo–Congolese treaty could very easily have also had a friendly talk about what Baudouin and Kasavubu were going to say; and reached an agreement over what they should *not* say, so as to avoid upsetting public opinion in both countries. But no such talk took place. Lumumba, Gizenga, Delvaux, Bomboko and Kashamura on the Congolese side had met Eyskens, Wigny, de Schrijver, Lilar, de Vleeschauwer, Lefebvre, and Harmel on the Belgian side; but no word was said of the speeches to be made on 30 June.

At the point when the treaty of friendship, aid and cooperation was officially and solemnly signed by the Belgian ministers and their Congolese opposite numbers King Baudouin's speech for the next day was already written; and he himself, already on his plane to the Congo, was due to arrive at four that afternoon.

At that same moment, the Belgian ministers who were there – especially Eyskens, Wigny, de Schrijver, de Vleeschauwer and

*See Appendix 1.

Ganshof van der Meersch – were well aware that Kasavubu was going to say nothing in his speech about the negative aspects of Belgian colonialism. It might have occurred to them to wonder what Lumumba would think; but the men who wielded power in Belgium had not yet given up their general insolence towards us. There were of course a number of Congolese ministers who were still moderate; who felt good will and honourable intentions towards their colonizers; and who were not dominated by this question of equality. There were also a number of foreign visitors who could clearly see the drama being played out in Léopoldville.

They realized that Lumumba had every reason to be furious over some of the attitudes which the Belgian authorities were displaying towards the Congo and its people. What other prime minister – African, Asian or European – would not have felt angry and insulted at such treatment?

On 29 June, as Lumumba spoke to us, he gave all the signs of a man physically exhausted by the superhuman efforts he had been making for the five months since his release from prison. We wondered how long he would be able to carry on at his present pace. He was overworked and worn out. He was disappointed too, yet he still felt some confidence and hope. He had decided to let himself be neither influenced nor condemned by any foreign powers. But he certainly exaggerated the value of the fact that his was the legitimate government, with its constitutional and democratic prerogatives. His faith was more than the facts warranted, and he overestimated the support of the Congolese masses, who were disorganized politically and not yet decolonized mentally. He was too trusting towards his declared friends, and lacked prudence where his enemies were concerned – making it all too clear that he knew their game and was ready to out-manoeuvre them.

Lumumba simply would not believe, would not recognize, that his government was a pathetically fragile edifice which might not stand up to the first gust of wind – whether natural or contrived.

The Congolese head of state was to have almost exactly the same powers as the King of the Belgians. Constitutionally he had no mandate for decision or action except when decision and action were advised and endorsed by two ministers. Every official act of the head of state was the responsibility of the Congolese government. This idea satisfied Belgium since it was something more easily accepted and understood there than an executive presidential rôle. The bad faith of the Belgian ministers here was appalling: had they wished, they could directly or indirectly have advised Kasavubu to submit his speech to the Congolese government for approval. Properly speaking, in fact, it was both the right and the duty of Lumumba's government to prepare and approve the speech before submitting it to the president at all.

What were Kasavubu's own motives in all this? Was he afraid of something? Did he think he would be forced to read a text that ran counter to his own ideas and opinions? If so his fears were groundless. He should have known the limitations of the president's power; and if he did not, then it was up to the Belgian government to remind him, if their intention was genuinely one of friendship and cooperation. But far from doing so, the Belgians who met Kasavubu appeared to enjoy circulating the rumour that the Congolese head of state was independent-minded; that he preferred to write his speech himself rather than be at the mercy of the central government and risk the interference of Lumumba. I was in a position to refute such rumours of his independence categorically: I knew for a fact that parts of the speech given by Kasavubu on 30 June were entirely conceived and written not by himself at all but by foreigners.

Philibert Luyeye, Kasavubu's private secretary, together with Youlou, the then president of Congo-Brazzaville, had redoubled their activities since Kasavubu's election as head of state.

Luyeye, as Kasavubu's trusted private secretary, met a number of different people in the course of carrying out his chief's directives, and passed on written or verbal messages. As for Youlou, his ascendency over Kasavubu was such that he exercised supervision and control over most of the important steps that Kasavubu took. He frequently seemed to forget that his friend and colleague in Léopoldville did not in fact have the same privileges attached to his title as president. Youlou was head of both state and government, whereas Kasavubu was only head of state. Youlou could have prevented Kasavubu from making the unconstitutional blunder of failing to submit his speech to the government. But Youlou hated Lumumba, and was therefore quite unable to be objective or logical. It was not only the Belgians who exploited the rivalries between the two Congolese leaders.

The programme for the celebrations was arranged by Belgian colonials whose names we did not even know. And everything took place in such a disorganized way that it was not unreasonable to suspect some plan to sabotage the celebrations. Certainly a Congolese government existed already in the legal sense but the Congo was not yet independent. That government had only come into being five days before independence and the preparations to celebrate the event had obviously been made well before that. The leading members of the colonial administration remained in ubiquitous control.

King Baudouin arrived in Léopoldville on 29 June at 4 p.m., and the whole Congolese government, together with the head of state, were present to meet him. On the way to the airport there had been a certain fuss over protocol among the ministers, some of whom were only too ready to be uninformed about the estabblished rules of precedence. In theory this problem had been resolved, having been discussed and decided during the first Council of Ministers. But the ministers were still intent on pressing their competitive claims, and though superficially unimportant and innocent this indicated an unfortunate state of affairs. One minister would order his chauffeur to drive faster and overtake the car of a colleague who was perhaps younger and less famous than himself. The idea of there being an established order of precedence was forgotten.

King Baudouin's arrival at Njili airport (more than twelve miles from the centre of the city) passed off without any mishap. It proceeded with a quite remarkable dignity, in fact. The King got into a luxurious American convertible, alongside the Congolese president. The cortège went through the town amid public rejoicing and a general craning of necks.

Then, as it reached the statue of King Albert I, an incident took place which could have spoilt everything: a Congolese came up to the King, snatched up his sword, and ran off in triumph.

The King remained completely unperturbed. The man was chased and restrained by those responsible for keeping order. The cortège had stopped. Everyone at once suspected the worst; but happily it turned out to be an isolated incident, involving only one eccentric citizen seeking attention, and celebrating the joys of independence and the end of colonialism in his own way.

Had it been a premeditated action to create disorder, we should all have panicked: in effect, the maintenance of order and security was still in Belgian hands, still the responsibility of foreigners. Though we sat so comfortably in our sumptuous official cars, driven by uniformed military chauffeurs, and looked as though we were ruling this large and beautiful country, we were in fact ruling nothing and a prey to whatever might happen.

We were, then, still at the mercy of a security system established by our Belgian colonizers. Though for some months they had been running the Congo in preparation for 30 June, they were not actually doing much to prepare for handing over their functions to the Congolese. Many of them still wanted to prove that they were the masters, and that any attempt to manage without them would result in disaster. The colonial administration continued to bear all responsibility, and the Congolese who had come to power only gave the appearance of being in command.

30 Independence: 30 June 1960

It was a historic day for the Congo and for Africa. Lumumba had warned us the day before that there might be some kind of incident, and had also talked to other friends whom he thought influential, in the hope of finding some solution to the diplomatic problem that would arise if Kasavubu did not change his attitude.

The Belgian ministers in the Congo had been indirectly informed of the Congolese prime minister's indignation. The question is whether they in turn had warned the king of the facts, and of the tension between Kasavubu and Lumumba. I do not believe they had. What they had probably told him was that Lumumba was excitable as always; but that they themselves had the matter well in hand, and that there would be no awkwardness.

The official ceremony to mark the proclamation of independence was to take place at 11 a.m. Early in the morning, I was at Lumumba's home, on the Boulevard Albert Ier. He had telephoned me to come at once, and I found him dressed only in trousers, an open-necked shirt and slippers, in the drawing room. With him were four Congolese – among them, Joseph Kasongo, president of the chamber of representatives, and two secretaries of state – and two Belgians, one of whom was a colonial lawyer I knew well. They were deep in talk, discussing a text, and apparently a very important one. Kasongo was obviously annoyed. He was shortly to preside over the solemn session in the Palais de la Nation. One of the other Congolese was adopting a philosophical pose and hesitating to give a definite opinion. The Belgian lawyer was relaxed, and seemed pleased to be there with Lumumba in his own drawing room, when so many Europeans found the greatest difficulty in ever meeting him privately. Lumumba handed me the text: 'Sit down and read this and tell me what you think of it. Quickly.'

My first reaction puzzled him. I was taken aback, and showed it; not by what the text said – which was the simple truth – but at the thought that anyone could think in terms of haste when it came to composing and discussing a text so important in the history of our own country and of Africa as a whole.

I was alarmed because, by every argument of political shrewdness and subtlety, there seemed no need for Lumumba to say these things so brutally on this particular historic day, and before so distinguished an audience. I tried to assess the atmosphere of the discussion before I joined it, and carefully looked at all those present before saying to Lumumba: 'I quite understand your point of view, but I don't see what I can do.'

The Belgian lawyer smiled slightly; the two Congolese secretaries of state remained impassive; Kasongo looked distressed. The only really active person in the room was a young Belgian with a beard, who called everyone *tu*. I knew him only by name. He had worked against colonialism in Stanleyville, which had won him the good opinion and trust of Lumumba and other important members of the MNC; but I soon realized that he was not there to safeguard Congolese interests. The text I had just looked through certainly represented for him a kind of externalization of his own bitterness against his colonizing compatriots, whom he saw as having made money and still making money out of the Congo to the detriment of its people. His thinking was that of a young Belgian socialist militant whose only weapons of revenge were insult, and who felt a genuine revulsion for any subtler methods of diplomacy.

On hearing my reaction, Lumumba explained: 'You see, Thomas, Kasavubu has not changed his mind. I told you that yesterday. It's too late now. Will you work out with these others here how to tidy up the text, and make it acceptable – a bit less explosive? It has to be delivered very soon, so there's no time to lose.'

Less than an hour before 11 o'clock, a Belgian officer came to tell the prime minister that it was time to set out for parliament.

Protocol demanded that the entire Congolese government be present before the foreign guests came in. Lumumba went upstairs to his bedroom and dressed quickly. Kasongo had to leave us to go to parliament. He was obviously upset, and said to me in Lingala: 'Thomas, I'm counting on you to do your best to tone down that speech.'

I went up to the prime minister while he was dressing, with one of the secretaries of state. Between us we had not enough time to read and correct the whole text of the speech. Some words we simply replaced with less violent ones. Three or four paragraphs we totally excised; trying to tone them down would have taken too long. We told the prime minister what we had done, and begged him to pass over such sections.

Downstairs, the Belgian officer was getting impatient. He realized that the prime minister was not yet ready, and that the text we were working on must be important since Lumumba would not leave without it. At his insistence, Lumumba finally left his private house to join the rest of the government. They were waiting for him at his official residence, not far from Parliament House, beside the river Congo, in the Boulevard Tilkins.

The secretary of state and I followed him in the second car of the cortège. We carried on as best we could re-reading, correcting, and softening the text of the speech. We had to rest content with putting our alterations and additions in the margin. Every page was riddled with amendments, and we were afraid that its author would find it hard to read. Once we got to the official residence Lumumba gave us a few moments to explain the changes we had made. Regretfully we handed over the text of his speech, so hastily amended. He was delighted, indeed almost jubilant. He promised us he would change it as he went along: in fact, he resolved to read part of the text, to leave out a few paragraphs, and to improvise as the atmosphere of the gathering might seem to suggest.

Lumumba's determination was inflexible. No one on earth could have stopped him that day from making his speech at that solemn session when independence was proclaimed. Belgium had presented him with a challenge by purposely slighting him, and he intended to meet it.

Protocol decreed that he sit beside Gaston Eyskens, the Belgian prime minister. That fact did not trouble him at all. Abbé Youlou was there too. King Baudouin was sitting with Kasavubu on a separate platform.

Joseph Kasongo presided over the meeting, and kept a close watch on the reactions of Lumumba, and the various foreign dignitaries present. Joseph Ileo, president of the Senate, was beside him.

The King of the Belgians made his speech in a firm voice, but with great emotion:

Mr President, Gentlemen,

The independence of the Congo is the conclusion of a work conceived by the genius of King Leopold II, which he undertook with tenacious courage, and which Belgium has continued perseveringly. It marks a decisive moment not only in the destiny of the Congo itself, but, I can surely say, of all Africa.

For eighty years, Belgium has sent to your land the finest of her sons, first to free the Congo basin from the appalling slave traffic that was decimating its populations; then to unite ethnic groups which had been enemies but have gradually come together to form the largest of the independent African states; and lastly, to call to a happier life all the various areas of the Congo represented by those gathered together here in a single parliament. . . .

When Leopold II undertook the great work which today finds its consummation, he did not come in the guise of a conqueror, but of a civilizer.

From its foundation, the Congo has opened its frontiers to international trade without Belgium's ever having exerted a monopoly for her own exclusive interests.

The Congo has been given railways, roads, waterways and air routes which, by bringing your people into contact with one another, have fostered their unity and given your country worldwide opportunities. . . . Thanks to the mission schools, and also those supported by the authorities, primary education has been widely extended, and an intellectual élite has begun to be formed which your own universities will rapidly enlarge.

An ever-increasing number of qualified workers – in agriculture, industry, craftsmanship, commerce, and administration – are bringing about in all classes of the community that emancipation of the individual which constitutes the basis of all genuine civilization.

We are happy to have thus, despite the gravest difficulties, given to the Congo the elements needed to prepare a country on its way to development.

The great independence movement taking place all over Africa has been best understood by the authorities in Belgium. In response to the unanimous wish of your peoples, we have not hesitated to grant you that independence at once.

It is for you, gentlemen, to prove that we were right thus to place our confidence in you.

From now on, Belgium and the Congo will stand side by side as two sovereign states linked by friendship and determined to provide each other with mutual help. So, today, we put into your hands all the administrative, economic, technical and social services, as also the organization of justice without which no modern state can survive. Belgian officials are prepared to collaborate sincerely and intelligently with you.

Your task is enormous, as you yourselves are the first to recognize. The main dangers you face are: the lack of experience of self-government among your peoples; tribal struggles, which have done such harm in the past, and which must at all cost be prevented from recurring; and the attraction foreign powers may exercise over some areas with a view to profiting from the slightest sign of weakness on your part.

Your leaders know what a hard task it is to rule. Whatever party they belong to they must make their first concern the interests of the country as a whole. They must teach the Congolese people that independence is not achieved by the immediate satisfaction of mere enjoyment, but by work, by respecting the liberty of others and the rights of minorities, by tolerance and order – indeed without this last no democratic régime can survive.

I would like here to give special praise to the *Force Publique* which has carried out its difficult mission with unfailing courage and devotion.

Independence will call for effort and sacrifice from all concerned. Institutions will have to be modified to suit your ideas and your needs, so that they will become stable and balanced.

You will also have to form administrative cadres, and to experiment as to how best to intensify the intellectual and moral development of the people, preserve the stability of your currency, and safeguard and develop your economic, social and financial organizations.

Do not place the future at risk through over-hasty reforms, nor replace the organizations that Belgium has given you unless you are quite sure of being able to provide better ones.

Watch carefully over the continuance of your medical services, for their interruption would be disastrous indeed, resulting in the re-appearance of illnesses which we have conquered. Watch too over the scientific work which is a quite inestimable intellectual inheritance we are leaving you. Never forget that to have an unemotional and inde-pendent system of justice is indispensable for social peace; to guarantee a respect for the individual's rights confers upon any state great moral authority in the international sphere.

Do not be afraid to turn to us. We are ready to remain at hand and help you with advice, and in training the technicians and officials you will need.

Africa and Europe are complementary, and, if they cooperate, can achieve great things. The Congo and Belgium can play a leading rôle in such fruitful and constructive collaboration, and mutual confidence.

Gentlemen, the entire world is watching you. When the Congo makes its own free choice of a life-style, I trust that the Congolese people will preserve and develop the inheritance of spiritual, moral and religious values which we share, and which can overcome all political vicissitudes, all differences of race or nation.

Remain united, and you will show yourselves worthy of the great part you are called on to play in the history of Africa.

People of the Congo, my country and I recognize with joy and emotion that on this 30th of June 1960, the Congo, in full agreement and friendship with Belgium, has attained independence and inter-national sovereignty. May God protect the Congo!

Kasavubu, in his turn, faithfully read out the text that had been composed for him:

Your Majesty, Your Excellencies, my dear compatriots,

At this solemn moment, as the Republic of the Congo stands before the world and history as fully independent and sovereign; at this moment when we feel most intensely the irrevocable and final nature of the step we are taking, we cannot help considering the seriousness of our responsibilities, and we ask God, in a spirit of profound humility, to protect our people and guide all their leaders.

Before anything else, I should like to express most warmly the gratitude we feel towards all those who have worked, whether privately or publicly, for our national emancipation, and all those who, through-out our vast land, have been unsparing in giving of their strength, their sufferings, and even their lives, in order to realize their bold dream of a free and independent Congo. Think of those workers on the building sites and in the factories, those who have cultivated our plains and valleys, and also of all those intellectuals of every age who have felt an irresistible longing for freedom rising in their hearts, and have remained faithful to their ideal and done all they could to fulfil it. Think also of our women, who, never flinching, have given courage to their sons and husbands in all their splendid struggles, and have even fought beside them in the heat of the battle.

The independent Congo which you have all worked so magnificently to create thanks you with an infinite gratitude and solemnly assures you that you will never be forgotten.

Now let us look to the future.

Independence is dawning on a land whose economic structure is outstanding, well balanced and firmly united. But the lack of universal national awareness among our peoples has given rise to some disquiet, which I should like to dissipate today by reminding you of all the progress already achieved in this area and which is our surest guarantee that we shall succeed in travelling the rest of the way.

After all, what vast differences there were, when our country was first founded, among peoples who all did their share in preserving the distances between them: even apart from variations of language, custom and social structure, think of the vast distances that separated us, and the lack of modern means of communication at the end of the last century. We could only get to know one another through contact. A great many peoples living within this vast land felt nothing in common with one another at all. You have reminded us, Your Majesty, how much the advancement of travelling arrangements has contributed to bringing the country together in a network of mutual exchange, which helps enormously in bringing individuals closer. Economic development, also, has resulted in the building of cities for workers and centres where those from different ethnic groups have learnt to live together, to understand one another better, and insensibly to achieve a certain osmosis. Exchanges are becoming more frequent, the regions are coming gradually to collaborate in their development. The advances in education, the formation and diffusion of newspapers and periodicals, the increase in radio stations – all these things have contributed, first in the towns, and then in rural areas, to the creation of a public opinion which has gradually been growing into a genuine national consciousness.

Belgium then had the wisdom not to resist the movement of history; understanding the magnificent ideal of freedom which inspires all hearts in the Congo, she has been able – an unprecedented step in the history of peaceful decolonization – to let our country move directly and without any transition from foreign rule to full national sovereignty.

But, while we rejoice at this decision, we must not forget that it is now for us to take up the work, and draw together the elements that must form our national identity, to construct our nation in unity and solidarity.

For this purpose we have at our disposal a wide range of means, but we must be sure to use them with wisdom, without either haste or delay, but working in harmony with the natural rhythms of life; we must neither march forward too swiftly, leaving people behind, panting by the roadside, nor must we be content to sit back and happily admire what we have so far achieved. National awareness has for a long time been leading the peoples of the Congo towards a greater sense of solidarity: it is for us to do all we can to foster this movement of national identity.

In this striving for greater national cohesion, there will be a very special rôle for the central institutions of our country, and above all for the work of the legislative chambers. There are some among us, gentlemen, senators and deputies, who have only just made contact for the first time with those chosen by other provinces. It has been astounding to discover how closely linked are all our ideals and concerns. I am convinced that you will make these sessions a real crucible for forging an ever stronger national consciousness.

All over the country, we shall have also to further the acceptance of everything good that eighty years of contact with the West has brought with it: the language, the indispensable tool for satisfactory relationships; the legislation which has imperceptibly influenced the development of all our varying customs and gradually brought them closer together; and finally, and most important of all, the culture. There is already a basic affinity of culture among all the Bantu; in addition, our contact with Christian civilization, and the roots that civilization has put down among us, will give new life to our old blood, and bestow on our cultural manifestations a peculiar originality and impulse to advance. We shall be concerned to foster the flowering of this national culture, and to help our people at every level to recognize its message and deepen it. This will be a truly essential mission, for culture must be the true unifying agent in a nation.

This effort, together with an understanding of the elements that make for national unity, must be the prime concern of us all. No one living in this country can refuse to take his share in this vital obligation.

In this vast worksite of fourteen million people – which is what our country is – we shall be there to enlighten and guide all those who dedicate themselves to this task with enthusiasm.

It is this community of effort, of suffering, and of work that will most certainly unite all the Congolese into one large, independent and stable nation. We shall thus, by our actions show the world that we are worthy of the trust the people have placed in us – which many countries have already accepted. We shall not disappoint them.

In the name of the nation, I proclaim the birth of the Republic of the Congo.

Kasavubu's original text included some further paragraphs. At the last minute, he decided not to give them, though they would have given great pleasure to the Belgians. I append them here by way of interest:

Your Majesty,

Your presence at the ceremonies of this memorable day provides a further outstanding indication of your concern for all these peoples whom you have loved and protected. They are happy to be able, today, to express both their gratitude for the good things you and your illustrious predecessors have done for them, and their delight in your understanding of their aspirations.

They have heard your message of friendship with all the respect and enthusiasm they feel for you, and will long remember in their hearts the words you have spoken to them at this deeply moving time.

They will appreciate the value of the friendship offered them by Belgium, and will set out with enthusiasm along the path of sincere collaboration.

You, gentlemen, who represent foreign powers, you have been ready to share our joys, and have done us the honour of coming in force to celebrate these historic days with us. It will therefore not be difficult to establish friendly relations between our country and all of yours in the future.

You see around you the great excitement among all our people, and you must feel our desire to succeed and do well; I ask you then, to present to the world this hopeful image you will take with you when you leave the Congo – it is the true image.

The rest of the programme provided, especially for the Belgian ministers, a definite proof that they had been mistaken in under-estimating Lumumba's courage and determination.

The Belgian authorities had forgotten that the session would be under the chairmanship of Joseph Kasongo. A week earlier, Lumumba had succeeded, against all expectations, in getting Kasongo elected to the enviable post of president of the chamber of deputies. Who could be naïve enough to think that Kasongo would dare to oppose Lumumba publicly ? The situation might have been totally different had Joseph Ileo been presiding over the session.

Lumumba had long been decolonized in his own mind, and since 24 June he had been the prime minister of the Congo. He should have been accepted and treated as such by all foreign governments, including the Belgians. Kasongo invited the prime minister to the platform, and Lumumba gave his speech, which was at once taken as an insult and affront to the King, to the Belgian government and indeed the whole of Belgium. Here is the official text of what he said:

Men and women of the Congo, who have fought for and won the Independence we celebrate today, I salute you in the name of the Congolese government.

I ask you all, friends who have fought unrelentingly side by side to make this 30th of June 1960 an illustrious date that remains ineradicably engraved on your hearts, a date whose significance you will be proud to teach to your children, who will in turn pass on to their children and grandchildren the glorious story of our struggle for liberty.

For while the independence of the Congo has today been proclaimed in agreement with Belgium, a friendly country with whom we deal on an equal footing, no Congolese worthy of the name will ever be able to forget that that independence has only been won by struggle, a struggle that went on day after day, a struggle of fire and idealism, a struggle in which we have spared neither effort, deprivation, suffering or even our blood.

This struggle, involving tears, fire and blood, is something of which we are proud in our deepest hearts, for it was a noble and just struggle, which was needed to bring to an end the humiliating slavery imposed on us by force.

Such was our lot for eighty years under the colonialist régime; our wounds are still too fresh and painful for us to be able to forget them at will, for we have experienced painful labour demanded of us in return for wages that were not enough to enable us to eat properly, nor to be decently dressed or sheltered, nor to bring up our children as we longed to.

We have experienced contempt, insults and blows, morning, noon and night, because we were 'blacks'. We shall never forget that a black was called *tu*, not because he was a friend, but because only the whites were given the honour of being called *vous*.

We have seen our lands despoiled in the name of so-called legal documents which were no more than a recognition of superior force.

We have known that the law was never the same for a white man as it was for a black: for the former it made allowances, for the latter it was cruel and inhuman.

We have seen the appalling suffering of those who had their political opinions and religious beliefs dismissed; as exiles in their own country their lot was truly worse than death.

We have seen magnificent houses in the towns for the whites, and crumbling straw huts for the blacks; a black could not go to the cinema, or a restaurant, or a shop that was meant for 'Europeans'; a black would always travel in the lowest part of a ship, under the feet of the whites in their luxurious cabins.

And finally, who can ever forget the firing in which so many of our brothers died; or the cells where those who refused to submit any longer to the rule of a 'justice' of oppression and exploitation were put away?

All this, brothers, has meant the most profound suffering.

But all this, we can now say, we who have been voted by your elected representatives to govern our beloved country, we who have suffered in body and mind from colonialist oppression, all this is now ended.

The Republic of the Congo has been proclaimed, and our land is now in the hands of her own children.

Together, brothers and sisters, we shall start on a new struggle, a noble struggle that will bring our country to peace, prosperity and greatness.

Together we shall establish social justice, and ensure that everyone is properly rewarded for the work he does.

We shall show the world what the black man can do when he is allowed to work in freedom, and we shall make the Congo the focal point of all Africa.

We shall take care that the soil of our country really provides for the good of her children.

We shall review all the laws of the past, and make new ones that are just and noble.

We shall put an end to all suppression of free thought, and make it possible for all our citizens to enjoy to the full those fundamental freedoms spoken of in the Declaration of Human Rights.

We shall effectively suppress all discrimination of every kind, and give everyone his true place as dictated by his human dignity, his work and his dedication to his country.

We shall set up a rule of peace – not with guns and bayonets, but peace of heart and goodwill.

And for all this, my dear fellow-citizens, you may be sure that we can count not only on our great forces and immense resources, but on the aid of many other countries whose collaboration we shall always accept when it is sincere and not an attempt to force us into any political alignment.

In this connection, even Belgium, who, having at last understood the way history was going, has no longer tried to prevent our independence, is ready to give us aid and friendship, and a treaty to that effect has just been signed as between two equal and independent countries. Such cooperation, I am sure, will profit both our countries. For our part, while remaining on the watch, we shall respect the engagements into which we have freely entered.

Thus, both within and without, the new Congo which my government creates will be a rich, free, and prosperous country. But if we are to achieve this object quickly, I must ask you all, legislators and citizens of the Congo, to do everything in your power to help me.

I ask you all to forget the tribal rivalries that dissipate our energies and make us the laughing-stock of foreigners.

I ask the parliamentary minority to help my government by making their opposition constructive and keeping it strictly within legal and democratic channels.

I ask you all to hold back from no sacrifice that will ensure the success of our magnificent enterprise.

Lastly, I ask you to show unconditional respect for the lives and goods both of your fellow-citizens and of the foreigners living in our midst.

If those foreigners behave badly, they will be expelled from our territory by law; if, on the other hand, they behave well, then they must be left in peace, for they too are working for the good of the Congo.

The independence of the Congo marks a decisive step towards the liberation of the whole African continent.

This, then, Your Majesty, Your Excellencies, Ladies and Gentlemen, my dear fellow-citizens, my brothers by blood, and my brothers in the struggle, this is what I wanted to say to you in the name of the government on this wonderful day of our full and sovereign independence.

Our government, strong, national, and popular, will be the salvation of this country.

I urge all Congolese citizens, men, women and children, to set resolutely to work to create a prosperous national economy and thus guarantee our economic independence.

Honour to those who have fought for national liberty!

Long live the independence and unity of Africa!

Long live the sovereign and independent Congo!

Looking back on events coolly and objectively, I cannot help wondering who should really take the blame for Lumumba's speech, which the Belgians considered so appallingly arrogant.

Why did Kasavubu not submit his speech to the Congolese government for approval?

Why did the Belgian ministers in Léopoldville not use their good offices before the ceremony to achieve a meeting between Kasavubu and Lumumba? I am convinced that, had there been such a meeting, many subsequent diplomatic disasters could have been avoided.

Certainly Lumumba's speech was inopportune and discourteous. But what are we to say of Kasavubu's unfounded mistrust? And what of the whole paternalistic attitude of the Belgians, so unregenerate in the speech made by the King?

31   Patrice Lumumba: Alone in Power

The functioning of the first Congolese government seemed to me from the first to be bizarre and unique; though excusable in view of its members' lack of experience, organization, equipment, coordination, of almost everything.

Lumumba's first disappointment came when he suddenly recognized the impossibility of getting a government formed a week before independence to function normally – especially when that government was made up of people who had never before held the responsibility of state office. His second disappointment arose from the fact that in accepting the leadership of a government to unite the nation, he was inevitably forced into certain concessions and compromises; he had to work with people who, though they were his political opponents or personal enemies, were henceforth to be effective members of his government, charged with important responsibilities.

His first serious mistake was his refusal to come to terms with this state of affairs – even only temporarily, until he could arrange matters better. Having become a statesman, Lumumba acted towards those he distrusted without any pretence of diplomacy or manoeuvring of any kind. He was too self-confident. In accepting him as prime minister, the anti-Lumumbists were simply giving themselves more leverage. Why did Lumumba never realize this, and act accordingly? We shall probably never know. He knew how to win power, but it seems that he never made any plan for keeping it, despite all the alliances that were formed against his government, and against him personally.

He did not collaborate smoothly with Kasavubu, the head of state, before independence. And Bomboko, too, complained that contacts with foreign delegations were being made by all the ministers together, and Lumumba in particular, rather than by himself, whose job it should have been. The Belgian General Jannsens, head of the *Force Publique*, had a very poor opinion of Lumumba, and though Lumumba knew this he hesitated to demand his dismissal before 30 June. Albert Kalonji, delegate from the Kasai province where the Congo's diamonds were to be found, was more arrogant than ever. He declared publicly that Lumumba had grabbed the position that rightfully should have been his; and that he therefore intended to act, and not rest content with being merely a member of parliament. And Kalonji was to be reckoned with: he really thought himself a kind of 'king' by divine right. Moïse Tshombe, established by the Belgians as provincial president of Katanga, showed every intention of dealing with Kasavubu as an equal. He looked upon Congo-Léopoldville as a neighbouring but foreign country, with which an autonomous or independent Katanga might negotiate certain economic, financial, cultural, military and other agreements. He had no intention of being treated like the other provincial presidents; he and his friends considered Katanga not a province, but a state.

All the circumstances that were to bring down Lumumba's government were already in evidence. Everyone's personal bitterness and hatred centred on him. He felt this, but had not the realism, or perhaps the cynicism, to elude the ambushes that awaited him.

He was a jovial politician, an excellent strategist, an eloquent speaker and a supreme tactician, but he had not the time he needed to make use of these qualities as a statesman. Events, time, circumstances, his cumbersome and unfriendly entourage, all forced him to improvise, to make rush decisions, ever more numerous errors, and to fall open-eyed into the traps set by his opponents.

As Roger Verbeck says:

Lumumba had too generous a view of human nature. He believed in the virtue of truth, and thought one had only to denounce a scandal for it to stop. He underestimated the power of the enemy, those monopolies he hoped to break up by fervent oratory. It was the same optimism that made him sure he had only to appeal to the progressive masses all over the world in order for them to rush to the aid of the Congolese people.[1]

The Belgians who thought that they knew Lumumba and his political ideas were the first to be astounded at finding that he had been elected prime minister. In reality, Lumumba himself had not changed, but his friends had changed their opinions of him. Some wanted the privilege of proclaiming themselves publicly his intimate friends; others considered themselves as benefactors to whom Lumumba owed a certain gratitude. Both groups were proud of this former Post-Office employee who had become prime minister, but they could never in their hearts believe that Lumumba would henceforth serve the interests of his people. And he, while remaining affable to his old friends, both white and black, could never forget his new status and responsibilities.

Lumumba's dream had always been to lead the Congo, to become the equal, and if possible, the superior, of the most illustrious leaders in the history of African liberation. His immediate ambition was to be the head of the Congolese government, 'the boss'. One surprising fact seems to have determined Lumumba's political life: close friends declared that he was predestined not to live long. He was convinced of his mission to free the Congo, but he also firmly believed that he had only a short time at his disposal, and must do as much as he could as quickly as possible. This would certainly explain his impatience, his impulsive behaviour, his mistrust of all those who advised him to wait, to give himself time, to consider his actions carefully and think before he spoke.

I can remember one most significant instance of this. I myself once advised Lumumba not to become the leader of the first government, given the unstable political alliances that would be needed for him to be accepted as prime minister by the Western countries which had such enormous financial interests in the Congo. After the elections, Lumumba had a comparatively comfortable majority inside parliament, and that majority would make it possible for him to control the government more easily than to lead it. My suggestion was ill received, despite the tactful

1. op. cit., p. 196.

way I had framed it. I knew rather more than did Lumumba's Congolese entourage about the nature of Western opposition to Congolese nationalism, and of the kind of reaction that his slightest political or diplomatic mistake would be apt to provoke.

I had, therefore, suggested to Lumumba that he get himself elected president of the chamber of deputies, and propose Cyrille Adoula for prime minister. This was at the time of his first visit to my father's home. Everything was still in the realm of possibility, since none of the major posts in the republic had yet been filled. Adoula had just been co-opted as senator with difficulty. Politically he was no danger to Lumumba, who knew him well; they had worked together in the beginnings of the MNC; at the diplomatic level, Adoula was well known as a socialist but anti-communist trades unionist, though in point of fact he did not believe in Marxist socialism. He had the advantage over Lumumba of being a *Mwana ya Lipopo* – a 'son of the capital' – and knew far better than Lumumba the intricate pattern of friendships and enmities among the people of Léopoldville. Lumumba had lived in Léopoldville only since 1957.

His own political allies and most of those who supported him in parliament were provincial politicians only just discovering the marvels and glitter of the capital. The vultures from all over the world who had been sent to stay in Léopoldville to safeguard Western interests had already gone quite far in corrupting the naïve among them, especially those who hoped to get rich quickly and easily. Furthermore, though Lumumba and Adoula were opposed politically, they did not personally dislike each other.

Events in the Congo would undoubtedly have been very different had Kasavubu been president with Adoula as prime minister, dependent on the support of Lumumba as president of the Chamber, and of Alexandre Mahamba as president of the Senate. The hostility which crystallized around the person of Lumumba, both inside and outside the Congo, may well have gradually weakened. Lumumba would in this way have partially disarmed the plots against him, and would have gained the time and perspective necessary to reorganize his party, by including his genuine friends and removing his implacable enemies. Albert Kalonji, the deputy from South Kasai, and Moïse Tshombe, the provincial president of Katanga, would probably never have gone so far in their ambition and hatred as to proclaim the secession of their two provinces. Furthermore, the Belgian mining companies which were behind these secessions might well have found it wiser not to pursue such dangerous plans. The Catholic Church, which worked through Congolese intermediaries, both priests and laymen, and through Belgian professors at Lovanium, might perhaps have behaved more realistically. It would have abandoned its exaggerated fears of seeing communism overrun central Africa, persecuting its missionaries.

Such a distribution of responsibilities would temporarily have satisfied Belgian financial interests as well, and indeed those of Europe and America generally. In short, the main beneficiary of such a compromise would be Lumumba – who would emerge a few months later as the strongest, most popular and most astute of all Congolese politicians. For a time he would have been the *éminence grise* in the government, while carefully and methodically making ready for the fusion and unification of the various nationalist political parties whose uncontested leader he would in the process become.

It was clear from the exchanges of opinion and the discussions that took place before the investiture of Lumumba's government that he would never be able to govern the Congo in peace and stability.

Those who knew him personally were convinced that he would, sooner or later, try to overthrow Kasavubu, so as to combine the functions of head of state and head of government. Many of those who had only heard about him were afraid of him, especially if they happened to be Catholic and conservative. People who had no admiration for him made no effort to understand and judge him in the context of the Congo, nor to recognize his merits. They condemned him out of hand. And the people who described themselves as 'Patrice's friends' were certainly too numerous for all of them to be loyal and sincere; they were not, many of them, to be taken seriously.

Ultimately, Lumumba found himself lonely and confused, in spite of his glamorous, powerful and honourable position. Public opinion was used to its picture of Patrice as a handsome young man, an elegant politician, a perfect orator, a manipulator, an ambitious man; it was not possible to think of him as lonely, confused and defeated.

Seated in his chair, in his new office, Lumumba saw pictures of Ryckmans, Jungers, Pétillon, Cornélis, the four Belgians who had been governors-general of the Congo since the Second World War. They had all sat in that same chair to do their governing, at that same table, in that same room.

He felt the overwhelming burden of the Congo – more than a nation, almost a continent. Up till then, he had idealized and magnified it: the Congolese were unhappy because of the Belgians; that the Congo was not united and free was due only to the imperialists. In the future, Lumumba was to be blamed for whatever went badly, and to receive little congratulation for what went well. As for the imperialists, he would have to stop openly insulting them, and, on the contrary, cooperate with them as far as he possibly could, in order to preserve a united and prosperous Congo, till he could act with greater freedom. Otherwise, those same imperialists would speak of the Congo as an independent country; yet see it in reality as dependent and still colonized. They would not need Lumumba; they could manage quite well without him.

There were two great thorns in his flesh: how was he to secure the internal and external security of his country; and how could he prevent the mineral wealth of its land from becoming the cause and source of its people's misfortune? In other words, how was he so to control the colonial *Force Publique* as to make what had been an instrument for repression, the guarantee of national independence; and how to stop the anger and dissatisfaction of the capitalists from producing the secession of Katanga and Kasai, and the balkanization of the Congo?

Though he was in power, Lumumba felt far from content. He still had to fight. His fight now was to win *real* independence for the Congo; merely nominal independence was not enough. With this great aim to spur him on, and inspired by who knows what supernatural faith, Lumumba was prepared to sacrifice himself if such a sacrifice had to be the price paid for the effective liberation of the Congolese people. He could no longer be influenced by events: he wanted to direct them, to change them in line with his ideals and convictions. Instead of seeing people as they were, he imagined them as he wanted them to be.

Lumumba was almost obsessed by this struggle to the death against colonialism and imperialism in all their forms: economic, financial, military, political, cultural, ideological. There was not a soul who could have persuaded him that it was a struggle that would take years, possibly even generations, to win; and that he was wrong to rush at it headlong, alone and effectively powerless. Lumumba fought alone, because he alone knew why he was fighting and how.

The criteria he considered basic for true independence were indeed noble, but they called for more than just watchfulness and skill if they were to be gradually achieved. The first criterion was to be a government made up solely of native Congolese, and a fully Africanized administration. The second was to be firm control by the national government of what General de Gaulle called 'the three levers for wielding power abroad, i.e. the diplomacy to express it, the army to uphold it, and the police to protect it'.

Now that he was prime minister, Lumumba was hoping that he could apply these two essential criteria immediately, and he thought that by so doing he would make his government an independent authority, and the Congo a genuinely sovereign state.

Without bothering to take the vital precautions needed, Lumumba determined to take control of the army and police out of the hands of the foreigners. He attributed to such men the intention – admitted or otherwise – of being prepared at any minute to use their commands against his government.

Lumumba planned to entrust all the responsible positions in the army and the police to Congolese of firm convictions; men whose devotion to their country was not in doubt. He believed that the skill needed to do the job could then be learnt; it would depend on individual suitability, training, education, and good will on the part of those chosen. Or so he intended. But unfortunately Lumumba announced all this before ever being in a position to put his ideas into practice. His enemies therefore had all the time they needed to prepare their campaign against them. More than once, Lumumba had to act hastily, and even to improvise decisions of major importance; aware that the realities of life were far from harmonizing with his intentions and ideals. His fine nationalist principles needed both time and genuine support if they were to be put into effect in the Congo. He gradually discovered that many of those whom he had selected as collaborators or friends were nationalists in name only, and that in their hearts they intended to work for a cause very different from his. A number of them gradually dissociated themselves from him altogether.

To Africanize the administration remained an absolute imperative for him. Most of the appointments he had made to positions of responsibility were not properly considered. He made a point of simply not seeing self-interest, revenge, jealousy and ambition where it existed, nor the marked tribalism in so many of his fellow-citizens. He made the further serious error of minimizing the dislike that the former colonizers felt for himself: as, for instance, the directors of the powerful Union Minière du Haut-Katanga, the Kivu settlers, and all the various business groups which were determined to get him out of power. In their methodical way, those groups were already one step ahead of Lumumba; many of his self-styled political allies were purely nominal friends.

32 The Problem of the *Force Publique*

Lumumba combined the functions of prime minister and minister of national defence. It was his intention to reorganize the *Force Publique* totally. He did not intend to get rid of the Belgians (who were the only officers) immediately; on the contrary, he was depending on some of them, especially Colonel Henniquiaux, to help him in the work of reorganizing and decolonizing what was to become the Congolese National Army (ANC).

Since March 1960, Lumumba had been considering a memorandum put out by the central committee of the *Fraternelle des anciens militaires congolais de la Force Publique*. His plan for reorganizing the *Force Publique* coincided in the main with the points made in that memorandum. This I knew because he had talked it over with my father, whom he intended, when the time was ripe, to bring into his government as defence minister. As an old soldier, my father knew most of those in the army, of his generation, who had been the authors of the memorandum. Here are the major points from it:

Fraternelle des anciens militaires congolais de la Force Publique
Léopoldville, 18 March 1960

... We are bold enough to believe that our country owes us some gratitude, and that those involved in the administration should try to express that gratitude in some concrete form. If such is their intention, we submit to them our wishes here, in the hope that these will be looked at with the care they deserve. We take the same occasion to submit to them our views and considerations on the pressing problems of the moment, especially those relating more or less closely to the security of the new nation.

1. PUBLIC FUNCTIONS

(a) *Ministry of National Defence*

The former soldiers of the Congo would like this portfolio to be given to one of their number, if possible a non-political man. To this purpose, the man who makes up the first Congolese government would have a choice of twelve candidates presented to him by our fraternity, each group having the brief of presenting one candidate per province.

(b) *Functioning of the Ministry of National Defence*

The former soldiers would stress, in order that military secrets be secure, that the responsibilities of the officials in the Ministry of National Defence be given to those who have served as soldiers in preference to other candidates. It should be an absolute condition that anyone wishing to work in this ministry will have done his military service.

(c) *National Security*

It is no secret that the new Congolese state is subject to the covetousness of foreign powers. It is equally true that there are some citizens and leaders whose self-interest would not yield to any scruples about safeguarding the superior interest of the nation, and who could be corrupted to serve those foreign powers.

To provide against the ultimate disorder which might result from political trickery and personal ambition (attempts to overthrow the established authorities, plots against individuals, etc.), the job of safeguarding the security of the new nation should be given to former soldiers. Not merely do these have a strong civic sense, but their military training itself provides a far from negligible advantage. It is inconceivable, indeed, that the security of our country should remain in the hands of foreigners, some of whom were to the very last firm opponents of our achieving independence (AFAC, settlers etc.).

(d) *The Police Force*

Ex-soldiers are also ready to take over the running of the national police force. Their functions are indeed closely bound up with the defence of our national security, and it is vital that they be exercised as soon as possible by our own people.

2. TRAINING COURSE FOR EX-SOLDIERS

To carry out the various functions mentioned with a minimum of efficiency, it is vital that some ex-soldiers be at once given a crash course, which can later on be filled in and completed. In this way, by 30 June the present staff, made up wholly of non-Congolese, can be largely filled by our own people. *To achieve this rapid training, we require a fair share in the grant of fifty million francs which the government has just placed at the disposal of the Congo.*

3. METROPOLITAN BASES IN THE CONGO

We ex-soldiers would like to have demanded the pure and simple abolition of these foreign bases if the political problem posed by their existence did not link up with other problems of a social and economic nature. It seems, in effect, that these bases employ something in the region of 15,000 Congolese.

... One must not, however, underestimate the danger of their continuing indefinitely, especially since we know that a good number of the non-Africans living in this country fought against independence for the Congo, and have received it with coolness if not actual displeasure.

We therefore propose as soon as possible to bring to an end the duality produced by the presence on our country's soil of two armies, our own and a foreign one. To this purpose, economic programmes to be set up by the future Congolese government should consider as among their first priorities the absorption of the labour force now working in the metropolitan bases (in building the Inga dam, for instance; mining the bauxite in the Lower Congo; and undertaking various public works throughout the country).

4. REORGANIZATION OF THE *Force Publique*

This organization must change its name on 30 June. It must become the Congolese National Army. In this way not only its spirit, but also its organization can be changed.

Among the modifications to be made, we suggest both reducing the length of active military service to eighteen months or two years, and enlisting all young men capable of doing military service. The latter will then be obligatory, though of course this must depend on how much money the new state can afford to spend. As a result the wives, apart from those of regular soldiers, will no longer be able to come with their husbands. To minimize the possible disadvantages of this social reform, enlistment in the army must take place at the age of eighteen.

A real effort must also be made gradually to Africanize the leadership in the army. Here one may call r..t only on soldiers and former soldiers, but also on young men who have got secondary school diplomas and who could go through a technical military training course of six months or so and emerge as junior officers. The best-suited among them might carry on their training in military schools abroad, until we have schools of our own.

We ask all the presidents of our groups throughout the country to be willing to contact all the political leaders of their provinces and give them the viewpoint of the former soldiers about all the various matters discussed above.

THE CENTRAL COMMITTEE

Belgium had totally neglected to Africanize the leadership of the *Force Publique*. While the administration contained senior Congolese officials, and there were Congolese coming out of the universities both in the Congo and in Belgium, one could only deplore the total absence of Congolese officers – whether training in military schools abroad, or working in the Congo.

On 23 April 1960, two months before independence, Lieut.-General Janssens, the commander-in-chief of the *Force Publique*, was still making suggestions about the 'need for a firm and loyal army, capable of enforcing the decisions of a wise, prudent and strong government'.[1]

This leading Belgian officer, whose military competence was unquestionable, had far more need than the Congolese of an immediate and enormous injection of mental decolonization. Indeed, he thought it perfectly natural to declare, on 23 April, to a group of Congolese political leaders:

To cross the difficult peak of the transmission of power and the first months of the new state, the *Force Publique*, the only force available, ought to pass intact into the service of the Congolese government, with its leaders, its traditions, its discipline, its unique hierarchy and above all its morale, unchanged.

1. Ganshof van der Meersch, *Fin de la souveraineté belge au Congo*, 1963, Brussels, *Institut Royal des Relations Internationals*, p. 402.

He added that in his opinion it was not yet time to disturb the force with innovations; for an army in the process of reorganization was in no condition to carry out its work. General Janssens considered that political changes in the army might be thought of once this critical period was over, and stable government assured – but not until then. At present, he concluded, the authority of the existing officers had to be publicly recognized and even increased; for a revolt against them would be a revolt against the Congolese government. The spirit of revenge among the rank-and-file was to be feared. As for promoting Congolese, and Africanizing the leadership, the commander-in-chief considered that this should be guided by the following principles: 'Everyone must be of service according to his merits and abilities, rank depending on ability rather than on skin colour. The replacement of the Belgian command must be effected from below, and gradually.'[2]

This incredible statement was made to politicians who in eight weeks' time were to be the chief authorities in the land. They were Joseph Kasavubu, Patrice Lumumba, Anicet Kashamura, Rémy Mwamba, Paul Bolya and René Myahgwile: men who since March 1960 had in theory been ruling the Congo as its provisional government under the leadership of the Belgian governor-general Henry Cornélis. They formed the Collège Exécutif Général – a Belgian, paternalist adaptation of the gradual transfer of power as effected by other decolonizing states.

In May 1960, some six weeks before independence, Belgium appointed Ganshof van der Meersch, a former advocate-general in the Court of Appeal, as minister without portfolio charged with general African affairs. He was to live in the Congo. His mission there consisted of 'coordinating measures relating to the main-tenance of order, overseeing the normal functioning of the judiciary, and stimulating the action of the administration'.[3]

The Congolese, hearing for the first time the head of the *Force Publique* express his ideas and suggestions, suddenly grasped what kind of military hero Belgium was keeping at the head of their colonial force in the hope supposedly of gradually and pro-

2. Ganshof van der Meersch, op. cit., p. 402.
3. Ganshof van der Meersch, op. cit., p. 52.

gressively leading the Congo towards full and complete independence.

One wonders whether Janssens knew anything of the memorandum I quoted above, which the Congolese politicians saw as the only opinion worth considering in regard to the existing situation in the *Force Publique*. Once they had become respectively president and prime minister of the Congo, it was an inexcusable error for Kasavubu and Lumumba not to have demanded the instant dismissal of Janssens. Having had the unhoped-for luck of discovering his opinions several weeks beforehand, Kasavubu and Lumumba could hardly have expected the Holy Spirit to descend upon the General and make him automatically a decolonizer and a progressive!

The insolence and arrogance of Janssens towards the new Congolese authorities did not remain in the realm of theory. The impression he gave of being himself the sole guarantee of any continuing authority in the independent Congo was reinforced by the arrival in May 1960 of fresh Belgian troops at the military bases of Kamina in Katanga and Kitona in the Lower Congo. General Janssens had worked out a plan for dealing with 'disturbances' – his '*Plan Trouble*' – which, had it been put into force, could have paralysed the political and civil authorities in the Congo and brought the whole country under military control by the *Force Publique*, aided and supported by the troops from Belgium now in those bases.

Janssens fostered his public image and took trouble to fraternize with the new Congolese authorities. I was one of those he invited to come and have drinks with him on 28 June (in order to 'get to know me better'), but as I was out of the country I was unable to accept.

33 Hints of Katangan Secession

Lumumba sent me to Brussels on a lightning mission: I was to find out to what extent financial and Catholic groups in Belgium were supporting the secessionist tendencies of Katanga and Kasai. I was also to make contact with some influential non-Belgian friends: to let them know of Lumumba's fears in that direction, and find out from them what was being said in Belgium.

In fact, since Lumumba's nomination to the post of prime minister, Tshombe, his colleagues and their advisers were doing all they could to avoid collaborating with the central Congolese government. They began by denouncing the so-called secret agreement between Lumumba and CONAKAT: it seemed that it had been agreed to name Lumumba as head of government on condition that Kasavubu became president and Bolikango vice-president (a post not mentioned in the *Loi Fondamentale*). The ministries of defence and of the interior were, it seems, not to go to supporters of Lumumba.

In Léopoldville, we had followed with great interest the Belgian manoeuvres to get Tshombe made head of the provincial government in Katanga. On 17 June, Tshombe had come to Léopoldville in the hope of making contact with the newly elected members of parliament there. My brother Philippe and I met him briefly in the lobby of the Hotel Memling. Tshombe, whom I knew quite well, seemed to be somewhat amused by the political confusion in the capital, as compared with the peace and cordiality reigning in Elisabethville. He even suggested paying our expenses to attend the independence celebrations in Katanga:

'If this disorder continues in Léopoldville, the Congo will lose Katanga,' he said.

'Don't be too sure of that,' I replied.

He roared with laughter and went off, repeating his invitation to visit Katanga.

Less than a week before Congolese independence, Katanga seriously threatened to proclaim its secession: Lumumba's presence at the head of both the government and the ministry of defence meant to Tshombe and his friends, both white and black, in Katanga, the certainty of disorder in the Congo. They were even more indignant at the nomination of Jason Sendwe – a political enemy of Tshombe's – as commissioner of state for Katanga; in other words, the eyes and ears of the central government in that province.

Tshombe and his Belgian advisers decided to act earlier than they had meant to. In Léopoldville the Belgian colonial authorities, who could not have been unaware of Katanga's secessionist leanings, showed a sudden zeal in collaborating with the new Congolese authorities to nip any such plan in the bud. A great deal of pointless fuss was made over the presence in Elisabethville of François Scheerlinck, a former Belgian *Sûreté* agent in Katanga, and friend and personal adviser to Tshombe and Munongo for many years. Scheerlinck had just been entrusted by them with the pompous title of Special Ambassador of Katanga. His mission was to take him to Brussels, New York and Washington.

The colonial *Sûreté* made great play of requisitioning his hotel room, arresting him, and deporting him from Congolese territory. He was sent to Léopoldville for questioning, and on 27 June was put on a plane for Brussels. I was on the same plane, and we took off very late because we had to wait for 'Ambassador' Scheerlinck, held by the *Sûreté*. Was he in fact among friends and accomplices; or had he really been under interrogation in the interests of the Congo?

The plane took off several minutes after his arrival. I watched this so-called ambassador, who was in no way affected by what had happened to him in Elisabethville and Léopoldville. He knew that it was merely a matter of a little delay; and that in a few days he would once more be free to carry out his mission for his 'dear friends', Tshombe and Munongo.

Having left the Congo on the evening of 27 June, I was back in

Léopoldville at dawn two days later. My report to the prime minister was quite categorical:

Influential groups in Belgium – both religious and financial – were convinced that Lumumba would foster communist infiltration into the Congo. Therefore they were determined that he be removed from power as soon as possible after 30 June, and the Congo restructured on a federal basis, with the cooperation of Kasavubu, Tshombe and Kalonji.

Lumumba listened attentively. He was grieved; he sincerely believed himself doomed forever to be misunderstood, both by his own people and by Europeans, all of whom condemned him before even hearing the evidence: 'But why, for God's sake, can't these Belgians *wait* before they pass judgement on me?' That was his only comment on my report.

It was agreed all over the West the day after Lumumba's speech on 30 June: it was the beginning of the end for this man as a politician.

Contrary to all the counsels of prudence and moderation that he had been given, Lumumba would not 'play the game'. Politics, it is said, has its unspoken laws, and one must conform to them, at least on the surface. Now Lumumba had revealed himself as refusing to conform, and therefore as a danger to Western interests in central Africa.

King Baudouin had decided to fly straight back to Belgium after the official session in the Palais de la Nation. It called for all the persuasiveness that those about him could muster to make him change his mind.

In the hall, each one of us did all he could to explain and interpret in moderate terms the speech that Lumumba had made. I had to talk, among others, to Monsignor van Waeyenbergh, the rector of Louvain University, and Professor Hallstein, the president of the European Common Market commission. It was no easy task to explain Lumumba's good faith to them, and convince them of his determination to make the Congo a major African country and not a Soviet satellite.

In the meantime Lumumba had been conferring with the

Belgian government, Prime Minister Eyskens, and also Wigny and Ganshof van der Meersch. The special envoys from the socialist countries had no chance of any interview with him.

The incident to which his speech gave rise took its place in the context of the relationship between Belgium and its former colony. After over an hour of anxious waiting, of discussions, justifications, explanations, a compromise was found: the King would not leave the Congo at once, and Lumumba for his part agreed to give a 'little speech of reparation' in the form of a toast during the banquet that was to be held in the gardens of the Palais de la Nation.

During that banquet I was sitting beside Pierre Harmel, the Belgian minister for cultural affairs. We spoke with some hesitation, avoiding as far as possible all mention of the earlier meeting. The toast proposed by Lumumba was considered by most of those present as a necessary compromise, but it certainly did not erase the shock of his earlier speech. It went as follows:

At this moment of the Congo's accession to independence, the whole government would like to pay solemn honour to the King of the Belgians and to the fine nation he represents for the work done here in three-quarters of a century, for I do not want my ideas to be misunderstood. [*Applause.*]

The head of state will pray with His Majesty by the tombs of the pioneers and the statue of Leopold II, the first sovereign of the independent state of the Congo. [*Applause.*] Since their day a city has been built of which we can be proud, a city which can be admired by the members of all the foreign delegations, and which is only one aspect of the modern Congo.

It is to the Belgians that we owe these splendid achievements which are today the pride of the independent Congo and its government. [*Applause.*]

To that Congo, Belgium has granted independence without delay or restriction, complete and total independence.

We hope that this realistic political act, which makes Belgium honoured today throughout the world, will lead to a lasting and fruitful collaboration between two independent sovereign peoples, equal, but linked by friendship.

I propose a toast to the health of the King of the Belgians [*Applause*].

Long live King Baudouin, Long live Belgium, Long live the independent Congo!

The Congolese prime minister was applauded, of course. But despite his good faith, Lumumba himself was well aware that the breach caused by his previous speech was not so easily to be mended.

34 Revolt of the Congolese Troops

On 2 July Baron Jan van den Bosch, former secretary general for foreign affairs, arrived in Léopoldville to take up his new post as Belgian ambassador to the Congo. Rothschild, who also had ambassadorial rank, and whom I had known as Spaak's chief assistant, was one of van den Bosch's two immediate colleagues.

The other was de Ridder, who also had ambassadorial rank. For some months he had been diplomatic adviser to Governor-General Cornélis. Though the Congo was now independent, he was still in Léopoldville, but was now packing his bags and making his farewells. . . . The same was true of minister Ganshof van der Meersch. The security services were still run by Major van de Waele, the chief administrator. And the *Force Publique* was still completely ruled by General Janssens.

In the 'independent' Congo, the Congolese government was, in fact, working parallel with the former Belgian colonial administration.

Confusion reigned in Lumumba's offices, and also those of Gizenga, his deputy. Blacks and whites were working there, men and women with strange titles; some, relatives or friends of Lumumba or Gizenga; others carrrying out special missions – sometimes even without any direct authorization from either minister.

In the ministry of foreign affairs Bomboko, Mandi and I were busy trying to get things sorted out. To Bomboko the whole idea of organization was unfamiliar and altogether too complex; I myself was trying to get my letters of credence ready as quickly as I could for my departure to New York.

It was the first time we had had to compose letters of this sort, and we were completely in the hands of the president's office and of Belgians trained in foreign affairs. Meanwhile we got a telegram from Hammarskjöld in New York pointing out the difficulty of deciding the name under which our country should be admitted to the UN, given the fact that there was another, ex-French, Congo next-door to us, whose application for membership was also under consideration.

Stéphane Tchitchelle, the minister of foreign affairs of Congo-Brazzaville, came to Léopoldville so that together we might reach an agreement over what name each country should adopt. Bomboko was otherwise occupied, and left Mandi and me to negotiate with the delegation from Brazzaville.

We took the opportunity to consider other problems of mutual interest to our neighbouring countries. Abbé Youlou, president of Congo–Brazzaville and friend and adviser to Kasavubu, had come to the independence celebrations. He knew, therefore, how the Western delegations had reacted to Lumumba's speech. The backstairs relations which the Belgians hoped for between Kasavubu and Tshombe could only take place through the good offices of Youlou, who hated Lumumba, both because of tribal differences, and differences of principle. Youlou was one of the Lari tribe (from the Lower Congo). Politically, he was allied with France; ideologically, he was violently anti-communist. To him, Lumumba represented the domination of the Bangala tribes (from the Upper Congo), and the infiltration of communism into both areas.

Our discussions resulted in a decision to give the former Belgian Congo the title of Republic of the Congo, or Congo-Léopoldville; and the former French Congo that of Congolese Republic, or Congo-Brazzaville.

Independence was still being celebrated all over the Congo in various ways. In the capital, Lumumba and Gizenga's offices became the centre of gravity for the entire government; and, generally speaking, all Congolese felt it quite natural to go there whenever they felt like it, and for whatever reason.

As for the *Force Publique*, it had for months been keeping order, somehow managing to protect the Republic against any disturbance. But its soldiers were also first and foremost Congolese. They were not going to put up with having their organization, now the Congolese National Army, remain indefinitely under the command of the same old colonial officers. They had the same grudge against the Belgian officers as our politicians and civil servants had against the Belgian colonial officials.

To the Congolese troops, Lumumba was the only person who could remedy matters. They were right, in that the national army was the responsibility of Lumumba as minister of defence. But unfortunately they had no personal access to him; as the days went by, they felt more and more strongly that while independence meant something for civilians and for the politicians, it had brought no change for them.

General Janssens's behaviour on 4 July at the army camp in Léopoldville – when he personally demoted a Congolese n.c.o. – as well as certain opinions he had let fall, unleashed an open protest movement among the ordinary soldiers. These determined upon a generalized campaign of disobedience to their white officers, and went in groups to the minister of defence to express their many grievances.

The Holy Spirit certainly did not work the hoped-for miracle. Despite our dislike of General Janssens, some of us did respect him, for he at least had the courage to say aloud what most of the Belgians in the Congo thought. But – such is the irony of fate – the Belgians began to blame the general for the same reason they had blamed Lumumba: saying in public what the majority of his compatriots said in private.

In Thysville, where the colonial administration was now carefully keeping a section of *Force Publique* shock troops, there was the same protest and the same spirit of revolt.

On that same day (4 July) Lumumba convened the Council of Ministers to talk over the grievances of the troops and consider what to do about them. 'There can be no question of merely reforming the *Force Publique*,' said Lumumba, 'it must be revolutionized.'

The ministers did not all agree with this; nor even with the idea of dismissing General Janssens. The communiqué eventually put out by the Council was, therefore, not such as to satisfy the soldiers. They had been in a state of tension well before independence because of the colonial administration's fears of disturbances that might mar the occasion, and were ready for almost any kind of violent action against the authorities.

At the same time General Janssens felt that he had been insulted by the communiqué. The ministers had not consulted him and this he could not tolerate. On 5 July he was pleased to put his anger into writing, to his immediate boss, Lumumba. But his style remained that of a colonial leader talking to a colonized subordinate.

I have the honour respectfully to draw your attention to the matter of the morale of the *Force Publique*, and to inform you of the fact that if certain things continue to be said and done we can only fear the worst from the troops.

I beg to stress this point, and I repeat formally and officially that if methods unreasonable and incompatible with the spirit of military discipline continue to be used we shall be courting disaster. The declaration made on 30 June 1960 by the prime minister at the solemn session of parliament astounded both officers and men. The communiqué put out on the radio on the evening of 4 July has now caused serious disturbance among our men.

The enclosed letter from Mr Nyembo, secretary of state for national defence, undermines all the laws of discipline.

Add to this that the increase in public disturbances since 1 July has brought disappointment and surprise to our ranks, because we all believed that the Congolese government was a completely popular one. The result of all this is that there is real danger of a loss of effectiveness among the Congolese army just at the time when their country has greatest need of them.

Since I am not in the habit of contradicting or having to repeat myself, I beg you respectfully to take this as a final and serious warning.

The commander-in-chief
Janssens
Lieutenant-General

General Janssens illustrated his ideas by a simple equation which he wrote with his own hand on the blackboard for all the soldiers and officers of the *Force Publique* to read:

After Independence = Before Independence[1]

1. Ganshof van der Meersch, op. cit., p. 408.

In short, the Belgian general himself gave the signal for his *'Plan Trouble'*, but in reverse. The revolt broke out, with mutinies all over the Congo. Officers were arrested; their shoes removed, they were made to kneel with their arms in the air. And that was only the beginning. Worse was yet to come. It was too late to stop the revolt of the national army. Fantastic rumours circulated all over the country. The response of authority in the West was inevitable: Lumumba had set the Congo on fire! The socialist states interpreted it differently: 'The Congolese were revolting against the continuation of Belgian colonialism.'

The cold war had come to the Congo.

Meanwhile, General Janssens and his family took refuge in the buildings of the Sûreté Coloniale. Courageously, Lumumba faced the soldiers in Camp Leopold II, and made the following speech:

As prime minister and minister of national defence, I come to give you the government's greetings. I add my own thanks to the *Force Publique*, now our national army, for the way they have kept order during the past months. We want our army to be a fine one, comparable to the armies of other independent nations. The first government of the Republic of the Congo has one overriding wish: to indicate our country's confidence in you, and make a marked improvement in your conditions. While waiting to work out new laws for our army, I have a piece of good news for you: all n.c.o.s and soldiers are promoted from the 1st of July 1960 by one grade, except for recruits in training – in other words, soldiers of the second class are to become soldiers of the first class; soldiers of the first class will be corporals; corporals, sergeants; sergeants, top-sergeants; top-sergeants, sergeant-majors; and sergeant-majors, adjutants.

Later promotions will depend on the merits of individuals. The new reforms we are planning for the army will abolish all traces of racial discrimination among the troops. I want especially to stress the discipline which must be the rule among soldiers. Such discipline is needed if we want our republic to have a fine army of which our nation can be proud. Let me remind you that those who represent the government among you are your officers, junior officers and n.c.o.s, all of whom have sworn to serve our country loyally. Officers, junior officers, n.c.o.s and other ranks, I trust to you all to lead this country to a happy future.

He had not consulted his ministers. Those of them who were

still reformists yielded when faced with the evidence of revolt in the very core of the national army. Powerless before the new situation, we watched the occupation of the capital and other cities of the Congo by Belgian troops stationed in Kamina and Kitona.

The massive exodus of Europeans began: they went to Brazzaville, Northern Rhodesia, Angola, Uganda, Burundi, Ruanda, the Sudan, Ubangui; all the countries bordering on the Congo which had suddenly become so many promised lands. The Europeans' one idea was to escape.

Janssens was one of the first to go; he left for Brazzaville by helicopter.

Some of the simpler of the Congolese troops were talked into believing that Lumumba had brought in Russian soldiers to disarm them. Belgian propaganda thus succeeded in achieving a real psychological somersault: the Congolese began to turn against Lumumba, whom they identified with the communists. The rooms which the Soviet delegation had in the Hotel Stanley were invaded by Congolese troops. They manhandled the Russians, but did not do them any real harm. When informed of this, Lumumba asked Bomboko to take charge of the security of all foreign delegations, and make it possible for the Soviets to leave unhindered. Bomboko begged me to collect them from the Hotel Stanley and drive them under military escort to Njili airport.

The head of the Russian delegation was delighted to see me. But though remaining calm, he made a most energetic protest in the name of his government at the unfriendly way that his delegation had been treated. I simply rejected his protest, and made it clear to him, through the Russian interpreter, that the Congolese government was doing its best to ensure the safety of its guests; my presence was proof of the fact, and I had been ordered by the prime minister and the minister of foreign affairs to remain with the Soviet delegates until their plane took off from Njili.

We then left the hotel, to go under escort to the airport, where an unfortunate incident very nearly took place. The special Soviet plane was surrounded by Congolese soldiers, who were anxious to go aboard in order to inspect all the luggage. Belgian propaganda had borne fruit: the Congolese soldiers honestly believed that Lumumba had brought in Russian troops. There was a rumour that the Soviet plane at the airport was the last one to have arrived: others had arrived earlier, and left again after depositing Russian soldiers. This plane must therefore be inspected. The Soviet delegates let me negotiate with the Congolese soldiers, and agreed to get into their plane, leaving their luggage behind for the moment.

Bomboko met us at the airport, and between us we managed to make the soldiers understand that the Congo was independent, and that we must not treat some foreign visitors with more honour than others. Innumerable delegations had come and gone without incident, and the same must be the case with the Soviet. Bomboko and I would go to the door of the plane and make certain that there were no Russian troops concealed there, and that the delegates' cases contained nothing suspicious.

The luggage was taken into the plane, and Bomboko and I were invited by the head of the Soviet delegation to come aboard to say good-bye, and reiterate the friendly sentiments that the Congolese people felt towards the Russians.

We were offered a glass of vodka. Bomboko improvised a toast which pleased everyone. The Russians left for Moscow, after their days – some pleasant, some not – in the Congo. We then returned to the prime minister's office to await further developments. The same Congolese who believed in the presence of Russian troops were equally convinced that General Janssens had already asked General Gheysen, the Belgian commander-in-chief, to give Belgian troops the command to go into action on Congolese soil.

The Belgian ministers de Schrijver and Ganshof van der Meersch, who had left the Congo a few days earlier, came back for three days to assess the situation, and if possible to restore order to their former colony. What happened exceeded anything anyone could possibly have foreseen. Certainly some trouble had been expected, but hardly this. Every plan that had been made proved useless because they were all plans worked out by the colonial power, and did not take into account the legitimate grievances of the people they had colonized. The Africanization of the leadership, which was the basic issue of the upheaval, was also the one basic principle for any kind of peaceful decolonization. Indeed, while condemning the violence perpetrated by the Congolese, international opinion did recognize that Belgium herself had sown the seeds of it.

The fury with which the Congolese troops attacked their Belgian officers, and the appalling treatment meted out by civilians to any Europeans they took to be 'Flemings', were a kind of violent expression, or externalization, of the profound bitterness which Belgian colonialism had produced.

Belgium was suddenly being made aware of her disastrous mistakes; her Congo had seemed a model colony to those very same people who were now blaming her for having given the Congolese everything that was supposedly useful and pleasant, while resolutely refusing to give them what was necessary. She had made the Congolese into baptized colonials – but not into African citizens who could take their place proudly in the modern world.

The 8th of July was a memorable day. By then panic had spread everywhere. The European exodus was general, and an extraordinary Council of Ministers met under the chairmanship of the head of state and made certain revolutionary decisions. No longer were there any who supported mere reform: they had all been turned into revolutionaries by the sheer force of events.

The meeting was held in a hall at the army camp itself. We were almost like prisoners, for the soldiers on guard outside would not let us leave the camp until we had made decisions that could at once be put into force.

From time to time the door opened and two or three Congolese soldiers would bring in more Belgian officers, barefoot, their shoes in their hands, whom they then forced to kneel in a corner of the hall with their arms upraised.

Despite the general discontent, there remained a certain discipline among the Congolese troops. They treated the Congolese authorities with some respect, and were convinced that we would make the needful decisions that had never occurred to the Belgians.

Kasavubu was in the chair, with Lumumba beside him, and we

were all present. The main purpose of this extraordinary council was the Africanization of the leadership in the army, and general maintenance of order. Given the state that things were in, the council accepted the suggestion that the camp commandant be elected by the troops themselves. Their choice was limited, as only three or four Congolese had the rank of adjutant – the highest rank achieved by any native after more than half a century of colonization!

Adjutant Justin Kokolo, the senior of the four Congolese eligible, was chosen to command Camp Leopold II. The Council of Ministers then proceeded to nominate a Congolese to take over the work of reorganizing the army and its command, with the assistance of Belgian and other foreign military advisers. The choice for chief of staff seemed to lie between two of Lumumba's ministers: Maurice Mpolo and Joseph Mobutu. Up to then, Mpolo, minister of youth and sport, had given evidence of having some influence over the mutinying troops. But some members of the government were afraid of him – especially Kasavubu – and some Bakongo ministers suspected him of wanting to bring about a military *coup d'état* if he were given charge of the army.

Joseph Mobutu, private secretary to the prime minister, was equally anxious to restore order and discipline since the rising, and he was calmer, less excitable and more thoughtful than Mpolo. Lumumba valued them both; but while he admired Mpolo's bravery in the face of danger, he preferred the calmness and carefulness of Mobutu.

A kind of unspoken campaign began among the ministers discussing the problem. Taking advantage of a break, Lumumba asked me whether my father might not be ultimately a good candidate for commander-in-chief. He thought this might avoid a collision between Mpolo and Mobutu and their two sets of friends. He would, for that reason, have preferred to find a third candidate, and keep them both in his government. I unhesitatingly replied that Kasavubu and the Bakongo ministers would certainly fight against my father as a candidate. But he decided none the less to introduce the suggestion indirectly.

The mention of my father's name brought matters to a head. Kasavubu was sure that there would then be a military coup. He received the suggestion in such icy silence as to scotch it completely, and thus the fact that Bomboko, Lumbala and Delvaux all supported Mobutu was decisive. Mobutu was named chief of staff of the army, and given the rank of colonel.

It was further decided that the minister of defence should appoint a Congolese to replace Janssens, who was to be formally dismissed and expelled from the country. This man must be chosen from among the ranks of soldiers or ex-soldiers who had reached the rank of chief sergeant-major in the *Force Publique*.

Later it was announced that Victor Lundula, at present in Jadotville where he was mayor of one of the communes, had been appointed as general and would carry out the functions of commander-in-chief. Eight days after independence was declared the Congo at last had a Congolese general and a Congolese colonel: a Congolese commander-in-chief and chief of staff. Surely Belgium should have felt the deepest shame at never having found a single Congolese capable of becoming even a lieutenant.

These revolutionary decisions once made, it was important to make them known at once, so that people might be reassured and the independent Congo make a fresh start. The troops were summoned, and hurried to take their places on the huge barrack square as usual. All this took place without a single white officer being present or giving orders, and with the Congolese adjutants taking temporary command.

Kasavubu, followed by Lumumba and the other ministers, went to the platform. The president made a short introductory speech, and then asked Lumumba as minister of defence to announce to the troops and the nation the revolutionary measures decided by the government. The press and radio put out the following communiqué from the secretariat of the Council of Ministers:

An extraordinary Council of Ministers comprising the head of state, Mr Kasavubu, the prime minister, Mr Lumumba, and the rest of the government, was held this Friday at the army camp.

The Council received in audience the parliamentary commission of inquiry led by Mr Kasongo, president of the Chamber of Representatives. It also received a delegation of students from the University of Lovanium.

The head of state and members of the government first listened to delegations from the Congolese army, who put forward the reasons for their dissatisfaction. The basis of the trouble is the fact that all leadership in the army remains exclusively in the hands of European officers, even now that the Congo is independent.

After some discussion, the head of state and members of the government have decided to give positions of command to Congolese soldiers, so as to create a national army directed and commanded by its own people. The new structure of the army has been provisionally determined as follows:

– The head of state will *ex officio* be the supreme commander of the army.

– The prime minister and minister of national defence will control the army as provided for in the governmental structure as approved by parliament.

– A state committee for the army has been formed and put under the authority of a Congolese officer.

– All groups, battalions and companies will be put under the command of Congolese.

From today, Camp Leopold II is to be put temporarily in the charge of Adjutant Justin Kokolo.

Similar measures will continue to be taken in other parts of the country, with both the police and the civil administration.

The Council of Ministers wants to make it clear that these reforms do not involve the dismissal of any Belgian commanders and officers prepared to serve the Congo loyally. The government guarantees them their income and security, and the safety of their families and goods. All that is asked of them is to work with the new régime which is part of the natural working-out of Congolese independence.

The Council also makes it clear that, contrary to rumours current this morning, the prime minister, Mr Lumumba, has not been killed or arrested. The group of Europeans who wanted to make an attempt on his life were immediately arrested by the soldiers on guard at his home. These men are at present in prison. A judicial inquiry has begun to deal with them.

There will be a curfew from six p.m. onwards in Léopoldville and the surrounding areas. Gatherings of more than five people are forbidden until further notice.

Firm measures will be taken against any citizen, whatever his social position, who tries to disturb public order.

The head of state and all members of the government solemnly appeal to the whole population, to all soldiers and police, to re-establish order and return to work. The needful arrangements are being made to secure the safety and protection of people and property.

The army camp in Léopoldville is now completely orderly again. The soldiers have accepted with enthusiastic applause the steps taken by the government in their regard, and have given a firm promise to return to the discipline that every army requires.

35 The Secession of Katanga

Moïse Tshombe was in Léopoldville on 8 July. I met him in the doorway of the prime minister's official residence, where he was trying to convince someone in the office that he should be allowed in to talk to Lumumba.

This was before the extraordinary Council of Ministers, and Tshombe did not know that the Council was to meet at Camp Leopold. After we had exchanged greetings, he said, 'My dear Thomas, I have come specially to see the prime minister. There are two possibilities: either he is refusing to receive me, or his staff do not wish me to see him. What I have to say to Lumumba is most important for the future unity of the Congo.'

'But', I said, 'the prime minister is already at Camp Leopold. Come there with me and I will tell him myself that you want to talk to him.'

When we were meeting in council, I could see Tshombe, wearing a shirt and no tie, watching us from among the soldiers and other onlookers who had got into the camp. I had asked Lumbala, secretary of state to the presidency, to arrange for Lumumba and Tshombe to meet. I had also stressed to Lumumba how important it was for Tshombe to be in Léopoldville, and urged him to meet him, and he promised me he would.

The next day I saw Tshombe getting into a car outside the Hotel Memling. He was on his way to the airport, where a special plane was waiting to take him at once to Elisabethville. His last words to me were most significant: 'I came specially to see Patrice Lumumba, but I have not been able to see him. I am going back to Katanga now, but Lumumba will regret having ignored me.'

The huge American car drove off, bearing Tshombe and his friends away. That same evening, the province of Katanga officially accepted Belgian military intervention to ensure the safety of the mining companies, and the protection of the Europeans who were beginning their flight to Northern Rhodesia and Angola.

In Katanga especially, the colonial administration continued to run things, with the collaboration of the directors of the mining companies and powerful European settlers established in Katanga. Tshombe and his provincial government were instruments in the implementation of the policy of Katangan secession. Schoeller, the former colonial governor of Katanga, had not yet packed his bags and said good-bye; he was still there, and still acting as though he were the legitimate authority.

The former Belgian colony consisted of six provinces. The Belgians were willing to accept that four of those six should behave as though the Congo were no longer a colony; but when it came to the other two, Kasai and, above all, Katanga, Belgium felt sure of receiving support from the West in continuing to keep them under her control for a long while yet.

On Sunday, 10 July, at dawn, on the orders of Wigny and Gibson, respectively Belgian ministers of foreign affairs and defence, and at the request of the European leaders in Katanga, dozens of Belgian paratroop commandos landed in Elisabethville, disarmed the Congolese troops, and systematically occupied the town. Thus the province of Katanga began its return to official Belgian guardianship.

The next day, two days after he had said good-bye to me in Léopoldville, Tshombe made history by taking on a responsibility of which he certainly did not fully grasp the consequences. First he decreed that the territory of Katanga was in a state of emergency:

I hereby inform the inhabitants of Katanga that, given the seriousness of the situation, the government of Katanga has, this day, decreed a state of emergency throughout the province. Furthermore, the provincial government has placed in command of the *Force Publique* a Congolese adjutant whose name will soon be announced. The government has appointed M. Pius Sabwe chief commissioner of police in Elisabethville. Commandant Weber, officer of the Belgian forces and former officer of the *Force Publique*, will be in charge of liaison.

197

The provincial government is sure that order and peace will be kept. It formally guarantees this both to the European and to the Congolese population. The provincial government urgently requires that everyone, whether working in the public or private sector, return at once to his job. It also asks that everyone throughout the province as well as in Elisabethville should remain calm and return home. The government of Katanga insists that the traditional chiefs give the authorities their whole-hearted support.

We give the most stringent warnings to looters that they will be firmly and immediately punished. We are sure that all these steps will combine to bring peace once again to Katanga. The government counts on every one of you, and promises in turn its total dedication.

That same evening he read out the declaration of Katanga's secession – a declaration whose international repercussions he simply could not realize. Tshombe was longing to have his revenge on Lumumba; to him, probably, proclaiming the secession of Katanga meant the humiliation of Lumumba, and possibly even the overthrow of the government over which he presided. Tshombe's Belgian advisers and 'ambassadors', who had been 'expelled' from the Congo before 30 June, could come back in triumph to carry out their mission there as planned. Tshombe, the 'noblest Congolese of them all', read this statement:

Belgium has granted independence to the Congo, in conformity with her promise of 13 January 1959.

That promise, and the royal message that went with it, envisaged endowing us with democratic institutions; and, in line with the stipulations of the United Nations charter, which is committed to respecting the rights of all peoples to self-determination, it envisaged endowing us not with a servile copy of Western democratic institutions, but with a régime chosen by all the regions that combine to constitute the Congo, according to the conceptions and traditions desired by each.

Congolese independence has existed since 30 June 1960. What is the situation now?

Throughout the Congo, and especially in Katanga and in the province of Léopoldville, we see at work a tactic of disorganization and fear, a tactic we have seen used on a number of occasions, and in many of those countries now subject to communist dictatorship.

After the elections (which involved cheating in some provinces and some people being unable to vote at all) a single party won a majority and an extremist central government was established.

That government, from its inception, has ignored the stipulations of the *Loi Fondamentale*, and interfered in matters strictly within the competence of the provincial governments.

Thus the prime minister of the Congo took it upon himself to appoint state commissioners in the various provinces. Only intervention by the Senate put a stop to that manoeuvre.

Disturbances have arisen everywhere.

This tactic of disorganization and the erosion of authority is that which has always been used by propagandists and communist supporters.

It has not taken long to bear fruit.

Soldiers, throwing off all discipline, have since 5 July been carrying out acts of insubordination, using threats and brutality – especially against the European population – illegal requisitioning and arrest, looting and even murder.

The object of all these, and their planning, are sufficiently indicated by the repeated protests of the prime minister of the Congo against the sending of Belgian troops to protect human lives and goods.

We realize that what the present central Congolese government wants is nothing more nor less than the breaking up of the whole organization of the army and the administration, in order to set up a reign of terror to get rid of our Belgian assistants.

In this way it is hoping to replace the disbanded leadership as soon as possible with leaders it seems already to have chosen from among natives of communist-tending countries.

Katanga cannot bow to such actions. The government of Katanga was elected by a provincial assembly, itself elected on the basis of a programme of order and of peace.

In these circumstances, and given the danger we are in of being forced to an even longer subjection to the communizing will of the central government, the government of Katanga has determined to proclaim the independence of Katanga.

That independence is TOTAL. However, since we recognize the vital need for economic collaboration with Belgium, the Katangan government – to whom Belgium has just granted the help of its own troops in order to protect human life – begs Belgium to join us in close economic community.

We ask them to continue their technical, financial and military aid; and also to help us in reestablishing public order and security.

If Belgium refuses to fulfil this pressing need, and if she refuses to recognize Katanga as a free and independent country, and our government as the only legal government, then Katanga will appeal to

199

the entire free world, and ask all nations to recognize our right, like that of every other nation, to self determination.

That we address ourselves first to Belgium in this offer of economic collaboration, is primarily as a gesture of gratitude for all the benefits we have received from her.

To everyone living in Katanga, without distinction of race or colour, we ask that you gather together with us to lead our land and all our people towards political, social and economic progress, and to the well-being of us all.

We are ready to receive with open arms people from any other region of the Congo who wish to work with us for the same ideals of order, brotherhood, and progress.

God save independent Katanga!

Kasavubu and Lumumba were out of Léopoldville on 11 July. Travelling round the country on a peace-bringing mission, they were in Luluabourg, in Kasai, and preparing to visit Katanga.

Their plane had flown over the town and the airport of Elisabethville; but Godefroid Munongo, Tshombe's minister of the interior, came on a personal control mission to prevent the presidential plane from landing on the soil of independent Katanga.

Sitting dumbfounded in their plane with its Belgian pilot, the Congolese head of state and his prime minister became aware of the tragic fact that to the Belgians Kasavubu and Lumumba were still just colonized people.

The Belgians in Elisabethville were playing a completely successful game against Tshombe, Munongo, Kibwe, Kimba and their friends. These men naïvely believed that Belgium would hasten to recognize the independent state of Katanga, and that that 'paternal' move on the part of Belgium would be followed by further brotherly actions, such as recognition by the Federation of Rhodesia and Nyasaland, then ruled by Sir Roy Welensky.

Tshombe and his friends came to learn that their servile obedience to Belgium, their undermining of Congolese independence, was to do them no good. Their prayer, 'God save independent Katanga', was not in fact heard. Not a single sovereign foreign country accorded the secessionist province the expected official recognition – not even Belgium, in the cruellest blow of all.

The Belgian government of Eyskens, Wigny, de Schrijver, van der Meersch and the rest, who had continued endlessly lauding the superhuman virtues of the 'splendid people' of Katanga, were the same people who, in secret diplomatic messages, recommended all self-respecting states not to lower themselves to recognize a province which, though it called itself independent, had in fact merely returned to being a colony.

In Lumumba's absence, Gizenga presided over the Council of Ministers. The Belgian ministers de Schrijver and van der Meersch twice assisted at Congolese ministerial Councils, on 11 and 12 July. It was a dangerous experiment on our part. In fact, the Congolese ministers had not fully discussed it in advance, with the result that leading foreign politicians were given the unhoped-for chance of seeing at first hand the divergence of views among the Congolese leadership. Particularly on 12 July; for not only were the Belgian ministers present at the Council, but also the Belgian ambassador van den Bosch and even the American ambassador Timberlake, with his personal adviser.

There were some among us – for instance, Bomboko, Mandi, Delvaux and myself, with posts that concerned the Congo's relationships with other countries – who deplored this precedent of allowing foreign ministers and ambassadors to attend any of our Council sessions. It could hardly be an edifying spectacle to foreigners, and could only be to the detriment of our government.

Had Lumumba himself been in Léopoldville, such a precedent would never have been set. By allowing discussions between Congolese ministers and leaders from abroad, Gizenga seemed to be trying to prove to his colleagues that the Belgian military intervention in the Congo and the secession of Katanga were well-planned moves by the Western powers.

Clearly, from that time on, the Congo could count only on her true friends for aid and assistance, and those true friends would not be found among countries which had military alliances with Belgium.

Bomboko and I in particular were strongly opposed to the request for military assistance made by our government to the American government, through Ambassador Timberlake; especially since it took place in the presence of the Belgian ministers de Schrijver and van der Meersch and Ambassador van den Bosch.

It was a failure in diplomacy, and we knew in advance that it could only meet with refusal. Timberlake took this unexpected chance to get important military information from the Belgians, which he at once passed on to Washington.

On the pretext of being in a better position to support the Congolese request, Timberlake wanted to know the exact strength of the ANC and how they were deployed in the country. None of the Congolese ministers was able to answer his questions, and we had to call in the Belgian Colonel Marlière, an officer in the *Force Publique* whom Joseph Mobutu had retained in the capacity of advisor to the commander-in-chief. Marlière was delighted at being able to teach us something about our own security forces, their numbers and how they were deployed. Having received the information, Timberlake became once more the perfect diplomat, and informed us that he would pass on our request to Washington, with his own personal recommendations.

That same day Gizenga received a letter from Lumumba, asking him to make this official protest to Belgium against the intervention of Belgian military forces in the Congo:

Mr Ambassador,

In reference to paragraph 2 of article 5 of the Treaty of Friendship signed between the Belgian and Congolese governments, the Council of Ministers of the Republic of the Congo begs Your Excellency to remind His Majesty's government officially that 'all military action by Belgian forces stationed in the Congo bases will take place only at the express request of the Congolese ministry of national defence to the Belgian government'.

The Republic of the Congo is a sovereign and independent state. We must therefore stress the fact that it is only for the Congolese minister of national defence to call on help from the Belgian metropolitan forces, and deplore any intervention not so authorized.

I am, Mr Ambassador, yours most sincerely,

A. Gizenga (deputy prime minister)
(in the name of th Council of Ministers,
for the prime minister)

That same day, the government confirmed in writing its request to the American government, asking for a contingent of 3,000 men to be sent immediately to Léopoldville to neutralize the effects of the intervention by the Belgian army.

Before leaving Léopoldville for a tour of Kasai and Katanga, Kasavubu had had an interview with Ralph Bunche, the representative of the UN secretary general. Several ministers, including Lumumba, Gizenga, Bomboko and myself, were present. We discussed what technical and military aid from the UN might prevent the cold war between the East and the West from entering the Congo. The request we made to the UN as a result, via Bunche, was as follows:

HAVE HONOUR TO ASK YOU AS RESULT CONSULTATIONS 10 JULY BETWEEN MY GOVERNMENT AND YOUR REPRESENTATIVE HERE THAT UN PROVIDE REPUBLIC CONGO GENERAL TECHNICAL ASSISTANCE FOR CREATING LEADERS IN ALL AREAS MEANS OF INTERNATIONAL EXPERTS AND TECHNICIANS STOP THAT ASSISTANCE MUST BE SUBSTANTIAL ENOUGH TO HELP MY GOVERNMENT TO FORM AND CONSOLIDATE NATIONAL ARMY IN ORDER ENSURE NATIONAL SECURITY MAINTAIN PUBLIC ORDER AND RESPECT FOR LAW STOP I APPEAL YOUR EXCELLENCY TO REPLY FAVOURABLY TO THIS REQUEST STOP DEEPEST REGARDS FULLSTOP

PATRICE LUMUMBA
PRIME MINISTER

36 United Nations Troops Arrive

After the Council of Ministers on 12 July and the non-committal attitude of the American ambassador, it became clear that the only solution which could honourably bring to an end the military aggression of Belgium would be the arrival in the Congo of a UN force.

The official Congolese request to the secretary general sent through Ralph Bunche was therefore made more specific. A second, more detailed and urgent, telegram was sent to the secretary general, and signed by both Kasavubu and Lumumba, after the events of Luluabourg.

Belgian aggression in the Congo, and the secession of Katanga, had horrified the governments of most underdeveloped countries, who considered the Congo's attainment of independence as a crucial step in the whole fight for freedom in Africa.

Had Washington given an affirmative response to the Congolese request for military help, it would certainly have provoked a crisis within NATO. In point of fact, it would have been inconceivable for American soldiers to have come to the Congo to fight the Belgian military, who were already treating it as a conquered land. Furthermore, the socialist states, with the Soviet Union at their head, would have found in such an action good cause for their indictments of Western imperialism and neo-colonialism. Yet we could not hope to see international troops from the UN arrive before the security council had met, discussed and agreed in favour of sending them. Thus, in the meanwhile, the Congolese government decided, on 13 July to ask for military help from another African country – Ghana – which we knew to be well-disposed towards us and ready to help us quickly.

The Council of Ministers was presided over by Gizenga in Lumumba's absence. To prevent anyone's dissociating himself from it later, Gizenga had all the ministers present sign this request to the Ghanaian government:

THE COUNCIL OF MINISTERS OF THE REPUBLIC OF THE CONGO

In view of the delay in the UN's sending forces, of the gravity of the situation, and while awaiting the arrival of forces from the UN,

The Council of Ministers of the Republic of the Congo, met this day, 13 July 1960, under the chairmanship of the deputy prime minister, M. Antoine Gizenga, indicate their total agreement in asking the army of the Republic of Ghana to come at once to the assistance of the Congolese government.

The Council of Ministers have given notice of their decision to the Belgian Embassy, as also to the UN delegation in Léopoldville.

The Ghanaian government responded to our request with the following message:

Owing to the absence from Accra of the Belgian ambassador, the government of Ghana is using the good offices of the Belgian ambassador in London to transmit the following message to the Belgian government:

The government of Ghana has been invited by the government of the Republic of the Congo to provide military aid. The president will be in touch with the secretary general of the UN during the night so as to see how far it will be possible to use UN transport to convey Ghanaian forces to the Congo. In responding to the request for aid, the government of Ghana is not, of course, acting in any spirit of hostility to the government of Belgium. If the Belgian government so desires, Ghanaian troops might by arrangement with the Belgian commander on the spot replace Belgian troops in an agreed manner. In order to assist the planning of Ghanaian military aid, the chief of the Ghana defence staff, Major-General Alexander, will be arriving in Léopoldville tomorrow morning and will naturally call on the Belgian commander. The government of Ghana hopes that the present close cooperation between Belgium and Ghana will continue and that it will be possible for Belgium to give all assistance to the Ghana force in their mission. The president has asked me to instruct you to convey this message to the Belgian ambassador in London immediately. This is very urgent and immediate.

In the hope of hastening the intervention of the UN forces,

Kasavubu and Lumumba sent the secretary general of the UN a further telegram, stating their request more precisely:

In regard to the military help asked for by the Republic of the Congo from the UN, the chief of state and the prime minister of the Congo want to make it clear that

Primo: the aid asked is not for the purpose of re-establishing the internal situation of the Congo, but of protecting national territory against aggression of metropolitan Belgian troops.

Secondo: the help we ask should be given solely by a UN force of soldiers from neutral countries, not of the USA as suggested by certain radio stations.

Tertio: if aid asked for does not come soon, the Republic of the Congo will be forced to appeal to the Bandung Treaty powers.

Quarto: aid has been asked by the Republic of the Congo as a sovereign state, and not, as is rumoured, in agreement with Belgium.

Meanwhile, the American ambassador in the Congo informed us that his government would support the Congo's demand in the UN. That same evening, the 'Voice of America' radio made this statement as part of its African programme:

The White House has let it be known that the problem has been presented to the UN and must be treated collectively by them, and not by any one country. President Eisenhower added that, in the interests of the Congo itself, it is desirable that the troops asked for by Mr Lumumba's government be from countries other than the major powers.

The fact that Kasavubu and Lumumba were both out of Léopoldville resulted in various misunderstandings among the ministers in council. When discussing the internal situation of the Congo, it was easy for us to agree on all major decisions. But most of our colleagues felt out of their depth when considering the repercussions of the Congo situation at an international level; those who felt this trusted quite simply in the explanations given by Bomboko, Mandi, Delvaux and myself. But there were others whose only policy was to be anti-Belgian; they could not have cared less about any international consequences and considered us simply as tools of the West.

Most of my colleagues were anxious for me to go to New York

at once, to defend the Congolese viewpoint at the security council meeting of 13 July at 8.30 p.m. (NY time). But I did not want to be in the ridiculous position of leaving the Congo without being fully informed of the views held by my own government. Our country as yet *had* no foreign policy; and as long as Lumumba remained at the head of the government, his ideas had to be considered the most important.

I was in agreement with Bomboko on a number of points, but I could not fail to take account of the mistrust existing between himself and Lumumba. Matters were complicated further by the telegrams that Kasavubu and Lumumba kept sending. Having considered the possibility of appealing to the Bandung powers, they had now sent a telegram to the Soviet government, from Kindu, on 14 July.

Secret and urgent

To His Excellency the President of the Council of Ministers of the Soviet Union:

Given the threats to the neutrality of the Republic of the Congo from Belgium and various Western nations conspiring with her against our independence, we ask you to watch the Congo situation closely. We might be led to ask help from the Soviet Union if the Western camp do not stop their aggression against our sovereignty. Since Congolese territory is not militarily occupied by Belgian troops, both the president's and the prime minister's lives are in danger.

This was signed by both Kasavubu and Lumumba.

I knew that neither of them wanted the present disturbances in the Congo to continue; nor did they want any part in the cold war. Their telegrams represented means of pressure and propaganda rather than any wish to have Soviet or American troops replacing the Belgians in the Congo. However, to outsiders, things looked rather different.

Officially, upon my advice, the Congo had presented an official request for technical and military aid to the United Nations, dating from 13 July. Any foreign state wishing to help us could, if it wished to do so and belonged to the UN, act by means of that organization. Our request to Ghana, as was made clear in the text signed by all the ministers present, applied only 'until the arrival of the UN forces'.

On 14 July the security council adopted the proposal from Ceylon and Tunisia, by eight votes to none, with three abstentions [France, Great Britain and China (Formosa)].

The security council,

Considering the report of the secretary general on a request for United Nations action in relation to the Republic of the Congo,

Considering the request for military assistance addressed to the secretary general by the president and the prime minister of the Republic of the Congo,

1. Calls upon the Government of Belgium to withdraw its troops from the territory of the Republic of the Congo;

2. Decides to authorize the secretary general to take the necessary steps, in consultation with the government of the Republic of the Congo, to provide that government with such military assistance as may be necessary, with the technical assistance of the United Nations, until the national security forces are able, in the opinion of the government, to meet fully their tasks;

3. Requests the secretary general to report to the Security Council as appropriate.

On the day this resolution was voted, the Congolese government made a decision, which to some of us seemed politically unfortunate. The Congo broke off diplomatic relations with Belgium in a telegram sent from Kindu by Kasavubu and Lumumba. Gizenga, who remained in constant contact with them both, told us of this major diplomatic decision. The two leaders had acted in order to satisfy as best they could the pressing demands of the Congolese parliament, which had been urging this for some days as a spectacular response, likely to restore the prestige of the Congo all over Africa and teach Belgium a lesson.

The Congolese parliament had become a forum in which demagogic politicians could attract the open-mouthed admiration of their colleagues and work up enthusiastic applause. Deputy Albert Kalonji, for instance, who up to then had not yet been wholly 'conditioned' by the influence of the Belgians upon Tshombe, assumed the most extreme and outspoken anti-

Belgian position. In the public session of 14 July, he declared, before hearing of the Lumumba government's decision:

I am amazed to realize that we have, since independence, failed to see that colonialist-inclined Belgian agents are still at work in both the public and private sectors. Several of us have demanded that these people be repatriated at once.

While they stir up troubles we do nothing – it never occurs to us to get the government or the police to expel them. I have even been astounded to see a typical colonialist continue to fill a major post in the national army – I mean of course Colonel Henniquiaux. Who can say that he has played no part in the conspiracy ? Our friends know it – but I will not go into details now. I was horrified to hear that the chief of state and the prime minister were so disgracefully treated at the airport; surely this should call for a motion of complaint against the Belgian embassy ? We have already voted to break off diplomatic relations and will not go back on that, but the Belgian ambassador must leave *now*, and take in his diplomatic bag a written complaint to his government from our government and our legislative assemblies.

That same day, before the breaking-off of diplomatic relations had been announced, the Belgian ambassador, van den Bosch, wrote a letter to Gizenga, making clear his government's attitude on the resolution voted by the security council in New York. It was scarcely apologetic.[1]

Since 12 July, a Ghanaian goodwill mission sent by President Nkrumah had been in Léopoldville. The mission was to study what forms of aid the Congo needed, and what Ghana could do for us. It was made up of six members: Andrew Djin, the ambassador-designate to the Congo, Colonel Otu, the second-in-command of the Ghanaian army (they still had an Englishman in command, Major General H. T. Alexander), Ribeiro, Ghanaian ambassador to Moscow, and three other officials. With them the Ghanaian delegation had brought radio equipment to facilitate communication with Accra.

The Ghanaians had a number of difficulties to contend with upon their arrival. Both the town and the airport were under Belgian military occupation. Lumumba was still out of Léopold-

1. See Appendix 2.

ville. And since the Ghanaians spoke no French they had obvious problems in communicating with the Congolese authorities.

On the morning of 13 July Gizenga convened at his home a small council of ministers of whom I was one, to meet the Ghanaians. Our working session was suddenly interrupted by news from Camp Léopold where the troops were still in revolt against a number of Belgian officers who had not yet left. Mpolo, minister of youth and sport, was with us, dressed in military uniform. His rank did not matter much; in the absence of General Lundula and Colonel Mobutu, appointed only a few days previously by the Congolese government, Mpolo was acting commander-in-chief of the ANC. Gizenga had asked him to act in this capacity temporarily; and he was held in such awe by both soldiers and civilians that they called him 'General'. He wore a large revolver at his belt. On hearing of fresh disturbances at the camp he at once arose and decided to go there directly. Colonel Otu, who was quite evidently bored by the political discussions in which we were engaged, was delighted to be able to go to the camp with Mpolo and make contact with the soldiers.

The Ghanaian delegation did not report to Accra on the results of its mission immediately. President Nkrumah became anxious, and we therefore discovered two days later that General Alexander was coming as well. He had more luck than the original delegation, having also taken more precautions. The general in command of the Belgian troops in Léopoldville had him driven from the airport to the American embassy, and there he was received at once by Ambassador Timberlake, who helped him make whatever contacts he wished.

It was Alexander's first visit to Léopoldville, and he spoke no French. He had come with a more powerful radio transmitter than had the first group, so as to communicate directly with Accra.

The two Ghanaian delegations were slightly mistrustful of each other. General Alexander had got in touch with Ambassador Timberlake to make his mission easier, and this the other group did not like. He was British himself; and in view of both the position that Western countries were adopting in the whole Congolese crisis, and the relationship between the secessionist régime in Katanga and the British settler government in Rhodesia, General Alexander found himself suspected by the Ghanaians and Congolese alike. Though he was doubtless a fine officer, he stood for a viewpoint which the Congolese government and the mutinying troops of the ANC found it hard to accept. He suggested that a partial disarming of the Congolese troops would be the first necessary step towards the reorganization of the ANC. The Western ambassadors agreed with him. Ralph Bunche, the representative of the UN, was won over to the idea: only active troops should be allowed to carry arms, and all the others must hand them over.

Alexander's arrival introduced a certain confusion; especially since 'General' Mpolo was becoming established as effective commander-in-chief of the ANC, and was employing Colonel Otu more and more as his adviser.

After the security council vote on 14 July, the Congolese assumed that Alexander was the military leader of the international force sent by the UN. Meanwhile, the first Ghanaian delegation did its best to throw doubts on the intention behind General Alexander's partial disarmament proposal: not unconvincingly, since the latter had no hesitation in conferring, whenever he thought it necessary, with the Belgian general in command of the Belgian troops that had been occupying Léopoldville.

Mpolo's authority among the troops was continually increasing. In order to avoid misunderstandings, he came to Camp Léopold in company with General Alexander, who spoke to the Congolese soldiers and explained to them in guarded terms what he meant by disarming them. In brief, he explained, it was a question of applying straightforward military discipline by authorizing soldiers to carry arms when they were in action, and to give them up when not on duty.

On 15 July, Kasavubu and Lumumba returned to Léopoldville. Lumumba was very much on edge, and seemed to have come to the tragic realization that his enemies were pursuing a carefully worked-out plan, while he himself had been disorganized and had dissipated his energies.

The general impression in Léopoldville was that Kasavubu was a kind of hostage for Lumumba, a guarantee of his safety. And in effect, as long as Lumumba travelled in Kasavubu's company, most of the decisions that he made carried some weight for the Europeans in the various provinces who were living in a state of fear. Would he have survived those days of July 1960 had he continued to travel round the Congo *alone*, even flying over Katanga, and the airport at Elisabethville ?

On 15 July Lumumba came to inform parliament of the situation that he had found in the Congolese countryside, and the emergency measures that he had taken in agreement with Kasavubu. On this occasion he had a considerable personal success. He had a well-documented collection of evidence on what was happening in all the various areas known to be disturbed. Not a single deputy interrupted to accuse him; indeed, on the contrary, his long account was followed with great interest both by the deputies and by the foreign visitors and general public who filled the galleries. Several times he was cut short by applause, indicating congratulation and encouragement for some of the emergency measures that he had taken during his tour.

He showed himself patient and forbearing with the deputies. After his talk, he was asked various questions, all of which he answered in full. He even had the tact to leave Gizenga to give further information to the session on some points of detail. Everyone recognized the seriousness of the moment, and realized too that the prime minister and his entire government could not sit calmly in parliament while the country was in danger.

Lumumba's mastery of his audience, his power of persuasion, his elegance, his gestures, the force of his argument, all these produced a total impact which he was alone among the hundred deputies in the chamber in possessing. Everyone who had occasion to see and hear Lumumba at such times as this was aware that he was a remarkable figure, worthy of respect, a statesman carrying out, and fully conscious of, his responsibilities.

One instance of his influence over the Congolese parliament was the series of resolutions voted after this particular speech:

The Chamber of Representatives, met together this day in public session, having heard the account of the prime minister on the situation in the country, agrees to the following:

1. That on various occasions during their tour of the different

provincial states of the Congo, the head of state and the prime minister have been the object of harassment and outrage on the part of the Belgian population, both civilian and military;

2. That there are facts to prove that the tragic events which the Republic of the Congo is at present experiencing are the responsibility of a number of civilian and military nationals of the kingdom of Belgium;

3. That the unilateral intervention of Belgian armed forces against unarmed Congolese citizens is an act of aggression in flagrant violation of the Treaty of Friendship signed between Belgium and the Congo, a treaty which has in fact never been ratified by the Congolese parliament:

A. Has adopted the following resolutions:

– Evacuation within twelve hours of all Belgian troops wherever they may be stationed in the territory of the Republic of the Congo, and their official replacement by troops of the UN

– Immediate departure of the former officers of the *Force Publique* who are behind all the disturbances

– The treaties supposed to exist between the Congo and Belgium can only take effect on condition that the Belgian troops at present invading our country leave. The Congo is not anti-Belgian, but desires that our friendly relations be based on both countries' sovereign rights.

B. It protests violently against the violation of the neutral zone – the immediate neighbourhood of the Congolese parliament – by soldiers of the Belgian metropolitan forces, even while the two Chambers are actually in session.

C. It asks that UN troops be sent to Katanga.

I knew that Lumumba would not stay in Léopoldville for long, and was planning to leave with Kasavubu on another tour. That same evening I acted as interpreter for him with the Ghanaian delegation led by Ambassador Djin. Afterwards, he gave me twenty minutes to talk over our request to the UN and the resolution of the security council. He took this occasion to explain in confidence what tactics he wanted me to pursue in New York if I were to go there before his return. At the same time, we decided that he himself should travel to the United States for a personal meeting with the UN secretary general, and also to make contact with the American government.

1960 was election year in the USA. John F. Kennedy was the Democratic candidate, standing against the Republican, Richard M. Nixon, Eisenhower's vice-president. Lumumba asked me which one I thought would win. I recalled to him what President Roosevelt's widow had said in 1958 in Boston, when she introduced me to Senator John F. Kennedy: 'Here is the future president of the United States of America.' I was then at Harvard University. Now, two years later, it looked as though her prophecy was to be fulfilled.

In any case, it seemed to me that given the tragic situation in the Congo, it was essential for Lumumba to go there. The West had labelled him a supporter of communism ever since his speech on 30 June – an impression fostered assiduously by Belgian propaganda. Up till then, Lumumba still had a lot of sympathizers in America. Anti-Lumumba propaganda by Belgium could still fail there if he could only succeed in capturing American public opinion, giving his own personal account of the background to the crisis now ravaging the Congo, that former 'model colony'. I was convinced that the Americans were against the secession of Katanga – so profitable to Belgium and her European allies. A united Congo would be more advantageous to the Americans from all points of view.

Lumumba left it to me to arrange his visit to New York and Washington as soon as I could. Officially he was going to meet and discuss with the UN secretary general the ways in which the security council resolutions could be put into effect.

My own departure for New York was delayed a few days by the arrival in Léopoldville of the first UN troops. Ralph Bunche suddenly found himself acting commander-in-chief of the UN forces in the Congo, while waiting for the arrival of the Swedish general. I was continually at Njili airport with Bunche, to welcome military contingents arriving to serve under the UN command. General Alexander was also in a somewhat ambiguous position: he was the chief of the Ghanaian army, which had agreed to send a contingent to serve in the Congo; he was also the highest-ranking officer in the country at the time; he could therefore hardly avoid being in practice treated as the commander of the UN troops, working in cooperation with Bunche to get the

Belgian troops evacuated as the UN troops arrived to take over.

The day after the first landing, Bunche broadcast a message.[1] Kasavubu and Lumumba had left for Stanleyville, and there they made certain decisions which were badly misunderstood by the UN representatives in the Congo, and the secretary general in New York. In particular, they ordered the immediate evacuation of the Belgian troops, and denounced the UN's slowness to act. They also renewed their official request to the Soviet Union for military aid, despite the security council's resolution.

Ralph Bunche was very distressed; he thought that he had at last established a basis of confidence with Kasavubu and Lumumba upon which to build a sincere collaboration between the UN and the Congolese government. I had told him of my forthcoming trip to New York, and he had given the UN notice of my impending arrival. He suddenly decided that he himself would fly to Stanleyville for talks with Kasavubu and Lumumba, and get them to explain their latest step.

General Alexander, who up to then had not yet met Lumumba, suggested going along. Djin, the Ghanaian ambassador, had already gone there. Alexander undoubtedly feared that Djin would influence Lumumba's views by presenting his and Bunche's ideas as being inspired by Great Britain and America, both allies of Belgium.

Quite clearly there was already a crisis of confidence between the UN authorities and the Congolese government. In parliament, the chamber of representatives, with Kasongo at its head, approved most of the decisions being made by the government; the senate, under Ileo, did not. The UN representatives in the Congo, guided by Western diplomats in Léopoldville, exploited this divergence of opinion between the two chambers. Thus, the decision of Kasavubu and Lumumba to appeal to the Soviet Union was severely criticized in the Senate, and a motion of disapprobation passed against it.

Immediately upon his return to Léopoldville Bunche let the secretary general in New York know how his relationship with the Congolese government had deteriorated. Hammarskjöld decided to convoke the security council at once and get it to clarify exactly

1. See Appendix 3.

what was meant by the resolution that it had voted on 14 July.

It seemed essential that I should go at once to New York. I received this mandate from my government:

The Council of Ministers of the Republic of the Congo has met today and deliberated with the command of the UN forces in the Congo, consisting chiefly of Dr Ralph Bunche, and General van Horn.

In conformity with the decisions of the security council, the Council of Ministers asks the following:

    1. that the metropolitan Belgian forces be immobilized,
    2. that all such forces be put in one place,
    3. that all those forces be evacuated from the Republic's territory.

The command of the UN military forces have indicated their agreement on the three above-mentioned points, and will carry out the decisions of the Congolese government as and when the UN troops arrive. In view of the seriousness of the situation created by the presence and aggression of the Belgian troops, the Council of Ministers has asked that these decisions be implemented at once.

Mr Thomas Kanza, minister-delegate of the Congo to the UN, and Mr André Mandi, secretary of state for foreign affairs, will be present as observers at the special meeting of the security council to take place on Tuesday 19 July 1960. They have been ordered to inform the UN secretary general of the Congolese government's decision.

> Justin Bomboko (minister of foreign affairs)
> Antoine Gizenga (deputy prime minister, and
> President of the council of ministers)

37 The Congo at the UN

It was 20 July 1960, exactly twenty days since the former Belgian Congo had become the Republic of the Congo. The Belgian Congo no longer existed, in international law. We attached great importance to our country's admission as a member state of the UN. Some of us had even feared that Belgium might be able to prevent this from happening; but a telegram from Hammarskjöld on the 17th, announcing that our application was successful, had put an end to worries of that nature.

On the evening of 19 July, my delegation of three Congolese, plus General Alexander, embarked on a Globemaster in Léopold-ville, together with a group of American Protestant missionaries who considered themselves refugees. We had to make do with military comfort on board until we reached the airport of the American base in Morocco, where we embarked on the more luxurious plane that was to take us to New York in company with a hundred or so American soldiers, who were noisily delighted to be going home.

The American military leaders in charge of our reception had been informed of the presence of a general and a minister on their plane, and throughout the journey we received the special attention due to our rank: nothing was too much for us. In the Azores, where we landed, there was a red carpet on the tarmac, and the delights of the officers' mess. General Alexander appeared to be very well known in military circles.

In addition to André Mandi, my then private secretary André Matubanzulu was also of the party. We landed at Idlewild (now Kennedy) airport, and were at once surrounded by reporters, photographers and a crowd of sightseers; we were given all the honours of television, and the respects of the UN chief of protocol. It was all a bit surprising for us, but not especially thrilling.

I had advised everyone to watch carefully and see everything, to listen carefully and hear everything, but say nothing. The English language was Greek to my two companions, and in any case I had to be considerably more careful than they had: as head of the delegation I was considered its spokesman, and everything I said was scrupulously noted.

Though we arrived at the crack of dawn, the Afro-Asian ambassadors all had representatives to meet us at the airport.

Two hours after our arrival at the Barclay Hotel, we were taken to the UN in a huge black Cadillac. The crowd of journalists and photographers was there before us. At 10.30 precisely we met Dag Hammarskjöld, the secretary general, on the thirty-eighth floor of the UN building.

Before meeting him, I had learnt that he was a bachelor, always elegantly dressed, extremely intelligent, à subtle diplomat but also a cordial one. After the tedious business of the photographers, who followed us to the thirty-eighth floor, we began our working session. With his closest colleagues, to whom he introduced us all in turn, around him, Hammarskjöld sat down on one side of the table. Among those present were Andrew W. Cordier, executive assistant to the secretary general of the UN, and Heinz Wieschoff, adviser to the secretary general on Security Council affairs. With my two fellow-countrymen on either side, I sat down on the other side of the table. Our encounter lasted for about an hour, and was extremely friendly.

I was delighted to be meeting Dag Hammarskjöld at long last. In 1958 during my first stay in the US I had visited the impressive UN building for the first time, and seen it as a state within a state. I now imagined what it would feel like to be staying in New York, regularly meeting Hammarskjöld and taking part in the numerous important international deliberations that went on there.

Hammarskjöld lost no time in welcoming me briefly, summing up the UN point of view in a few words, and then inviting me to speak. He then asked me some questions and listened carefully to my answers. He suggested that I repeat my government's point of view a few hours later at the private meeting of all the ambassadors from the African and Asian countries to the UN, and invited me to meet him alone in his office for a few minutes before that meeting, which was due to begin at 3 p.m.

Our *tête-à-tête* that afternoon was the beginning of a sincere and fruitful friendship which continued for fifteen months – the last fifteen months of his life. The purpose of our private interview was principally that of doing all that could be done to 'save' Lumumba. I took the opportunity of letting him know what Lumumba's intentions were and what he understood by the idea of collaborating with the UN. Hammarskjöld followed with interest what I told him of Lumumba's internal problems on both personal and political levels, and was delighted to learn that Lumumba was so eager to come to New York and meet him. He asked me to let Lumumba know that it was his own intention to visit the Congo, but that he would wait to do so until after their meeting in New York.

I now for the first time really became aware of the extremely delicate position of the secretary general: if the UN action in the Congo were to fail, then either Lumumba or myself, if not both, would be the scapegoat; and the personal no less than the political consequences were likely to be disastrous. Lumumba must be made to realize this, and to do everything humanly possible to make our work in the Congo succeed. For my part, I must also do all I could to 'save' him and help the Congo.

Hammarskjöld's problems as secretary general of the UN consisted primarily in maintaining a balance between West and East; between the rich countries and the poor; between the former colonizers and the former colonized. If he was to survive as prime minister, Lumumba had to face up to the intrigues of both Eastern and Western countries, which coveted the wealth of the Congo; but also, as far as possible, to try to satisfy the ambitions of his opponents in parliament, and fulfil the promises he had made to the people as a whole.

The survival of Lumumba seemed to depend on his sincerely collaborating with the UN, and above all with Hammarskjöld. It seemed that their fates were linked for the future. Would they help one another, or destroy one another? I sensed in Hammarskjöld a rare if cold nobility of mind and a lofty ideal of humanism, and felt that I had managed to create the right atmosphere for the

Hammarskjöld–Lumumba meeting that was to take place four days later. Would the Congo take advantage of Hammarskjöld's skill and friendship, and so advance its cause with the help and support of the UN? Were the leaders of the great powers sincere in the trust that they expressed in the UN's ability to restore peace and order to the Congo?

In 1960 Hammarskjöld manifestly believed that the West had a sacred mission towards Africa in general, and especially the Congo; but he could at times be blinded by his determination to become a world hero of peace. It might be said that his whole life had been dedicated to making the UN secretariat-general the basis of a world government. He desperately hoped to achieve that objective – if only incompletely – through the UN's action in the Congo, and it was this that ultimately cost him his life.

As for Lumumba, he made the fatal mistake of underestimating both the influence of the USA in the United Nations and the powerful means that Hammarskjöld himself had at his disposal, together with the skilful and effective use that Hammarskjöld could make of his relationships with and prestige among the various member states. Lumumba simply did not grasp the nature of Hammarskjöld's secret ambition.

The former Belgian Congo was on the agenda of the security council. General Alexander, my travelling companion, gave Hammarskjöld's advisers and the UN experts an account of the Congolese situation from a military standpoint. He tried, I suspect, to get them to accept his own conviction that Congolese troops should be disarmed as UN troops arrived, which he hoped would neutralize some of the mutinous soldiers and permit a total reorganization of the ANC.

Whether he succeeded in this, I did not know. But general opinion among those working with the secretary general was that Belgium had a heavy responsibility to answer for in regard to the ANC. The Congolese troops had revolted because their ANC had remained a colonial *Force Publique*: they had inherited with independence the same Belgian officers, with their unchanged sense of superiority. In effect, the tragedy unfolding in the Congo could be traced to the total absence of any mental decolonization among the Belgians, and the total lack of any leadership among the Congolese capable of securing power effectively. Objectively speaking, though one might look at the problem from a number of angles, everything was ultimately the result of this twofold cause. This was the point I laboured in all the private interviews I had before the first session of the security council in which I took part, on that same evening, at 8.30.

I found the most heart-warming sympathy among the ambassadors permanently representing other African and Asian countries at the UN. On the diplomatic and tactical level that must be considered in the security council meeting, I got some sincere and useful advice from Mongi Slim (Tunisia) and Omar Loufti (Egypt), both personal friends of Hammarskjöld and experienced diplomats who carried a certain weight at the UN. In addition, Ambassadors Diallo Telli (Guinea), Alex Quaison Sackey (Ghana), Natan Barns (Liberia) and Tesfaye Gebrez Egzy (Ethiopia) were all enormously helpful. Though time was short, I also made a point of paying a brief courtesy visit to the representatives of the two major world powers – the USA and the USSR.

Henry Cabot Lodge was the American representative. He spoke perfect French and, with his elegant distinction, advised the path of moderation and wisdom; he dwelt on the prudent choice that the Congolese government had made in preferring to ask for help from the UN rather than from individual states. He put me at ease, and I felt that I had – apparently, at least – won his sympathy. He was favourable to the idea that Lumumba might eventually visit New York, but could not make any promises in advance of his being able to meet President Eisenhower or Vice-President Nixon in person.

Vassily Kuznetzov, first vice-minister of foreign affairs in the Soviet Union, was the head of his country's delegation to the security council. He was a great tactician, and much respected as a diplomat. Despite the frequently violent tone in the declarations of his government, I sensed that fundamentally the Soviet Union had no definite plan for coming to the aid of the Congo with any troops to confront the occupying army from Belgium. For the moment, the Soviet delegation persistently drew my attention to two points: the need to get Belgian aggression formally condemned by the council; and to have the resolution demanding the immediate evacuation of the invading troops put to the vote as soon as possible.

I tried as best I could to explain my government's position to Kuznetzov, and let him know of Lumumba's forthcoming visit to New York. The objective of my delegation was to win the sympathy and understanding of the eleven members of the security council, and especially of the five permanent ones – the USA, USSR, France, Great Britain and China (Formosa) – any of whom could defeat a resolution by simply voting against it.

At the meeting of Afro-Arab and Asian representatives I had briefly described the situation in the Congo and set out the four points my delegation wanted to put before the security council for embodiment in their resolution:

1. stopping the aggressive action of the Belgian troops in the Congo,
2. the evacuation of Belgian troops from the Congo,
3. a formal refusal by the UN to recognize Katanga as a separate entity; and
4. finally, a reiteration of our request for general technical assistance from various member states to be channelled through the UN.

After that meeting I was once again called to see the secretary general, to let him know the results of all my various interviews.

He asked me what I thought of a telegram he had received from Léopoldville, ostensibly sent by Lumumba, demanding a report of the security council session. He suggested that I find out whether Lumumba was still of the same mind as when I had left Léopoldville, or had since changed his views. There was no need for me to consult Léopoldville: I knew that as long as any messages that came from there were not those in code which I was waiting for, I could assure him that Lumumba had *not* changed his mind.

The secretary general was reassured; yet he now began entertaining the belief that Lumumba's personality was unstable, too undependable for comfort. He had been told as much; but since meeting me he had hoped that it was not true. The security council was still to meet at 8.30 as planned. It was 6.00 when I left Hammarskjöld, and I had arranged with Diallo Telli, the Guinean ambassador, to telephone Lumumba from his office.

While we were waiting for our call to Léopoldville I was able to go over the situation with André Mandi, and work out the position we should take in the Council in the light of the various contacts we had made and the advice we had been given.

I had not thought it necessary to write out my statement to the Council. Having noted down the four major points I wished to submit, and various other suggestions, I decided to speak simply from those notes. It seemed to me to be the better way, in that I should feel more relaxed, and could adapt what I said to suit the audience's response.

Lumumba was not there, so I spoke to Gizenga on the telephone. He assured me that Lumumba had not changed his mind, and was still waiting to hear from me before leaving the Congo. I promised Gizenga that I would telephone him immediately after the first session of the security council. I gave him a brief account of my first contacts in New York, contacts I felt to be favourable to our government. To my intense surprise I was told that some of my fellow-ministers and members of parliament had in fact asked Lumumba to go straight to New York and take my place. The reason for this was the fact that Pierre Wigny, Belgian minister for foreign affairs, was leading the Belgian delegation in New York; and it was rumoured in Léopoldville that Wigny was a friend of mine, and that our friendship might influence me so much as seriously to compromise my defence of the Congolese cause. It appeared that Lumumba appreciated this as a possibility, and had promised to investigate the matter when he got to New York.

I knew that my position as minister-delegate to the UN was somewhat envied by certain of my fellow-ministers and various other members of parliament. On 15 July, before I left the Congo, I had been questioned closely in parliament, along with Bomboko and Kashamura. There were a number of deputies who imagined that working sessions at the UN would be the same as those in the Congolese parliament; and they felt that they were better qualified than I to speak in the name of the Congo and her people because they had been 'elected by the people'. But fortunately I had enjoyed Lumumba's confidence, and was able to go forward with

223

his support; I was also on good terms with Bomboko and Mandi, both of whom had defended me warmly.

By about eight o'clock the security council chamber was already full; nearly all the permanent representatives to the UN were already in their seats. The press gallery too was almost full. Friends of the diplomats, and various other people who had managed to get tickets, were in the public gallery, while UN security men stood along the walls and in the gangways between the seats.

We arrived at the UN building in company with the diplomats from Guinea. We still had to greet the heads of delegations again briefly, before the session opened. I shook hands in all directions; I turned to the American ambassador, Cabot Lodge, for a quick word. He saw me and smiled: 'I don't think I need introduce you – I believe you already know the Belgian minister, M. Wigny.' Wigny was just behind me; he had also come to have a word with Cabot Lodge.

Wigny looked grave, as though prepared for a fight. Cabot Lodge and I were smiling. I turned to Wigny, and we exchanged looks that were rather cold and reserved: up to then we had avoided each other like two duellists before meeting in the field. We had each in turn been meeting the same people, putting forward the viewpoints of our respective governments; and each of us believed that he had convinced the various delegations of the merits of his own cause.

In a few minutes we were to be in verbal battle, in full view of world opinion: television, radio and the press were all there in force to report the Belgian–Congolese contest, just as they might report a boxing match. I had one advantage over Wigny: I was accorded the international sympathy usually given to the weak, the innocent party involved in aggression. Wigny seemed to be preparing to display the hypocritical regret of the aggressor, and indignation at being misunderstood by people who would not even look at the evidence.

The moment the session opened, the president-in-office, Ambassador Correa of Ecuador, invited Wigny and me to take the seats reserved for us at the council table, a horse-shoe shaped affair. The president made it clear that we were invited to take part in the council's deliberations, but had no right to vote.

The secretary general then gave a report on the events that had taken place since the resolution of 14 July had been voted, and the steps being taken to implement that resolution. He concluded by saying:

... we are at a turn of the road where our attitude will be of decisive significance, I believe, not only for the future of Africa. And Africa may well, in the present circumstances, mean the world. I know these are very strong words, but I hope this council and the members of this organization know that I do not use strong words unless they are supported by strong convictions.

I was then asked to speak. The audience seemed at first surprised to see that I was not reading from a carefully prepared text. I was quite relaxed, and found no difficulty in watching how the members of the council reacted. From time to time Mandi, who was sitting just behind me, handed me a note suggesting an idea arising out of the reactions he felt around him, or bits of news he had received.

In fact I stuck to the four points I had already put to the secretary general and to the various delegations at our private meetings. As far as possible I wanted to avoid creating any unnecessary excitement by using violent or provocative language; I took a line that was firm, moderate, courteous, and above all realistic – even towards Belgium, which could depend on the loyalty of her Western allies. For our part, we could be sure of the sympathy and friendship of states in Africa, Asia and South America; but all their sympathy combined could not get a resolution passed in the security council.

I was as well aware as anyone among all our friends that Lumumba was involved in a dangerous, perhaps mortal, struggle; for though the West wanted to save the Congo, it had had enough of him. I knew that basically my job was to defend the Congo *and* save Lumumba. Had I used violent language or a needlessly provocative tone in my first statement at the UN, I might have defended the Congo but I should certainly have helped to destroy the government of Lumumba.

Wigny spoke immediately after me. It was also the first time in his career that he had taken part in the debates of the security council. As I expected, he began his speech with a reference to white women raped before their children's eyes, little white girls raped, Europeans wounded and mutilated. He hoped to move international opinion by reading out heart-rending telegrams from Europeans – priests and laypeople, men and women – who had been the victims of the ANC revolt. Ultimately, he was aware that reading such accounts was not a weighty enough argument to change the minds of that large section of international opinion which saw Belgium as the prime mover in the whole Congolese tragedy. He had prepared a well-written speech that was most impressive, and a careful juridical argument: but since I had spoken only from notes, he decided to do the same, and recalled how Belgium had sent troops to the Congo 'because of her sacred duty to protect the life and honour of Belgian nationals', and that she would withdraw them as soon as and in so far as the United Nations could secure order and the safety of persons.

Following Wigny, I made use of my right to reply to improvise a second speech. And this time my tone was a little harsher to Belgian ears. It was intended to remind them as often as possible that the Congo was now independent and sovereign, and despite our dearth of leadership and expertise no longer a Belgian colony. In future, relations between Belgium and the Congo must be those of two friendly sovereign states. Never again would they ever be those of colonizer and colonized, master and servant.

After I had given these reminders courteously but in a slightly firmer tone, Wigny replied briefly to make sure he had been quite clearly understood; he wanted to suggest an international inquiry, and to reaffirm the good faith of the Belgians, 'aggressors against their will', who were only begging the UN to send its own troops soon so that the Belgians could withdraw theirs.

After this Belgo–Congolese oratorical duel, the members of the security council began their usual tragi-comedy. The situation in the Congo provided a splendid occasion for East and West to play against one another, with the third-world countries being used as counters.

Kuznetzov, the Soviet spokesman, was the first to speak.[1] He recalled that this Council had been convened at his country's request 'in order to hear the report of the secretary general on the implementation of the security council's resolution of 14 July 1960'. He continued:

We now know that the expansion of military intervention in the Congo is being accompanied by efforts to dismember the young state. As so often in the past, the colonialists are here trying to apply the principle of 'divide and rule'. They have succeeded in finding a stooge to be used to that end in the person of one Tshombe who, only a few days after the proclamation of the Republic's independence, came out with the idea of separating from the new-born African state one of its most important provinces, namely Katanga. . . . It is hardly surprising that the activities of Tshombe should have caused the financial and industrial moguls to exult. Behind these attempts to dismember the Congo can easily be discerned the desire of the Western powers to reserve for themselves the economically valuable areas of the former Belgian colonies, which are among the chief sources of enrichment for the capitalist monopolies . . .

The Soviet delegation fully shares the opinion of President Kasavubu of the Republic of the Congo and Prime Minister Lumumba that the present external aggression against the Republic of the Congo constitutes a threat to international peace. . . . In the light of what is happening in the Congo the measure most urgently needed is the immediate withdrawal of the aggressor forces, that is, the Belgian troops. . . . The presence of Belgian troops in the Republic of the Congo is an intolerable challenge not only to the government of that Republic, but to the whole world. It must be frankly stated that the stubbornness of the Belgian government would have been impossible had that government not been supported by powerful protectors in the shape of its military allies in the North Atlantic Treaty Organization.

In connection with the situation which has arisen, the Soviet delegation, on instructions from the Soviet government, submits the following draft resolution to the security council for its consideration:

'The Security Council,

Having heard the report of the secretary general of the United Nations on the question of aggression by Belgium against the Republic of the Congo,

1. United Nations Security Council Document S/PV 877, 20 July 1960; S/PV 878, 21 July 1960; S/PV 879, 21 July 1960.

1. Insists upon the immediate cessation of armed intervention against the Republic of the Congo.

2. Calls upon the member states of the United Nations to respect the territorial integrity of the Republic of the Congo, and not to undertake any actions which might violate that integrity.'

This intervention from the chief deputy minister of foreign affairs from the USSR was immediately followed by one from Henry Cabot Lodge.

Listening to the speech of Kuznetzov we realized that from then on all the debates would centre upon the cold war between East and West. The Congo would not really be the point of the debates, since the powers representing the two major world blocs wanted to settle their own accounts, and would seize upon any possible occasion of doing so in public. The Soviet speaker had publicly explained the colonialist game going on behind the scenes which was undermining the independence of the Congo and immediately endangering the very existence of our central government. He did us a great service by saying this, and by accusing in public – and for the historical record – those who were supporting 'little Belgium' in her work of subtly recapturing the Congo – militarily, economically and ideologically. Coming from a Russian spokesman however, such accusations were regarded by the West as malicious and indeed 'imaginary'; all the Western powers were at one in fearing the danger to their interests that would result from the success of socialism in the newly liberated countries.

The American delegate started his speech[2] by congratulating

the secretary general and his staff, including Mr Bunche, who have worked tirelessly in bringing about the reassuring presence of the United Nations on the troubled soil of the Congo. . . . The report of the secretary general is a message of hope for all mankind, a message that tells us that calm and quiet and order will come to the Congo soon.

Simply by taking up this kind of position in support of the secretary general, on behalf of the US government, he had thus already given their answer to the USSR and the communist bloc

2. ibid., S/PV 877–9.

– for the latter had little confidence in Hammarskjöld. He went on to talk about the withdrawal of Belgian forces:

> We think we can understand the feelings of everyone concerned in this problem. We can understand the fears of the Congolese leaders when troops of the former administering power returned to the Congo. We can understand equally well the anxieties of the people and government of Belgium and their feeling that they had to send urgent contingents to protect their nationals . . .
>
> It is regrettable to note tonight that the Soviet Union is evidently seeking to bring the cold war to the heart of Africa. Its demand tonight that the United States withdraw the few American technicians who are at present in Léopoldville with the approval of the United Nations is clearly another effort by the Soviet Union to obstruct the United Nations effort to restore order in Léopoldville . . .

Cabot Lodge's speech was far shorter than Kuznetzov's. That night the security council heard only five speakers: Hammarskjöld, Pierre Wigny, Kuznetzov, Cabot Lodge and myself. The session ended at 1 a.m. on 21 July.

At three o'clock in the afternoon we again took our seats (it was of course 8 p.m. in both Belgium and the Congo). Ambassador Mongi Slim of Tunisia spoke first. He and I had become good friends in the two days we had known each other. With his experience in the UN, really a world of its own, and his extremely subtle mind, he became one of those I found it most helpful to consult during my early days as Congolese ambassador to the UN. Slim and Omar Loufti, of Egypt, were the two Africans most respected and most likely to get a favourable hearing in the whole of the UN. Hammarskjöld regularly consulted them; and at a personal level they trusted him completely. I found the advice of them both enormously valuable.

In the international arena, Tunisia had sponsored the Congo's request to be admitted to the UN as a member. But Mongi Slim did not try to win any personal kudos for this; he was modest as well as subtle. In his speech he expressed matters very clearly but also diplomatically. He offended nobody; and made proposals amounting to a resolution whose terms all eleven members of the security council had found basically acceptable. It was quite a feat. He had worked it out in collaboration with the ambassador of Ceylon, Sir Claude Corea, who was the second speaker of the day. Their resolution was known as the 'Afro-Asian resolution' because it had been studied and approved by most of the African and Asian states which belonged to the UN at that time.

After Corea the next to speak was the Polish ambassador, Lewandowski. Poland was the only member nation of the Council openly to support the Soviet point of view and the projected resolution that Kuznetzov had put forward. The ambassador was an intelligent and indeed a respected man, but in this international forum he was pigeon-holed as the representative of a Soviet 'satellite'. The Congo could be grateful to him for saying aloud what we ourselves thought and felt, and it was encouraging to hear his speech; but we knew that it was falling on deaf ears, just as Kuznetzov's had done the day before. Here is part of it:

The Belgians called their armed intervention an emergency expedition to defend the life and property of the European population living in the Congo. But not until the Belgian troops moved in and aggravated the already existing bitterness against the Belgian administration and everything that was represented by it, did the situation become serious. The incidents provoked by Belgian soldiers and paratroopers, the full-scale attack launched by excellently equipped Belgian units, resulted in casualties. But strangely enough the Belgian press, followed by the public information media of other Western countries, gave wide and loud publicity only to the loss of life among Belgian soldiers and the European population, although the casualties among the Congolese were and are several times higher . . .

It is entirely unacceptable for any honest person to differentiate between human beings – alive or dead – because of their origin or colour of skin. But why then is there so much publicity in the West about the loss of life of people of European origin; and why are the killings of the non-Europeans so conveniently forgotten?

. . . The case of the Congo's fight for its independence has and will have far-reaching consequences. We live in times when the final distintegration of the colonial system is taking place. This process can be neither halted nor reversed. It will go on; it will bring freedom and independence to all peoples still remaining within the framework of colonial rule. But, as in the case of the Congo, we can see also that this process is not by any means a smooth one. Belgium's aggression

230

against the Congo is only one example. If it is not dealt with swiftly and decisively, there may be others . . .

After Poland it was the turn of Ambassador Amadeo of the Argentine, whose speech was similar to the one the US ambassador had given the day before.

The second session of the council rose at 6.30 p.m., only to reconvene at 8.30. At this third session Ambassador Ortona of Italy was the first speaker, followed by Ambassador Beeley of the UK. The latter openly attacked the statement of the Soviet representative, supported the action and the report of the secretary general, and unreservedly aligned his country with the position of the USA. Among other things, he had this to say:

Nine members of the council are agreed in regarding the threat of anarchy in the Congo as a grave misfortune. I see no evidence that the government of the Soviet Union shares this opinion. I think it is important that the council should be conscious of this fundamental difference of approach. Not only are many of the arguments advanced by the Soviet Union representative in his speech last night unintelligible on any other hypothesis than this; some of them are hard to understand on any hypothesis.

[*And on Katanga:*] Today we regard the Republic of the Congo as a single state possessing the same national boundaries as those of the former Belgian Congo. Her Majesty's Government in the United Kingdom has received a request for recognition from the authorities of Katanga but has not replied to it. We consider that the relationship between the province of Katanga and the other provinces of the Congo is a matter to be settled by the Congolese themselves. It is a domestic problem which cannot satisfactorily be resolved either by the intervention of outside states or by this organization. In this connection we remember the words of the secretary general before the council on 13 July 1960, which he reiterated yesterday at the 877th meeting. We agree with him that the United Nations Force cannot be a party to any internal conflict, nor can the United Nations Force intervene in a domestic conflict.

The British government was in something of a quandary over the secession of Katanga. On the one hand it could not openly denounce the 'Katanga lobby' that was so active and influential in Salisbury (Rhodesia), Johannesburg and London; on the other, it had to side with the US and Western interests in supporting the action of the UN in the Congo, so as to prevent 'communist infiltration' there and throughout Africa south of the equator, where the West had such enormous financial investments at stake.

The British government had a further fear: it had no wish to see the intervention of the UN Force in the Congo taken as a precedent for later international intervention in Rhodesia or South Africa.

So, for the three years of Katangan secession, the British government gave theoretic and verbal support to the UN action in the Congo, but did nothing to stop bankers and businessmen, who wanted to collaborate with the Belgians, from safeguarding their interests through the survival of their political pawns in Katanga.

Beelcy's speech was followed by one from the representative of Formosa – incorrectly known as the representative of China. Tshiang was his name, and he spoke in English. With only tiny variations, the speeches of the delegates of Italy, the Argentine, Great Britain and Formosa all supported the viewpoint of Cabot Lodge. They approved the projected Afro-Asian resolution, and rejected outright that of the Soviet Union.

The French ambassador, Armand Berard, who spoke after Tshiang, was full of praise for Belgium and her government. At the same time he extolled the magnanimity of de Gaulle's France in having given independence to fourteen African states that year:

On 11 July the Belgian prime minister told the parliament that the independence of the Congo was an established fact and would be respected by Belgium. His representative, Mr Loridan, communicated this solemn declaration to us here on 13 July. At this table, Mr Wigny, the minister for foreign affairs, reaffirmed the Belgian government's firm resolve. No one has the right to doubt Belgium's word. Its whole history shows that it has always honoured its commitments. France can bear witness to this, for it has twice found Belgium at its side in dramatic circumstances, when human rights and freedom were threatened. We cannot allow the slightest suspicion to be cast on Belgium . . .

My country is glad to do all it can to help dispel these fears. Need I remind you that over the last few months France has presented to the United Nations, one after another, requests for the admission of

Cameroun, Togo, Mali, and the Malagasy Republic? Soon it intends to present those of the Ivory Coast, the Republic of the Upper Volta, Dahomey, the Niger, Chad, the Central African Republic, Gabon, and the Congolese Republic headed by President Fulbert Youlou. Present events will not change in any way this policy of the French government and its determination to help these countries to attain independence in the best possible circumstances. Our African friends need not worry. Nothing can interfere with a development which France is the first to applaud and to promote.

The French representative congratulated the UN for its action in the Congo; he declared himself in favour of the projected Afro-Asian resolution.

After he had spoken, the president of the session spoke on behalf of his country, Ecuador. He wholly concurred with the point of view expressed by the representatives of Tunisia and Ceylon, in considering that ' the United Nations operation in the Congo is the first thoroughly concerted effort to deal with a situation which might endanger international peace and security, not only by removing its immediate and external causes, but also by dealing with its deeper causes . . .'

Before voting, the council heard the delegates of the two major world powers exercise their right to reply: Kuznetzov for the USSR, and Cabot Lodge for the USA. Both speakers tried to justify the positions of their respective governments – in the eyes of world public opinion, since their statements could influence neither the course of events nor the final voting. The Soviet Union knew in advance that her draft resolution had no chance at all of being accepted by the council members, so Kuznetzov 'had no objection to the draft resolution submitted by Tunisia and Ceylon being given priority'.

A vote was then taken by show of hands. All eleven members of the security council were in favour of the draft resolution of Tunisia and Ceylon, and it was declared unanimously adopted. Kuznetzov made a very short statement. 'In view of the fact that the security council had adopted the draft resolution submitted by Ceylon and Tunisia, the USSR delegation will not press for a vote on its own draft resolution.'[3]

3. ibid., S/PV 877–9.

It was a graceful way of avoiding diplomatic defeat. After the votes had been counted by the Soviet and French delegates, the president of the council allowed me to speak on behalf of the Congo for the last time. I thanked the council warmly for their vote:

If it is not the first time, it is certainly one of the few times that the security council has unanimously adopted a resolution of this kind. I extend my sincere thanks to the members of the Council.

. . . For the Congolese government the word 'speedily', in operative paragraph I of the resolution, can only have the following meaning: if the Belgian troops leave Congolese territory tomorrow, that will be satisfactory; if they can leave it today, that will be better. We are convinced that peace and tranquillity and mutual understanding between the different peoples in the Congo depend on the immediate withdrawal of the Belgian troops . . .

The government and people of the Republic of the Congo intend to defend the territorial integrity of their country at all costs and by every means. Attempts to create division will not succeed in the Congo. We are even convinced that they will no longer succeed in Africa. Africa, once divided, intends to unite again in order to become a force for peace and progress in the world . . .

I cannot conclude my statement without paying a tribute to the perseverance and eminent qualities of the secretary general, and of under-secretary Bunche, who is now at Léopoldville . . .

The United Nations will have prevented – and we hope that Belgium will respect the council's decisions – the Congo from becoming a battlefield and the cause of a Third World War. . . . In September 1960, the Congo will be very proud to be counted among the member states of the United Nations.

Wigny, for Belgium, asked to be given the floor to comment on my last statement. And what he said seemed to give indirect justification both for Katanga's secession and the aid which military, political, financial and official circles in Belgium had every intention of continuing to provide to Tshombe, Munongo and the rest in their stand against the authority of the central government in Léopoldville and their safeguarding of Western financial interests in the provinces of Kasai and Katanga.

Where Congolese unity is concerned, may I recall that this unity is

Belgium's doing? Before we came to Africa there was no Congo. Congolese unity was enshrined in the *Loi Fondamentale* adopted by the Belgian parliament this year in agreement with and on behalf of an independent Congo . . .

But since 30 June the Congo has been independent, and we are no longer entitled to intervene. . . . We are fulfilling our commitments regarding technical and financial assistance wherever it has been requested, provided that we are given the basic guarantees that are to be expected from any civilized state. For the rest, it is for the Congolese themselves to decide their fate. Neither the Belgian government nor any state, nor even the United Nations has the right to do it for them. . . .

As we heard these words from the Belgian delegate, we could not but wonder whether he was really speaking on behalf of the Belgian people, or, rather, of the Belgian and Western interests hanging on so desperately in Kasai and Katanga.

The final session ended at 1 a.m. on 22 July. About an hour later I was talking to Lumumba on the telephone, to let him know officially how the voting had gone and report to him on my impressions of how much hope we might place in the UN. Despite the lateness of the hour, Lumumba listened with great interest, but I sensed a certain scepticism in his questions. However, we talked for some minutes about his coming to New York, and our conversation ended with his saying, 'Cheer up Thomas, I trust you. Don't get too tired; go and have a good sleep – you certainly deserve it.'

38   Lumumba and Hammarskjöld

Travelling from Léopoldville via Accra and London, Lumumba got to New York on 24 July 1960 with a suite of sixteen: fourteen of them Congolese, and the other two, European women – an Italian secretary, Miss Gablai, and an adviser, Miss Vermeirsch.[1]

The whole party stayed at the Barclay, where I was already living along with André Mandi and my private secretary André Matubanzulu. Tom M'Boya from Kenya had arrived at the same hotel the day before Lumumba got there; the two men had known each other since meeting at the All African People's Conference in Accra in 1958, and could converse in Swahili without an interpreter. The American State Department had appointed one of its officials, Owen Roberts, to accompany Lumumba's party.

The prime object of Lumumba's visit was to meet the secretary general and discuss the implementation of the Security Council's resolution – especially in connection with the withdrawal of Belgian troops from the Congo and the general help to be given to our government by the UN. Lumumba was thus visiting the UN rather than the US government. Everything was done to make his visit to New York as much of a success as possible. I saw to this myself, with the valuable advice of my fellow-African ambassadors – especially Diallo Telli, Quaison Sackey, Mongi Slim and Omar Loufti. On three consecutive days, 24, 25 and 26 July, Lumumba had talks with Dag Hammarskjöld and his closest assistants and advisers.

He had a very heavy programme: he wanted to meet everyone in very little time. He was received by the group of Afro-Asian ambassadors to the UN; went to a reception at the home of the

1. The Congolese in the group were Okito, Kasongo, Mbuyi, Kiwewa, Yumbu, Weregemere, Kiangala, Mbeka, Baelongani, Mongita, Nzuzi, Salumu, Matiti, and Captain Mawoso.

doyen of African ambassadors, the Liberian; made a brief visit to Harlem; and closed his visit to New York with a brilliant press conference in the UN building.

Lumumba thought it a good opportunity, since he was in the country, to make contact with the authorities in Washington. I was told to lay the ground for this by arranging for Cabot Lodge to have a private talk with Lumumba in his hotel suite at the Barclay. It was agreed that he would meet President Eisenhower, as well as Secretary of State Christian Herter. Though the invitation to Washington was confirmed, the interview with the president remained only a possibility. Meanwhile there was an unofficial meeting between Lumumba and Kuznetzov – unofficial, but known to all the UN diplomats. This meeting took place in the private office of one of the African ambassadors, and I was there too. In fact he had two meetings with Kuznetzov. Nothing the least sensational was discussed, but the Americans at once placed a false and exaggerated interpretation on them. And for its own cold-war reasons Radio Moscow made a point of describing the meetings within hours of their taking place:

> The Congolese prime minister, Patrice Lumumba, now on a visit to the US, has just accepted the Soviet government's invitation to come to Moscow. No date has been decided upon, but observers think it will take place soon. The prime minister has had talks in New York with our deputy foreign minister, Mr Kuznetzov.

This piece of news had weighty consequences: I was officially informed by Cabot Lodge that same evening that President Eisenhower regretted that he would be out of Washington at the time of Lumumba's visit. Arrangements had, however, been made for the Congolese delegation to have discussions with Herter. So Lumumba, who had so longed for a chance to explain his position in person at the White House, was to leave the US without doing so.

We could not, of course, know the true reason for Eisenhower's diplomatic refusal to see Lumumba. We knew that Timberlake, the ambassador in Léopoldville, considered Lumumba to be a communist, or a crypto-communist at the least; but we had thought the president would be interested in having a personal

237

meeting with the prime minister of so large an African country –
and furthermore a country for which the UN was to risk its
prestige and indeed its whole *raison d'être*.

Lumumba was most annoyed by Washington's decision, and
wanted to give up the idea of going there at all. But a group of
Congolese friends – among them Okito, Kasongo, Mbuyi and
Mandi – some other African ambassadors and myself finally
managed to convince him that this would provoke a diplomatic
incident that might do him untold harm.

Lumumba's stay in New York was not a success in its main
purpose. His meetings with Hammarskjöld were not as relaxed
and friendly as we had hoped. Almost immediately after the
normal courtesies had been exchanged there arose a series of
misunderstandings and disagreements which dogged all their
talks. Okito, Kasongo, Mandi, Salumu and I were present with
Lumumba at all three meetings. We felt most uneasy, for we were
witnessing a real conflict of personalities, and one which could
have serious results on the whole future relationship between the
central Congolese government and the UN. The two principals
were equally determined to get their point of view across, and each
persistently underestimated the other. All the rest of us made
attempts to reason with Lumumba in Lingala; counselling tact
and diplomacy in the answers and suggestions that he made to the
UN authorities we were confronting and of whose good will we
had such need. But Lumumba remained extremely demanding
and impatient, while Hammarskjöld simply noted down his
suggestions and continued to promise continued assistance to the
Congo and its government.

I knew that Hammarskjöld was committed to 'assisting the
Congo and the central government'; but contrary to all my hopes,
he gave no hint of any intention to collaborate with Lumumba as
an individual. I was most disappointed; Hammarskjöld was a man
of deep feeling, and from my first arrival in New York I had
succeeded in creating an atmosphere of trust between us. He had
more than once helped and advised me, not as the secretary
general of the UN speaking to the Congo's ambassador, but as
friend to friend. I had hoped that Lumumba would be enough of a
diplomat to gain his friendship too, and thus be able to take

advantage of the intervention and general help of the UN to secure the authority of his government, and restore peace and order to the Congo. But everything turned out quite differently; and the conflict of views between the two men was crystallized in the composition of the joint communiqué to be issued after their third meeting. Hammarskjöld wanted to make it as vague as possible; whereas Lumumba wanted to lay stress on various decisive points they had discussed. Lumumba's draft communiqué was as follows:

On 24, 25 and 26 July, Mr Dag Hammarskjöld, secretary general of the UNO, and Mr Patrice Lumumba, prime minister of the Republic of the Congo, held three working sessions.

The Congolese head of government was accompanied by Messrs Joseph Kasongo, president of the Chamber of Representatives; Joseph Okito, vice-president of the Senate; Thomas Kanza, minister delegated to the UNO; André Mandi, secretary of state for foreign affairs; and Bernard Salumu, the prime minister's private secretary.

The prime minister informed the UN secretary general of the determination of the Congolese government and parliament to have Belgian troops withdrawn at once from the whole territory of the Republic, including the evacuation of their bases of Kamina and Kitona. He laid stress on the fact that peace cannot be re-established in the Congo unless the Belgian troops leave at once.

The prime minister also raised vital questions in relation to United Nations aid to the Republic of the Congo in economic and technical spheres.

The secretary general informed the prime minister of the actions he had undertaken as a result of the security council resolutions, and together they considered the possibilities and scope of economic and technical aid which the UN could usefully and effectively offer the Republic. In consideration both of immediate needs, and those of the more distant future, they reached certain conclusions in regard to the immediate dispatch to the Republic of the Congo of technical assistance staff (to include personnel for administration and security).

. . . In order to fulfil the requests of the Congolese government and the decisions of the security council, the secretary general of the UNO will leave New York for Brussels and Léopoldville within a few days.

Hammarskjöld's communiqué – which was ultimately accepted

by both delegations as the official one, leaving Lumumba free to express his views at his press conference – was as follows:

On 24, 25 and 26 July Mr Dag Hammarskjöld, secretary general of the United Nations Organization, and Mr Patrice Lumumba, prime minister of the Republic of the Congo, held three meetings, during which the prime minister put forward his views as to the withdrawal of Belgian forces from the territory of the Republic of the Congo, and other matters relative to the resolutions adopted by the security council.

The secretary general informed the Prime Minister as to the actions he had undertaken to implement the security council resolutions, and considered with him the possibilities and scope of economic and technical aid that might be usefully and effectively offered to the Republic by the United Nations. In regard to both long- and short-term needs, they reached certain conclusions as to the immediate dispatch to the Republic of the Congo of personnel for technical aid (including the fields of administration and security).

The talks between the secretary general and the prime minister will be continued in Léopoldville during the secretary general's second visit there at the beginning of August.

While the beginnings of mistrust between Lumumba and Hammarskjöld were being thus created in New York, Ralph Bunche in the Congo was having to deal with Gizenga's intransigent attitude over the withdrawal of Belgian troops and the need for UN troops to enter Katanga. According to the report produced by Lumbala on 27 July, it appeared that Bunche was faced with as obstinate and mistrustful a Gizenga as the Lumumba with whom Hammarskjöld was dealing.

The Congolese crisis had proved how quick the Western countries were to unite when it came to the protection of their interests and privileges anywhere in the world. And Lumumba had discovered for himself that American businessmen, whatever assurances they might give to the Congolese government, distrusted him personally, and paid heed to the counsels of prudence and reserve emanating from Brussels, London and Paris. It must be admitted that this situation enraged Lumumba, and that he was certainly anything but prudent or diplomatic in his private comments. He several times declared that 'the agreements made

240

by Belgium on behalf of the Congo will have to be reconsidered by the Congolese government, and ratified by our national parliament'. Such statements implied – at least to the ears of Western financiers – that Lumumba was prepared to cancel some of the economic and financial agreements which gave such profits to the West, and replace them with offers from communist countries.

During one meeting between Lumumba and a group of American businessmen the former declared:

The exploitation of the mineral riches of the Congo should be primarily for the profit of our own people and other Africans. We have decided to open the gates of the Congo to any foreign investors prepared to help us to get the fullest and most immediate value from our mineral resources and energy, so that we may achieve full employment, an improved standard of living for our people, and a stable currency for our young country. Belgium will no longer have a monopoly in the Congo.

One of those present, head of a New York bank, asked him: 'Do you know, for instance, that Congolese uranium is sold in the United States as Belgian uranium, according to a legal and formal agreement between ourselves and Belgium ?'

I guessed what Lumumba would say; and I said, in Lingala, 'You needn't answer that question.' But his reaction to my advice was 'Why ever not ?' And he replied to the American banker: 'As I have said, Belgium won't have a monopoly in the Congo now. From now on we are an independent and sovereign state. Belgium doesn't produce any uranium; it would be to the advantage of both our countries if the Congo and the US worked out their own agreements in future.'

The Americans present, all of whom represented powerful financial interests, looked at one another and exchanged meaningful smiles.

The things said by Lumumba in the US, both in public and in private, were not such as to amend the reputation he had achieved in the West as an anti-colonialist extremist.

Our many influential American friends, who had up to then

given Lumumba the benefit of the doubt, were disturbed by articles they read in the American papers, misinterpreting – of set purpose – the statements and reactions of Lumumba. The situation was deteriorating in the Congo, and it was becoming harder and harder for Lumumba – who was in continual communication with Gizenga by telephone – not to react with that fact in mind.

His visit to the US and Canada was anything but restful. He was wanted everywhere – praised by some, attacked by others. The black Americans in Harlem carried him in triumph, with the result that they provoked what amounted to a pitched battle with the police who were supposed to be protecting Lumumba. In their mass meeting at the corner of 7th Avenue and 125th St, speakers acclaimed Lumumba as 'one of the few blacks who has been brave enough to drive the white men out of Africa without a cent'. Others described him as 'a second Marcus Garvey'.

At their last meeting on 26 July, he and Hammarskjöld arranged to meet again in Léopoldville. That same evening Hammarskjöld left New York for Brussels, to confer with the Belgian government about putting the security council resolution into effect. Lumumba saw this trip in the worst possible light from the start, suspecting that there were private agreements between Hammarskjöld and the Western financial groups supporting Belgian manoeuvres in Katanga.

Lumumba had suggested that I go with Hammarskjöld as our UN delegate, so as to be present at any discussion that he had with the Belgian government. But we decided otherwise; in any case neither Hammarskjöld nor the Belgians would have accepted me. I was against the idea myself, if only because the whole atmosphere in Belgium was so fantastically anti-Lumumba and unfavourable to the central Congolese government. It was agreed, however, that as minister-delegate to the UN I ought to be present at the discussions that Hammarskjöld and his advisers were to have in Léopoldville with Gizenga (since Lumumba would still be away). I could not therefore be with Lumumba when he went to Washington or Canada; and my departure provided a good opportunity for Joseph Mbuyi, who was to be our future ambassador in Washington, to get himself known there and make friends. Hammarskjöld left on the evening of the 26th for

Brussels; and the next day I left for Amsterdam, together with Wieschoff, the secretary general's adviser, and my own private secretary Matubanzulu. After a few hours' rest in Amsterdam, we got on the K L M plane that was to make a special stop in Brussels to pick up Hammarskjöld on the way to Brazzaville.

My last interview with Lumumba in New York left me in no doubt as to the attitude he had instructed Gizenga to adopt towards the secretary general. Lumumba had become convinced that Hammarskjöld was working mainly for Western interests, and that he could not be trusted even as a man, because of his preconceived ideas about the means by which the Congo's integral security was to be preserved. Tragic though it may seem, Hammarskjöld, too, had similarly judged Lumumba; he no longer gave him the benefit of the doubt as he had before they met. To him Lumumba did not deserve the trust I had tried to win for him. In the plane from Amsterdam to Brazzaville, Hammarskjöld asked me to sit beside him, and we discussed Lumumba, the Belgians, the Congo, Katanga, and the UN. All he thought of Lumumba could be summed up in this phrase: 'Let him play with fire if he wants to – but he'll certainly get burnt.'

At Brussels airport I had stayed in the plane and watched through the window as Wigny bade Hammarskjöld good-bye at the foot of the gangway. The airport was full of people waiting to meet relatives who were fleeing from the Congo.

Relations between the Congo and Belgium were extremely strained. Press, radio and television had managed to create a general panic throughout Belgium: Lumumba appeared as the racist, the lunatic, the communist. The Belgians returning from the Congo reported every kind of atrocity, all faithfully repeated by Wigny at the security council. Even those who had not been molested at all displayed the utmost conviction in recounting imaginary or hearsay tales that would attract attention and sympathy. The Congo was thus made to appear a hell which it was sheer joy to get out of. Those who had managed to get away safe and sound were seen as heroes. What was incredible was that among those same colonial 'refugees' who described the anti-white and anti-missionary passions aflame in the Congo, many were ready to go back after only a few weeks of idleness and

243

nostalgia, claiming that they 'so loved the Congo and the Congo-lese' that they 'simply couldn't settle down in Belgium again'.

In the Congo, animosity was directed against the Belgians – not against all white people as such. The Congolese made a very clear distinction between the two, and called the Belgians 'Flemings'. It was more than sad to see the good relations that had been beginning to exist between us after the January Round Table deteriorate so quickly. There were many – some of them very influential – Belgians who were still determined to make Lumumba pay for his arrogant speech on independence day. Yet the true cause of the violent anti-Belgian feeling that had now taken possession of our people lay in what official and financial circles in Belgium itself had done and were still doing.

As we flew to Brazzaville, it was this burning topic which Hammarskjöld and I tried to come to grips with. From his talks in Brussels, he had formed the impression that the Belgians were unwilling to let anyone else tell them how they should deal with the Congolese, even after independence. 'They knew' the Congo and its people; they had their own ideas and opinions of Lumumba, Kasavubu, Tshombe, Kalonji, Bolikango and Gizenga; and they were simply not prepared to deal with such people on the same equal footing as they would with Nkrumah, Nasser, Sékou Touré – or even Youlou across the river.

Hammarskjöld was adept at concealing his disappointment. In Brussels he had received clear proof that the resolutions voted in New York did not suit the interests of powerful mining companies in Katanga and Kasai; and that therefore the Belgian government was in no position to force the economic and financial groups to support the implementation of the resolutions. Though he would not reveal his disappointment to Lumumba, he could not refrain from speaking of it to a few friends, both white and black. And in the plane it became clear to me as he spoke of the conclusions to which his brief stay in Brussels had brought him.

'I don't know what you think about the United States, Thomas,' he said, 'but it seems to me right now that America is the only ally the central Congolese government can count on, the only one that sincerely supports what the UN is doing in the Congo.'

At the airport the secretary general was greeted by President Youlou and his ministers, and also by Bomboko on behalf of Kasavubu and the Congolese government. Ralph Bunche was also there. I was delighted to see Bomboko and Bunche again. The presidential convertible with its escort of motor-cycles took Hammarskjöld to the river; there a guard of honour was waiting to escort us to Léopoldville, where a troop of UN soldiers was waiting to take over. He went directly to the UN headquarters in the Royal building. It was fortunate that I, too, had my apartment there, since he could always make use of me when he needed to get in touch with the Congolese government. Bomboko and I went to pick him up and escort him to the president for a courtesy visit. The interview was a cordial one – far more relaxed than Hammarskjöld's first meeting with Lumumba had been. Kasavubu was far more of a diplomat, and was well aware how much he needed the UN, both for the Congo, and to further his own ambitions as president.

When Hammarskjöld arrived in Léopoldville Lumumba was in Washington, but he kept in touch with Gizenga. The two major issues between ourselves and the UN were the immediate withdrawal of Belgian troops from our territory, and the sending of UN forces into Katanga.

Bomboko told me how much worse the situation had got; he even thought it possible that Lumumba's own friends, among them Gizenga, might consider organizing a *coup* to oust him. I told him of my impressions of the Security Council, Lumumba's visit to New York, and the secretary general. Before the latter's arrival in Léopoldville and since Lumumba's departure to New York, there had been several Councils of Ministers, some presided over by Gizenga, and others by Kasavubu. Not all ministers had been present at every meeting, and there had been a number of differences of opinion both about the Belgians, and about the situation in Katanga.

A number of our fellow-ministers were hoping that the resolutions of the Security Council could be put into force without any major problems, especially since there were UN troops on the spot who could, in case of need, use force. Some of our colleagues could not understand why UN troops should be sent everywhere in the Congo but not into Katanga; they could not accept the idea that the UN should ask Tshombe, Munongo and their partners to agree before sending soldiers into the province. They saw Hammarskjöld as a racialist and a capitalist lackey for suggesting that only white military units be sent to Katanga in order to avoid any armed conflict with the 'Katangan' gendarmerie, who were led and controlled by Belgians and white mercenaries.

At the Council of Ministers on 29 July the secretary general was able to discover the extent of Congolese mistrust. Accompanied by his advisers, Bunche and Wieschoff, he put forward the UN point of view and the way in which the resolutions that had been passed were to be put into operation. Gizenga was in the chair; he reiterated firmly the determination of the Congolese government to see the Belgians leave the Congo at once and Katanga occupied by UN troops.

The session was adjourned until next day. That evening Hammarskjöld conferred with various foreign diplomats in Léopoldville. Later he received Bomboko and me, and told us what he intended to say in reply at the next day's meeting. He had recognized that we trusted him, and asked us to help him as far as possible in his efforts to avoid introducing international complications into the Congo crisis. We were well placed to get our colleagues in the government to see reason. We did everything we could to prevent anything untoward being said or done at the three Councils of Ministers to which Hammarskjöld and his advisers came.

With the help of other ministers who were becoming aware of the complexities in the Katanga problem, we got most of the Council to trust Hammarskjöld, who had, after all, shown his good faith by coming himself to the Congo after his talks with Lumumba in New York. Yet despite all this, there still remained some who distrusted the UN and its secretary general. Bomboko and I were helpless to deal with what went on behind the scenes in the deputy prime minister's office. Madame Blouin, Gizenga's special adviser, together with a group of Congolese and a few foreign advisers, ran things there. This became crystal clear on the evening of the 30th, when the Congolese government gave a banquet in honour of the UN secretary general.

Bomboko and I had received an advice note from Gizenga's office that no official speeches were to be given, apart from a few words of welcome. When I told Hammarskjöld of this he was delighted, and willing simply to improvise an equally brief response. The banquet was given in a restaurant in the residential suburb where the rich settlers lived. At the chief table were Gizenga, several ministers (including Bomboko, Kashamura and myself), and the secretary-general with his closest aides. There were some ladies present, and I was accompanied by my sister Madeleine Sophie, who was in her last year at the Sacred Heart Lycée in Kalina. Protocol decreed that she sit at the chief table, almost opposite Hammarskjöld and next to Kashamura. Hammarskjöld enjoyed chatting with her, and she made him laugh by asking him how his wife was. He was not the least embarrassed, and replied that he was still a bachelor, and looking for a wife, to which she replied: 'Impossible! At your age, and in such an important position – I can't believe you aren't married!' The whole table laughed, and he joined in, not the least offended. The atmosphere was relaxed, and things were going beautifully; the food was good, and the wine also.

Just before dessert, some of us were surprised to see men from the National Radio setting up microphones and other equipment. Madame Blouin was holding a bundle, which turned out to be the mimeographed text of the speech Gizenga was to give. Hammarskjöld looked at me as if to ask what was happening, and I gave him a reassuring sign, for I sincerely believed that Gizenga intended no unpleasantness. A few moments later Gizenga stood up and went to the microphone. There was total silence, and in an emotionless monotone he read a speech, relating the high hopes with which the Congo had approached independence after almost a century's oppression, and how soon these had been dashed by Belgium's 're-conquest' of Katanga. He went on to speak of the trust that had been placed in the UN, the Congolese willingness to lay down arms and let the UN solve the problem; and then the discovery that the UN were doing no such thing. He concluded by begging Hammarskjöld to get the Belgians out, and ended with a formal phrase of welcome.

As he read more and more of his text, the atmosphere moved from gaiety to annoyance and embarrassment. Some of our colleagues had been told about the speech in advance, as had also some foreign diplomats. But there were few people present, either Congolese or foreign, who approved of any government's thus attacking a guest of honour without warning. Madame Blouin was already quietly distributing copies of the speech.

Hammarskjöld did not admit defeat: he stood up in turn, and went to the microphone to improvise a few words of thanks for the warm welcome and the banquet. He apologized for being unable to reply that moment to the questions raised in the deputy prime minister's speech, but promised to do so in the next few days.

He had saved the UN's face, and the banquet ended in a slightly more cheerful atmosphere. Bomboko and I arranged to see Hammarskjöld afterwards in the Royal building, and tried as best we could to explain to him that, despite Gizenga's highly embarrassing speech, our people still trusted him, and hoped that he would manage to hasten the departure of the Belgian troops and the end of Katanga's secession. Gizenga and his advisers had succeeded only in casting doubts on the sincerity of the central government in its declared intention of cooperating with the UN to restore peace and order everywhere in the Congo, including Katanga.

Two days after the banquet the secretary general gave an official dinner at the Kalina golf club, in honour of Kasavubu; who came in the company of various Congolese ministers, foreign diplomats and senior UN officials. Gizenga sent his apologies: the secretary general had decided to make this the occasion for officially and publicly answering his speech at the banquet two days before. Hammarskjöld spoke in French, and his speech was broadcast on the National Radio as Gizenga's had been. It was an appeal for trust and for time.[2]

The next day Hammarskjöld thought it advisable to give a second speech, this time to the Congolese people as a whole,

2. See Appendix 4.

telling them of the decisions of the security council and how they were to be implemented. He was anxious to put an end to the rumour that all he was doing was working for Belgian and Western interests by indefinitely delaying the entry of UN troops into Katanga. He spoke clearly on the radio, expanding what he had said at the dinner, and reassuring his audience that more troops would be coming and that eventually the situation in Katanga would be rectified.

On Thursday 4 August Ralph Bunche went to Elisabethville as Hammarskjöld's representative. He took with him civilian and military aides from the UN. At the Council of Ministers the Congolese government withdrew its demand that Congolese ministers should join the party. They had received details of the plan through a note from Hammarskjöld to Bomboko, promising that Bunche's trip would be followed on 6 August by the arrival there of the first contingent of UN troops.

While the UN and the Congolese government were engaged in this war of mistrust over the departure of the Belgian troops and the entry of UN troops into Katanga, Lumumba had left Montreal, where he had gone from Washington, and was on his way back to Africa via London, where he was greeted at the airport by Archibald Ross, under-secretary of state at the Foreign Office. Though only on a flying visit – of six hours – Lumumba managed to confer with the ambassadors of Tunisia, Ghana, Morocco, and Ethiopia. From London he flew to Tunis, to see President Habib Bourguiba, and there, too, he met the leaders of the provisional revolutionary government of Algeria, who spoke at length about the sins of French colonialism, and the anti-colonialist revolution in general. To give concrete expression to their support of the Congo's liberation struggle, the Algerian revolutionaries offered Lumumba the services of Serge Michel as press attaché. Henceforth, Madame Blouin who was doing anti-colonialist service for Gizenga, would have an opposite number on Lumumba's staff. From Tunis, he went on to Morocco to meet King Mohamed V, who must certainly have given him advice from the fruits of his own experience as a returned exile. From there Lumumba went to Conakry, where President Sékou Touré impressed upon him the advantages of an independence wholly without compromise;

without saying so much of the disadvantages attaching to such a form of liberation. Lumumba was completely hypnotized. In 1960 Sékou Touré was the only French-speaking African leader who could so impress Lumumba and so stir up the anti-colonial in him. After all he had heard from the Algerians in Tunis and the Guineans in Conakry, Lumumba had formed a very definite idea of French colonialism as being all of a piece with the Belgian. This was most unfortunate, for Lumumba badly needed to make friends in Paris if he was to cut the ground from under the feet of Youlou in Brazzaville, who was guiding Kasavubu's every decision while becoming friendly with Tshombe in Katanga and Kalonji in South Kasai. Lumumba thought – mistakenly, I believe – that he could only support the Guineans, the Algerians, and Moumié's Camerounians by declaring himself the enemy of France.

From Conakry, Lumumba went to visit President Tubman of Liberia, from whom he heard the same phrases of careful assurance and prudence that he had heard in Washington and New York. But Lumumba only listened with half an ear to Tubman's advice; he felt far more attuned to Sékou Touré, and above all to Kwame Nkrumah. Indeed, he visited Nkrumah the same day as leaving Monrovia.

Nkrumah had one advantage over all the other African leaders: he had known Lumumba personally since 1958, and had from the first assured him of his unreserved support for the Congo's liberation. Furthermore, on the level of material help, Nkrumah could rightly claim to have given financial aid to the Congolese nationalist leaders – both Kasavubu and Lumumba. Nkrumah had seen Lumumba before he went to the US and was pleased to see him again at the end of this, his first international tour as head of the Congolese government.

But before that second meeting, the Congolese crisis had produced a fresh situation in the international sphere. Ralph Bunche returned from Katanga on 5 August to report to Hammarskjöld on his talks with Tshombe and his secessionist party in Katanga the day before. The Congolese government was expecting Bunche's visit to be followed by the occupation of Katanga by

UN troops. But, to our surprise, we were told – again through a note to Bomboko – that Hammarskjöld was going back to New York and convoking the Security Council for further discussions – despite what he had said in his earlier note to Bomboko.

To prevent more misunderstandings, he preferred not to see Gizenga again. He was especially nervous of some further regrettable 'showdown' in Léopoldville, as a result of the various statements that Lumumba had made during his African trip. Above all, he had no wish to be in Léopoldville when Lumumba returned; thus perhaps stoking the fire instead of putting it out. Bomboko and I had the chance of a private meeting with him before he left for New York. He said 'I can't let Belgium call the tune. The UN must set the pace, and I need a more explicit mandate before I can act further.'

As soon as he learnt of Hammarskjöld's decision Gizenga got in touch with Lumumba. After consulting his personal advisers, the deputy prime minister made a speech on the radio, attacking Hammarskjöld for failing to keep his promise of sending troops to Katanga, and failing to inform him of his departure until the last moment. He strongly suggested that Bunche had been influenced by Tshombe and his Belgian advisers, and demanded that Hammarskjöld's previous promise be implemented at once.

Bunche's immediate reaction to this was to write a note to Gizenga, which was also made public to the press, and report to the secretary general.[3]

Nkrumah was meanwhile more active than any other African leader in defending the Congolese cause. At the moment when Gizenga was talking on Léopoldville Radio, Nkrumah was giving a press conference in Accra at which he denounced the action of the Belgians in the Congo in general, and Katanga in particular. The next day he welcomed his 'brother' and friend Lumumba for a two-day visit, during which several problems were discussed, and important decisions made that in the event were never to be put into effect. At the end of the visit the two men published a joint communiqué reaffirming their determination to liberate the

3. See Appendix 5.

whole African continent; condemning the behaviour of Belgium and demanding the immediate withdrawal of Belgian troops, including those in the Kitona and Kamina bases; and insisting on the recognition of the Congo's sovereignty and territorial integrity. They also agreed to convene an African summit conference in Léopoldville from 25 to 30 August.

In addition, they signed a secret agreement, which Nkrumah never made known until after the coup in Ghana in 1966. After Lumumba's death, Nkrumah had made several attempts to get 'Lumumba's surviving followers to ratify it; but since none of these ever became prime minister or head of state, the agreement always remained a dead letter. Nkrumah did me the honour of showing me the document in confidence in 1961, after Lumumba's death; since then he himself has published it in his book *Challenge of the Congo*, so there is no reason why I should not reproduce it here:

The president of the Republic of Ghana and the prime minister of the Republic of the Congo have given serious thought to the idea of African unity, and have decided to establish with the approval of the governments and peoples of their respective states among themselves a *Union of African States*. The Union would have a republican constitution within a federal framework. The federal government would be responsible for:

(*a*) Foreign affairs
(*b*) Defence
(*c*) The issue of a common currency
(*d*) Economic planning and development.

There would be no customs barriers between any parts of the federation. There would be a federal parliament and a federal head of state. The capital of the union should be Léopoldville. Any state or territory in Africa is free to join this Union. The above Union presupposes Ghana's abandonment of the Commonwealth.

Dated this 8th day of August 1960
Kwame Nkrumah   Patrice Lumumba

In 1960, when it was signed, this document was the fulfilment – on paper, at least – of the dream of two genuine African idealists who felt themselves endowed with a mission to unite Africa and all Africans. Certainly, one had to be idealistic in the extreme seriously to hope in 1960 – or even today – that Africa and its people would be prepared to accept a union of that kind.

From Accra, Lumumba went on to spend a few hours in Iomé (Togo) to meet President Sylvanus Olympio, before returning to Léopoldville where the situation was growing daily more explosive and out of control. And, it must be admitted, the statements that Lumumba had made abroad were not such as to promote calm or harmony with Belgium. Then, on his way back to the Congo after his two weeks' absence, Lumumba gave the following statement to the press:

I am proud to realize how all Africa is united with the people of the Congo in their heroic struggle against the last remnants of Belgian colonialism.

All the heads of state I have met during my journey through Africa have been unreserved in their condemnation of Belgian aggression, and the military occupation of the Congo by a foreign power.

His Majesty the King of Morocco, Mohammed V, Their Excellencies, Bourguiba, Sékou Touré, Tubman, Kwame Nkrumah and Sylvanus Olympio, the presidents respectively of the Republics of Tunisia, Guinea, Liberia and Ghana, and the prime minister of Togoland, who specially invited me to meet them, assured me of all the support and assistance the Congolese government might need in order to get the Belgian troops out of the Congo – especially Katanga.

They strongly condemn the manoeuvres of secession taking place in Katanga at the instigation of the government and imperialist circles of Belgium.

The manoeuvres of the imperialists in the Congo are visibly trying to create an explosion, not only in the Congo, but all over Africa, in order to enable them to continue with their commercial exploitation.

By use of the strategy always close to their hearts, 'divide and rule', the Belgian government want their operation in Katanga to succeed, so as to separate that province from the rest of the Congo. This new tactic is being pursued by means of the corruption of certain dishonest Congolese, notably Tshombe.

They have undermined the strength of our bank with gold and silver, by trying to create a new bank and new currency in Katanga.

Belgium has spent eighty years enriching itself with the wealth of the Congo, through the labours of the Congolese.

The gold and silver that the Belgian government has withdrawn

253

from our national bank will not impoverish our rich Congo: we still have gold in our land.

With our own money, the money of the Congolese people, the Belgian government has bought arms for thousands of francs in order to be ready to repress the Congolese people. Those arms are now in Katanga, and especially at Kamina.

NATO has taken part in this operation, as I was actually told by Ambassador van den Bosch, when things first began happening in the Congo.

Let me warn our aggressors: we would rather die than live under Belgian military occupation.

The Belgians tried to corrupt me, to buy me – but I replied that the Congolese people whom I represent, and who have elected me, want only to enjoy their freedom totally and completely. I added that we prefer poverty in freedom and dignity to riches in slavery and contempt for our Africanness.

Our ancestors had no bank-notes, but they were happy and they were humane.

It is money and love of money that have made some nations so decadent, and reduced the moral values of some peoples.

The Belgian government wants war. That is clear from their attitude.

One thing is quite certain: Belgium will lose whatever she tries to get by force, and will realize only too late that she has done so.

The security council of the United Nations twice adopted objective resolutions recognized by the whole world, and I continue, on behalf of the Congolese people, to honour the members of that council for the decision they made for our country. Unfortunately, that resolution has never been applied, owing to the behind-the-scenes manoeuvrings which we have discovered.

The secretary general of UNO, instead of combining his efforts with those of the legal government of the Republic of the Congo, as directed by the security council, went instead to negotiate with the Belgian government who are directly responsible for the tragic situation of Katanga.

Instead of replying to the request of the central government, the legal authority in the Republic of the Congo, the secretary general of UNO preferred to deal with the Belgian officers who were sent to Katanga to advise Tshombe.

Instead of agreeing to the legal government's request, expressing the wishes of the fourteen million inhabitants of the Congo, the secretary general of UNO preferred to deal with a traitor to our country, the Belgians' puppet, Tshombe.

While the peoples of Katanga beg day after day that UN troops be sent there, the secretary general rejects their legitimate request.

The secretary general of UNO has deeply disappointed the peoples of the Congo and of all Africa; Asia as well.

We have proved our good will and good faith in facilitating the success of the UN mission in the Congo. We have been patient now for a month, believing that the UN was going to help us get peace for our people, but we are deeply disappointed.

Tomorrow I arrive in Léopoldville. The government, firm in the authority vested in it by the whole Congolese people, and aware of its responsibilities, will resolve the Katangan problem for itself.

I should be letting down my people who have put their trust in me, were I not to answer their appeal. The whole Congolese people is asking most forcefully that I get the Belgian troops removed from the whole of the Congo without delay.

With no interest at heart save that of the people of the Congo, the members of the government will enter Katanga, and the peoples of the five other provinces will join us there. Perhaps the Belgian troops will kill us, but it would be an honour to have sacrificed oneself for one's homeland and its people.

With the support and help of all the peoples of Africa, we shall defend freedom all over Africa, and the territorial integrity of the young, sovereign and independent Republic of the Congo.

Home once more, Lumumba did not question or consult the Congolese who could have given him objective information about what had happened in his absence. He let his judgement be influenced by foreigners who claimed to be better informed. He would take no account of my view of Hammarskjöld – still less Bomboko's. He accepted the extremely subjective account of his so-called friends instead. All the right-wing groups – Catholic and commercial – were busy plotting to get Lumumba out of power. A number of possibilities were being canvassed, and there were certainly plenty of people all too willing to step into his shoes. (No one seemed to entertain the notion of displacing Kasavubu.) The anti-Lumumba groups spread rumours of a possible coup by Gizenga diligently so as to conceal their own plans; and Lumumba's informants were fanatical and naïve enough to believe them. A few hours after getting back, Lumumba asked Gizenga to lead the Congolese delegation to the Security Council which was to leave for New York that same evening.[4]

We managed to persuade Gizenga to let Bomboko take his place as spokesman for the delegation. Indeed, there were already rumours that the Belgians were fostering an entente between Kasavubu and Bomboko, Delvaux, Bolikango, Tshombe, Kalonji, Ileo, Adoula and Youlou. So it was a very good move to get Bomboko to speak out publicly against the Belgians and their manoeuvrings in Katanga.

Unlike the procedure at the security council meetings of 21 and 22 July, when I had read from my own notes, Bomboko read a text that we had all composed together. This reassured Gizenga, since he still remained head of the delegation and it would therefore be his responsibility to report to Lumumba and justify whatever attitude we might take. Bomboko's pronouncement of the speech prepared by the delegation won a degree of confidence for him, temporarily at least, among the more fanatical Lumumba supporters, who were already thinking of him as a 'traitor' to the Congolese cause. The speech, also temporarily, discouraged the Belgians who were trying to create open dissension among the Congolese ministers. It may be, of course, that despite Bomboko's nationalist declarations, Kasavubu and the Belgians were already secure in the knowledge that, when the time came, their protégé would follow instructions. He was convincing enough, certainly, as he read the speech.[5]

The French ambassador, Armand Bérard, was president of the council for August; Wigny had come back to New York to represent Belgium – the self-same Wigny who on 29 June had set his signature alongside Bomboko's on the Treaty of Friendship and Cooperation between our two countries.

The Afro-Asian resolution put forward by Ceylon and Tunisia was agreed by the Council with nine for and none against and two abstentions – France and Italy. At last, it seemed the secretary general had won his point, and, as he had said to us, Belgium

---

4. The delegation comprised Gizenga, Bomboko, Mwamba, Mpolo and myself.
5. See Appendix 6 for the most significant passages.

would no longer be calling the tune. The resolution (voted on 9 August) 'called upon the government of Belgium to withdraw immediately its troops from the province of Katanga under speedy modalities determined by the secretary general, and to assist in every possible way the implementation of the Council's resolutions'. It further declared that the entry of the UN force into the province of Katanga was necessary if the resolution were to be fully implemented.

Hammarskjöld had used every trump in his hand to win the vote for this resolution. Washington seemed now wholly on his side; and the gravity of the situation facing Belgium was abundantly clear from the fact that no attack came from the Western powers after comments of Hammarskjöld's such as this:

> The presence of Belgian troops now is the main cause of continual danger; by the term 'the speediest possible withdrawal of those troops in accordance with the security council resolutions', I mean a withdrawal that must be complete and unconditional. . . . I do not hesitate to say that the speediest possible – I would even say immediate – achievement of such a solution of the Congo problem is a question of peace or war, and when saying 'peace or war' I do not limit my perspective to the Congo. A delay now, hesitation now, efforts to safeguard national or group interests now in a way that would hamper the United Nations effort, would risk values immeasurably greater than any of those which such action may be intended to protect. This applies to all parties, first of all the one to which the security council has addressed its appeal.

Encouraged by the resolution of 9 August, and having received an assurance of cooperation from the central Congolese government in implementing the measures decided upon by the council, Hammarskjöld set off for Elisabethville on 12 August with military and civilian advisers, and with two companies of Swedish troops under his direct command.

This journey, and his interview with the Katangan secessionists, provided the occasion for a further convocation of the security council.

While we were in New York, and Bomboko was defending the central government's point of view before the security council, there was a bitter conflict raging in Léopoldville between Lumumba and his opponents as a group. He had, as I have said, sent Gizenga to New York, to give himself a chance to look into the rumours that Gizenga was planning a *coup d'état*. Further seized by the whole nightmare of Tshombe and the secession of Katanga, Lumumba gave little thought to Kasavubu, whom he considered a lazy man, physically weak, and politically a robot. This was a fatal error, for Kasavubu was in fact the crocodile sleeping open-eyed beside the river – in his sumptuous residence on Mount Stanley.

Though they had from the first been divided in their loyalty to Lumumba, his ministers accepted most of his suggestions without any major disagreement. Many of them, either out of fear or political calculation, did not dare contradict him, and the communiqués put out on the national radio often represented his point of view alone rather than decisions resulting from any genuine discussions amongst them all. So we were not surprised to receive the following telex message from the Ghanaian embassy on 8 August:

The Council of Ministers, met this Monday 8 August 1960, under the presidency of Mr Patrice Lumumba, the prime minister, has considered the situation in the country in general, and in Katanga in particular.

After some deliberation the Council has decided, in the higher interests of the country, and in virtue of its authority, to make these decisions:

1. A state of emergency is declared throughout the Republic.

2. The decision made on 15 July 1960 by the Congolese government that the Belgian ambassador van den Bosch be expelled from our territory must be put into effect. In addition, the embassy must be closed, and all staff withdrawn.

The decision made by the government, and ratified by parliament, to break off diplomatic relations with Belgium also means the closure of all Belgian consulates in Léopoldville, Coquilhatville, Luluabourg, Elisabethville, Stanleyville, Bukavu and Matadi, and the departure of the consuls general of each one.

3. All Congolese students and business trainees at present in Belgium must return. The Congolese government promises to send them to other countries to complete their courses.

4. The Council of Ministers has decided to call a summit conference of independent African states on 25 August 1960. It will be a conference of major importance for the whole continent.

The Council of Ministers reaffirms its total confidence in the prime minister, and recognizes the value of his dynamic action. It congratulates him on the outstanding success of his journey to the United States and other American countries, in assisting the defence of the Congolese people's interests.

39   A Broken Appointment

Once Lumumba had discovered America and got to know a number of African heads of state, his one great dream became to hold a pan-African summit conference in Léopoldville. Theoretically, the Congo had long been the ideal geographical centre of Africa; now that he was Congolese prime minister, he was determined to make it the active centre of African liberation and independence.

Lumumba was an idealist, and like all pure and sincere idealists, he often lacked realism; all too often he thought that to want a thing was as good as already having it, and that to conceive an original idea was as good as already putting it into effect.

Lumumba thought he had formed new relationships in the United States which would stand him in good stead; he believed that his point of view had been accepted by many who – from Washington, New York or Texas – influenced American political action in the Congo and throughout Africa. Lumumba could not have been more wrong, for the number of new friendships he had made, and new sympathies he had aroused, in the US was tiny in comparison with the number of those convinced by the anti-communist propaganda directed against him personally. Belgium had done her best to make the West permanently uneasy at seeing Lumumba at the head of the Congolese government. To the Belgians Lumumba was a communist, an anti-white, and an anti-westerner – and to the West, the Belgians knew Lumumba and the Congo better than anyone else did. Therefore it would have been far more to the point for Lumumba to try to put himself in a more favourable light with regard to the Belgians, than to try to denigrate the Belgians in the eyes of their allies and fellow white men in America.

Lumumba had his long-dreamt-of chance to have personal

talks with the African heads of state whom he visited on his way back to the Congo from America. Did he realize that these were all men who had been in power for some time, and that experience had taught them to be more realistic than he was ? What did they say, what did they advise – all these African heads of state, none of whom actually knew the Congo at all ?

I was not with the prime minister on his African tour. I did not at the time know what took place during his talks with his African colleagues. However, on his return to the Congo Lumumba once more found himself faced with the reality of the situation there, which was very different from the picture of it which was probably envisaged by those other African leaders.

His determination to achieve that pan-African congress in Léopoldville can in part be explained by his wish to discuss with other Africans problems common to them all; not just in theory, but in practice, starting from the actual situation in the Congo where imperialism and neo-colonialism were revealing aspects not before seen anywhere in the continent.

Lumumba was convinced that he would manage to convert the African political leaders to his ideas about pan-Africanism, the conception of African unity and solidarity, and the strategy needed in the struggle for African liberation.

A number of the political and diplomatic mistakes he made on his return home can be explained by this new objective to which his ideas and actions were now geared: the Congo was a prey to the west and must be set free by Africa and Africans. But who were those Africans ? What power had they to effect such a liberation ? What did they know of the Congo ? What did they think of the Congo and the Congolese, and indeed of Lumumba himself? None of these were questions Lumumba would consider. He had faith in Africa and its people; and the discussions he had had during his trip, and the things he had been told, had increased his faith in the potential of united African effort to an incredible degree. The vision he had of African countries rushing their troops to the Congo, under the command of the UN but 'for the aid of the Lumumba government', had blinded him to the limitations of African solidarity.

Dag Hammarskjöld, whom Bomboko and I saw often at that

time, had drawn our attention to the serious consequences of Lumumba's diplomatic, juridical and military misconceptions. Certainly we were all too aware of the harm done when Lumumba effectively broke off all personal relations with Hammarskjöld – in one of the worst diplomatic errors he committed during that August of 1960.

I had done my best to become a friend of the secretary general's from the moment of our first meeting in New York. I had urged upon Lumumba the need to recognize the immense rôle that Hammarskjöld could play in contributing to his political survival or downfall, as long as UN troops remained in the Congo. Hammarskjöld evinced the same friendship for Bomboko as for myself. We had created the necessary trust between ourselves and the 'boss' of the UN, who was wholly disposed to help the Congolese government maintain the unity of the Congo, and preserve the integrity of our country: two of the major points in Lumumba's political programme. Yet, alas, on the advice of those who intentionally or ignorantly served his downfall rather than his success, Lumumba himself saw things in very different terms from the realistic diplomatic policy which we were advising so strongly. It was in August 1960 that the fate of the Congo and the Lumumba government was finally decided. Rather than have one or two personal meetings in which they might have come better to understand each other, Lumumba chose instead to exchange a series of letters with Hammarskjöld, and neither Bomboko, minister of foreign affairs, nor myself, minister-delegate to the UN, were among that group of experts and friends of Lumumba who helped him compose those letters.

With his customary respect for protocol and the rules of diplomatic decorum, Hammarskjöld approached Bomboko and myself, getting us to read every letter from our prime minister, and the answer he proposed sending to each. Thus, quite without intending it, Bomboko and I became far better informed than those friends who were so disastrously advising Lumumba. We were in a position to know how Hammarskjöld was reacting to the letters he got from Lumumba, and what answers he sent after consulting the five permanent members of the Security Council.

In effect, by hurling this kind of challenge at Hammarskjöld instead of negotiating with him, the Congolese government was simply destroying itself, as became clearer and clearer from the tone of the letters exchanged between the two men. They were to have met on 15 August, at the written invitation of the secretary general and with Lumumba's agreement. The interview was fixed for 3.00 p.m. The prime minister was invited to come with his deputy, Gizenga. He had asked me to come along too; but, oddly enough, not Bomboko.

Personally, I was delighted at the idea of being able to take part in a meeting which promised to be such a decisive one. Dag Hammarskjöld had come back the previous evening from Elisabethville, where he had had talks with Tshombe; he was in a position to inform Lumumba of the exact situation in Katanga, and all the many intrigues going on there. In effect the UN secret service had far more complete and precise information than we did, on the whole network of financial and political powers behind Katanga's secession.

A meeting between Hammarskjöld and Lumumba would be of great advantage to them both, since if they were to succeed and survive, they *must* work together. I kept on repeating to Lumumba my conviction that his fate was becoming ever more tied in with that of Hammarskjöld; for by helping the Congolese government to preserve its country's unity and territorial integrity, the UN was standing with the central government against not only the secessionists in Katanga, but also all the forces inside and outside the country that supported them.

I was therefore expecting to see Lumumba and Gizenga at about 2.00 p.m., before the critical interview. But, to my surprise, Lumumba telephoned to tell me that the meeting was not to take place after all, and that I need not bother to come to his house. It was then noon. Lumumba had summoned together his 'experts and friends' – some Congolese, some foreign – and together they had decided that the meeting would be useless. Instead they had worked out and written a letter which Lumumba sent to Hammarskjöld by special messenger. Within half an hour, Bomboko and I knew what the letter had said, and what Hammarskjöld's reaction to it was.

Three days later, after a further exchange of letters with

Lumumba, the secretary general flew back to New York, having convened another meeting of the Security Council to discuss the Congo.

Dag Hammarskjöld and Patrice Lumumba never met again.

40　Lumumba and his Enemies

After his failure to meet him on 15 August Lumumba thought he could best defeat Hammarskjöld by making a public speech as soon as possible, rather than by attempting any kind of discreet diplomatic action. Hammarskjöld himself had returned to New York, where he swayed opinion strongly against Lumumba and his government. For the first and last time in his life he had met and talked with Tshombe: another point in his favour as against Lumumba, who had not seen Tshombe since independence day. The two Congolese hated each other now absolutely. To Katangan secessionists Lumumba was *the* communist, *the* dictator to be feared above all others – or so they had been assured by the Belgians and other Westerners. To Lumumba and his supporters Tshombe was the quintessential puppet of Western imperialism: they could not see him as a person any longer but only as a type.

On 16 August Lumumba gave a press conference in which the salient points were these:

I have invited you to this conference, first to tell you of an important decision which the present situation has forced our government to make, and also to make clear to you exactly what that situation involves.

Yesterday you received from the UN their version of the differences between the UN secretary general and our government. They have tried to turn these into a question simply of personalities.

I want first of all to make it clear that the secretary general of the UN is a high official in an institution which we respect enormously – which is why we called upon its help.

Therefore all we are concerned with here is to consider the mission he has been given, and the way in which he has carried out or failed to carry out that mission . . .

Through the attitude of the Belgian colonial forces, through misunderstandings created by interested individuals or groups, incidents are occurring daily of a kind that the presence of the UN troops should long ago have prevented.

Furthermore, all the Belgian magistrates departed leaving their offices in indescribable disorder, with the result that we no longer have any civil courts.

We have decided to take immediate steps to get rid of the trouble-makers once and for all, so that our people may recover their dignity, and law may once again be restored in the Congo.

Scarcely had the journalists sent off their reports on this press conference when he summoned another – the very next day, in fact. He enlarged upon what he had said: that the Congo still had faith in the UN, and that all that was in question was the manner in which the secretary general was carrying out his mandate. For the secretary general was acting as though the central government did not exist: having talks with Tshombe, and allowing the cold war to penetrate to the Congo; permitting Belgian troops to massacre Congolese in Katanga; and turning a blind eye to the conspiracy between Tshombe and the Belgians. Though Hammarskjöld had promised that the security council would not meet until the Congolese delegation had arrived, the council was in fact now doing so. Lumumba then closed with an impassioned reaffirmation of the Congo's sovereignty, and her determination to maintain it.

Meanwhile we were on our way back to New York for the second time that August. The delegation was again led by Gizenga, who had been ordered firmly by Lumumba to act as the spokesman himself. I suspected that Lumumba's inquiries had led him to conclude that any possible coup would be led by Bomboko and the Belgians, rather than Gizenga. In addition to Gizenga and myself, the delegation included Mandi, Pierre Elengesa, adviser to the prime minister, and Mpolo. But before our delegation had managed to put the Congo's point of view to the security council Lumumba once again spoke on the radio in Léopoldville, on Sunday 21 August, a few hours after the security council session had opened. He assailed the terrible record of Belgian colonialism, which had destroyed Congolese artistic and moral values 'in the name of civilization and religion'. It had taken away the Africans' self-respect, and attempted to turn them into people with no personality of their own who would be merely imitators of the West – propaganda tools whose only function was to work in silence and resignation. He spoke of the long humiliation endured by Africans in being unable to move freely in their own country, while white people could do so; of curfews, the repression of local religions, and exploitation; of how the Belgians, once they realized that independence had to come, tried to form political parties to support their interests, determined to maintain their economic domination of the Congo. He urged the Congolese to abandon their internecine struggles and unite against all attempts by the former colonial power to 'divide and conquer', and ended with the cry, 'Long live the sovereign and independent Republic of the Congo!'

In the security council Gizenga read the text we had worked out together. He read it without any emotion; though it was harsh, if not positively unjust in places, in its attitude to the secretary general.

Wigny, who represented Belgium, made it clear during his speech that he felt the strongest personal dislike for Gizenga; but the latter, despite all our pleas, decided not to make use of his right to reply either to Wigny or Hammarskjöld. The only speech he made was our prepared one; otherwise, he simply listened immovably to the various speakers. He was not loquacious by nature, and certainly never spoke for the pleasure of hearing his own voice. Here are the most important extracts of what he did say:

After the brutal and unjustified aggression which was unleashed against the Congolese people, the government of the Republic immediately appealed to the United Nations for help in the peaceful settlement of the conflict . . .

The security council entrusted the implementation of these resolutions to the secretary general and recommended that he should consider all operations in full cooperation with the central government.

The secretary general, who is surrounded by all the prestige and authority of the United Nations, immediately began sending United Nations troops to the Congo. We hoped that the secretary general would at once clarify his intentions regarding the Katanga problem, so that all ambiguous interpretations could in future be avoided.

You all know, however, in what circumstances the commander-in-chief of the United Nations forces went to Katanga: first, our government was not consulted; second, negotiations were held with the rebel Tshombe in the presence of Belgian government representatives sent to Katanga; third, contacts were established with tribal chiefs sent for military purposes to Elisabethville, and with Belgian advisers; fourth, at the secretary general's request, following negotiations with Tshombe, the security council was reconvened before the implementation of the resolutions adopted only a few days earlier, while the central government was left in complete ignorance; fifth, the result of the Katanga negotiations was made public in a press conference held by Mr Tshombe himself, when he announced that the entry of United Nations troops into Katanga had been postponed, and that the secretary general was to leave the following day for New York where he had requested a new meeting of the security council.

As you know, everything happened just as the puppet Tshombe had stated, and the secretary general left the next day for New York, after addressing a note to our government stating that he had to leave in fifteen minutes. ... In view of the numerous clarifying statements made throughout the meeting [9 August], we were entitled to expect, this time, a final settlement of the Congolese problem.

The secretary general returned to the Congo more determined than ever to carry out the task he had already started. At Elisabethville he stated that he was convinced in advance that he could work fruitfully with Mr Tshombe. There were official negotiations between the United Nations representative and this puppet of the Belgians and their allies who were under orders to carry out in Katanga the plan of aggression directed by the Belgian government against the Republic of the Congo.

As a result of these negotiations, Mr Tshombe was able to tell the press that he was 'satisfied with his talks with the secretary general' who had just 'ratified the ten points of his ultimatum except for a few details'. The secretary general then sent a report to the security council from Elisabethville, the contents of which you know.

In all conscience, the government of the Republic of the Congo and the Congolese people cannot agree to being handed over to neocolonialism in this way. We cannot accept this because we are convinced that no nation in the world can accept further domination once it has won back its independence. If the council's resolutions were to continue to be wrongly interpreted, they would lead not to the complete liberation of the Congo, but to the effective reconquest of our country ...

268

The Congolese government has no easy task in preserving among the Congolese people the necessary atmosphere of good will towards the foreigners called upon to work in its territory. Because of this extreme sensitiveness created by the continual tension in which our people live, any mistake, however small, committed by a person connected with the United Nations, is attributed to the secretary general, who is identified with the United Nations as a whole in all its activities, not only by the Congolese people, but by African opinion in general.

For this reason, the Congolese government would very much like to see the secretary general share his heavy responsibilities with a group appointed by the security council. I should recall here the suggestions made by the Congolese government in this respect, which are based solely on factual considerations.

This group, which must, of course, include the secretary general, should not be confused with a committee of censure nor with a purely advisory committee. It would be made up of nationals of neutral Asian and African countries and would operate permanently on Congolese territory in close cooperation with the central Congolese government and the commander of the United Nations Force.

It might perhaps be useful to recall some of those mistakes, already clearly set forth by our prime minister in documents which have since become official United Nations documents. Let us mention briefly some of the facts.

The central government has not yet understood the reasons which prevented the secretary general from consulting it before he visited the Congolese province of Katanga.

The Congolese government has noted an unfortunate parallel between the so-called conditions laid down by the rebel Tshombe and the decisions taken by the secretary general in implementation of the Security Council's resolutions concerning Katanga . . .

Had he consulted the central government of the Republic of the Congo, the secretary general would have learned that Tshombe's demand, which was, in effect, a Belgian one, had no other aim than to allow Belgian military personnel and civilians to disguise themselves as United Nations troops without being discovered . . .

With regard to these intrigues, I would draw the attention of the council to the arrest in Léopoldville of at least seventy Belgian paratroops wearing the uniform, arm-band and beret of the United Nations. I have with me a United Nations pass numbered 000090 which was given to Major Dieu, managing director of the Belgian Sabena Airline; aircraft of this line have on several occasions endangered the internal security of the Republic by bringing insulting and provocative pamphlets from Brussels . . .

In the secretary general's lengthy report to the council was one passage which was especially telling in relation to the future attitude of the UN to Lumumba, both as a politician and as head of government. Hammarskjöld, who knew better than any of us the game that the Belgians were playing in Katanga and Kasai, actually said this:

. . . With this short summary of the Belgian withdrawal, and with the resulting vacuum filled by the United Nations, we should be entitled to regard the chapter of the Congo story, which describes the situation as one of threat to international peace and security, as being close to the end. *This is said in the firm expectation*, of course, that we need not envisage a risk from any new developments in the Congo outside the framework firmly established by the security council and contrary to the attitude on action by foreign troops that the council has taken in this as in other cases. It is said also *in the firm expectation that the Government of the Republic will take such measures as are within its power to assist the United Nations Force in carrying out the council's decision* and, thus, helping to bring about the order and stability necessary to avoid future eruptions. Other chapters are to unfold, but they relate to the construction of the state and the laying of foundations for a balanced political, economic and social life for the people. In the long run they are more important than the chapter which has come to an end, but they are only indirectly within the sphere of the responsibility of the security council, whatever importance they may have for the United Nations in its effort to help Africa to achieve its rightful place in our political and economic world of today . . .

As far as Hammarskjöld was concerned, Belgium had preserved appearances by officially withdrawing its troops; yet he knew quite well that Belgium had taken care to keep a few in the military base at Kamina, and had also hurried to provide a military framework for the Katangan *gendarmerie*, which it had thoroughly equipped and reorganized. All that now remained for the UN was to help, whether they liked it or not, with the 'construction of the [Congolese] state and the laying of foundations for a balanced political, economic and social life for the [Congolese] people'.

So there was the UN, which was supposed not to interfere in

the Congo's internal affairs, obliged it seemed, less to assist the Congolese government, than in effect to direct it along the path it thought best for the economic, political and social life of the country and its people.

It was on this that Hammarskjöld was hoping either to 'convince' or 'defeat' any Congolese leader who disagreed with him as, during the past few weeks, both Tshombe and Lumumba had been trying in their different ways to do. To forestall any objection that he was acting in his personal capacity, Hammarskjöld formed a consultative committee, with himself as chairman, composed of the representatives in New York of those states which had provided contingents for the UN force in the Congo (that is to say, Canada, Ethiopia, Ghana, Guinea, India, Indonesia, Ireland, Liberia, Mali, Morocco, Pakistan, the Sudan, Sweden, Tunisia and the UAR). These were to give their governments' advice on the workings of the UN Congo operation.

Meanwhile our delegation left New York, to return home via Paris. In forming his consultative committee in New York, Hammarskjöld had completely disregarded our suggestion of a college which would give him practical assistance, rather than merely advice which he might or might not choose to follow. Gizenga decided to publish a communiqué explaining the Congolese attitude on 25 August, from Paris. In it, among other things, he deplored the delay in withdrawing Belgian troops; explained the difference between the college we had proposed and the consultative committee actually formed; and suggested that the next security council meeting should take place in Léopoldville, so that the delegates could see the situation for themselves. He reasserted the importance of *all* Belgians leaving, technicians as well as the military, and their replacement by UN personnel.

We were staying at the Crillon in Paris, and the French government had provided us with bodyguards who remained with us, two at a time, during our whole stay. They were armed and could thus ensure our protection, but they could also keep an eye on every contact, every move we made.

That same day in Léopoldville, Lumumba was officially opening the pan-African conference of foreign ministers. In theory, this was to be a preparatory conference for the pan-African summit conference to follow, but events decreed otherwise.

The trouble was that Lumumba was tending more and more to forget the existence of Kasavubu, while the latter was more watchful than ever, and carefully noting every tiniest error that Lumumba made. It took the bloody incidents on the opening day of the conference to make Lumumba at last aware. These were clearly produced and organized by young Bakongo and Baluba fanatics who supported Kasavubu and Kalonji. They gave pause to the foreign heads of state who had been invited to Léopoldville and who now decided that they were good reason for refusing to come there. So the conference was limited to discussions of the Congolese crisis and African solidarity in general, among foreign ministers only.

Bomboko was chosen to preside over the conference, which lasted from 25 to 30 August. As soon as we got back to Léopoldville, Bomboko asked me to take his place at the head of the Congolese delegation. This gave me a chance to see once again the various friends I had made in New York, and make some new ones too – for the conference had brought together a great number of distinguished Africans – Mongi Slim of Tunisia, Boumendjel of Algeria, Kojo Botso and Quaison Sackey of Ghana, Diallo Telli of Guinea, and many more.

A few days before the pan-African conference opened, Ralph Bunche resigned as Hammarskjöld's personal representative in the Congo. It was hard to know whether his resignation was by his own choice or enforced, considering the fact that he seemed physically exhausted and psychologically disheartened by the number of attacks being made openly and in private on both him personally and the UN in general. In choosing a replacement Hammarskjöld had consulted the Indian prime minister, Nehru, who offered him the Indian ambassador to Pakistan, Rajeshwar Dayal, a brilliant diplomat and the perfect combination of English education and Indian aristocracy. He was given the job at once, but only came to the Congo on 8 September.

Having opened the pan-African conference, Lumumba set off for Stanleyville on 27 August with a group of ministers,[1] photo-

1. Among them were Christophe Gbenye, minister of the interior; Marcel

graphers and reporters from the Information Service. He was fighting against time, knowing it to be working against both him and his government. Though he had liked, and indeed initiated the idea of the African conference in Léopoldville, he could not personally devote his full attention to making it a success.

What he wanted above all was to get South Kasai and Katanga successfully occupied by Congolese army forces, without any help from the UN, while the summit conference was actually taking place in Léopoldville. Only the Soviet Union, it seemed to him, could and might provide the central Congolese government with the help that it needed to plan and carry out a methodical invasion of the rebel provinces. Lumumba had talked it over in New York with Kuznetzov, and more recently in Léopoldville with the new Soviet ambassador, Mikhail D. Yakovlev. Unfortunately for him however, the West could not help interpreting such Soviet assistance as being similar in kind to the assistance openly given to Tshombe by the Belgians. Yet in effect, when it came to Katanga, Belgium and the West had stepped in to safeguard their own interests and material advantage, whereas the Soviet aid to the central government was directly aimed at ending the secession of Katanga, and ultimately at ending Western control of our vast mining resources.

The Soviet Union could hardly fail to be aware of the international implications and repercussions of its offering such aid to the central government. Furthermore, the Soviet spokesmen who had discussed the question with Lumumba or various of his ministers were only half convinced of the final success of an invasion of Katanga by the ANC. The foreign view – whether Western, African or communist – on the fighting abilities of the ANC troops was far from encouraging. But to Lumumba it was a matter of life and death. He had defied Hammarskjöld and the UN; he had proof of concerted Western action in the Congo's mining provinces; and he could really now depend only upon himself, the ANC, and the Soviet Union – the one powerful nation apparently prepared to give him the help that he needed in

---

Lengema, secretary of state to the presidency (as successor to Mobutu since the latter had been appointed Colonel of the ANC) and Captain Mawoso, the prime minister's chief ordnance officer.

the way of arms, equipment and, above all, transport. The Soviet Union, which up to that time had not drawn breath in its fulsome praise of Lumumba, was now being obliged to do something concrete in order to win his full confidence. The West had not dreamt that Lumumba could get hold of adequate transport to make his troops really mobile; and the arrival in Matadi of more than a hundred Soviet military trucks, as a gift from Russia, and of sixteen Ilyushin transport planes in Stanleyville, finally set the seal on Lumumba's political downfall.

The strategy of the military invasion of Kasai and Katanga was discussed in Lumumba's office, and was known only to a few of his most intimate friends and advisers. General Lundula, commander-in-chief of the ANC, was one of the most fully informed; as was Jason Sendwe, Tshombe's political rival, and undisputed leader of the northern Katangan Balubas. Lumumba was counting on the revolt of Sendwe's supporters in Katanga to bring the apparent success of Tshombe's supporters to an end politically.

Christophe Gbenye, minister of the interior; Grenfell. minister of state without portfolio; and Marcel Lengema, private secretary to the prime minister, were the only ministers fully involved in the planning. Mobutu, chief-of-staff of the ANC, only took part in some of the talks, and certainly cannot be said to have been wholly trusted. However, discretion was not the strong point of Lumumba's entourage; both he and Gizenga had far too many outsiders, advisers or self-styled friends milling about their offices. It was the easiest thing in the world for anyone with connections in high places to get information about Lumumba's plans and intentions. Among such associates would seem to have been some who were actually being paid to hand out communiqués so worded that every slightest plan of the prime minister's could be read between the lines. Lumumba's *chef de cabinet* was Damien Kandolo, a close friend of Albert Ndele, Joseph Mobutu and Victor Nendaka. Here is an extract from one such communiqué, describing Lumumba's return to Léopoldville:

The prime minister, M. Patrice Lumumba, who made an official visit to Orientale province on Saturday last, returned to Léopoldville yesterday. He arrived at Ndjili airport at 4.30 p.m., and was accompanied by M. Christophe Gbenye, minister of the interior; M. Marcel

Lengema, private secretary to the prime minister; and Captain Mawoso, his chief ordnance officer; as also his press attaché, and photographers and reporters from the Information Service, and the rest of his suite.

On disembarking, he was greeted by M. Mwamba, minister of justice; Mr Sendwe, commissioner of state for Katanga; M. Lutula, minister of agriculture; M. Bolamba, secretary of state for information; M. Kiwewa, secretary of state for foreign commerce; General Lundula; Colonel Mobutu; his private secretary, M. Kandolo; and others . . .

The prime minister and minister of national defence then had a long talk with troops of the national army who are to embark this evening for Luluabourg, where they will start military operations. He encouraged the troops, urging them to serve the nation with loyalty, and above all to work with a good team spirit and preserve at all times the strictest military discipline. He also promised various financial and other improvements in their conditions, thus raising their morale enormously. He followed this up by a public meeting at which he told everyone what had been decided.

Communiqués of this sort were certainly not dictated by Lumumba, but were the work of agents planted among his entourage, whose job it was to indicate to their employers and friends, who were determined to oust Lumumba, just how the land lay. Other Africans, with more experience than the Congolese in the armed struggle against imperialism, were sadly disappointed by the indiscretions in the Congo. When a secret meeting was proposed to discuss matters with the prime minister, one of these had no hesitation in saying in so many words: 'In the Congo there are no secrets. Every meeting between even two Congolese behind locked doors will sooner or later become a public gathering.'

It was sad, but during those final days of August 1960 the Congo was like a vast glass tank full of fish of all colours and sizes; and the moment any bait was thrown in, they would fight one another to the death to get hold of it. The Belgians had thrown in as bait the secession of Katanga and Kasai; the Americans' bait was the UN, which they supported with all the power and money they had; the Afro-Asians enjoyed making anti-colonialist and anti-imperialist declarations, while the Soviet Union threw in its trucks, planes and technicians whose object was to drive imperialism out of the heart of Africa – a colossal bait but, alas, a deceptive one.

The Americans believed that it was their duty to keep a watch on every move, every action, of the Soviet Union in the Congo. And this they could do everywhere except perhaps in Stanleyville, Lumumba's political fiefdom. On 27 August he arrived there to receive the Soviet planes in person; while at the same time the team of eight Americans who arrived were manhandled by ANC soldiers at Stanleyville airport. This was the occasion for several diplomatic protests: the UN protested to the Congolese government, as did the American ambassador, Timberlake. The tone of both protests suggested that the Congolese government had no right to prevent the Americans from watching – indeed, even from supervising – Soviet activities on the soil of the Congo. The Swedish Major-General Carl von Horn, commander of the UN forces in the Congo, gave his full support to the American protest, and promised that no such incident should ever again occur while he was in charge of the UN operations there. Andrew Cordier, Hammarskjöld's private secretary, had arrived in Léopoldville on 28 August. Bunche having left, and Dayal not yet arrived, he became acting head of the UN in the Congo.

On 31 August, when all his available troops had entered into action against the secessionists in Kasai and Katanga, Lumumba delivered the closing speech of the pan-African conference in Léopoldville. In it he tried to run with the hare and hunt with the hounds: praising the UN's work in the Congo, and at the same time declaring that the Congo and Africa could not stand by idle as the UN hesitated to use force to re-unify the Congolese state. Cordier's presence in Léopoldville presaged a whole new turn of events in the Congo, and certainly not one that would be to the advantage of Lumumba, who had accepted aid from the Soviet Union outside the framework of the UN. Cordier was Hammarskjöld's right-hand man; he was, like Bunche, an American, but less hesitant and more resolute. Timberlake found in him a valuable ally; during the few days that he was in the Congo at the head of the UN, Cordier could be described as having been in effect the Congolese head of state, with Timberlake as personal adviser and vice-president.

276

Lumumba was not slow to recognize the situation, and was therefore moderate and conciliatory in his closing speech – as witness the following extracts:

... The colonialists have created a completely false problem. That problem, as you all know, is the tragedy of Katanga, behind which lies concealed a whole organization for sabotaging our national independence. That organization, which is now acting in devious ways, through intermediaries, has but one aim in view: to foment disturbance, to create problems for the government and discredit it in the eyes of other nations through a carefully planned propaganda, and so reconquer the Congo. And all this with the single object of fostering their own selfish interests.

It is not Africa itself that the colonialists are interested in, but the wealth of Africa; and everything they do in Africa is determined by what is best for their own financial interests, at the expense of the African people. They will stop at nothing to get hold of that wealth.

Fortunately for us, the Congolese people and government have been on the watch. Our struggle is purely and simply for the liberation of our country, the establishment of peace and true social justice.

The Congo has acceded to independence in conditions such as have existed in no other African country. Whereas elsewhere, former colonies' accession to independence has been preceded by intermediate stages, in the Congo such was not the case: we achieved our sovereighty without any transition. From being one hundred per cent a colony, we were suddenly one hundred per cent independent.

We took over the leadership of our country on 30 June 1960, and the Belgian government, leaving us no time to become organized, unleashed a brutal aggression against our republic on entirely false pretences. Our response to these acts of violence and provocation was to appeal to the United Nations ...

That differences of opinion have arisen between the government of the Republic and the secretary general of the United Nations is because, in all their actions in the Congo, the representatives of the United Nations have never consulted us, as the Security Council resolutions proposed.

Such incidents would have been avoided if there had been from the first a spirit of cooperation between the representatives of the United Nations and those of the government of the Republic. We have never doubted the value of the work done by the United Nations in Africa. There can be no one who is not aware how many disasters have been avoided throughout the world through the concerted efforts of the United Nations . . .

Peace will not exist fully in Africa unless the West puts a full stop to its colonial enterprises there.

Let me insist that there is no feeling of hatred or hostility on the part of the government or people of the Congo towards Belgium or any other European country.

Yet the moment the Belgian government announces that it is withdrawing its troops from Katanga, it replaces those leaving with fresh ones. Thus a hundred Belgian police recently arrived in Katanga in the guise of 'technical advisers' who were to 'train' and 'organize' Tshombe's police force.

Furthermore, before he left Elisabethville, General Gheysen, the commander of the Belgian occupying troops in Katanga, demanded the creation of a neutral zone between Kasai and Katanga, and the neutralization of the Kamina and Kitona bases. But the Belgian general did not stop at making recommendations; he went straight into action. So the roads, bridges and all the strategic points of Katanga were carefully mined by the Belgian army on express orders from the government in Brussels.

In addition, the entire white population of Katanga has just been mobilized. Every European has been given an official order of requisition, countersigned by the commandant of the Volunteer Corps and the Belgian administrator of the area . . .

The 'Volunteer Corps' is a military organization founded and established on the spot by the Belgian government – thus proving its determination not to leave Katanga.

What they are trying to do is abundantly clear: while apparently withdrawing their troops, they are in reality renewing and reinforcing their occupation personnel, both by sending fresh troops in the guise of 'technicians', and by mobilizing all the Belgians actually living in Katanga. In the name of the government and people of the Congo, I want to make it clear that there can be no question of neutralizing the Kamina and Kitona bases; but only of wholly and completely evacuating them.

We do not want any foreign military bases in the Congo, even one supervised by the United Nations.

Not a single square yard of Congolese soil must belong to any foreign power whatever, and nothing can be done, nor will anything ever be done, in this country except by decision of the one government which alone guarantees the legality and sovereignty of the Congolese people . . .

In the end the Conference had voted resolutions, which were simply declarations of intent and encouragement, involving no commitment on the part of any of the states concerned. The Conference declared the need to preserve the unity and territorial integrity of the Congo; condemned secession wherever it might occur and any colonialist manoeuvring to divide the Congo; and pledged its total support to the central Congolese government, the only legitimate and legal authority in the new state. It promised to help that government within the framework of the UN; paid tribute to the UN's peace-keeping work in the Congo, while hoping for more complete collaboration between the UN and the central Congolese government; and, finally, launched an urgent and solemn appeal to all Congolese leaders to preserve the unity of the state, and to maintain harmony and cooperation among themselves in the higher interests of the Congo itself and of Africa as a whole.

In regard to the proposal for a summit conference of African heads of state, the Conference restricted itself to stressing the desirability and importance of such a meeting, but left it to the heads of states to decide among themselves what diplomatic consultations should precede it.

The Conference enabled some of us to discover the divergences of opinion among Africans in regard to the Congolese problem, divergences resulting from the outside interests and commitments of each country. Certain of them – for instance Liberia, Morocco, Tunisia, and Ethiopia – impressed us as being uncertain of the stability of the Lumumba régime, and as accordingly withholding their total support until such time as the Congolese government was more secure. The delegates from these countries let it be understood that their presidents or kings had a political maturity and an experience of statesmanship which they had not found among the Congolese leaders in Léopoldville.

Lumumba's closing speech was greeted with applause, despite the general uneasiness prevailing behind the scenes. (Indeed, several delegations had suggested that Lumumba give Kasavubu the honour of closing the Conference; but the prime minister was obdurate.) The next day Kasavubu gave courtesy audiences to various of the African delegates, in order to receive from them the good wishes of his fellow African heads of state. At the same time, this made it possible for them to discover for themselves just where Kasavubu's ideas parted company from Lumumba's.

France and Belgium seemed to be the principal targets among Western countries in the attacks that the delegates made against imperialist action in the Congo. Lumumba drew closer and closer to the Algerians, the Guineans and the Moumié group from Cameroun – in other words, the anti-French African bloc; while Kasavubu was improving his relations with France through the good offices of Abbé Youlou and his French advisers in Brazzaville, and was also preserving his contacts with Belgium via his then political allies – notably Ileo, Kalonji, Bomboko, Delvaux, and Tshombe himself.

Lumumba could not be everywhere at once. Military victory against the secessionists in Kasai and Katanga was his major preoccupation, together with consolidating the support of such African countries as Ghana, Guinea, Mali and the UAR. But the west was lying in wait for him. No one can fight a war without money; and in fact the financial situation of the Congo was increasingly serious. Highly placed Belgians who still ran the country's administration were making fun of Lumumba behind his back, with his arrogant speeches and his determination to crush their puppets, Tshombe and Kalonji.

In Geneva, ministers Nkayi and Delvaux, and their American and Tunisian advisers, were negotiating with Belgium the liquidation of the central bank of the Congo and Ruanda-Urundi. Their talks were not restricted solely to the main purpose of the conference: the Belgians took the occasion to consider one by one the problems of Belgo-Congolese relations – among which was obviously the possible political elimination of Lumumba. As for the overt object of the conference, the Congo proposed the creation of a national bank of the Congo, and the setting up of a monetary council there.

The Congolese delegation had been in touch with Kasavubu; and Lumumba does not seem to have been informed in any detail of the viewpoint being put forward by the Congolese. In Lumumba's view, Albert Ndele, private secretary of Nkayi, minister of finance, and himself acting secretary general to the ministry of finance, was the brains and the moving power of the Congolese delegation in Geneva. Lumumba thought that via Ndele the Belgians would put into effect the resolutions made in Brussels at the Economic Round Table, where Ndele had been one of the young Congolese representatives.

In the ensuing battle between Lumumba and Ndele it became clear that the prime minister was gradually losing control over his own government. Ndele, who was a distant relative of Kasavubu, was dismissed from his job as private secretary to the finance minister, and then shortly afterwards on 1 September reinstated by order of the Council of Ministers.

That same day, we began to hear on foreign radio stations the news of the ANC's advances in the secessionist province of South Kasai. We learnt that several people had been killed, and that the ANC was moving successfully towards Katanga. Joseph Ngalula, appointed prime minister of south Kasai by the secessionists, was finding it difficult to prevent the ANC's advance; and Albert Kalonji, the self-appointed emperor of South Kasai, had fled from Bakwanga to Elisabethville, to ask for help from his friend and accomplice Tshombe.

Tshombe himself badly needed his police force (formed by Belgian officers) and white mercenaries as well, because the ANC was determined to follow its invasion of Kasai by invading Katanga. Tshombe and Kalonji realized the mettle of the ANC troops from the military reports they received, and they got in touch with Kasavubu through the intermediary of their Belgian advisers. An *Abako* delegation came to Elisabethville, with Kasavubu's full approval, to meet with Kalonji and Tshombe.

At the Council of Ministers on 1 September Rémy Mwamba, a Katangan politician and minister of justice, demanded that Lumumba inform the Council of what was happening in Katanga. Here is the episode as officially recorded:

In reply to M. Mwamba's question on the Katangan affair, the prime minister put before the Council all the arrangements made for the invasion of Katanga. 'As authorized at the last session of the Council, I have obtained ten planes, five helicopters, sixty assistants, and food for 10,000 people for six months. The president of the provincial government of Stanleyville is arriving today to be given precise instructions. The UN leaves us a free hand in regard to invading Katanga.'

The UN secretariat was in fact now in a strong position, since from then on it could blame the Soviet Union and Belgium equally: both were foreign countries which had sent personnel and equipment to the Congo independent of any UN channels.

On 4 September Hammarskjöld drew the attention of the permanent Belgian representative at the UN to the presence of Belgian officers among the Katangan *gendarmerie*, in the guise of 'technical aid' quite outside the UN operation; and furthermore, to the presence of 'individuals' – white mercenaries – who had volunteered to help. On 5 September he demanded an explanation from the Soviet delegation of the presence – on Congolese soil – of IL-14 type aircraft with crews, technicians and non-flying staff. Ten such planes, said the note, had come from Stanleyville and landed on 2 September in Luluabourg, carrying Congolese troops to reinforce the Congolese armed forces in the Bakwanga area of Kasai. The secretary general further asked for information regarding the delivery of 100 Soviet trucks (GAZ-63 type), which the Soviet government had been promising the UN since 22 July.

While the Belgians could not justify their direct military aid to Kasai and Katanga except in terms of safeguarding their financial interests and reinforcing the secessions they had themselves inspired and organized, the USSR could, on the other hand, say definitely in a note to the secretary general that 'the sending by the Soviet Union of help to the government of the Republic of the Congo – in the form of civil aircraft and motor vehicles – was not contrary to the terms of the resolutions of 14 and 22 July 1960, since the said resolutions set no limit on the right of the government to ask for or be given direct bilateral aid'.

Following the end of the pan-African Conference, and the news of the ANC's victory over the South Kasai secessionists, anti-Lumumba circles began organizing themselves more actively around Kasavubu in order to create a constitutional crisis, which would divert Lumumba's attention in other directions, and hold back his advance into Katanga. Once again, the initiative came from Westerners for whom Lumumba was a crypto-communist, and Katanga an oasis of peace which had at all costs to be preserved.

While most of us were seeing Lumumba every day at the Council of Ministers, Kasavubu was carrying on his own consultations in his residence. He placed great weight on the various warnings he received on all sides: from Western diplomats and special Belgian envoys – from Congolese parliamentarians and even ministers whose loyalties were divided between himself and Lumumba.

Some Belgian envoys, together with the *Abako* delegation, had even succeeded in informing him that Tshombe would agree ultimately to a reconciliation with the central government if Lumumba were removed from power. Despite the unending stream of visitors urging him on, however, Kasavubu hesitated to confront Lumumba openly without feeling secure of support in parliament, where Lumumba had achieved greater popularity than he had. As for the army, it would be difficult to turn General Lundula against Lumumba; he had, therefore, to find some means of acting in Lundula's absence and without his knowledge. So Colonel Mobutu began to assume great importance, for he was number two in the military hierarchy of the ANC. He had had no part in planning the invasion of South Kasai and Katanga; and was now given, as so-called assistant, the Moroccan General Kettani, to help him reorganize the ANC – which meant that the Moroccan general was to see how best to swing the ANC's allegiance from Lumumba to Kasavubu. Moreover there was a secret radio station supporting Kasavubu, Kalonji and Tshombe – operating in Brazzaville under the wing of Youlou, the Belgians and the French – which might prove decisive, if Kasavubu could not get support from parliament.

Once assured of Mobutu's loyalty, and of Kettani's assistance in taking over the army, and having at his disposal a propaganda medium that could not be appropriated by the other side, Kasavubu became more and more ready to create a constitutional crisis. And the presence in Léopoldville of Andrew Cordier, an American citizen in touch with American financial circles, issuing warnings in the name of the UN, was another factor that determined Kasavubu in hastening to carry out his decision. Since 28

August Cordier had been working actively to put an end to Russian intervention in the Congo.

But Kasavubu, over-prudent as always, decided to move step by step, thus gaining the time he needed to study the reactions of Lumumba himself and of his political allies, both Congolese and foreign. Jef van Bilsen, Kasavubu's Belgian friend and private adviser, was the last European to talk with him, only a few moments before he carried out his decision to dismiss his prime minister.

Since the end of the pan-African Conference the press and radio in the West had been announcing a worsening situation in the Congo. The presence of Russian planes and trucks, with crews, technicians and interpreters, on Congolese soil, was interpreted as a threat to international peace and security. The fact that those transport planes and trucks would help to conquer Katanga convinced public opinion in the West that the Congo as governed by Lumumba was already more than half-way to being a communist and anti-Western power.

All propaganda of this kind was part of the necessary psychological preparation for a major diplomatic coup in the Congo, a coup inspired and supported by the Western powers.

On 1 September 1960, parliament could not sit because there was not a quorum present. Joseph Kasongo, speaker of the chamber of representatives, took the occasion to draw the attention of the deputies to the number of active parliamentarians in the Congo. Of 137 deputies, he said, more than ten chose no longer to be present at any sessions; these were the Katanga deputies who supported Tshombe's CONAKAT, and the members elected by Kalonji's MNC. The assembly was also informed that certain deputies had been arrested because, according to Kasongo, they had been caught *flagrante delicto*, and were therefore not protected by parliamentary immunity. The session was then adjourned until 5 September, when it opened at 10.25 a.m. There were at least two points on the agenda: a speech from Kasongo, on his trip to the USA and elsewhere with the prime minister; and debates on parliamentary immunity, with a motion demanding the temporary release of the arrested deputies.

On his trip to the U S A, Kasongo spoke in much the same tone as the prime minister had used a few days earlier when describing the manoeuvres of the Belgians to ruin the Congo financially. Here are some of the most important things he said:[2]

We arrived in Washington where we were officially welcomed with a nineteen-gun salute; we were given rooms in the presidential guest house, where all important guests stay. On the day of our arrival we were received by the American secretary of state. ... We took the opportunity of asking to become members of the World Bank and the International Monetary Fund. ... We had also intended to choose this moment to ask for a loan. It was then that we discovered that Belgium had made a contract in the name of the Congo to borrow 120 million dollars. To justify this, she had alleged that the money would be used to form a metalled network of roads out of the Le-kenge, the Kasai/Katanga, the Kingu/Bukavu, Stan/Bunia, Stan/Bukavu, and Leo/Matadi roads, and then to build airports, in Stanleyville and elsewhere. ... We were told that of the 120 million dollars, Belgium had already received 79 million, and was still to receive 41 million. We were told that we could not touch this remaining money, because Belgium had not yet given receipts to show how she had spent the 79 million she had received. We were asked to pay back the advance. We replied that we had not had any of it, and were in serious financial difficulties which would make it impossible to do so. Belgium was supposed to have repaid 14½ million dollars at the beginning of the previous August, but had not done so. So, we were told, there were two things we must do: (1) fulfil the terms of the contract relating to the repayment of funds lent; and (2) show that the work had been carried out. If these two conditions were fulfilled, then we could have the remaining 41 million. ... It goes without saying that, given the money and the gold reserves of which we had quite simply been robbed, no return to diplomatic relations with Belgium could be contemplated until it had been returned in its entirety, and the money borrowed 'for us' shown to have been spent as intended. Both our wealth and our hard work had been exploited.

As regards the arrested parliamentarians, the chamber passed a resolution demanding the temporary release of all its members at present in prison, especially Bolikango and Bondhe.

2. *Annales Parlementaires, Chambre des Représentants de la République du Congo, Séance publique du lundi 5 Septembre 1960.*

The arrest of Jean Bolikango, leader of the Bangala and once a candidate for the presidency, gave fresh fuel to the animosity that the Bangala people had felt in the past for Lumumba. From that point on, Lumumba's circle of antagonists was complete; those who were planning his political downfall could now count on agreement among all those Congolese politicians whose common denominators were their pro-westernism and their hatred of Lumumba. It was a gamut running from Kasavubu to Tshombe, by way of Bolikango, Kalonji, Ileo and Bomboko.

On 5 September, at about 8.15 p.m., Kasavubu finally mustered his courage, secure in the support of the West and the UN secretariat. He took up the microphone of the Congolese National Radio to announce the dismissal of Lumumba and six of his ministers.[3] The speech he gave fell like a bomb among Congolese and other Africans, but brought a sigh of relief all over Europe and among the European inhabitants of the Congo. I was in my apartment at the Royal during his speech, and did not happen to hear it myself. I had invited the Congolese who were to be sent to work as permanent diplomatic representatives of the Congo in New York to an informal meeting to talk about their mission.

My sister Madeleine Sophie who had heard the speech rang me at once to tell me what had happened. I turned on the radio, and I and my future colleagues heard the rebroadcast of the speech. My first reaction was to find out what Lumumba felt about it. I telephoned him at his residence, and his answer was brief: 'There will be an extraordinary Council of Ministers in an hour's time, but first of all I must ask that everyone hear what I also have to say on the radio. I am going there now.'

I got in touch with Mpolo who was enraged, and at once suggested that we get Kasavubu arrested and sent to Stanleyville. Lumbala also wanted to do this: 'Kasavubu has sold out to the Belgians. He is playing the same game as Tshombe. He was never really against Katangan secession anyhow, because he always had the idea that sooner or later the lower Congo would secede as well.'

3. A. Gizenga, R. Mwamba, C. Gbenye, A. Kashamura, A. Bolamba and J. Lumbala.

A few minutes later the National Radio was handed over to Lumumba, who gave a hastily prepared response to Kasavubu. It was then 9 p.m. This is what he said:

The National Radio has just broadcast a statement by the head of state, M. Joseph Kasavubu, a statement demanding that the government I lead be dismissed.

In the name of that government and the whole nation, I should like to make a formal refutation of what he has said. The government has had no discussion on the matter with the head of state. Having been democratically elected by the nation, and received the unanimous confidence of parliament, our government cannot be dismissed unless it should lose the people's confidence. At present the government still has their confidence, and the entire nation is behind us.

Having determined to defend the people, even if it costs us our lives, having refused to sell our country to the Belgian colonialists and their allies, having refused to give way to the demands of those who are still trying to exploit our nation, this government will defend the people's rights with honour and pride. We shall remain in power and continue the work we have been given to do.

I beg that the people who have placed their trust in us remain calm in face of the attempts to sabotage our national independence. It was we ourselves who elected the head of state, though he did not have the confidence of the whole people.

People of the Congo, lift up your heads. The enemies of our country and the collaborators of the Belgian imperialists have today shown themselves for what they are. All Congolese officers and n.c.o.s remain at your posts to defend your country just as you did so heroically against the Belgian aggressors.

But Lumumba then went further, deepening the constitutional crisis and creating confusion in the minds of everyone. At about 9.30 and again at 10.00 that same evening the radio twice broadcast a second speech by the prime minister. This one was longer, and left no possible opening for reconciliation or compromise. Among other things, he said this:

Let me inform you that a Council of Ministers will take place this evening to consider the situation created by M. Kasavubu's unexpected statement which can only be called a public betrayal of our nation. I was not consulted, nor was a single minister, nor even a single member of parliament. ... The government can only rejoice tonight in its victory. Yes, it is a victory, for the people are at last really able to see who is defending and working for them, and who is working for the Belgians; who is for the country and who against it; who is loyal and who is not. ... Following the lead of the MNC, the PSA, the BALUBAKAT, the CEREA and all the other nationalist parties who are the parties actually in power now no longer can give him their confidence. Now he is no longer head of state. The government must take over the sovereign privileges of our republic. ... Parliament will also take a stand, and I beg that the United Nations and the free world do not interfere in the internal affairs of the Congolese state, nor become accomplices in the manoeuvres of the Belgians – for it is by a Belgian manoeuvre that Kasavubu has done what he has done today, a plot worked out by Belgian and French imperialists. Whenever I have been to M. Kasavubu's office, I have always found those people there, and it is they who have set up this plan. ... I ask the United Nations not to depart from their mission, not to get involved in the differences now existing between the government and Mr Kasavubu. We shall resolve them ourselves by democratic means in our own parliament, in the framework of our own national institutions; we ask them not to complicate the situation but to let the Congolese people themselves, sovereignly, resolve their problems. ... Brothers, keep together, go forward hand in hand and victory will be ours. There is no longer a head of state in our republic, only a government by and for the people ...

At about 11 when we were all at the prime minister's residence for the extraordinary Council of Ministers, the situation would have been comic were it not so tragic. We were there, meeting and discussing, without the least idea of what the next day was to bring. I caught traces on people's faces of all kinds of contradictory emotions – worry, hypocrisy, fear, satisfaction. Chaos was upon us in the Congo. The state, still without any constitution approved by the national parliament, already faced jurists with a problem of constitutional law which the Belgians had not foreseen when formulating and imposing the *Loi Fondamentale*.

In the night of 5-6 September Kasavubu, president of the republic, had dismissed Lumumba, prime minister, and various other ministers in a broadcast on the National Radio. On that same National Radio, the head of government had told the world that he was in turn dismissing the head of state who had only been elected by parliament thanks to the support he got from Lumumba and his followers.

Henceforth every man and woman in the country had to opt for one or other of the two leaders; while the Western and communist powers all decided as best suited their particular financial or ideological interests.

Lumumba summoned us as an improvised Council of Ministers at 11 that night. Both ministers and non-ministers came, and we stayed until 3 a.m. Throughout the meeting there remained one mystery troubling all but those responsible: who were the two ministers who had countersigned Kasavubu's order of dismissal?

We felt we might be thought guilty until proved innocent; any one of us, apart from the six dismissed ministers, might have been a signatory of the president's declaration. The meeting ended without our discovering who the men concerned were; but those who had not come to the meeting were inevitably suspected. After naming those present,[3] the official account went on to say:

The Council was to act on the unexpected speech on the National Radio given today, Monday, 5 August 1960, at 8 p.m. by M. Joseph Kasavubu, head of state.

The prime minister, head of the legal government of the republic, informed the Council that he had not been contacted by the head of state, nor had the latter ever put forward the smallest complaint or comment of any kind on the action taken by the government since its formation up to the present.

On the contrary, they had always worked as a team ever since the unleashing of the Belgian aggression had become a wider issue than any internal differences in the country.

The government elected by the people had, since the vote of confidence in both chambers, won a majority far larger than the quorum

3. Lumumba, Gizenga (deputy prime minister), Ilunga (minister of public works), Mulele (minister of national education), Mpolo (minister of youth and sport), Mwamba (minister of justice), M'Buyi (minister of the middle classes), Lengema (secretary of state to the presidency), Lumbala (ditto), Bisukiro (commerce), Sendwe (commissioner of state for Katanga), Okito (vice-president of the senate), Finant (president of the Stanleyville provincial government), Asumani (senator), I. Kalonji (senator), Medie (senator), Kashamura (minister of information), Wafwana (deputy), Mobutu, Keleke (vice-president of the provincial assembly of Stanleyville), Mandi (secretary of state for foreign affairs), Kanza (ambassador to the UN), Muzangi (private secretary to the president of the provincial government of Léopoldville).

demanded by law. The confidence shown in the government by the nation had not ceased to grow.

On 29 August 1960 the Senate unanimously voted a motion to give the government whatever powers it might need to succeed in its mission of pacification.

The Council concluded, after a thorough examination of the situation, that the coup attempted by the head of state is the result of a conspiracy which has been in preparation for some time among Belgian and French imperialist circles, and certain local elements in their pay.

The Council further stated that for some days representatives of the Belgian and French governments, notably van Bilsen, Christian Jayle, director of information in Brazzaville, and others, have held regular meetings with the head of state in his office.

The Council also notes that the members of the national parliament were not consulted by the head of state before he made his statement.

After long consideration, the Council made decisions which will be set out in a press communiqué to be published as soon as possible.

There followed a long communiqué which the prime minister read himself over the radio at 5.30 that same morning of 6 September – two hours after our meeting had broken up. The communiqué repeated the accusations against Kasavubu, saying particularly that he had violated the *Loi Fondamentale*, and had committed an act of high treason, which automatically made it illegal for him to continue to carry out his constitutional functions.

Another Council of Ministers was called for 11 a.m. that day. This time all the ministers were there, some anxious and frightened, others enraged and aggressive. I recall myself as having said something of this kind:

Gentlemen, I believe I am one of those who know Kasavubu fairly well, owing to his antagonism towards my father and my family. He is a timid and extremely prudent man, and takes great care in making his decisions, especially when he is announcing them publicly. Let us be therefore very cautious in considering what has happened since yesterday evening. Kasavubu would never have dared to make that speech, had he not first had certain negotiations and received certain formal guarantees. So let us try to find out just what those guarantees are, and who the powers are behind him – for although he is slow to take decisions, once he has made up his mind he will never retract.

Delvaux was the first to agree with me: 'I think M. Kanza is right. If Kasavubu has taken a decision, then he has some guarantees and won't withdraw. So let us be very careful as to how we react.'

Bomboko was present among us; he said nothing, but after what Delvaux and I had said, he stayed for a few moments longer to see what Lumumba's reaction would be. Then he asked me to go outside with him. In the garden he said to me: 'Listen Thomas: what has just happened is a lesson for Patrice. I am sick of all these pointless discussions. You be careful; I'm off to President Kasavubu, and will telephone to tell you what happens, and you let me know the news from your end.' I asked him whether he had countersigned the dismissal. 'Not yet,' he said, 'but I think I shall. Patrice treats us like a bunch of kids. He must be taught a lesson.' 'But Justin,' I said, 'must it really be you who signs? There are only two of us ministers who are graduates. If you sign, then all graduates will look like traitors; and then, you are foreign minister; and if you sign the act of dismissal, it will carry more weight at the international level than anyone else's possibly could. For God's sake think what you're doing.' 'I will; and whatever happens I'll ring you tonight around nine.'

Bomboko got into his ministerial car and drove off. I went back into the Council; but not to take part in the discussions so much as to sit and think, while my colleagues got involved in arguments that seemed to me as pointless as they were illogical. Almost all of them still did not know – or at least claimed not to know – which two ministers had countersigned the dismissal. The ministers whom Kasavubu had not dismissed thought that they would remain in office if Kasavubu were eventually to win the day. Yet, it emerged Kasavubu had dismissed Lumumba and the six ministers verbally only; when he spoke on the radio, no such dismissal order had been officially signed by him and countersigned by two ministers in office as the *Loi Fondamentale* demanded. None the less, he had received promises from more than one minister to countersign the dismissal if required.

On 6 September, after the Council meeting, Bomboko and Delvaux agreed to add their names to Kasavubu's statement; and thus, less than three months after the declaration of our independence, plunged the Congo into a major constitutional crisis. Bomboko telephoned me that evening at about nine as promised. He confirmed his own decision, and told me of Delvaux's intention to countersign the presidential order. I remember saying: 'No one can know the full consequences of what you have done. But by countersigning the dismissal you are certainly speeding up the establishment of total chaos in the Congo, and the only people who will gain from it will be outsiders. Kasavubu and Lumumba need each other. It would be much better to try and bring them together, instead of encouraging misunderstanding, conflict and hatred between them – after all they are our two "fathers of independence".'

As soon as the news was out, the government – that is the prime minister and those ministers still loyal to him – determined to dismiss Delvaux and Bomboko and have both arrested at once. Bomboko was sought in vain: he had taken refuge in the presidential palace, well guarded by UN troops. Delvaux on the other hand had taken no such precaution and was arrested.

On 7 September parliament was to debate the president's dismissal order and hear the prime minister's reply to it. Both chambers were to meet in an extraordinary joint session, but the Senate decided against such an arrangement. So the Chamber of Representatives on its own debated the two points on the agenda. Just before, I saw Delvaux handcuffed in the prime minister's official residence. Lumbala was beside him. For Lumumba had ordered his private secretary Lumbala to keep Delvaux in his residence until further instructions.

During the session, Delvaux unexpectedly entered the hall and went straight to the rostrum, where he said:

My dear brothers, I should like to know on what basis the government has arrested me. I have come from Camp Léopold, because I countersigned the head of state's decree of dismissal. I did so in all legality, because I can no longer watch the country in the state it is in; as a member of the government I cannot accept foreign planes landing on our soil, bearing arms of every kind from Russia. I signed this act to fulfil my duty as a citizen, to save my country. This morning I was arrested at my home, and subjected to an interrogation by the minister of justice, notes of which were taken by the secretary of state to the presidency. I was then taken to Camp Léopold. I hereby resign from the government.

This dramatic statement, ending with a no less dramatic resignation, was loudly applauded from the benches of the opposition. The session was very rowdy, with heated debates and extremely excitable speakers. It was declared open at 11.55 and closed at 4.50 p.m. after close on five hours of debate. In his reply to all the pro-Kasavubu deputies, Lumumba gave parliament details of information up to then unknown to the public at large and even to the majority of the members. We all listened with unwavering attention. The opposition members tried from time to time to interrupt him, but no one was in a position to contradict him, since he had an enormous amount of evidence and everything he said could be verified. He took an impish delight in actually naming those present, to give them a chance to deny anything that might not be true, but no one stood up to deny anything.

It is interesting to record the prime minister's version of the situation, so I quote here extracts from it, out of the parliamentary annals of the session.

As for the arrest of certain members, I must first of all give you a general explanation: certain delegates, abusing the trust placed in them by the people, spent the parliamentary vacation carrying out activities which were to the benefit neither of those who had elected them, nor of the nation as a whole . . .

The case of M. Bolikango: Before going to Equateur Province, he came with me, together with M. Dondo. Dondo said to me: 'Lumumba, it was you who conspired to get M. Kasavubu elected head of state when there were two candidates put forward. You had the majority in parliament, and you could have got M. Bolikango elected, but you did not do so because you were afraid of the Bakongo. We are going to Equateur, and there will be bloodshed, because we shall create the Republic of Equateur.' . . . They formulated a document stating that a Republic of Equateur must be proclaimed, and a break made with the central government, thus giving up all hope of unity for the Congo . . .

M. Bolikango was in Lisala, where he urged on the Bangala soldiers

293

to drive out their Bakongo fellows. I received telegrams from the Lisala *gendarmerie* denouncing this manoeuvre, and warning me that if I did not order the arrest of Bolikango within two days, they would do it on their own authority. It was the provincial president of Equateur, a *Puna* delegate, and his government, largely made up of *Puna* members – of whom Bolikango is the party leader –, who demanded his arrest; it was not Lumumba, nor the central government who ordered it. When the members of Equateur government arrived in Léopoldville, the *Puna* members living there put pressure on them and even threatened them to try to force them to go back on their own declarations. But the provincial president still went to see the minister of justice to ask why he had not had the *Puna* party leader arrested.

M. Bolikango was arrested. When I learnt of this, MM. Ngenge and Ngwenza pointed out that despite what he had done, the arrest of M. Bolikango would create a sensitive situation; they asked me to do everything I could to prevent his imprisonment. I made arrangements: the minister of the interior went to Coquilhatville to settle the question amicably. He came back, and we heard no more. A short time after, I received a telegram telling me that M. Bolikango had been arrested. Where? At Gemena. On whose orders? The provincial government's. Police took him from Gemena to Coquilhatville, and the provincial government sent him here under escort. The law allows provincial governments a large measure of autonomy; so if someone is arrested by the provincial government for committing grave crimes proved by military witnesses, how can I, Lumumba, contradict them and order him to be freed? Either we respect the law or we do not. In Belgium, for instance, no individual would ever – just because he was a member of the opposition or the president of a party – proclaim the province of Antwerp as an independent republic, thus making nonsense of territorial unity. If such a thing happened, I am quite certain that that man, who ever he might be, however important, would be arrested at once . . .

And what is happening now? . . . Aircraft [are] sent from the Forminière Office in Brussels filled with arms and ammunition. The planes bear the symbol of 'Air Kasai'. We have intercepted all the telegrams whereby this deal was arranged. A headquarters has been established in Brazzaville, and Baluba elements are crossing the river and embarking there to take munitions to Bakwanga on board Belgian and French planes, some of which have been intercepted in Luluabourg. Two of these Baluba have been made generals, and a third colonel in Kalonji's army. . . . The Belgians and French have violated our national territorial integrity. You all know how serious it is to fly over another country's air space without permission. These planes came by night, and since the airfield of Bakwanga is not properly lit, they came down in Luluabourg, where they were stopped by our troops. . . . I received a telegram from the provincial government of Kasai telling me of the arrest of the crew and seizure of the plane. . . . If you have been following Radio Brazzaville, you will have heard that 300 men have left that province for Bakwanga, armed to the teeth by the Belgians. Such arms as you have never seen. It is a vast conspiracy. Is this democracy? Tell me if any government in power now, or tomorrow, or the day after tomorrow, could tolerate such activities? If so, then opposition and democracy would mean that anyone can create his own little republic whenever he wants, and go to the French for arms to massacre his own brothers! . . . Yet when we take steps to put an end to this kind of outrage and send troops to arrest the trouble-makers, you accuse us of suppressing freedom!

What is still going on at this time of crisis? The *Abako* has arranged to send emissaries to Katanga (so Radio Brazzaville tells us), forming a delegation made up of members of the *Abako*, *Puna* and MNC-Kalonji. They have boarded a plane in Brazzaville for Elisabethville; there is ample proof of this, and it has even been reported on the radio. It is quite clear that the *Abako* are accomplices in the whole Katanga affair. It is my duty to proclaim their guilt, and I have never shirked telling the truth, for I did not appoint myself a minister but was freely elected just as you were; I have a right to defend the people to the end.

The affair of M. Kasavubu: Frankly, I have personally enormous admiration for M. Kasavubu. He has always been a close friend of mine, and never, either before independence or since, have we had the slightest disagreement. Up to now we have worked in complete harmony. . . . Furthermore, to show you that I have never felt any antagonism towards M. Kasavubu, I must tell you that the fact that he is head of state now is because of me; it is thanks to me, Lumumba, that M. Kasavubu was raised to that honour. [*Loud applause from the majority, and cries of 'Bravo!' from M. Colin in his seat.*]

There were two candidates: Kasavubu and M. Bolikango; each came to ask me to use my parliamentary majority in his favour, and I said to them that I myself did not wish to be head of state because I was still too young and would prefer to work, and that I should like one of them to occupy the position. I knew that even some of the opposition deputies did not wish M. Kasavubu to be elected, because he was a separatist; they preferred M. Bolikango. Today has shown how right their fears were . . .

The affair of Russia: Much is said about communism, and there are all kinds of stories going the rounds about me. Do you realize, my dear friends, that there are people playing the imperialists' game? During the electoral campaign the Catholic missions had leaflets printed which they distributed everywhere. Did the people listen? No! They voted for us – but I need hardly remind you of the fact since you know how the elections went. I find it somewhat amusing to be called a communist, for I am not one, and never will be. The facts are these: since becoming prime minister I have been visited by all comers – businessmen from the US, from France, from Germany, from Belgium, and so on, all proposing one agreement after another. I accepted none of them, and it is because they realize that they cannot corrupt our government that they are waging this campaign against it . . .

My last contacts with M. Kasavubu took place on Saturday. I should like to tell you what occasioned our meeting. . . . The minister of finance, an *Abako* delegate, recently went to Geneva with M. Delvaux to negotiate the matter of our national bank, and the money of ours which the Belgians had confiscated. (You must realize that on 30 June, when independence was proclaimed, our gold reserves reached a value of 3,764,000,000 francs, while by 15 August we only had 1,764,000,000 – owing to a magical disappearance of 2,000,000,000 francs which Belgium had paid into their national bank in Brussels, supposedly in order to open a bank in Ruanda-Urundi.) This bit of trickery was discovered by our mission in Geneva. M. Delvaux is in fact present, and can bear me out, as can the rest of the delegation.[4]

The Belgians now say that they agree to return this money to us. M. Delvaux telephoned me from Geneva to ask my authorization for signing the project for our national bank, which he thought a good one. I told him I could not agree, that he must not sign but must bring it back to be considered by the Council, who would study it point by point, line by line, and then, if they approved it, would in turn submit it to parliament. M. Delvaux did as I had said, and the project was brought back by the delegation and given to me on Friday last. The minister of finance and M. Delvaux told me how the meeting had gone. Article 6 of the project, referring to the Monetary Council which was to govern the bank, stipulates: 'The Monetary Council is directed by a temporary chairman appointed by the head of state at the suggestion of the UN secretary general. It also comprises a treasurer, and four members appointed by the head of state at the suggestion of the

4. *Annales Parlementaires, Chambre des Représentants de la République du Congo, Séance publique du Mercredi 7 Septembre 1960.*

minister of finance in consultation with the United Nations.' [*Dis-approval in the Chamber.*]

I told the minister of finance and M. Delvaux that this was un-acceptable, and that I could never agree to it. We are a sovereign state, and shall create our own national bank. Why should the UN secretary general appoint a chairman, so that every other state can know our political and financial situation, and then they can all conspire together to get our currency devalued? It was out of the question. It is up to us, to our own government, to choose the people we trust, and put them in our bank – not up to the secretary general to force people upon us who may well be spies. If we need technicians, then we shall ask for them; but if independence means anything at all, no one can force us to have foreign governors for our bank, the very life-blood of our state. The Council did not approve the project, and we asked a special commis-sion to examine the whole matter afresh, a commission made up of M. Nguvulu and other ministers.

Just at that point, various members of parliament wanted copies of the speeches I had made at the opening and closing of the pan-African Conference. I had sent the texts to the national printing press to have them copied, but the manager of the press apologized, saying, 'I still have an urgent job to finish – printing 500 copies of a text describing the creation of the national bank.' I was astounded to hear the manager talking about printing this kind of legal text which would in effect create a national bank when it had not yet been signed by the government or even seen by parliament. I asked to see the text. I read: 'Joseph Kasavubu, President of the Republic. To all whom it may concern . . .' How could the government have any responsibility for this when neither I nor anyone else had been informed of it? The head of state and the minister of finance – who is a Mukongo – were arrang-ing between themselves to create a national bank with the help of the secretary general of the United Nations. [*Boos and cries of disapproval from the Chamber.*] As soon as I discovered this, I wrote the following letter, with the heading 'Note to M. Nkayi': 'Mr Minister, I am surprised to discover that you have submitted to parliament the pro-jected law to create a central Congolese bank without my being informed, nor the government's having made any decision. This pro-jected law, which was not approved by the government, has been sent to the printers. During the meeting yesterday, 2 September 1960, at which you were present, the Council of Ministers decided to submit the project for the creation of a national bank to a special commission for examination. This commission has not yet presented its conclu-sions. No projected law can be put before parliament without first

297

being approved by the Council of Ministers responsible for the government's political action. I should like an immediate explanation of this matter from you.'

If what I say is not true, let M. Delvaux who was there, and who was in Geneva with the finance minister, prove the contrary. How can it have happened that this project, still under examination by the commission, should have already been sent to the printers ? M. Nkayi, the finance minister, tells me that it was not he who gave it to them, but that it may have been done by the head of state; all he himself did was to prepare a report for me! I telephoned the head of state; on Saturday I went to his office, and we spoke among other things about various problems relating to the situation as a whole. I informed him of the state of affairs in Kasai. [*Against some opposition, Lumumba proceeded to read out the text of Kasavubu's decree of dismissal.*]

. . . 'I have appointed as prime minister, the appointment to take effect immediately, M. Joseph Ileo. M. Ileo is given the duty of forming a new government.' So you see, the government is already established! They may not have any vote of confidence from parliament, but this morning he summoned Colonel Mobutu, who went to his house and received orders as follows:

'We, Joseph Kasavubu, head of state,

In view of the *Loi Fondamentale* of 19 May 1960, and especially Article 22 of that law, order:

Article 1: M. Lumumba, member of the chamber of representatives, is dismissed from his functions as prime minister and all other ministerial functions.

Article 2: MM. Rémy Mwamba, Christophe Gbenye, Anicet Kashamura, Antoine Bolamba, Antoine Gizenga and Jacques Lumbala are dismissed from their respective functions as minister of justice, minister of the interior, minister of information, secretary of state for information, deputy prime minister, and secretary of state to the presidency of the Council of Ministers.

Article 3: M. Joseph Ileo, senator, is appointed prime minister, minister of national defence and minister of justice. [*Boos.*]

Article 4: Our prime minister Joseph Ileo is asked to put these orders into effect immediately [*Boos and laughter from the government benches*]. Given at Léopoldville this 5 September 1960.'

This is not the original document, but was composed only when he realized that the government would denounce what he had done as illegal.

Fellow-parliamentarians, let us as brothers and comrades, forgetting anger, forgetting party interests whether they be MNC, PSA, PNP or *Abako*, pay no attention to any of this; let me ask you whether M. Kasavubu, by his action, has not insulted parliament?[*Cries of ' Yes !'*] Can he in fact do anything of this kind? [*Cries of 'No !'*] Even if the government no longer had parliament's confidence, a *formateur* should be chosen by the majority, as is done in other countries, for only the majority party can be sure of a vote of confidence from parliament. If some individual is called upon, he can stand alone before parliament, and with 100,000 francs or so he may buy two or three deputies, but he will never enjoy parliament's confidence, because he will never have the majority he needs ...

We may point out innumerable illegalities in the dismissal order signed by the head of state and countersigned by the two ministers, MM. Bomboko and Delvaux – though I regret the incidents to which the latter was subjected this morning.

He would be the first to tell of the fine spirit of collaboration in which he and I have worked up to now. I believe in his sincerity – and I am not just saying this to smooth things over. On the 17th of last month when he was in Europe he wrote me this: 'My dear Patrice, you know very well that I have always personally opposed and attacked you in the past. I beg you to forgive me, and assure you that from now on we shall work in harmony, and my one wish is to return to tell you this face to face.'

I have never had any quarrel with M. Delvaux, and he knows in what spirit I have worked with him. Remember that parliament demanded the dismissal of three or four ministers; I still have in my possession the motion demanding the dismissal of MM. Bomboko and Delvaux. That is true, is it not? You voted for that motion? And it was I who prevented its being put into effect. I told M. Delvaux that I did not want to dismiss any ministers, and would try to effect a reconciliation between him and yourselves. If I had been against M. Delvaux he would not be a minister now; and the same is true of M. Bomboko, for you were the first to condemn him publicly here, and even now pressure is still being put on me to dismiss him ...

Some individuals have established a radio station: 'The Voice of Freedom', costing millions of francs, and broadcasting every day on the same wavelength as the national radio – one station is transmitting from here with the complicity of the Mukongo people, the other is in Katanga. The Katangans and the Bakongo peoples are combining in a campaign against the government; who can be giving them the money to do it except the imperialists? [*Applause.*]

Finally, we have spoken of Lovanium University. We wanted it to become a state university. The whole university, all the students, have been mobilized, and yesterday meetings were held in support of M. Kasavubu, and with his knowledge . . .

The imperialists are very strong, and rich, and we are still politically weak, letting ourselves be deceived and influenced too easily. When we were fighting here, when I was put in prison for demanding immediate independence, was it the Russians who were advising me then ? . . .

When our brothers were fighting everywhere, was it Russians who were instigating us to demand independence ? Who was it that exploited us for 80 years except the imperialists ? They thought of the Congo with all its wealth as their national preserve. When the French, the Americans and the Belgians come to the Congo, they see it as their right, but that the Russians come they find intolerable.

King Baudouin's grandmother, Queen Elisabeth of the Belgians, is president of the Belgo-Russian friendship society. Is she a communist ? . . .

I remember a time, not long ago, when the president of the Belgian chamber of representatives, M. Kronacker, went to Moscow. Radio Prague announced the fact. Was he considered a communist ? Was he accused because of his trip of having sold Belgium to Russia ? But now, if Lumumba or Gizenga or anyone else from the Congo goes to Moscow, the press goes wild. Anyone else can go, but not the niggers! The son of the Belgian foreign minister is in Moscow now, studying in the university. Every year, Belgian parliamentarians go to Moscow on missions, and no one objects. But when it comes to us, we are advised not to go. Why ? Have we not the right to travel when we want to ? Either we are a sovereign state or we are not. In other words, we want to be neutral; we do not want to follow the American political line, nor the Russian; we want to stay right where we are – in the middle. [*Applause.*]

It is because I have refused to make concessions to those who continue to try to exploit us that they criticize me as a communist; I am not a communist. Let me remind you all that my parents were married in the Catholic Church. My family is Catholic. My children are receiving Catholic instruction at the Athénée in Léopoldville – where they could equally be receiving Protestant instruction or simply teaching in ethics; they are being brought up as Catholics and Christians, and that you can verify for yourselves.

In Africa anyone who is on the side of the people and against imperialism is a communist, an agent of Moscow! But anyone on the imperialists' side, anyone in their pay, is a fine man whom they cannot praise highly enough. That is the true position, my friends . . .

When parliament rose, the deputies voted purely and simply to annul the 'mutual dismissals' of the head of state and the prime minister (sixty votes for annulment to nineteen against).

From 7 September onwards, the situation in the Congo was no longer in the hands of the Congolese. Despite parliament's wisdom in advising the head of state and the prime minister to achieve a reconciliation, the idea was immediately attacked and discredited by Western pressure groups, acting through the intermediary of certain deputies. Kasavubu himself announced that parliament had no right to nullify his decision to dismiss the prime minister.

In Washington, President Eisenhower set the tone by publicly accusing the Soviet Union rather than Belgium of causing anarchy in the Congo. In his statement, on receiving the American crew who had been manhandled by the Congolese troops in Stanleyville, and presenting them with decorations, he declared:

... The United States deplores and takes a most serious view of Russia's unilateral intervention which is thereby aggravating an already serious situation which finds Africans killing other Africans. ... The constitutional structure of the Congo republic is a question which should be worked out peacefully by the Congolese themselves. This objective is threatened by the Soviet action which seems to be motivated entirely by the Soviet Union's political designs in Africa.

Such a statement, coming from the White House, gave heart to all those who were against the Lumumba régime and working hard to turn the Congo into a satellite of the Western powers.

In Katanga the Belgians and their Congolese pawns rubbed their hands with glee. In Léopoldville, Andrew Cordier had effectively taken over the reins of government, and he arranged things in favour of Kasavubu and the interests of the West. He had first given Kasavubu a bodyguard of Moroccans to surround the presidential palace, where Ileo, Bomboko and the rest were also staying. Cordier decided that the National Radio must be closed down at once, as well as all the national airports, save only those in Katanga where the Belgians were making the rules.

For the radio, he sent one of his colleagues to remove a vital piece of equipment which made broadcasting impossible until it was returned; for the airports, he allowed free passage to the UN's planes, but formally forbade all ANC troop movements, and especially any movement of Soviet helicopters or planes. Cordier had not time to consult Hammarskjöld in New York before making these decisions; he gave orders as the UN's chief in command in the Congo, and only informed his superior after the event. Hammarskjöld had no option but to support the decisions of his American assistant who was acting, according to subsequent explanations, so as to preserve international peace and security, and to prevent civil war in the Congo. To the Americans the secession of Katanga was no threat to international peace and security. Thenceforth, the Congolese people received their news from Radio Brazzaville and the more powerful Radio Elisabethville; furthermore a station, Radio-Makala, was put up in Brazzaville for the Belgian mercenaries and technicians working on behalf of the Kasavubu, Kalonji and Tshombe alliance.

Having successfully carried out his mission, Cordier returned to New York in order to reassure the member states of the UN who were learning more and more about the UN's overt intervention in the Congo's internal affairs. Rajeshwar Dayal, the Indian diplomat appointed to be Hammarskjöld's special representative, got to Léopoldville on 8 September. He was not slow to recognize the results of Cordier's work, and the fact that the Congo was no longer being governed by the Congolese. He thought it right to try to help the Congolese get their country's fate back into their own hands. As a defender of English-style democracy, he wanted to encourage the functioning of the national parliament, and to reconcile the head of state with the prime minister through the good offices of a parliamentary reconciliation commission.

But events taught Dayal that the pace was to be set by Cordier and America, and not by himself and the Afro-Asians.

On 12 September, the security council refused to give a decision on who held legitimate power in the Congo. There were actually two Congolese delegations present in the council chamber: the first, led by Justin Bomboko, had been sent by Kasavubu; the second, led by me, had been sent by Lumumba's government. Neither delegation was admitted officially as representing the Congo; neither could take part in the deliberations of the council. So the Congolese problem was discussed in the security council without any contributions from the Congolese actually present. It was almost a mirror image of what was going on in the Congo itself. The Congo's fate was thenceforth to be determined by foreign powers; as for the Congolese people, no one cared too much, since they were, it was said, incapable of resolving their own personal and political problems.

On 13 September parliament voted full powers to Lumumba's government. We had not long to wait to see America's reaction to that. The very next morning Kasavubu gave the entire national parliament leave of absence. Meanwhile, the Moroccan General Kettani played the final stroke in a peaceful *coup d'état*, with the help of Colonel Mobutu and money as the determining factor. Behind the scenes, Tshombe and his Belgian advisers were offering substantial financial rewards to the ANC. (Tshombe also publicly congratulated Kasavubu on his decision to dismiss Lumumba.) The Congolese troops had had no pay for a month, and were ready to give allegiance to anyone who would offer them money – ready even to lay down their arms for them. Kettani was the assistant to van Horn, the Swedish general: in other words the UN gave Kettani the money he needed to make the coup successful.

Colonel Mobutu had a personal crisis of conscience: Kasavubu had ordered him to arrest Lumumba, but Lumumba reminded him of their former friendship, and suggested that he should take orders from him, as prime minister and minister of national defence, and arrest Kasavubu instead. Mobutu's heart was swinging between the two; but his heart could not go on swinging indefinitely, for the Americans had no time to lose in their fight against Soviet influence in the Congo. Furthermore, the Congolese had presented the world with the idea that they were people who would not hesitate to jettison all loyalty and dignity to achieve their own personal or political ambitions.

On 14 September it was over. Mobutu's heart – and those of most other Congolese military leaders – stopped swinging. Orders were given to swing all hearts – by kindness or by force – in favour of Washington's decision, in other words, in favour of Kasavubu.

General Lundula was placed under house arrest; Colonel Mobutu nervously proclaimed the 'neutralization of the politicians' and takeover of power by the army. Within the ANC, he could count on the support of Colonel Kokolo – a fellow tribesman of Kasavubu's – who was in command of the capital's military camp; and also of Colonel Bobozo (apparently his own uncle), who commanded the crack troops at Thysville.

The following speech was given by Mobutu on the National Radio:

Dear Fellow-Citizens,

To get our country out of its impasse, the Congolese army has decided to neutralize the head of state, and the two rival governments now in office, as well as both houses of parliament until 31 December 1960.

This will give the politicians time to come to an agreement, the better to serve the higher interests of the country. As each of them will realize by tomorrow, this is no military *coup d'état*, but merely a peaceful revolution; no soldiers will be put into power. We shall appeal to neutral Congolese technicians and foreign technicians chosen by ourselves to save our country from chaos. The vast social, economic and financial problems the Congo faces are known to you all. The army will help the country to resolve all these various problems, which are becoming daily more acute. Will everyone keep calm and clear-headed; will everyone go freely and tranquilly on with his work.

The army is there to ensure the safety of goods and people. From now till the end of this short revolutionary period, every one of you will learn to be grateful to the Congolese national army, for I hope with all my heart that by then we shall have saved the honour and won the esteem of our country.

Long live the Congo; long live the Congolese national army!

The National Radio went back on the air, and the airports began to function again, guarded by the UN; all communist diplomats and technicians – Russians and Czechs – were expelled from the country; and the military invasions of Kasai and Katanga were simply brought to a halt. Kalonji, Tshombe and their friends were no longer rebels, but 'brother politicians'. In brief, the Congo had become an international, and more specifically an American colony.

Having agreed to pay a third of the cost of the UN operation in the Congo, to say nothing of all the 'invisible' expenditure needed to keep the country within the Western sphere of influence, the Americans were in command. The Congo became rather like a business company in which the largest shareholder could determine how the governing board was to act. By paying most of the expenses involved in preserving order and peace in the Congo, the USA thenceforth took it upon itself to behave as the major shareholder. Resolutions were voted in New York – whether in the security council or the General Assembly – only if approved and dictated by Washington, in consultation with its Western allies; and only the most meagre concessions were made to the Afro-Asian nations to preserve appearances – for they were, after all, the people who had sent their troops to the Congo under the UN flag.

From 14 September on, the Congo openly became a satellite country of the Western bloc, and any representatives of other countries wanting to intervene there must first make sure they had the written or understood approval of Washington. Helping the Congo through UN channels in fact meant interfering in the foreign affairs of the Congo with the approval of Washington. The US were satisfied by the advisers consulted by Mobutu; and through him, went forward to the temporary de-Belgianization of the Congo, without pushing Americanization to its fullest extent. For the Americans realized that they still needed the help of the Belgians, who knew the Congo far better than they did – but, while making use of them, they continued to 'decolonize' the Belgians psychologically by teaching them to act in the future as go-betweens in the Congo rather than as masters. Americans and Belgians worked in close collaboration in the Congo, but wherever there arose any conflict of interest, it was the Americans who carried the day.

Kasavubu and Lumumba were besought to think again, and to ally themselves with Washington for their own survival. This was the diplomatic advice contained in the broadcast message of Mobutu – and it applied to every politician in the country. He had kept in contact with both men; but whereas Kasavubu did what he was told like a sheep, Lumumba openly defied this young man whom he himself had promoted to colonel. Through the Algerian Serge Michel, his press attaché, Lumumba announced on 15 September: 'Colonel Mobutu, commander-in-chief of the armed forces, has been corrupted by the imperialists so as to carry out a *coup d'état* against the legal and popularly elected government.' There then followed a series of psychological and political disappointments for Lumumba and his supporters.

41 Farewell to Lumumba

The internal situation in the Congo was by now incredibly confused. Despite the presence of UN troops in the country, no one could see any quick solution to what was sadly called the 'Congo crisis'. At the constitutional level, there was a unique situation of the conflict between head of state and head of government. Joseph Ileo, Kasavubu's nominee to displace Lumumba, did not dare face his investiture by Parliament, as the constitution (the *Loi Fondamentale*) required. Meanwhile, the Congolese parliament had voted full powers to Lumumba's government, annulled Kasavubu's dismissal, and created a parliamentary commission to effect a reconciliation between president and prime minister. Since 14 September 1960, the Chief of Staff, Joseph Mobutu, attempted a military coup d'etat. Colonel Mobutu had not actually seized power himself, but been content to 'neutralize' the head of state, the prime minister and the whole of parliament.

In the hope of enabling the politicians to work out an honourable and acceptable compromise, and especially of thereby improving his own position, Mobutu was proposing to hand over power to a group of young Congolese 'intellectuals', some of whom had not even completed their studies. They were to leave their studies to become 'excellencies and ministers' for a few weeks, or even months, and then go back to continue their studies as before. Most of these students were studying in Belgian universities. No one knew what had actually happened to the government formed by Ileo at Kasavubu's request. The group of students adopted the title 'College of General Commissioners'.

On 20 September 1960, the Republic of the Congo (Leopoldville) was admitted as a member state to the United Nations but Mr Boland, the Irish ambassador then presiding over the General

Assembly, declared that the seat reserved for its delegation must remain empty in view of the confusion reigning inside the country. Since the constitutional crisis, there had been two delegations in New York fighting for the seat – my own, sent by Lumumba, and Bomboko's which was known as the Kasavubu delegation. There were all kinds of attempts by Kasavubu and Bomboko to prevent our reaching New York at all; I was turned back at Brazzaville airport with my delegation by order of the president, Abbé Youlou, and we were unable to board the Air France plane from there to Paris. Lumumba approached Dayal, and we embarked at Leopoldville on a UN plane for Paris, where we took an Air France plane on to New York.

The member states of the UN were divided over the Congolese question just as they were over the role and the character of Hammarskjöld. The general impression was that 'Mr H's continuing as Secretary General would depend on the success of the action undertaken in the Congo. Some states supported the theory that Lumumba was the legal and constitutional prime minister, and that therefore my delegation should occupy the Congo (Leo) seats in the General Assembly. These were for the most part the same states that disagreed with Hammarskjöld's interpretation of the Security Council's resolutions on the Congo. To them he was acting a bit too obviously on the advice of the USA and its allies. Krushchev made a fiery speech against him, nicknaming him the 'valet of Washington'. To the other member states, Kasavubu had therefore to be internationally recognized as the only legal spokesman and official office-holder. To them, Hammarskjöld was blameless, was doing his best, and acting in perfect conformity with this Security Council's mandate. Above all, he was, by the UN presence, fighting against communist infiltration into the Congo, the very heart of Africa. All the socialist member states, and the African and South American states that might be considered progressive were sympathetic to Lumumba's ideas, and supported my delegation. The western countries, and the so-called moderate countries of Africa, South America and Asia aligned themselves with the American viewpoint, and became fanatical defenders of Hammarskjöld and Kasavubu.

I was well aware of what was in effect going on. The UN forces in the Congo were waging a 'holy war' against communism, *not* coming to 'help and assist the Central Congolese Government'.

.   .   .

The college of commissioners general set up by Mobutu, whose president was Bomboko, was larded with members who were fiercely anti-Lumumba. On 8 November Kasavubu gave his speech to the UN General Assembly in New York. He had been literally rushed there by the Americans, who wanted to get him accepted internationally. The pro-Lumumba countries were quite incapable of preventing this international acceptance of Kasavubu and his delegation. Only the most naïve could really believe that he too had been 'neutralized' by Mobutu and the ANC, for the American game was all too obvious. In the constitutional confusion reigning in the Congo, the Americans needed a 'legal' and Congolese entry to permit their manoeuvres and confound their critics and opponents all over the world; so, to do this, they decided to get Kasavubu into the UN, as an individual who could embody the Congo as a nation. Once recognized by the UN, Kasavubu could ratify every initiative from Washington which was then, in the eyes of the world, acting fully in conformity with the wishes of the president of the Republic of the Congo, and in collaboration with the UN authorities there.

On 23 November Kasavubu's delegation was admitted to the UN General Assembly by 53 votes to 24, with 19 abstentions. With American support, Kasavubu had become internationally recognized as the only legal and legitimate authority in the Congo. But in being considered undisputed leader of the Congo by the West (though his leadership was contested elsewhere), Kasavubu was forced also to be the instrument of the US, the UN, and all the politicians who were so determined to get rid of Lumumba once and for all.

Over the months, the Egyptian ambassador in Léopoldville had become a personal friend of Lumumba's. Lumumba wanted to make plans regarding steps to be taken to ensure his political career; in fact what was at stake was his personal survival. He felt that he could not comfortably do anything while he was in his closely guarded house with his wife and children.[1] The children at least should be sent to some place of safety outside the country. Egypt was the one country he considered: for Nasser, he thought, was the one man who would take the risk of giving sanctuary to his children. The Egyptian diplomats had assured him that as long as their government approved, they were ready to take the great risk of getting the children secretly out of the Congo – and it really was a tremendous risk. Few of the African diplomats accredited to Kasavubu who had at one time gravitated around Lumumba would have dared such an exploit.

Lumumba consulted the ambassador, and was promised an answer as soon as possible; it was too urgent a matter for delay. When asked, Nasser at once agreed with great pleasure. He was pleased to be able to do at least something concrete for Lumumba who, though so much acclaimed by every 'African revolutionary' in speeches, was being given no tangible help during the present impasse in the Congo. Thus, a few days later, Lumumba's two children, wrapped in blankets, were put by Egyptian diplomats onto a SABENA plane that was leaving Léopoldville for Brussels, but stopping *en route* in a European capital near the Mediterranean, where the children were to change planes for Cairo.

The operation was carried out with smoothness and skill. The children travelled under a false Egyptian name, 'Abdel Aziz'; it was the name of the diplomat who took them, and they were being passed off as his own children. The plane was to leave late, well after midnight. The children, being very young, were asleep in their blankets. They were taken in a car with a UN registration to the foot of the gangway, before the other passengers embarked. Two Egyptian diplomats took them from the car to the plane where they were laid to sleep on reserved seats in the back row. The Belgian air hostess wanted to unwrap them from their

1. Although Kasavubu and Lumumba were 'neutralized', Kasavubu was free to receive visitors and had access to all persons he wanted to meet, while Lumumba was under house arrest and prevented from having visitors or sending for friends or officials.

blankets, but did not insist when it was explained to her that they were exhausted and deeply asleep.

For those at the airport who knew the trick that was being played under the very noses of the UN, it was a moment of great anxiety. It would have needed only the slightest slip for the children to have been stopped from leaving the Congo altogether, and the incident of their attempted departure would have had acute diplomatic repercussions. Lumumba was immensely relieved to hear that the plane had taken off, and that his children had got out of the dangerous country of their birth safe and sound.

They finally arrived in Cairo. President Nasser met them personally several times, and though he had never known their father, he did at least ensure that his children never became the innocent victims of the cruelty of his political adversaries. It was in Cairo that they heard that their father, execrated in 1960, was officially entitled a 'national hero of the Congo' on 30 June 1966.

On Saturday 26 November 1960, the eve of his escape, I had my last talk with Lumumba on the telephone. The Moroccan officer in charge of security had made it possible for us to talk several times before this. In fact, since his two elder children had gone to Cairo, Lumumba was living at home with his wife, their youngest child and two other members of his family. The telephone was cut off by the Congolese Sûreté, whose director was Victor Nendaka; but the UN had installed a telephone for the use of the soldiers who were ensuring the prime minister's safety. I had an apartment in the 'Royal' building, where the Congo's UN services were housed. Lumumba was allowed no visitors. The Congolese soldiers who surrounded his house made sure that no one went in. So the telephone was our only means of communication, apart from handwritten notes which we could send to him through Moroccan messengers. The members of the Lumumba government still in Léopoldville, and still loyal to him, often came to my apartment to talk to him on the telephone.

Those under threat of arrest by the Sûreté could also take refuge in my apartment; the building was guarded by UN troops who demanded a special pass before letting any visitors into it. On the eve of Lumumba's escape I was in my apartment with my father, several ministerial colleagues, and other political leaders including Jason Sendwe and Alexandre Mahambe. I talked to Lumumba for more than ten minutes, trying to dissuade him from attempting the journey to Stanleyville. His newly born baby had died, and this provided him with a pretext for going to Stanleyville where the funeral was to be.[2] Having failed to make him change his mind, I passed the telephone over to the three other friends who were there. My father spoke last of all; but despite the respect that Lumumba felt for him, he too failed in his attempt to persuade him of the danger he would be in from the moment he left his official residence and the protection of the UN forces.

Picking up the receiver for the last time, I made one more appeal to Lumumba: 'Things won't stay like this for ever; even if you have to stay in your house for years, I am convinced that sooner or later you will emerge victorious. Your enemies will be forced to appeal to you under the pressure of those who still have faith in you. If you leave your house now, I can only bid you farewell for ever. The imperialists will seize you, and you can hope for no mercy from them.'

Lumumba then made his prophetic remark: 'My dear Thomas, I shall probably be arrested, tortured and killed. One of us must sacrifice himself if the Congolese people are to understand and accept the ideal we are fighting for. My death will hasten the liberation of the Congo, and help to rid our people of the yoke of imperialism and colonialism.'

Remembering that our conversations were certainly being tapped by the security forces, Lumumba added almost jokingly, 'Thomas, don't take what I've been saying too seriously. I shan't leave here, because I am counting on having an interview with the UN Conciliation people who are coming to Léopoldville any day now. But I shall be sending you written instructions, and I want you to follow them to the letter.'

Less than an hour later I was visited by the Moroccan officer who acted as intermediary between us, bringing me Lumumba's written message. In it he told me that, on the most mature consideration, his decision was firmly made: he was leaving his house

2. The dead body had been flown to Stanleyville by plane.

the next night, and ordered me to put out a communiqué twenty-four hours later that would confuse any search parties.

So, on 29 November, more than twenty-four hours after Lumumba's escape, when the news had already appeared as a rumour on foreign radio stations, I got the press agencies to put out a communiqué on behalf of the Congolese prime minister. I denied – somewhat hopelessly – the rumours that he had escaped, and confirmed his decision to stay in Léopoldville until the UN Conciliation Commission got there. In this way I carried out his order to do my best to make it difficult to find him. It was little enough.

42 Lumumba's Murder

I had faith in Lumumba. Had he not been assassinated, he would certainly have come back as head of the government. His political enemies both inside and outside the Congo were as convinced of this as we were. Murder was in fact the only sure means of preventing his return to power. The election of the young senator John F. Kennedy as president of the US gave encouragement to us all, and led us to hope for a new turn of events in the Congo. Kennedy was elected at the end of November, but did not of course take office until the January following. Lumumba had sent the president-elect a long telegram of congratulation, in which he expressed his trust in the new president's progressive and liberal ideas, and the profound hope of our people that he would use his influence to achieve a political solution to our tragedy within the framework of the UN. Officially, Kennedy never acknowledged the telegram; but our American friends who had helped us get it through to him had reassured us of Kennedy's determination to do everything he could towards the establishment of peace and stability in the Congo.

There were influential circles in America where Lumumba's return to power was dreaded. The Belgians who were openly identified with the secession of Katanga and Kasai certainly could not hope to continue with their exploitation of the Congo and its people for long if Lumumba took up his office again. For them there was, therefore, a real problem of how Lumumba could be removed once for all from the political scene. The first stage had been achieved with his dismissal by Kasavubu.

The second stage, though actually far more difficult, was in fact made easier by Lumumba himself with his fatal escape from his guarded official residence in an attempt to rejoin his supporters in Stanleyville.

314

There remained only the third stage: his physical elimination.

The candidate intended to succeed Lumumba as prime minister was Albert Kalonji, the 'emperor' of South Kasai. Kalonji was prepared to put an end to the 'secession' of his province, if by doing so he could become prime minister of the Congo. He had come to see that South Kasai could not survive as an independent state, and that in continuing his secession he was merely providing a buffer for Katanga whose secession had been officially condemned and attacked by the UN.

The physical elimination of Lumumba once decided, it remained to work out the practical details. At that point there was no doubt that it must take place before John F. Kennedy took office on 20 January 1961.

At the end of December I was in Conakry, in Guinea, where I had sought asylum, and where I was treated as a minister officially representing Lumumba's government. Sékou Touré, the president of Guinea, gave me truly brotherly hospitality, and invited me to take part in the discussions of his Council of Ministers. It was there, in the presidential palace, with all the Guinean officials and their wives, that I spent New Year's eve.

The decision to eliminate Lumumba had been suspected by those political leaders of Africa who supported him and the cause for which he was fighting. It was a question of acting quickly, of arousing international public opinion, if Lumumba was to be saved. After a hasty diplomatic consultation, it was decided to hold an African Conference from 3 to 6 January in Casablanca, involving all the heads of state and of government of the independent African countries which appeared to be non-aligned, in order to plead the cause of the legal Congolese government under Lumumba. The Congo was therefore, the major theme of the Conference.

Among the participants were His Majesty King Mohamed V of Morocco; Nasser, Nkrumah, Sékou Touré and Modibo Keita, presidents respectively of the United Arab Republic, Ghana, Guinea and Mali; and also Ferrat Abbas, president of the provisional government of the Algerian Republic. For diplomatic reasons there was no official Congolese representative; however I was there, as also was Antoine Kiwewa, who had joined me in Conakry. We were both accepted as part of the Guinean delegation, and were thus able to take part in the Conference.

We had conferred beforehand, both in Conakry and Casablanca, with presidents Nkrumah, Keita, and Sékou Touré; and had in fact travelled to Casablanca on the same plane as Keita and Sékou Touré. The international support for Lumumba and his government evinced by the Casablanca Conference was most reassuring; but it was powerless to prevent the carrying out of the dreadful plan of the Western powers and their Congolese henchmen in Brazzaville and Léopoldville.

From Casablanca Kiwewa and I went back to Conakry. In the meantime, Gizenga had decided to assume the functions of head of government, since the prime minister had now been arrested and imprisoned in the para-commandos' camp outside Thysville. Colonel Louis Bobozo, a Congolese, was in charge of the camp; apparently he had invited Lumumba to dine with him on Christmas Day, and even threatened to set the illustrious prisoner free if no political solution could be found.

Before leaving the Congo, I had had talks in my apartment with most of my colleagues, ministers and members of parliament who were leaving discreetly for Stanleyville. Some of them got there safely, though after most hair-raising adventures: General Lundula, for instance, had disguised himself as a woman to get out of Léopoldville, and went to Stanleyville by boat; Mulele and Mwamba, who were part of Lumumba's escort, had spent days and nights in the bush before finally reaching Stanleyville. There were others who never got there at all, like Joseph Mbuyi, who was killed by his political enemies and his body cut into pieces; and there were those who were captured – like Lumumba, Mpolo and Okito – arrested, imprisoned and finally murdered in Katanga. Other ministers, such as Kashamura, Lutula, and Gbenye, managed to get to Stanleyville without any serious trouble at all.

The socialist and progressive countries that supported Lumumba had sent special envoys to Stanleyville, all with ambassadorial rank and with credentials which they presented to Gizenga on arrival. Among them were Mali, Yugoslavia, China, the USSR, Ghana, Guinea and Egypt. As regards foreign affairs, Gizenga gave Mulele the job of supervising all diplomatic missions abroad, and got him to establish himself in Cairo from where he could have a free hand in making contacts throughout Africa and Asia. Gabriel Lassiry and André Mandi had joined him there, and also Bernadin Mungul-Diaka.

Before Kiwewa and I left Conakry for Cairo, we heard on the radio the news of the mutiny in the para-commando camp in Thysville, where Lumumba, Okito and Mpolo were being held. We later heard from a trustworthy source that the Congolese troops had mutinied and almost succeeded in setting the three prisoners free; the news had produced panic among Lumumba's opponents in Léopoldville and throughout the Congo. There had even been a rumour that the soldiers were going to put Lumumba back in power. This might in fact have happened, had not Lumumba made another mistake in his political calculations: when they heard news of the mutiny, Kasavubu, Mobutu and Bomboko had rushed to Camp Hardy to confer with Colonel Bobozo. The troops had actually taken the prisoners out of their cells; but despite this agreeable surprise, Lumumba was in no mood to discuss terms with the political-cum-military trio from Léopoldville – still less to accept any compromise they might have to offer. It appeared that Okito and Mpolo were open to any compromise that would mean freedom for them; but Lumumba – whether as a spontaneous or a politically calculated move – rejected any kind of concession and preferred to go back to his cell.

The trio, according to our informant, realized the danger that threatened the Léopoldville régime, and had, 'in a brotherly spirit', offered Lumumba the job of deputy prime minister in the *de facto* government of Joseph Ileo, whom Kasavubu had named premier on 5 September 1960.

Lumumba's categorical refusal enabled the three from Léopoldville to convince the troops that it would be wiser for them not to trust Lumumba, 'a man who prefers prison to power'. Thereupon the mutiny ceased, and the soldiers were suitably rewarded for their good behaviour. But the leaders were aware that they would not be secure in their citadel as long as Lumumba remained in gaol only fifty kilometres from the capital. He could easily subvert the soldiers and lead them in a victory march on the city. The only reassurance for the régime was Bobozo's presence at Camp Hardy; for he was respected by his troops, and at the same time a member of the same tribe as Mobutu, probably a fairly close relative.

Kiwewa and I, on our way to Rome from Conakry, landed without incident in Cairo. We were delighted to see Mulele, Mandi and Lassiry on our arrival, and found that Mulele was well dug in at the African department of the Egyptian presidency. He had been received more than once by Nasser, and was in continual contact with Mohamed Fayek, his private secretary. He was also in regular communication with Gizenga in Stanleyville.

We decided to work together on foreign affairs, and coordinate our diplomatic activities. I was given the job of going back to New York, and confirmed by Gizenga as ambassador to the United States, the United Nations and Canada; while Kiwewa was appointed ambassador to Ghana, Guinea and Mali. Mandi, who had been secretary of state for foreign affairs in Lumumba's government, was asked to go back to Stanleyville as acting minister for foreign affairs.

In Cairo, I discovered from Mulele himself how Lumumba's escape had taken place, and the story of his arrest near Mweka by Congolese troops. These had been led by 'Major' Gilbert Pongo, a Congolese politician from the Lower Congo who had unofficially become an officer and an inspector at the Sûreté. His hatred for Lumumba and Lumumbists verged on the paranoiac. According to Mulele, the whole Lumumba convoy could easily have got to Stanleyville had Lumumba not delayed to harangue the locals wherever they went, and accepted courtesy invitations in various villages.

The most tragic, and last, of his political miscalculations was his voluntarily giving himself up to the Congolese soldiers sent from Léopoldville to arrest him. 'That was just too stupid,' said Mulele. 'I should never have believed Lumumba would be quite so sentimental and so over-confident.'

Lumumba was travelling with his wife Pauline, and their youngest child, Roland. There were nine cars in the group altogether, and despite various delays and rash actions, all had

318

gone well up till then. The party knew that Léopoldville had alerted every military checkpoint to arrest Lumumba and his companions before they could get to the border of Orientale province, where soldiers sent by Gizenga were waiting to escort them.

Mulele, Mwamba and several other friends kept stressing to Lumumba the need for the utmost haste if they were to get there safely; but he did not seem to be in any hurry, and would let pass no chance of stopping and talking to people in every village. He was even bold enough to chat with Europeans they met on the road – who of course got in touch with Léopoldville the minute that his back was turned.

On the day he was arrested, Mulele said, Lumumba was on the far side of the Sankuru river, which he had just crossed by ferry. Mulele, Mwamba and several others were with him. But Pauline and the child were still waiting for the ferry to come back for them, and the Congolese soldiers got there just in time to prevent their getting across. Everyone with Lumumba grasped the immensity of the danger, which now, with the arrival of the soldiers, had become imminent. Everyone who could talk to Lumumba as an equal, which meant in fact Mulele, Mwamba, Kemishanga, Mungul-Diaka and Lubuma, did everything they could to persuade him to continue to make for Stanleyville, and not go back to his wife and child.

It was hopeless; Lumumba would not listen; and to the intense disappointment of all those with him, returned to the other bank. It was the last time they saw their leader; some, for instance Mulele and Mwamba, had the presence of mind to say good-bye, but others were too overcome with emotion.

Lumumba was arrested and taken back to Léopoldville via Port-Francqui, where Gilbert Pongo, wild with excitement, took charge of him, to lead him into the capital in handcuffs.

I was once again in my Léopoldville apartment, when Lumumba was brought back to the capital, at about 5 p.m. on 2 December 1960. Okito, who was already in custody in the military camp at Binza, telephoned me at about 7 p.m. and in great haste gave me the news of what had happened there since Lumumba's arrival.

319

'Patrice has been beaten like a dog,' he said; 'he had his clothes taken off – Thomas, I beg you to get the UN people to do something – otherwise our prime minister will quite certainly be killed. . . . Good-bye.' I hung on, but he had rung off.

I at once went to the sixth floor, to the offices of the civil and military authorities of the UN. There I met the Indian general, I. J. Rikhye, who had the job of military adviser to the UN secretary general's representative in the Congo. I passed on Okito's unhappy message, and expressed my extreme anxiety about the lives of Lumumba and the other prisoners. General Rikhye was troubled, yet felt that there was nothing he could do about what was happening at Binza. 'The UN can't interfere in the internal affairs of the Congo. We protected Lumumba as long as he stayed in his residence in Léopoldville. But from the moment he escaped, the UN could take no further responsibility for him.'

It was a great pity that I was not able that day to meet Ambassador Rajeshwar Dayal, Hammarskjöld's personal representative in the Congo. We were on very friendly terms, and I had survived the wave of arrests of Lumumba supporters largely because he had agreed to place me under UN protection as long as I stayed in my apartment in the Royal building. Dayal himself could not have done any more than Rikhye, but I should have had the satisfaction of being able to pass on Okito's message through him direct to Hammarskjöld.

Several days after Lumumba's arrest, I escaped almost miraculously from the Congo by way of Brazzaville; Dayal had warned me that certain of my compatriots now 'in power' in Léopoldville were planning to arrest me because of my persistent refusal to become a member of the college of commissioners. André Mandi and I had refused to abandon the constitution by becoming 'ministers' in this illegal government, made up of students and a few viciously anti-Lumumba officials. Mandi was a personal friend of Mobutu, who therefore helped him to get out of the country for his own protection.

The same day we got to Cairo from Conakry, Mulele arranged an interview for us with Mohamed Fayek at the presidency. We had told him that it had been decided that I be sent again to New York, and had asked him to ask the Egyptian ambassador to the UN to give me what help he could when I got there.

Two days later, I embarked for New York on a TWA plane, via Athens, Rome and Paris. The members of my delegation[1] to the UN, whom I had left behind in New York in October, were delighted to see me back. They had been taken under the wings of the ambassadors of Guinea and Ghana – Diallo Telli and Alex Quaison Sackey.

My return to the US and the UN gave tremendous encouragement to all the Congolese who supported Lumumba's cause. Everyone hoped that the political solution to the Congolese crisis would come from there. I at once got in touch with Hammarskjöld, via his adviser Heinz Wieschoff, and it was a pleasure to meet again. Dayal had let him know of my escape from Léopoldville; for two or three weeks the commissioners in Léopoldville had not managed to follow my movements, and were most disagreeably surprised to hear that I had reappeared in New York at the head of the delegation of the 'legal government' of the Congo.

We agreed to keep in touch with Hammarskjöld through Wieschoff. The American state department were not too pleased by the presence of our delegation in New York; but they must have thought we might be of some use in achieving some future reconciliation with the Congo in the context of the United Nations. We were allowed to act as the official representatives of the Stanleyville government, which was recognized by something like a third of the UN member states. We were very busy, and much sought after by American groups of all political shades, anxious to learn about the Congo and the dramatic events there since independence.

Financially, we received help from the governments that supported Lumumba. From time to time Gizenga also got money

1. They were young men I had chosen myself in Léopoldville and who had gradually become more and more familiar with the general atmosphere of intrigue there: Alphonse Lema, Marcellin Tshitenzi, François Misano and Daniel Vibudulu. They were very hardworking, and had done all they could to maintain the support evinced by friendly countries towards the government and person of Lumumba. They were also popular among the black Americans in Harlem, Brooklyn, the Bronx and elsewhere.

through to us via Mulele in Cairo. Our delegation was living near
both the UN building and most of the embassies of the countries
friendly to our cause. I greatly appreciated the moral support of
President Roosevelt's widow; she introduced me to various
American Women's Clubs, and also into the local committees of
the Democratic Party.

Three days before Kennedy's official entry into the White
House, we heard the tragic news of the transfer of Lumumba,
Okito and Mpolo to Katanga. It was on 17 January. The transfer
had been carefully worked out by Nendaka, chief of the Sûreté,
in collaboration with his Belgian advisers and such Congolese
colleagues as Damien Kandolo, Fernand Kazadi and Jonas
Mukamba.[2] The day after the news came through, I saw Mrs
Roosevelt again, and told her that if Lumumba and his friends had
not yet been assassinated, they certainly would be before 20
January.

From the moment of my arrival in the country I had done
everything I could to make clear to Americans and everyone else
the fear we 'Congolese nationalists' felt for our leader's fate if he
remained in the hands of his political enemies without the supervision of the UN. The 20th of January was *the* day. If Lumumba
were still to be alive after that date, he would be safe, and might
even be approached by the UN with a view to helping solve the
political crisis in the Congo. That was what the 'progressives' in
the American Democratic Party wanted. In more than one
conversation, I had been given to understand that the new American government, which would come into power on the 20th, was
planning a far more open foreign policy, and intending to exploit
every possibility of reaching agreement with Lumumba or with
his followers in Stanleyville. I was pretty certain that Mrs
Roosevelt would let Ambassador Stevenson at the UN know about
our conversation immediately, and that through him it would
reach the White House.

Two days later, on the 19th, I heard of the deaths of Lumumba,
Okito and Mpolo, through the indiscretion of one of the members
of the delegation representing the anti-Lumumba régime in

2. G. Heinz and H. Donnay: *Patrice Lumumba, Les cinquante derniers jours de sa
vie*, Ed. Crisp, Brussels and Paris, 1966, pp. 104–11.

Léopoldville. The man had written a note to a colleague, and one of my Guinean friends had looked over his shoulder and noted the two words *Patrice akufi*. The Guinean came to me at once to ask what it meant. Thus the news of the deaths quickly got round. The ambassadors of all friendly countries were notified at once, as were Mulele and Gizenga. But from the public at large it was kept secret. Up to 10 February, the speculation continued on whether or not Lumumba was alive. Meanwhile the new government in the White House, though already informed of Lumumba's death, did its best to dissociate itself from the triple murder, carried out with the tacit agreement of some 'invisible' power in Washington.

Ambassador Stevenson won great sympathy by publicly demanding that the security council get Lumumba released, and use his help in finding a solution to the Congo problem.

The most intense confusion was in Léopoldville and above all, in Katanga, where Tshombe's henchmen – Munongo and Kibwe – were considering how best to announce to the world the supposedly perfect crime. Their Belgian friends were gradually abandoning them, for the government in Brussels was fearful of reprisals against Belgian settlers when the news became official. On 10 February, Godefroid Munongo, Katanga's 'strong-arm man', gave a sinister press conference, during which he announced to the world the news of the alleged escape of Lumumba, Okito and Mpolo.

In the Congo, cynicism and crime have always gone hand in hand. At that press conference Munongo appeared even more of a cynic than a criminal. The journalists, though laughing at him behind his back, acted quite innocently. Abbé Youlou of Brazzaville was on an official visit to Katanga at the time, and it is hardly necessary to say that he had discussed the whole 'Lumumba case' with his hosts, and made helpful suggestions to them.

Having read the account of Munongo's press conference put out by the press agencies, my delegation decided to publish a communiqué stating that we had reason to believe that prime minister Lumumba, vice-president of the Senate, Okito, and the minister of youth and sport, Mpolo, had been brutally murdered on the day they arrived in Katanga. Our delegation considered Munongo's declaration to be a careful manoeuvre to prepare

323

public opinion all over the world for the official announcement of the assassination.

At the time, I. E. Berendson was the UN's official representative in Elisabethville. Up to then, he had limited his activities to passing on messages and reports of a relatively vague and diplomatic nature to Léopoldville and New York. On the morning of 10 February, he had to make rather more of an effort, and consider just what the 'Lumumba case' would mean to international opinion. That day two important gentlemen were being specially sent from Léopoldville by Ambassador Dayal: the Ethiopian General Iyassu, commander-in-chief of the UN force in the Congo; and Knecht, chief of police from Geneva, on loan to the UN to help reorganize the police force of the Congo. These men, despite their rank and their mission, had to submit to the whims of Tshombe and Munongo, who would make appointments which they failed to keep, and were in fact gradually coming to realize that their crime could not long remain hidden. On 13 February Munongo, with his customary cynicism, but this time with a certain note of guilt in his voice, announced to the press that Lumumba, Okito and Mpolo had been massacred by the people of a small village.[3]

That same day in New York, the security council had met once again to continue its discussions on the Congo. The session got somewhat out of hand, and almost ended in confusion: some black Americans who favoured Lumumba's cause burst into the council chamber, causing uproar, and scuffling with UN security men. The secretary general and Ambassador Stevenson were their main target. The session was suspended for a few minutes, and the president of the council ordered the public gallery to be cleared before talks could go on. My delegation was permitted to remain: we held courtesy permits granted us by Hammarskjöld's own orders.

The announcement of the three murders gave rise to a series of demonstrations all over the world, directed particularly against Belgium and the United States. They were reaping the evil they had themselves sown.

3. See Appendix 7 for the full text of Munongo's statement to the press.

By an irony of fate, Gilbert Pongo, the politician-cum-soldier who had directed Lumumba's arrest, was captured in Bukavu on New Year's Day by troops still loyal to Lumumba. He was imprisoned in Stanleyville, from where he made several attempts to win his own liberation by begging his 'friends and superiors' in Léopoldville to liberate Lumumba. He was in company with a group of politicians who had once been faithful friends of Lumumba's, but had since 5 September turned against him and put themselves at the service of the 'authorities' in Léopoldville, to help in the ideological and political recapture of Orientale and Kivu provinces. Among them was Alphonse Songolo, Lumumba's minister of communications.[4]

The murder of the first Congolese prime minister unleashed a wave of political crimes throughout the country. Nothing could now prevent summary executions taking place. Southern Kasai, Albert Kalonji's empire, was nicknamed 'the national butcher's yard'; for all the politicians in Léopoldville who spoke openly against the Léopoldville régime of politicians, students and soldiers, were sent to Bakwanga and killed there in cold blood.

At almost the same time as Lumumba reached Katanga, Congolese whom I knew well were being systematically sent from Léopoldville to Bakwanga, where they were first mutilated, then butchered like animals. Among them was Pierre Elengesa, whom Lumumba had intended to be ambassador to Moscow, and Jacques Lumbala, private secretary to the prime minister.[5]

Lumumba's murder had a strange effect upon his personal and political enemies who had been playing the 'strong men' in Léopoldville and Elisabethville since September. Nearly all of them are still obsessed by the idea of proving their innocence and clearing up the misunderstanding to which they have been subjected. Truly among the most dreadful of all human suffering is to be uncertain in one's mind as to one's own guilt or innocence.

'Alive, Lumumba was a character who aroused the most

4. An unofficial list published in New York gave the names of senators Gilbert Fataki, Victor Iloko, Maurice Mandiangwe and Josias Fele; and deputies André Azanga, Victor Baleongani, Jean-Pierre Okita and Ernest Nzambi.

5. In the same group were J. P. Finant, the president of Orientale province, and Nzuzi, the president of the youth group in the MNC.

contradictory passions wherever he went. Dead, he still weighs upon the life and destiny of the Congo and all Africa.'[6]

6. G. Heinz and H. Donnay: *Patrice Lumumba, Les cinquante derniers jours de sa vie*, Ed. Crisp, Brussels and Paris, 1966, p. 8.

43 Lumumba: A Hero Too Late?

I don't suppose history will ever stop giving us surprises; indeed, the Congo is supremely a land of surprises.

Moïse Tshombe nearly became the 'saviour' of the Congo on his return from exile. But history decided otherwise, and the Congolese people found themselves under the leadership of Mobutu, who was to recall the 'testament' of Lumumba, in which he wrote:

Ma foi restera inébranlable. Je sais et je sens du fond de moi-même que tôt ou tard mon peuple se débarrassera de tous ses ennemis intérieurs, qu'il se lèvera comme un seul homme pour dire *non* au colonialisme dégradant et honteux et pour reprendre sa dignité sous un soleil pur.

At one point in Congolese history, Mobutu was one of Lumumba's political protégés, an active member of the MNC, Lumumba's personal representative in Brussels, a secretary of state in his government.

Can it be that this man, Lumumba's former friend and confidant, will succeed in putting his old leader's ideas into practice, and achieving the things he tried to achieve but failed?

Six years after his death, the Congo was to discover that Lumumba, denied by his own people, was held in the highest honour by other peoples, in Africa and elsewhere. The Congolese could only redeem themselves – through the voice of Mobutu, now president – by hastening to proclaim him a national hero. Better late than never!

Here are some excerpts from Mobutu's speech:

... Glory and honour to that illustrious Congolese, that great African, the first martyr of our economic independence:

Conflict in the Congo

PATRICE EMERY LUMUMBA

On this historic day, 30 June 1966, when our country is taking its first steps towards winning economic independence, how can we fail to recall that great figure Patrice Lumumba, for great he was, and great he will remain. It would be hard indeed to forget that important passage in his historic speech of 30 June 1960, that profession of faith, that masterly exposition of what the Congo must do to achieve its economic independence: 'I urge all Congolese citizens, men, women and children, to set resolutely to work to create a prosperous national economy, and thus guarantee our economic independence.'

'Economic independence' – two key words in that magnificent speech by the noblest of all Congolese fighters, on that memorable day which marked the victory of the Congolese people over eighty years of a repressive colonial régime, a régime of exploitation and humiliation . . .

In the name of the government, we ask you now to keep silent for a minute in memory of the man we proclaim officially today a national hero: Patrice Emery Lumumba . . .

We wish to inform you that the government has decided that from this day forth, the boulevard from the military airport of Ndolo to the international airport of Njili, which has been known up to now as the Boulevard Léopold III, will be the Boulevard Patrice Emery Lumumba.

Furthermore, a statue will be put up in his memory, on the corner of this same boulevard, at the highest point of the road to Lovanium university.

Politicians in the Congo re-open the issue of Lumumba's death from time to time when they feel it will serve their purpose, but the mystery surrounding it remains unsolved. I am convinced that whether Mobutu be guilty or innocent, the truth will some day come to light, because Lumumba's ghost continues to haunt the corridors of Congolese politics. Lumumba is now dead but Mobutu is very much alive and has been ruling the Congo since his second coup d'etat in 1965. Furthermore whether Mobutu can be absolved of all complicity in the plot which sent Lumumba to his death in the Katanga remains, for the moment, one of Congo history's great unanswered questions. His efforts to make Lumumba an international symbol might be interpreted as a sign that his own conscience on the question is not entirely clear since in practice no concrete action has been taken.

In this connection, an article in *Jeune Afrique* in 1966 stated 'All Congolese Governments before Mobutu came to power have looked upon Lumumba's murder as a strictly internal matter, and have declined to co-operate with international agencies anxious to investigate it. General Mobutu has now brought the issue into the open once more by setting up a subscription fund, open to contributions from all over the world, to erect a monument to the "Congolese hero".' Ten years later, in 1976 nothing has been done yet.

The mystery of Lumumba's murder, how, why and on whose orders he was killed, is bound to be solved sooner or later. Perhaps Mobutu will provide the key, possibly in spite of himself and as a result of his political downfall. In any event, the truth will some day be revealed, if only because of someone's indiscretion or inability to keep silent any longer.

The term 'Lumumbism' is now part of the vocabulary of modern political speech. It is accepted, yes, but not really very clearly defined, and though in fairly common use, can be given very different meanings.

To some, Lumumbism is the symbol of faith in a great future for the Congo, wholly free and united. To others, it spells danger for our country, it is an ideology to be fought, a kind of soft-pedalled racism in reverse. In my view, Lumumbism should mean the ideal Lumumba dedicated himself to; the ways he recommended for achieving it and along which he trusted others to follow him. The essence of Lumumbism is the awareness that everyone must fight, in his own sphere and according to his own abilities and chances of success, to take part in the whole liberation struggle of oppressed peoples and subjugated countries.

Lumumba never made any secret of his intentions or his objective: to free the Congo – even, and indeed particularly, after it had been given nominal independence – by means of a popular revolution, and the mental decolonization of its people, and also through the moral support and practical help of those African countries that were already free. Popular revolution implied a

329

revolution in institutions, society, politics, economics and culture.

Lumumba was convinced that all of Africa had a duty to help liberate the Congo. Without a genuinely independent Congo there could never be a united and really free Africa. On the other hand, he also considered that the liberated Congo had a moral and material obligation towards helping the rest of Africa to achieve a speedy liberation.

Though Lumumbism originated in what had been the Belgian Congo, its scope went far beyond the boundaries of a single nation. In our day, Lumumbism has a meaning for all of Africa. Indeed, Patrice Lumumba has become a symbol for all those, nationalists and revolutionaries, who are fighting for the liberation of their homelands.

Very often, to accede to national sovereignty has meant only a superficial change in relationship – not a fundamental one – between the metropolitan country and the colony. Often too, the former colonizers have succeeded in making independence a kind of umbrella to cover their own direction and control of the new state by means of solid institutions, and permanent and powerful pressure groups. They have found and been prepared to pay dependable agents from among the former colonized, to get legislation passed that would favour their interests.

Lumumba's convictions and statements about such neo-colonialism were tremendously courageous – and his courage was all the more admirable in that, as prime minister, he was faced with such manifold and complex problems. Some of these were inevitable, but others were created simply in order to paralyse his government. Lumumba confronted his problems with enormous determination, but was terribly lacking in realism. Neo-colonialism was strong enough to restore the ideas and conceptions against which Lumumba spent his life fighting. Alas, though he fought bravely indeed, he fought with few resources. And he was beaten.

But if Lumumba did not succeed as a ruler, that may in the end, paradoxically, have made him far more powerful a figure in history.

44 Nasser and Lumumba

'What do you think about the Vietnam war?' asked Nkrumah.

'Perhaps we should talk about Ghana rather than Vietnam', replied Nasser.

'There is nothing to say about Ghana. Everything is perfectly calm. As you know, I have just come from there and I made sure of that before I left.'

'I doubt it. If I were you, I should go straight back to Ghana, and forget Vietnam for the moment.'

Gamel Abdul Nasser was silent and drew on his cigarette. Kwame Nkrumah, now somewhat nervous, remained outwardly calm. For a few seconds he said nothing. He had been put firmly in his place by a colleague, a brother, and who knows, perhaps also a political rival.

This was part of a conversation memorable mainly in that it took place only five days before the military coup in Ghana of February 1966. The President of Ghana was paying a visit to the President of the United Arab Republic. He was stopping in Cairo, on his way to Vietnam, where he was to be the guest of Ho Chi Minh. His journey was to take him to Pakistan, India, Burma, China, North Vietnam, and the Soviet Union. He was travelling in a Ghana Airways VC10, his suite consisting of ministers I knew quite well personally, and including more than sixty people all told. Among them were Alex Quaison-Sackey, Minister of Foreign Affairs, and former Ambassador to the United Nations, and Kwesi Armah, Minister of Commerce and former High Commissioner to London. The Ghanaian delegation was fortunate to be making this princely journey, which was to have taken them to three continents – Africa, Asia and Europe. Who could tell what might happen if the Ghanaians were successful in their mission to Hanoi? Indeed, it was probable that

Nkrumah intended to call at London on his way back, to let the British Prime Minister, Harold Wilson, know where matters stood.

Nasser was in fact a most attractive character – honest and sometimes brutally frank if you knew him well and were in his confidence. In so far as he may be considered an African head of state – which he was after all, for Egypt is part of the African continent – one may quite truthfully say that he was the best informed political leader and the best organized statesman in Africa. (I do not here include the Union of South Africa because I do not know it.) Nasser was very well informed. Among African leaders he was one of the few who were not caught unaware by events or shaken by ideas brought in by outsiders. With him everything was carefully thought out and categorized. His strategy was one planned by himself, either alone or with a small group of intimates. The various tactics he used were generally dictated directly by objectives he had determined upon. This concept of political action fitting in with a well planned strategy, and tactics adapted to fit the situation of the moment, was probably the best result of his military training and career.

My own first conversation with President Nasser was in New York in September 1960. During the unforgettable session of the General Assembly of 1960, the Congo seemed to be at the hub of every debate that took place. A number of heads of governments and foreign ministers were also in New York at the time, and I had a chance of talking over the problem of the Congo with many of them, especially Nikita Krushchev, Ahmed Sukarno of Indonesia, Pandit Nehru of India, Tito of Yugoslavia, Sekou Touré of Guinea and Fidel Castro of Cuba. Apart from heads of government, I was also in touch with various foreign ministers who had come for the session, and the diplomatic heads of permanent missions in New York. Every delegation, in its speech at the General Assembly, had some opinion to put forward about the Congo, and incidentally, of course, on the Congolese. The Security Council had not succeeded in voting a single resolution acceptable to all of its eleven members; the Congolese problem was being put before the General Assembly. It was during that memorable session that Krushchev banged his shoe on the table while Harold Macmillan was speaking.

The UAR was a member of the Security Council. I had become friendly with its ambassador, Loufti, a former Egyptian judge, and a close friend of Dag Hammarskjöld. (In fact, a few months later, Loufti became one of Hammarskjöld's assistants.) He arranged an audience with his President, Nasser, for me which took place in one of the UN reception rooms. I was delighted and proud to meet this man of whom I had heard so much – good or bad depending on which paper I was reading or which radio station I was tuned to. Though tall, Nasser is not the giant his photographs sometimes suggested. His smile seemed to conceal a certain shyness or perhaps nervousness. I felt him to be shy by nature; he certainly looked it. His handshake was not as firm as one would have expected from a man of his authority, whose national and international decisions were so much discussed. I was barely 27 and Nasser was probably partly interested in meeting me because of my youth; also, Omar Loufti, it seems, had praised me highly to his President before our audience. In New York, I had acquired a certain celebrity – for three reasons: Firstly, I was the first Congolese to have addressed the UN Security Council, secondly, I was, to many people, 'too young' to be a minister and an ambassador; and thirdly, I was the official spokesman, in the international arena, of Patrice Lumumba. In 1960 Lumumba was seen as an extraordinary phenomenon, possibly a good one, but certainly a historic figure in being the incumbent leader of that great, new, troubled Republic of Congo.

My English was not sufficiently fluent to carry on a political and diplomatic exchange of views with President Nasser. So I spoke French. He understood French well, but he preferred to speak English with foreigners provided he could trust them, especially when time was short; otherwise, he would speak Arabic and have an interpreter. Though he understood my French, he had an interpreter to make absolutely certain of missing nothing. Omar Loufti was present so, also was the president's chief adviser on African Affairs.

Nasser had never met Lumumba; nor was he ever to do so. He asked me to tell him about my Prime Minister, and also about the other 'celebrities' who emerged in the Congo since independence, especially Kasavubu, Gizenga, Bomboko, Tshombe, Nendaka, Munongo, Kalonji and Mobutu. I was under no illusion – Nasser already knew a lot about my now celebrated compatriots. All he wanted was to compare, and perhaps complete, his information with what I told him. We went on to talk about what Patrice Lumumba and his government hoped for from the UAR Government, and Nasser, in particular.

I was in New York when Mobutu made his semi-coup on 14 September 1960. I could have talked to him every day on the telephone if I wanted to, but in fact only did so three or four times. Mobutu liked to confer at great length on the telephone with his close 'friend' Jacques Lumbala, who was part of my delegation in New York, and a Secretary of State to the Presidency. As I listened to their conversations, I learnt things I had not known before and gained some understanding of situations which had previously seemed to me wholly mysterious.

In every conversation on the telephone, I insisted that Mobutu make clear to us his precise constitutional position, so that we might explain the Congolese imbroglio to other people. His answers suggested a certain confusion on his part, and a certain unplanned element in his 'coup'. To many observers around the world, Colonel Mobutu's intervention in the Congolese political affairs was an 'unfinished military coup'.

Thus, at the time of my first meeting with Nasser, the situation inside the Congo was confused and desperate. But he knew more than I did about the intrigues at work behind the scenes among the great powers in relation to the Congo, and more particularly in relation to Lumumba himself. From New York it appeared to the majority of the delegations that the Congolese politicians were, unconsciously, and probably unwillingly, being manipulated by invisible but extremely powerful forces. The average outsider might well conclude that independence had been granted to the Congo without the agreement or assent of its people, since within only a few days, all was disorder.

Six days after the proclamation of Independence, the soldiers mutinied against their Belgian officers. Within twelve days, one of the country's provinces declared itself independent as Katanga; Albert Kalonji felt it his vocation to liberate the people of Kasai province by proclaiming himself 'emperor', and declaring his empire autonomous. Belgium, the former colonial power, did not hesitate to invade the major Congolese towns, sending in paratroops without the agreement of the Congolese government. Within a month, soldiers from all over the world were disembarking in the Congo in order, in official terms, 'to assist the Congolese Government to safeguard national independence, and to maintain and secure their territorial integrity'. They came from Guinea, Ghana, Senegal, Mali, Liberia, Tunisia, Morocco, Egypt, Sweden, Ireland, Canada, Denmark, Indonesia, Malaya, India, Pakistan . . .

These UN troops had come to the Congo at the express request of the Central Congolese Government. Then, as if that were not enough, those in power began playing the game of mutually dismissing one another: Kasavubu discharging Lumumba, Lumumba sacking the head of state, Mobutu neutralizing everyone – the head of state, the prime minister and the parliament – but not actually dismissing them, nor actually taking power himself. It is impossible to say whether he failed to complete his coup from fear, from diplomacy, from political strategy, or out of necessity.

At the UN in New York, we were the focus of much interest, since no one at all seemed to understand the Congolese, still less the Congo. Justin Bomboko, Kasavubu's special envoy, was now the darling of the western and so-called moderate countries. As Lumumba's representative, I had the sympathy of the socialist, the non-aligned and the revolutionary countries.

Nasser summoned me to complete his information, so as the better to determine what attitude his government should take – both publicly and behind the scenes – on the whole Congolese problem. I could get nothing much out of this extremely experienced politician and strategist, sparing as always with words. From his questions and his few answers to mine, I did realize how cold and calculating was his mind and his contempt for Kasavubu, Mobutu, Bomkobo and above all, Tshombe.

I got Nasser to agree unhesitatingly to everything I asked on behalf of the Lumumba Government. He was pleased to learn that I was doing my best to get Lumumba to come to New York in person during the General Assembly session, and encouraged me to keep trying. 'I believe,' he said, 'that Lumumba should leave the Congo and get to know the people who are in New York personally. It is a chance he won't have again.' And he went on to say, 'his presence in New York would be a great help in the discussions. It must be realized that the Congolese problem is far from being as simple as people think.'

Nasser smoked a great deal. I noticed that he was never without a cigarette in his hand. He had a friendly smile, and I found it hard to believe that this agreeable man could be as wicked as he had been made out to be in the western press. More than once during our interview, I sensed that he considered the Congolese to be ill-informed or ignorant, in general, of the intrigues going on behind the scenes before and after independence. 'Tell Lumumba to be very careful; the imperialists don't like him, and they will have his skin if they can.' This kind of phrase kept recurring. He did not make it clear just why the imperialists hated Lumumba, but the phrase, and the tone in which he said it, were quite enough to rivet my attention. We spoke of the UN, of Hammarskjöld, of the behaviour of the UN troops in the Congo and of the Belgian game, especially in Katanga and Kasai.

Nasser professed not to understand why the United Nations should be supervising the political, diplomatic and military activities of the Congolese Government, when the opposite should have been the case. 'Lumumba should have known more about the United Nations before requesting them to send an international force to the Congo,' he said. 'Now, the damage is done, since he is not in a strong position. I shall consult other African heads of state and try to find an honourable solution to the problem within the framework of the United Nations.'

He expressed strong doubts on the ability of small nations to do anything positive in the situation. 'Tell Lumumba that the Government of the United Arab Republic responded to his appeal by assigning Egyptian troops to the United Nations,' he said. 'But we and other member states must fulfil our obligations to the United Nations and cannot act independently in the situation. Lumumba must somehow get out of the Congo and come to New York, where he could inform us of his intentions, and we could try to find ways and means of giving him some practical help.'

Apart from making statements of a general nature and giving me some useful advice, President Nasser assured me that his Government would support the legally-constituted Congolese Government and its Permanent Mission to the United Nations in any circumstance.

My talk with Nasser made me yet more aware of the serious-ness of the situation in the Congo. Though a powerful man and great strategist, he was also very diplomatic; he was not pre-pared to compromise his own position for the Congo, and still less for the Congolese who were only names to him, though he had information about them all. In any case, Nasser was going to do nothing without consulting the other heads of state. In the matter of information, the UAR Embassy in Brussels had been extremely active in the months preceding Congolese Inde-pendence: I was quite certain that the Egyptian diplomats had the fullest possible information on all the Congolese politicians who has visited Belgium. I knew the head of the UAR diplo-matic mission in Brussels well, from the time when I was there as an official of the Common Market (1958–1960). He was most active, and well aware of the writing between the lines in Belgian–Congolese relations. Owing to the amount of Belgian investment in Egypt, the Ambassador was in continuous contact with the same financial group who dictated what went on in the Congo and who hated Patrice Lumumba.

Deep in myself, I understood the rules of the game. The UN forces were conducting in the Congo a holy war 'against com-munism'. They had not come to 'help and assist the Central Government'. To make quite sure of this, I made special inquiries as to the financing of the UN operation in the Congo. Basically, the Western powers were providing more than half the expenses involved – and by 'Western', I mean the NATO countries and their allies, whether military, political or economic, all over the world.

Now that Colonel Mobutu had created further constitutional confusion by neutralizing the political leaders and parliament, the Congo had become for the non-initiated a kind of mad and incomprehensible clockwork puzzle.

The general Assembly was ready to vote in favour of admitting the Congo (Leopoldville) to membership, while its seat there must remain empty until its internal constitutional problem be somehow acceptably solved.

I was well aware of the manoeuvres and pressures going on behind the scenes to get Bomboko, Kasavubu's man, seated, but I needed definite evidence of this to present to Lumumba. I got from Nasser the encouraging promise that the UAR delegation would support the delegation of Lumumba's legal Government. Nasser promised that he would do his best to get support for his plan from all the countries who considered themselves progressive or neutralist. My fear was the latter, if under serious pressure from the West, and especially America, would simply drop Lumumba and everything he stood for.

For the rest, I had to keep in touch with Loufti and the UAR delegation. I was to be called again to see Nasser if necessary, since he wanted to be kept informed about Lumumba, and eventual internal developments in the Congo. Before I left him, Nasser stood up, shook hands with me, and said once again 'Tell Lumumba to be careful. If he comes to New York, he must be more careful still. And you must be careful too,' he added, smiling. 'People are watching you, and at present your enemies are far stronger than you are.' I replied, also smiling, 'I'm well aware of how strong my enemies are. But I'm convinced that sooner or later truth will win. I shall make a point of passing on your ideas and advice to the Prime Minister – I'm hoping to see him in a few days' time.'

Lumumba was unable to get to New York during the 1960 session of the General Assembly for various reasons: Kasavubu and Mobutu's refusal to let him leave the Congo, the Americans refusing to give him a visa and the lack of any absolute safe means of transport out of Leopoldville.

Therefore, in his name, and that of the Government which had sent me to the UN, I made all the contacts that seemed necessary and useful with heads of Government and Foreign Ministers then at the UN. My job was made easier by my having in my delegation Jacques Lumbala, an intimate friend of Mobutu with whom he was in daily telephonic communication. Lumbala seemed very well informed as to the attitudes, intentions and ambitions of his friend, and the details of his partial coup. It would seem that they must have discussed the whole thing in detail before we left Leopoldville, and it was in a way amusing to hear him later on describing how the whole affair was developing.

Mobutu and Lumbala were certainly friends, close friends even. But how sincere were they towards one another? Lumbala was perhaps a little too emphatic over his influence on Mobutu; the way he spoke almost seemed to suggest that he had been the brains behind the 'coup', directing it by telephone from New York. As Secretary of State, Lumbala helped me considerably to explain to foreign delegations what kind of person Mobutu was, and why he had determined on 'neutralizing' the politicians and the parliament and temporarily given power to his group of students. The developments that followed were tragic indeed for him. He knew too much, and was brutally murdered in early February 1961, together with the group of 'Lumumbists' who had been sent from Leopoldville to Bakwanga (in South Kasai) a few days after Lumumba's own murder.

Having made all my most important contacts, I thought it best to return to Leopoldville and present Lumumba with the results of my labours. I was particularly pleased to be going back to find out what was really happening at home, and curious to discover Lumbala's true role, and precisely what his influence was over Mobutu. I arranged for him to return to Leopoldville ahead of me, since I did not wish to leave New York before Bomboko, which would have been both politically and diplomatically a mistake. Bomboko was busy trying to persuade western and pro-western delegations to support Kasavubu in his political struggle for power against Prime Minister Lumumba whom he used to define as 'communist puppet'.

Lumumba had a great admiration for Nasser, though he did not know him personally. He was most interested to hear his views on the Congo question and also his advice, but was rather dis-

appointed at Nasser's stress on the carefulness demanded of anyone so hated by the imperialists. 'But,' said Lumumba, 'the
imperialists hate him too. The West don't even want to hear his
name mentioned. They want his skin, just as much as they want
mine, so why does he pursue his revolutionary and anti-imperialist
policy?' In irritation, he continued 'Prudence, prudence . . .
everyone advises prudence. Africans are a lot of cowards. They
take us for innocents – helpless innocents. All the Nassers and
Nkrumahs and Sekou Tourés make fine speeches on the Congo,
but they don't know what they are talking about. They would
have been better employed arranging to get me to New York to
make my own speeches about the Congo and the Congolese.
After all, I'm a head of government just like them, and my
country is far larger and richer than any of theirs . . .' And warm-
ing to his theme, he turned his rage against his fellow-citizens:
'that idiot of a Kasavubu – he knows nothing about anything to
get him elected head of state, and there he is now trying to get
me arrested and killed. There's gratitude for you. And Joseph
(Mobutu) – how can he dare to talk of "neutralizing" and then
leave Kasavubu completely free? The Congolese really are fools.
I never thought that Joseph, after all the help I gave him, and my
appointing him to the Army just because he was so loyal, could
treat me as he has.'

Lumumba was in his shirt-sleeves. He was silent for a moment,
and then went on even more furiously: 'Prudence, carefulness.
. . . If Nasser had been careful would he have nationalized the
Suez Canal and enraged the whole Western world?' Since this
seemed like a question, I took the chance of slipping in a word:
'What Nasser really meant by that was that you should not act
without careful planning. You must work out everything methodically, because the fight is far bigger and fiercer than we realize.
It isn't just a political battle between Kasavubu and Lumumba,
or a constitutional struggle between the head of state and the
prime minister; far more is at stake than that.' I finished what I
had to say by telling Lumumba that he had been wrong from the
first in paying too much attention to the many who flocked to him
in Leopoldville with their advice. The time had come to think
out the whole Congolese question for himself, and create a

strategy and tactic that were truly his own. My conclusion from all the talks I had had in New York, was that no one anywhere else was going to sacrifice himself for the Congo or its people, still less for Lumumba. They might use his name; they might make political and diplomatic capital out of the Congolese tragedy. Our self-styled friends said fine words about us, but they would *do* nothing. The UN troops in the Congo were paid by the West and their allies. Those who declared themselves our friends were contributing only a tiny proportion of the cost, and some nothing. They were gradually being denied the right even to speak. They had thought that words might achieve something, but they had forgotten that wars are fought with money. Whether or not we wanted it, the UN force would be indirectly ruling the Congo for some years to come, and we must make our plans accordingly, and stop making snap-decisions, based on illusions and suppositions, that could only antagonize the senior UN officials.

My interview with Lumumba ended on a somewhat more friendly note. After his raging against his so-called 'African brothers' and 'socialist comrades' who had stood by and let him fail, Lumumba realized that he must at last start working out his plans for himself, and still alone, confront the diplomatic and political realities of life. He had hoped that the so-called progressive African countries would have had the courage to withdraw their troops from the UN Force and form an 'African' army to 'help and assist the legal Government of the Congo' to preserve its national independence and maintain its territorial integrity. And indeed a few African countries had withdrawn their troops under the command of the UN and made them go back home without creating an African army however.

The destiny of the Congo was conducted somewhere else than in the official residence of the Prime Minister, where we were. As for the fate of the Congolese, I understood a long time before that it was in the hands of God, because nobody was paying attention to it . . . except individuals like Lumumba and his associates, who, being so consciencious and idealistic were still convinced of being responsible for the happiness and misfortune of those millions of Congolese whose they had win the heart, love and the votes.

45 Who was responsible for the Murder

I cannot, for certain, put forward the names of those – fellow-countrymen and others – who were more or less directly involved in the calvary that took Patrice Lumumba, Maurice Mpolo and Joseph Okito to their deaths. Lumumba was the victim of a conspiracy worked out abroad, and put into effect in the Congo with the willing or unwilling help of his own compatriots.

In August 1962, I was received in audience by President Kasavubu. I was then head of the Congolese Diplomatic Mission in London. Cyrille Adoula was Prime Minister and Justin Bomboko Minister of Foreign Affairs. This latter had summoned me to Leopoldville for consultations over the attitude of Britain and Rhodesia to the secession of Katanga.

My audience with the president was in the nature of a courtesy visit. Protocol had officially fixed a 15-minute interview for me; but to the surprise of everyone, Kasavubu kept me for two hours. Normally taciturn, he seemed that day to feel a psychological need to talk to me as man to man, or perhaps father to son. He knew what accusations I had made against him at the United Nations at the time of his constitutional battle with Lumumba. Furthermore, there still remained a certain degree of mistrust between himself and my father, which neither of them would move to alleviate.

Kasavubu spoke to me of his innocence throughout the operations leading to Lumumba's murder. He spoke of his own good faith in relation to Lumumba's dismissal in September 1960, and the unforeseen and uncontrollable consequences of Lumumba's obstinacy.

I listened with the attention a son would give the confidences of his own father who he suspected of criminality. Like Lumumba, Kasavubu is no longer with us. In the history of the Congo, he will remain the man who – whether alone, or upon advice from other people – laid the scene that opened with the dismissal of Lumumba and closed with his being murdered in Katanga. Could he have prevented Lumumba being sent to Katanga, or had he become simply a tool in the hands of a group he could no longer control?

In April 1964, I received Moise Tshombe in private, we talked at some length.

In exile in Madrid since 1963, Tshombe was getting ready for his political comeback in the Congo. He was supported by western financial interests who promised to get him established at the head of the central Congolese government. After the 30 June 1964, the date when the UN forces were due to leave the Congo, there was no longer any question of Katanga's secession, but the central Congolese government needed a new head.

Tshombe needed me, both personally and politically. My name stood high on the list of those Congolese whom Tshombe and his masters thought they might hope to 'use' to get him back and ensure his political success in the Congo.

He had come from Madrid to London as a guest of the Institute of Race Relations, who had invited him to give a lecture on the future of the Congo.

I was no longer a Congolese diplomat, having resigned my job on 15 December 1963. My conversations with Tshombe were therefore purely of a private nature. Tshombe yielded to my every demand. Though quite evidently protected and watched by two Scotland Yard detectives, Tshombe made no secret of his urgent wish to talk with me. I had refused to go the Savoy Hotel where he was staying, but I had been to his lecture. With his two detectives, Tshombe came to see me twice in the apartment where I was staying in Knightsbridge. He had the pleasure and relief of unburdening his conscience during our two meetings. He wept – which was both moving and pathetic – the tears of a man who had suddenly come to appreciate the immense gravity of the secret weighing so heavily on his mind.

Two months earlier, in an attempt to win the confidence of Africans, and regain power in the Congo, Tshombe had given

343

an interview and a press conference in Madrid which were a sensation at the time. Openly and without any beating about the bush, he made accusations against his compatriots who had been in power in Leopoldville in 1960 and 1961, and who sent Patrice Lumumba to him in Katanga, 'half dead'. He made a most admirable effort to be heard and declared innocent, but no one believed him.

To history, Tshombe and Munongo will always appear as two of those Congolese who knew every detail of the developments leading up to and culminating in the murder of Lumumba, Mpolo and Okito, and who also knew just where their bodies went to.

Victor Nendaka, supreme head of the Congolese Sûrete,[1] knew better than anyone all the complications of the political and diplomatic operation which finally brought Tshombe, the exile, back to the Congo as Moïse the 'saviour' in July 1964. In fact, he was one of the major agents in the whole operation. At one time, Nendaka was a friend of mine and a lieutenant of Lumumba. Though his unlimited powers as administrator-in-chief of the Sûrete made him the 'terror of the Congo', Nendaka remained subtle, skilful and pleasant to meet. But he had the conscience of a cynic, and the reputation of being a man who could inflict the most appalling tortures on those who fell into his clutches. His methodical but tortuous mind made him a past master at setting traps, both for friends and enemies – in fact he *had* no real friends, for even those who felt themselves his friends were afraid of him, and well aware that he liked them only for their usefulness. He gave nothing for nothing, and could not conceive of doing something to please a friend without the friend's doing something for him in return. He was also the quintessential detective.

Of the tiny group which really held power in Leopoldville, Nendaka was probably the brains and the energy, but he liked to pass as simply an official carrying out other people's orders without argument or deviation. He was, in fact, the type of man who

1. He was appointed to the post by Kasavubu in 1960 after the Lumumba government's dismissal, and retained it until 1965.

believes his work consists in seeing that decisions once made are meticulously carried out. IIis group of intimates were often known as the 'Binza Group', because they met together in the Binza district, where most of them lived; it was said that the chief members were Joseph Mobutu, Justin Bomboko, Damien Kandolo and Albert Ndele. At times Kasavubu, Adoula, Joseph Litho and Roberto Holden also numbered among them.

In May 1963, Nendaka came to London to see the head of Scotland Yard, and to meet the secretary-general of Interpol to discuss the admission of the Congo as a member of that organization. I was present at those interviews, and he gave an impression of being delighted to see me again, and being able to renew an old friendship. It was a real bit of luck for me to have this chance of exchanging views with him on the thorny problems of the Congo, among others the death of Lumumba.

On 3 May 1963, he wrote this in my visitors' book:

En souvenir de mon passage à Londres pour rendre visite à mon ami Thomas Kanza. Je te souhaite bon courage et du succès dans ton avenir. J'ai beaucoup d'admiration pour ton courage exceptionel d'avoir, malfré les difficultés, réussi à imposer notre représentation dans un pays dont la politique des dirigeants nous semblait hostile, surtout dans l'affaire Katanga. Encore une fois, tous mes voeux de bonheur et de sincères amitiés.
Victor Nendaka, 3. 5. 1963
accompagné A. J. Hubert, A. Zamundu, M. Makalangi, J. P. Lemba, G. Amoury

Nendaka had almost all the information about Lumumba's death – down to the tiniest details, from the time of his escape from his residence in Leopoldville up to his arrest, his imprisonment in Thysville, his removal from there to Elisabethville and his death. and everything that happened in Elisabethville afterwards. He would have had no trouble in remembering the names of all those involved – black and white – the dates and places were they met, the money they spent, either by cash or into bank accounts.

As head of the Sûrete Nationale, he personally directed the

tragic journey of Lumumba, Okito and Mpolo: their removal
under escort from Binza to the army camp at Thysville, and
from Moanda to Elisabethville. Though not there in person, he
had made a point of sending one or more of his most trusted men
to bring him back every smallest detail.

Lumumba has been dead for almost fifteen years. He was murdered in cold blood in Katanga. By whom? On whose orders?
Why? How?

Future generations will know the answers to these questions
better than we do. Meanwhile, the secret is known to a handful
of men, Congolese, non-Congolese, European and American.
Will they ever speak out? And if they do, will they tell the
truth?

Whatever happens, the truth *will* gradually emerge, because
there does exist certain evidence, and because of the inevitable
and calculated indiscretions of those who know more than they
will say; for 'dead, Lumumba still lies heavy on the life and
destiny of the Congo and all Africa'.

History will record that the following Congolese, holding these
positions in 1960–61, were informed of the details of the deaths
of Lumumba, Okito and Mpolo:

Joseph Kasavubu, president (now dead)

Joseph Mobutu, commander-in-chief of the ANC

Justin Bomboko, president of the College of Commissioners,
spokesman for foreign affairs, and also one of the signatories
of Kasavubu's dismissal of Lumumba

Victor Nendaka, chief of the sûreté

Damien Kandolo, Lumumba's private secretary, and later a
colleague of Nendaka's

Jonas Mukamba, a colleague of Nendaka (he escorted Lumumba to Katanga)

Ferdinand Kazadi, Commissioner responsible for Defence;
former leader of the secessionist troops of southern Kasai,
and right-hand man of Albert Kalonji (Lumumba's escort
to Katanga

Moise Tshombe, president of secessionist Katanga (now dead)

Godefroid Munongo, Katanga's Minister of Home Affairs

Albert Kalonji, national deputy and self-styled 'emperor' of
southern Kasai

Joseph Ileo, appointed by Kasavubu as prime minister to succeed Lumumba, and formerly President of the Senate

Joseph Kiwele, Minister in the Katanga government (now
dead)

Jean-Batiste Kibwe, Minister of Finance in Katanga

Albert Delvaux, national deputy, minister responsible for relations with Belgium in the Lumumba government, and a
signatory of Kasavubu's dismissal of Lumumba.

Samalenge, Minister of Information in Katanga (now dead)

Pius Sapwe, chief of police in Katanga

Evariste Kimba, Minister of Foreign Affairs in Katanga (now
dead)

In addition to these Congolese, we must add Abbe Fulbert
Youlou, the then president of Congo (Brazzaville). He was actually in Elisabethville on the day Lumumba's death was announced
by the Katangese authorities.

Responsibility of Lumumba's death must be shared among various people, whom we may divide into four groups:

The first group comprises those Congolese who were personal
and political enemies of the Prime Minister. They were brought
together by representatives of international financial monopolies,
and western secret services working to combat communist influence in Africa, with the definite intention of getting rid of
Lumumba, first politically, and then physically.

The second group is made up of a handful of Congolese who
called themselves Lumumba's friends and thus persuaded him
to leave his official residence in Leopoldville and attempt the
mad escapade of driving by car more than a thousand kilometers
from Leopoldville to Stanleyville, where ten of the ministers
still loyal to him were waiting for him under the leadership of
Gizenga. The arrest, imprisonment, and later, the murder, of
Lumumba would have been almost inconceivable had he not
made the fatal mistake of leaving the protection of the UN
troops guarding his home. Those of his friends who advised
and helped make possible that escape have been aware how

impossible it would have been for him to arrive safely in Stanley-ville. Were they really so naïve and ignorant, or irresponsible; or was it a conspiracy?

The third group includes the students and others who, on pre-text of giving the Congo a better government than the politicians, allowed themselves to be purely and simply made use of and manipulated, in the framework of the College of Commissioners. Though their complicity was involuntary, future generations will find it hard to understand the ambition of these young men to govern, effectively to rule the Congo in a period as tragic as it was chaotic.

The fourth group of those responsible for Lumumba's mur-der consists of all those foreigners, whether African or other, who either helped to make it possible, or by direct or indirect means demanded its commission.[2]

2. The United States Senate published in 1975 '*An Interim Report of the Select Committee to study governmental operations with respect to Intelligence Activities*'—The report concerned the 'Alleged assassination plots involving foreign leaders'. The reading of this report (pp. 13–70) reveals in detail how the United States govern-ment under President Eisenhower was determined to 'get rid' of Patrice Lumumba as part of normal duty of the Central Intelligence Agency in the Congo. The U.S. CIA was not acting alone. Its activities were coordinated with other western secret services in the Congo, mainly Belgian, French, British, Portuguese, South African.

46 From Lumumba to Mobutu

Today, the former Belgian Congo is called the republic of Zaire. This country – at times known as Congo-Léopoldville, Congo-Kinshasa, and the present republic of Zaire – is very much a land of surprises. It is also been known as the Congo-Lumumba, the Congo-Kasavubu, the Congo-Tshombe. Zaire is the Congo-Mobutu.

The name Zaire was imposed by general-president Mobutu in 1971. It is not accepted by all the inhabitants of the country. I may be wrong, but I have the feeling that sooner or later, the name Zaire will change again to Congo. For that reason, I will continue to use both names to identify the ex-Belgian Congo.

Of the problems and difficulties facing the Congo-Zaire, it is useful to mention those of a lasting nature and those which are only accidental.

The permanent characteristics are threefold: the vastness of the territory, its enormous wealth, and its geographic position on the African continent. Those who speak of the Congo often forget that it is an immense territory – ten times the size of Great Britain, five times that of France, three times that of Nigeria, eleven times the size of Ghana, and eighty times that of Belgium. Superimposed on a map of western Europe, the Congo would cover Belgium, France, Holland, Denmark, Sweden, Norway, Luxembourg, Spain, West Germany, Portugal, and Switzerland. Thus, the size of the Congo is a permanent feature which must be taken into account when any interpretations of political events in the Congo are made or when the country is compared to other African states.

Secondly, the Congo is rich. The potential wealth of the country is enormous whether one considers the agricultural possibilities, or the mineral which has yet to be accurately estimated, or the potential resources of energy. The wealth of the Congo has aroused the envy of the outside world. Indeed, much of the interest shown in the Congo is inspired by an awareness of this wealth, which is a source of prosperity in a country, but which may also bring strife, and much unhappiness.

Lastly, there is the geographic and strategic position of the Congo. Situated as it is in the heart of Africa, the Congo has frontiers with Angola, Zambia, Ruanda, Burundi, Tanzania, Uganda, the Sudan, Congo-Brazzaville, and the Central African Republic. Many of the people on the borders of the Congo have relatives in the neighbouring countries. The geographic position of the Congo is of particular interest to those foreign groups or powers which have drawn up plans – political, economic, or military – to be implemented there.

Besides these three permanent difficulties, there are some temporary problems – the results of historical accident – that of Belgian colonization with all its subsequent repercussions: educational, political, economic, and military implications.

The first of these concerns education: the Belgian colonial administration favoured the education of the Congolese masses in the local vernacular. The system did not provide for a higher general instruction based on modern progressive conceptions of education. Belgium secured social and material well-being for her colony in subjection. Belgium had always been afraid to form an intellectual elite qualified to replace European civil servants and technicians. This paternalism had grave consequences. There were fewer than twenty Congolese university graduates in 1960, though now there are more than twenty hundreds.

Secondly, Belgian colonial authorities did their utmost to stifle any political awakening among the Congolese. It was only after persistent local agitation and pressure from other countries that Belgium granted political rights to her Congolese subjects. In 1960, there were almost as many political parties as there were major tribes in the Congo. This was used by the Belgians to prove that the Congo was not ripe for independence. Today, the number of political parties has been officially reduced to one. Not many Congolese now seriously envisage the creation of political parties on a tribal basis.

Thirdly, communications developed in the Congo by the colonizers had one main objective: to ensure easy access to the Atlantic Ocean in the west, and to the Indian Ocean in the east – for the exportation of products and raw materials. Inter-regional communication was never regarded as a major consideration. This lack of foresight later had serious social consequences on the national emancipation of the Congolese people. Moreover, the Belgian colonial power strongly maintained and protected the monopolistic privileges introduced into the Congo from the time of King Leopold II onwards.

In the military sphere, Belgian colonial administration never envisaged the building of a Congolese army as such. The *Force Publique* which existed before 1960 was rather a police force for the maintenance of law and order throughout the country and was under the direction of Belgian officers. The higher posts in the army, the police, and the public services have been the exclusive preserve of the Belgians. No Congolese had any hope of rising to the lowest commissioned rank in the army. The whole of the *Force Publique* (today the Zaire National Army) was subject to extremely harsh discipline and soldiers received very low pay. This situation made it impossible to build up a cadre of Congolese personnel to man the services. Here again, Belgian short-sightedness had tragic consequences.

Belgian methods of colonization profoundly affected the thinking of the Congolese masses. They created false notions, false fears, and false conceptions of reality. Any thought which did not have its roots in the Catholic religion was deemed 'not conducive to the public good'. However, with time, a few Congolese began to discover other ideologies, other conceptions of politics, society, and religion. But the habit of thinking along narrow lines is not easy to lose. Many errors of judgment, some of them tragic, have been made because of this.

The Congo since 1960

On 30 June 1960, the Congo became an independent and sovereign state. The basic cause of political instability lies in the economic system and the exploitation methods of the former colonial power. The viability of the Congo as a nation depends

351

partly on reorientation of the economy towards those interests especially beneficial to the country and to Africa as a whole. Since independence, the Congo has been no longer under Belgian paternalism but under a 'collective western paternalism'. Since independence, one can rightly say that the Congo is economically 'an international colony'. It is a humiliating fact that, in spite of all that has happened, many principal decisions on which the whole future role of the Congolese people depend have been made more often in Europe and in America than in Africa. Not so many Congolese are aware of the strong financial, economic, and military links which exist between various industrialized western countries. Therefore it is difficult for them to know the truth about the history of the Congo-Zaire. It is even more difficult but not impossible to know exactly what happened in the Congo and what the future holds for the Republic of Zaire.

Who is Mobutu?

I hope that time will permit me to write a book on *The rise and fall of Mobutu* dealing with the internal affairs of Congo-Zaire and the politics of general-president Mobutu. I recognize that my short and quick evaluation of a man in the middle of his political career will be reviewed and extended one day when Mobutu will no longer be head of state of Zaire.

Like Patrice Lumumba, Joseph Kasavubu, and Moise Tshombe before him, Mobutu's era will be one day part of Congo's history. No one is immortal and no one is indispensable in any given country.

A brief look at Mobutu's role in Congolese affairs during the colonial period and the time of Lumumba's leadership has been already mentioned in this first volume of my political memoirs.

Joseph-Désiré Mobutu is now Mobutu Sese Seko Kuku Ngendu Wa Za Banga and general-president for life of the Congo-Zaire.

Since 1966, Mobutu has been following in Lumumba's footsteps, and it seems that through Mobutu many of the ideas and thoughts of Lumumba have been made public and preached all over the country as Mobutu's thoughts and ideas. The *Preamble* of the *Manifesto of N'Sele*, the document which founded the Mouvement Populaire de la Revolution (MPR), Mobutu's political party, states as its aims: to build up a truly independent Congo, to adopt nationalism as its doctrine, to restore the authority of the State and its international prestige, to give priority to the economy over politics by achieving sound financial situation, stable currency, and controlled economy.

It could be said that Mobutu has been trying very hard to emulate Patrice Lumumba and to achieve the various basic goals mentioned in the N'Sele Manifesto. Apparently, Zaire is no longer an underdeveloped country but underequipped. In his speech at the United Nations on the 4 October 1973, Mobutu stated, 'We, in Zaire, prefer the term "equipment" to that of "development" and there is no disgrace in recognizing that we are behind in terms of equipment in comparison with many countries in the world . . .'[1]

Mobutu enjoys great confidence in the Western World. Quoting from the press conference he gave in Washington during his official visit to the United States in August 1970, Mobutu answered as follows when asked about guarantees for investments in the Congo:

. . . We have settled all conditions to guarantee the foreign investments in my country. Political stability, a hard-working nation unified behind its leader, resources that many of you have called unbelievable, the investment code we issued a year ago, these are the guarantee conditions we offer and I don't believe foreign investors need more. Besides what is clearly spelled out in this investment code, we never thought of touching foreign properties or, if you will, of nationalizing them. This is excluded from my policy, excluded from my economic standpoint.

However, it should be noted that, in November 1973, Mobutu announced the nationalization of all foreign agricultural companies operating in Zaire, although he promised compensation for seized properties. He did not limit the take-over to large foreign companies controlling cotton or palmoil production, but

1. Address by His Excellency General Mobutu, General Assembly, United Nations, New York, 4 October 1973, UN Documents A/PV. 2140, p. 51.

extended it to 'farms, cattle-raising, small trade, and real estate agencies' as well as plantations. In his words, the 'time has come for the Zaire citizen to become owner of the grounds of his ancestors'. He also announced that one of his goals was national control of all Zaire's copper ore, which would, according to plans, be processed in Zaire after 1980.

Other measures announced at that time by Mobutu included a take-over in the insurance field, the organization of a new shipping agency, and creation of a new state-controlled contractor group. To avoid frightening the capitalist world, Mobutu's decrees were called 'zaireianization' and not nationalization. Only Mobutu himself understands fully the difference between the two concepts. More recently, Mobutu has reversed most of his former decrees by de-nationalizing what he has previously nationalized or 'zaireinized'. Many observers are now convinced that Mobutu is an opportunist with an extraordinary instinct of survival and without any given ideology in the western sense.

Beyond Mobutu and authenticity

An old African proverb says that 'it is only those who walk that have dust on their feet'. Since 1960, Mobutu has been walking. But, since 1965, he has been doing better – he has been running. Only the passage of time will fully reveal what Mobutu has been able to accomplish in relation to what Zaire will have lost, gained, or overcome during this long walk and seemingly exhausting race.

One must recognize and accept the fact that, in his increasingly accelerating race, Mobutu hopes to give a new direction to the history of his country. But, of greater interest, he believes of having initiated the birth of a new concept – perhaps a new ideology – which cannot as yet be judged. It is a question of authenticity, or better still, of authenticism.

To attempt a definition of *authenticity*[2] is not easy. Is it a doctrine or an ideology? Is it a *leitmotif* for progress, or merely the rallying call of a carefully considered policy? It should be

2. 'Authenticity' will henceforth be translated as ideality, self-consciousness, self-awareness, self-realization, etc.

possible to qualify this concept of self-identity as a theory, a doctrine, and a political alternative.

One must avoid, however, becoming the prisoner of a specified definition. These formulations will be refined as they evolve and are put into practice.

There is a dynamic to ideas just as there is one to history and human lives. The belief in the concept of 'authenticity' appears to have become the raison d'être of Mobutu's policy, the tool on which he sharpens his thoughts and his beliefs about his country, about Africa, and perhaps about the world in general.

Can this doctrine of self-identity be made into a religion? Once launched, of course, ideas can no longer be controlled by their originators; for they give rise to fanatics and zealots who evolve, deform, or shape them into extremes which their inventor might possibly not have desired, but which he will be unable to prevent or to guide.

In the course of exercising military and political power, Mobutu recognized a certain usefulness, the necessity even, of turning to 'authenticity'. Mobutu's actions and decisions, his general policy and outlook upon world problems, seem to be based upon 'authenticity'. As noted above, it will take some time before one could define exactly what Mobutu understands by this philosophy or ideology. When he is confronted by critics, Mobutu summarizes his thoughts by saying that authenticity is

a dictate of conscience for the people of Zaire that they should return to their beginnings and search for the values of their ancestors in order to appreciate those which contribute to the country's harmonious and natural development. It is the refusal of the people of Zaire blindly to espouse imported ideologies. It is the affirmation, by a man of Zaire or by any man wherever he may be, of the mental and social structures that are his own.[3]

And so, in order to avoid referring to the ideas of Patrice Lumumba, to separate himself from the positive neutralism of Kwame N'Krumah, and to reject the fact that Zaire is practically

3. Address by His Excellency General Mobutu, General Assembly, United Nations, New York, 4 October 1973. UN Documents A/PV. 2140, p. 51.

under military rule or to use Ahmed Soekarno's term, a 'guided democracy', Mobutu has found this new explanation and motivation for all his actions and decisions. Mobutu's search for originaity, his pride in being African, his obstinate insistence on being accepted as such, his ambition to be equal to other eminent strongmen and heroes of the history of Africa or the world, his excessive self-esteem, all of this and perhaps more, could be the origin of the birth and promotion of authenticity.

In the Congo-Zaire, authenticity has been made an official and national ideology under the name of 'mobutuism'. This is the term used in the existing constitution. Fortunately, instead of preaching and practising the new religion of 'mobutuism', many Congolese have started looking beyond Mobutu and authenticity, since the history of the Congo, that of the Congolese people, will remain dynamic and not stagnant.

Mobutu's Foreign Polisy: a tightrope diplomacy

In his foreign policy, Mobutu has been unpredictable and opportunistic. Early on, in the 1960s, he was known as being pro-Israel and against the Arabs, pro-West and against the Communist World. In the 1970s, without any kind of prior warning, he has become, at least in his official statements, a non-aligned African leader; since 1972, the Republic of Zaire has been active in all international conferences, siding – on paper and in theory – with other non-aligned countries. Mobutu's speech at the United Nations on 4 October 1973 is still considered a masterpiece of opportunistic diplomacy. He denounced racial segregation – apartheid in South Africa; he broke diplomatic relations with Israel by a now-famous phrase: 'Zaire has to choose between a friendly country, Israel, and a brother nation, Egypt. But between a friend and a brother the choice is clear, and our decisions are made in full independence and freedom from all pressures.'

Secretly he had assured the racist regime in South Africa that he was not really going to fight them with arms, only with words; as for Israel, he kept his long-term agreement with the Israelis to continue supervising and training his intelligence service throughout the world and at home.

Earlier on in this speech he had described the Middle-East situation from the Zaireian point of view:

In the Middle-East there exist three kinds of reflexes: the reflex of fear, for the Israeli people; the reflex of despair, for the Palestinian people; and the reflex of humiliation, for the Arab people . . .
Zaire, which has now reached the moment when it must choose, must dispel all misunderstandings and remove a certain ambiguity resulting from its African vocation.

Later on in that United Nations speech, Mobutu denounced the injustices committed by the rich countries towards the poor countries. He claimed that Zaire could not be in the pay of the great Powers that harbour racists among them for the sake of their alliances.

The foreign policy of Zaire under Mobutu is a tightrope diplomacy. Mobutu is and remains a great friend of the Western powers; he owes much to these powers since Zaire has been kept well within the Western orbit. This fact acts as a limitation to Mobutu's initiatives, thinkings, and decision-making. During the last few years, Mobutu has been active among the more progressive African countries and militant non-aligned countries of the Third World. The central question here is the extent to which the Western world will continue to support and use Mobutu in his foreign policy, which seems to serve the vital interests of the USA and the Western bloc and which does not fall within the revolutionary context as outlined by Patrice Lumumba.

Like the late General Charles de Gaulle, Mobutu exalts the prestige and grandeur of the state. In most of his actions and decisions, he tries very hard to rehabilitate the former Belgian Congo in the face of international opinion. In the Manifesto of Mobutu's political party, the MPR, it is said that 'Congolese revolution is nationalist and pragmatic, with nothing to learn from other borrowed ideologies such as capitalism, socialism, or communism.'

The foreign policy of Zaire has been called 'sound' in the Western press and some commentators have gone so far as to suggest that this foreign policy could provide the model for all Africa.

Mobutu impressed the world when explaining the importance of Zaire in world affairs. He quoted the well-known revolutionary thinker Frantz Fanon who wrote that: 'Africa looked like a revolver whose trigger is placed in the Congo.' It is precisely for this reason that the foreign policy of Zaire could determine the evolution or stagnation of the situation in Black Africa. The Western powers were stunned to hear Mobutu announce that from now on he feels committed to the liberation of Africa and Africans. In fact, he said:

It is therefore an imperative political duty for Zaire to make its material and military contribution to all its neighbours that are still subjected to colonialism of any sort. Zaire as a whole is mobilized to fight against all the racists and colonialists of Southern Africa. If we must place our finger on the trigger of the African revolver of Frantz Fanon, Zaire is ready to shoulder all its responsibilities. All countries that call themselves our friends will be on our side, and in practical fashion. For as far as we are concerned, such passivity in this field is equivalent to complicity. My country is ready to undertake this sacred struggle, whatever may be the sacrifices involved. And we shall never retreat, regardless of what may happen, regardless of what it may cost.[4]

This verbal commitment follows the lines of Patrice Lumumba's nationalism. Whether this statement can be interpreted as calculated audacity or heroic determination is a question which would be at this point difficult to answer. It is now a fact that in the Angolan war of liberation, Mobutu was used as usual by the USA, the Western powers and the white racists of South Africa.

During his early days in power, General Mobutu enjoyed the backing of Israel – the aid and assistance of Israeli civilian experts and Army officers. This well-known alliance did not prevent Mobutu from joining – in theory – the ranks of the non-aligned heads of state who decided to support the struggle of the Palestinian people in the Middle East. Addressing the General Assembly in October 1973 Mobutu went further that day and broke off diplomatic relations with Israel, 'until Egypt

4. Ibid., pp. 59–60.

and the other Arab countries involved shall have recovered their territories at present under occupation'. Despite this spectacular gesture, Mobutu is still a very close friend and supporter of Israel. His verbal support for the liberation movement is also extended to Asia. The Zairese President encouraged the people of Vietnam, Laos, and Cambodia to determine their futures without foreign intervention. Zaire has established diplomatic relations with both North and South Korea from the time Mobutu visited Peking in January 1973, and about the same time Zaire broke off diplomatic relations with Formosa. In fact, the new and close relations between Zaire and the People's Republic of China may result in some interesting developments in central and southern Africa. Many political observers who were puzzled by the sudden change in Mobutu's attitude *vis-à-vis* Communist China have recognized that this new attitude is in accordance with American general policy opposing China with USSR. In the 60s, Mobutu said that no communist Chinese will set foot in Kinshasa as long as he is the president of Zaire. When the Peking's regime was admitted to the United Nations Zaire was one of the few non-aligned countries to have abstained.

Mobutu's first visit to Peking was in January 1973 with the approval and encouragement from Washington, eight months after the American president Richard M. Nixon had also discovered Peking and the communist Chinese. Mobutu returned home fascinated by the Chinese-inspired policy of self-reliance through self-help. He interpreted this policy as being similar to his concept of authenticity. Mobutu visited China for the second time in December 1974 and the third time in May 1975. A few years ago, any close relations between the People's Republic of China and Congo-Mobutu could have been interpreted as being a form of Communist infiltration in the heart of Africa. Today, the presence of more than seven hundred Chinese communists in Zaire is accepted as being the normal technical assistance from one friendly country to another. For Mobutu, the Chinese are now Chinese and not Communists; the Americans are Americans and not capitalists; the North-Koreans are Koreans and not Communists; the French, the British, the Germans and the Belgians are Europeans and not neo-colonialists. The only communists left in the world – as seen by Mobutu – are the Soviets, the Cubans, and the East-Germans.

It is still to be seen whether Mobutu's authenticity will remain distinctly African in the face of the growing influence and permanent contact with foreign and imported ideologies.

Mobutu seems to answer this question by pretending to look at the world today as being divided not in terms of a Communist and non-Communist world, but in terms of well-equipped and under-equipped countries. He confirmed this view when he said:

We should always have present in our minds the fact that the world is at a crossroads. It is no longer divided by ideology, nor even all that much by race or by political geography, but rather by economics, and this is the real essence of the question of relations among the peoples of the world today.[5]

One wonders why it took Mobutu so long before discovering the realities of international politics.

In 1960, Patrice Lumumba was labelled 'communist' and was murdered because he wanted the Congo to deal freely with all peace-loving countries of the world.

Under Patrice Lumumba, the Congo was the trigger of the revolver which could have liberated the African continent. Time will show if it is still true under Mobutu. Congo-Zaire remains the country of surprises.

Lumumbaism preceded Mobutuism and it seems that Mobutuism is paving the way for socialist revolution in Zaire. The country has reached the point of no return.

5. U.N. speech, 4 October 1973.

Appendix I

GENERAL TREATY OF FRIENDSHIP, AID AND
COOPERATION BETWEEN THE CONGO AND BELGIUM

29 June 1960

The major parties to this contract
Considering that it is in their common interest to maintain between them the bonds of friendship and solidarity, with respect to the sovereignty of each of their two independent states
Have arrived at the following agreements:

Article I

The major parties to this contract conclude between them a General Treaty of friendship, aid and technical cooperation. They will undertake mutual collaboration on an equal footing, and act in consultation on all matters of common interest.

Article II

The Belgian government will place at the disposal and under the authority of the Congolese government, in agreed conditions of common interest, staff to help in the administrative, judiciary, military, cultural, scientific and educational spheres.

Article III

Aid and cooperation in the social, economic and financial spheres will be determined by agreed conventions of mutual advantage.

Article IV

The agreements discussed in Articles II and III will be based on the resolutions and labours of the Round Table Conference and the Economic and Social Conference.

Appendices

Article V

In order to secure that the Congo is represented, and its nationals and interests protected throughout the world, the Belgian government will collaborate with the Congolese government; particularly –

In being prepared to represent the Congo wherever the Congolese government may wish

In placing at the disposal of the Congo, in so far as the Congolese government may ask, members of the Belgian ministry of foreign affairs

Article VI

Any military intervention by Belgian forces stationed in the bases in the Congo will only take place at the express demand of the Congolese minister of national defence. Later agreements will determine the handing over of the Belgian military bases in the Congo, and the exact forms of cooperation desired by the two governments.

Article VII

The governments of Belgium and the Congo will exchange diplomatic missions which will enjoy a special status in addition to the ordinary powers, privileges and immunities accorded to every embassy. The heads of these missions will take part in the Committee of Ministers provided for in Article IX. They will also, on invitation, be able to be present at committees of the ministers of the other contracting party. These prerogatives will enable them to have a particular status in international protocol.

Given the importance of the problems to be dealt with between the two states, the Congo may be represented in Belgium by a minister of the government of the republic.

In order to carry out the programme of aid and cooperation mentioned in Articles II, III, V and VI of this treaty, the Belgian diplomatic mission in the Congo will include a technical aid mission.

Article VIII

As regards matters of commerce, shipping and public decisions of any kind, the two contracting parties agree to grant each other as favourable a treatment as they would grant any other state by reason of a special agreement, and not to give any other state a more favourable agreement than they grant each other.

Article IX

In order to secure the fullest effective collaboration as desired in Article I, the governments of the two contracting parties and their representatives will arrange regular meetings and discussions.

Article X

Any litigation arising out of the application of this treaty which cannot be decided at once by the application of Article IX, will be worked out through an arbitration procedure established in a separate agreement.

Article XI

Separate agreements will be made to define the application of the agreements planned in Articles II, III, V, VI, VII, VIII, IX and X.

Article XII

The treaty will apply indefinitely. Each of the contracting parties may abrogate it at any moment by giving a year's notice, dating from the 31 December of any year.

The Prime Minister of the Congo P. Lumumba	*The Prime Minister of Belgium* G. Eyskens
The Minister of Foreign Affairs of the Congo J. Bomboko	*The Minister of Foreign Affairs of Belgium* P. Wigny
	The Minister of African Affairs A. E. De Schrijver

Appendix 2

At a meeting held on the evening of 13 July, the Congolese government expressed its wish that Belgium should withdraw the troops at Njili airfield, Léopoldville, before 5 a.m., 14 July.

At the same meeting, Mr Kanza, minister for United Nations affairs, also announced that the Congo had addressed a complaint to the security council about the presence of Belgian troops on the Republic's territory.

The security council has taken the following decisions on the subject:
1. Belgian troops shall be withdrawn, and 2. United Nations troops shall be sent.

The permanent representative of Belgium stated that Belgian troops would stay until the United Nations troops had the situation well in hand. Although this statement was not approved by Tunisia and the Soviet Union, it was expressly approved by the other members of the council, including the United States.

The Belgian government therefore asks me to inform you:

1. that Belgium is ready to implement the decisions of the United Nations and
2. that Belgium accordingly undertakes to withdraw its intervention troops when and where public order has been effectively restored by United Nations troops.
3. Belgian troops will remain as long as necessary to ensure security.
4. The Belgian government asks the Congolese government to co-operate in the re-establishment of security.
5. The Belgian government draws the attention of the Congolese government to the grave responsibility that it would incur should it act against the decision of the highest international authority.

6. The Congolese government should, in particular, avoid any steps constituting unnecessary provocation and dangerous incitement.

A few hours later he received a letter from the prime minister:

Your Excellency,

I have the honour to confirm to you the decision made by the chief of state of the Republic and his government, to break off all diplomatic relations with Belgium, dating from 14 July 1960. This decision has been indicated by telegram to the prime minister of Belgium in Brussels, to the secretary general of the United Nations, and to yourself.

You may find it useful to see the full text of the telegram, which follows:

FOLLOWING FIRST BELGIUM'S FLAGRANT VIOLATION OF THE TREATY OF FRIENDSHIP OF 29 JUNE WITH THE REPUBLIC OF THE CONGO AS TO THE CLAUSE STATING THAT BELGIAN TROOPS COULD NOT BE USED ON CONGOLESE TERRITORY WITHOUT EXPRESS REQUEST BY THE GOVERNMENT OF THE CONGO AND SECOND BECAUSE OF THE ATTACK ON OUR TERRITORIAL INTEGRITY WHICH BELGIUM HAS COMMITTED IN PROVOKING THE SECESSION OF KATANGA WHICH ATTACK WAS PROVED FIRST BY THE BELGIAN TROOPS' REFUSAL TO PERMIT THE CHIEF OF STATE TO LAND IN ELISABETHVILLE TUESDAY 12 JULY AND SECOND BY THE NOMINATION OF A BELGIAN OFFICER TO COMMAND THE ARMY IN KATANGA, OUR GOVERNMENT HAS DECIDED IN CONSEQUENCE OF THE ACT OF AGGRESSION AGAINST THE REPUBLIC OF THE CONGO TO BREAK OFF ALL DIPLOMATIC RELATIONS WITH BELGIUM FROM THIS DAY 14 JULY 1960.

Furthermore, during today's session, the parliament of the Republic of the Congo has unanimously approved the decision made by the head of state and the government in breaking off relations. This will of course involve the closing of the Belgian embassy in the Congo and the departure of all its staff.

A return to diplomatic relations with Belgium can only be considered after the departure of the Belgian troops, and the evacuation of the Kamina and Kitona bases.

Parliament has decided that the Belgian troops at present operating in Léopoldville, Luluabourg, Elisabethville, the Lower Congo, and throughout the territory of the Republic shall leave today, the 15

July 1960, all the places where they may be by six p.m. precisely.

I ask you, therefore, to make all arrangements to have the decision of our parliament scrupulously carried out.

The Belgian troops at present in the Congo, for instance those stationed in Kitona and Kamina, must leave the territory of the Republic within 12 hours, starting from six p.m. today.

Our government, thanks to the aid given us by the UN and Ghana, will itself ensure the protection both of our own nationals and of all foreigners.

As a sovereign country, there can be no justification for a foreign country, in this case Belgium, to meddle in the internal affairs of the Republic of the Congo. The sending of Belgian troops to the Congo, decided unilaterally by your government in violation of Article 6 of the treaty of friendship and aid signed on 29 June 1960, constitutes an act of aggression. I wish also to point out to you that today's session of the parliament of the Republic of the Congo has refused to ratify that treaty, since your government has already violated it by sending troops to occupy the Congo.

Let me here express the sentiments of friendship of the Congolese people towards all Belgians of good will who remain in the Congo, whether as technicians, businessmen, or in other capacities.

Your obedient servant,

Patrice Lumumba
Prime Minister

Appendix 3

The first troops from the UN arrived at Njili airport last night, Friday. They were Tunisian. The first contingents of Ghanaians came by air this morning. A lot more troops will be following in the next few days; they will be drawn from the armies of Ethiopia, Ghana, Morocco and Tunisia.

I want to make certain points about these troops absolutely clear. They will bear arms, but will only use them in legitimate self-defence. They come here as friends of the Congolese people. Most of them come from independent African nations, sister-nations of this one. But they are made up of mixed elements, with both officers and soldiers liable to be white or black, all working together whole-heartedly.

The UN forces in the Congo are forces for peace. They will do everything they can to help restore calm, harmony, and safety for all, whites as well as blacks, in this troubled land. They will function exclusively under the control and command of the UN.

The UN's appeal for food to prevent a serious crisis here has met with a wonderful response. Large quantities of foodstuffs are on their way here by air, and we have worked out a system of distribution in consultation with the government.

I would like to ask you all not to expect miracles. The UN has gone into action very quickly, for it was only last Tuesday that I received the appeals addressed to the UN by the Congolese government. It will take some time to put everything to rights, and to close the wounds so recently inflicted. There has been enough of violence. Too many people have been hurt; too many killed. There now exist tension, fear and bitterness that are dangerous indeed. I hope that everyone – both government and people – will give evidence of patience and moderation in the next few days. This alone can save your marvellous country from disaster.

367

Appendix 4

It is a privilege and an honour for us, the representatives of the United
Nations, to welcome you today, Mr President, as our guest on Congolese soil, in a demonstration of the close cooperation established by
your government with the United Nations, acting as we are upon your
request, and for as long as may be necessary to achieve the end in
view.

Cooperation is always based on trust. And trust is in turn reinforced by experience of good cooperation. Franklin D. Roosevelt,
during the dark days of the great depression, told his compatriots that
the only thing they must fear was fear itself. Altering his expression,
but with a similar meaning, I should like to say that, in our cooperation, the only thing we need mistrust is mistrust itself. Our relationship
has only just begun, but we know one another well enough to realize
that there is absolute harmony as to our mutual objectives, and as to
the relationship between the UNO and this Republic as one of its
future members, as well as the rôle of the UN in working disinterestedly
for your service.

We shall try, by giving a help whose nature and scope must be
determined by your needs as you see them, to supply what you lack,
and give you the support you need. But we want to do so only to the
degree that, and for as long as, the creative forces of the Congolese
people and nation cannot take care of your needs by their own vitality
and their own resources.

During troubled times, and under conditions of a complexity rare in
modern history, it is only too natural that misunderstandings should
arise under the stress of intense emotion and the difficulty of seeing our
way clearly through the complex of factors with which international
politics has to cope. It is above all at such moments that one must
'mistrust mistrust itself', for it is that that ruins relationships, weakens
our common effort, and undermines the very structure of society.

Gentlemen, you have an immense task – the task of giving the Congolese people and nation new life in peace and unity. You have come into the modern world and the framework of the great international family with the intention to follow a direct line determined by the interests of your people, and to create for them a destiny to correspond with their traditions and ideology.

In view of the overriding importance of integrating this Republic harmoniously into the great family of nations, part of the immense task you have before you is to explain to your people just what the United Nations is, what are its ideals and goals; and you must help them to realize that it will give you impartial support in your difficulties.

A great nation is not created in a day. Nor can the nation's rôle in the community of nations be made comprehensible in a matter of hours. The close cooperation we have established puts you in an exceptionally good position for fostering the integration of the people of this country into the world of today, as represented here and now by the UN.

You know that the UN action to help you was unanimously voted by the security council. This may give you some indication of your future destiny. A world divided over the Congo can only weaken you; a world united in supporting you will make the Congo stronger and more secure.

At every step, every turn of the road, a wrong choice of direction may imperil such unity. I am convinced that you are anxious to avoid any such wrong choices. You are undoubtedly equally anxious to avoid divisions among all peoples, especially the people of the Congo. In your attempts to find the right direction, look upon the UN flag as the symbol of a world united in supporting you and ready to give you a say in its councils – so that you will also be able to make your national contribution to the international cooperation whose colours that flag bears.

We are at the beginning of what will be a long road – your road. During the difficult first steps, we shall be happy to go with you, hand in hand. But after the first steps, once you feel secure in your own strength, and sure of your direction, you will walk alone – not of course abandoned by the United Nations, but with the same relationship with it that the other member countries also have: you will have access to its forum, receive the benefit of the experiences it has gained in its work, and you will be protected by the equilibrium to which all our efforts are directed for the purpose of that final peace we hope to see established.

In conclusion, Mr President, let me once again present you our best wishes, and renew the assurance of our assistance, which will be guided solely by the goals and principles of the United Nations' Charter, and thus remain ever free of any particularist influence, whether of a single group or a single ideology.

Appendix 5

Mr Deputy Prime Minister,

Your broadcast speech of 6 August 1960 relating to the situation in Katanga has been brought to my attention. I am writing because I want to make it clear that your statement is incorrect as regards the behaviour attributed to me, and I am sure that you would wish the facts to be correctly reported.

Your declaration speaks twice of negotiations between Mr Tshombe and myself in Léopoldville. I am surprised to see my talks with Mr Tshombe described in this incorrect way, since you were present at my interview with Mr Kasavubu on the night of 5 August, during which I gave a detailed account of my visit to Katanga, pointing out quite clearly that, during all my talks in Elisabethville, I stuck strictly to the mandate defined by Mr Hammarskjöld – which was to prepare the ground for the withdrawal of the Belgian troops and the entry of UN troops. I engaged in no negotiations of any kind with anyone in Elisabethville.

I note too that you refer to a declaration made by Mr Tshombe to the press after my interview with him. Is it possible that my own two press statements, one of which was made at almost the same time as Mr Tshombe's, can have escaped your attention? Since they would seem to have done so, let me sum up here what I said:

1. First statement, the night of 4 August: 'Bunche simply said that he would present the secretary general with a detailed report on the day's discussions. He explicitly said that he could make no decisions.'
2. Second statement, the morning of 5 August: 'I am in Elisabethville on Mr Hammarskjöld's instructions, to hold talks about the arrangements that must be made for the arrival of UN troops in Katanga and the implementing of the security council resolutions. To this point I have stuck. The UN is not concerned with the internal political affairs of this area, though clearly such affairs will affect UN operations. I have not taken, nor will I take, any decision here, and I have no

authority to do so. My function is to present as complete a report as possible to Mr Hammarskjöld of what has happened since my arrival yesterday afternoon.'

I will not discuss here the other parts of your statement, especially certain passages about the secretary general which I consider to be mis-statements. Since your statement has been published, I know that you will agree that it is desirable that this letter from me, rectifying the facts, should also be made public.

Appendix 6

... I wish also to thank the secretary general and his colleagues for the way and the spirit in which they have carried out the very delicate task of implementing the resolutions adopted by the council . . .

However, in view of the present difficulties, which are caused solely by the Belgians, the Congolese people has shown and is continuing to show a certain impatience and sense of urgency. This cannot be interpreted as a sign of mistrust. If there is any mistrust it is of Belgium, which as a member of the United Nations of long standing might be expected to set us an example of compliance with the resolutions adopted by the security council.

Everywhere, as you see, United Nations forces entered the Congo without meeting any resistance on the part of either our soldiers or our people, despite certain manoeuvres in regard to which we have damning evidence. Why then is there resistance in Katanga? The resistance is factitious. The opposition is created and kept alive by the Belgian government. It is entirely without politico-sociological, military or legal justification . . .

It has been proved that United Nations troops have been the subject of propaganda that is completely at variance with the spirit in which the United Nations wishes to undertake its operations in the Congo. It has been stated that United Nations troops were coming to Katanga not to restore order but to introduce communism and, should the occasion arise, to endeavour to strengthen Mr Lumumba's authority. This is the explanation of the opposition of the tribes in Katanga. We are convinced that with the departure of the Belgian troops, the apparent authority of the Katangan leaders in foreign pay will disappear . . .

While these operations [laying down of arms by Congolese], proving our goodwill, were being carried out, Belgian troops systematically looted our garrisons, collected the weapons and took them away. At

373

the same time, looting organized by the Belgian administrative authorities was draining the coffers of the Republic of the Congo, in the anticipation that the country's economy would collapse, which would have had very serious social consequences.

What is happening in Katanga ? The military occupation of Katanga by Belgian troops was carried out on the initiative of the Belgian authorities, without the Congolese authorities even being advised that it was taking place. When the troops arrived they supported Mr Tshombe and, as it were, forced him to proclaim the secession of Katanga from the rest of the Republic of the Congo. The Congolese soldiers unwilling to accept this decision were simply driven out of Katanga by the Belgian military command. The only opposition to the entry of the United Nations forces into Katanga is coming from Belgian forces reinforced by the political militia of the CONAKAT party, who have become, as if by magic, a so-called Katangan resistance force under the command of a Belgian general . . .

Before the recent incidents no problem had arisen between the provincial government of Katanga and the central government. The problem of Katanga, of which there is so much talk today, has been created artificially by the Belgian government. In fact, plans for secession, also encouraged by the Belgian authorities, have fortunately been discovered in the other provinces. I have documents on this subject available for the Council to study . . .

It is therefore incorrect to say that the problem is an institutional or constitutional one, since our Assembly, which, as I have said, is a constituent body, will shortly have to consider the most suitable structure for our young Republic. Nor, in consequence, can it be regarded as a domestic issue so long as foreign troops remain in the Congo. The immediate withdrawal of Belgian troops from the entire territory of the Republic, including Katanga and the bases at Kamina and Kitona, is the *sine qua non* for peace, order and unity in the Congo . . .

Appendix 7

TEXT OF GODEFROID MUNONGO'S STATEMENT TO THE
PRESS, ELISABETHVILLE, 13 *February* 1961

13 February 1961

Gentlemen,

I have brought you here to tell you of the death of Lumumba, and his
accomplices, Okito and Mpolo.

Yesterday evening, a Katangan from the Kolwezi area (no more
details) arrived at my private house to tell me that Lumumba, Okito
and Mpolo had been massacred yesterday morning by the people of a
little village quite a long way from the spot where the car was found –
so far indeed that we are still wondering how the three fugitives managed to get there.

Since receiving this news, I have informed Mr President Tshombe,
and the major local authorities.

This morning, we went to the place by plane. 'We' were various
people capable of identifying the three bodies: Mr Minister Kibwe,
Mr Minister Kitenge and myself.

We were accompanied by a doctor who was to provide a death certi-
ficate if they were in fact Lumumba, Okito and Mpolo. They were
identified, without any possible doubt, and their death can be established. The bodies were buried at once, where I shall not say, if only
to prevent pilgrimages being made there in the future.

Nor shall we reveal the name of the village where the unhappy
exploits of Lumumba and his accomplices came to an end. For we do
not want those Katangans – we shall not even say what tribe they
belong to – to be subjected to reprisals by any Lumumbists later on.

Nor do we wish to be subjected to any pressure to charge those
Katangans with murder, for though they may have acted somewhat
precipitately (particularly excusably so, in that they believed the
fugitives to be armed), we cannot honestly blame them for having rid
Katanga, the Congo, Africa and the world of a problem which some

people have exaggerated out of all proportion, and which therefore threatened to poison human lives all over the world.

That village will receive the reward of 400,000 francs promised by the Council of Ministers. And I now have nothing more to say of the circumstances in which the fugitives died.

I should be lying if I were to say I was sorry that Lumumba is dead. You know my feelings: he was a common law criminal . . .

I realize of course that the UN will say the whole thing was a plot, and that we killed him ourselves. That is only to be expected . . .

I will speak frankly as I always do. We shall be accused of having killed them, and my answer will be: 'Prove it' . . .

Even had we executed them (which is being said everywhere, but nowhere proved), I would categorically deny that the UN has any right to make a judgement in the case.

Appendix 8

My Dear,

I am writing this without knowing whether you will ever get it, or when, or whether I shall be still alive when you read it. Throughout my struggle for the independence of my country I have never for one instant doubted that the sacred cause to which my friends and I have given our lives would triumph in the end. But what we have wanted for our country, the right to honourable life, to untarnished dignity, to unrestricted freedom – these things have never been desired on our behalf by those important officials in the UN in whom we put our trust, and upon whom we called for help, because, whether they knew it or not, they were directly or indirectly supporting the colonialism of Belgium and her friends in the West.

They have corrupted the minds of some of our compatriots, others they have simply bought, and they have played their part in distorting truth and shackling our independence. What else can I say? Dead or alive, free or imprisoned by the colonialists, it is not I who matter. It is the Congo, it is our poor people whose independence has been turned into a cage in which we can be watched by those outside, either with positive pleasure, or with benevolent compassion. But my faith remains unshaken. I know, and I feel in my heart, that sooner or later my people will shake off all their enemies, inside and outside our land, and that they will rise as one man to say 'no' to the shame and degradation of colonialism, and to assume once again their dignity under clear skies.

We are not alone. Africa, Asia and the free and freed peoples all over the world will always stand beside those millions of Congolese who will not give up the struggle until the day when no colonizers and no mercenaries are left on our soil. I would like my children, whom I am leaving and may perhaps never see again, to be told that the Congo has a great future, and that it is up to them, as to every other Congolese, to carry out the sacred task of rebuilding our independence and our sovereignty; for where there is no dignity there is no freedom, and where there is no justice there is no dignity, and where there is no independence there are no free men.

No brutality, no agony, no torture has ever driven me to beg for mercy, for I would rather die with my head high, my faith unshaken, and a profound trust in the destiny of my country, than live in subjection, seeing principles that are sacred to me laughed to scorn. History will have its say one day – not the history they teach in Brussels, Paris, Washington or the United Nations, but the history taught in the countries set free from colonialism and its puppet rulers. Africa will write her own history, and both north and south of the Sahara it will be a history of glory and dignity.

Do not weep, my love; I know that my country, which has suffered so much, will be able to defend its independence and liberty.

Long live the Congo! Long live Africa!

Patrice

Appendix 9

THE LUMUMBA'S GOVERNMENT:
WHERE ARE THE MINISTERS TODAY?

I. *Ministers*

1. Prime Minister: Patrice Lumumba (murdered).
2. Vice-Prime Minister: Antoine Gizenga (in exile).
3. Foreign Minister: Justin Bomboko (alive and in Zaire).
4. Foreign Trade: Marcel Bisukiro (dead).
5. Minister Resident in Belgium: Albert Delvaux (alive and in Zaire).
6. Justice: Rémy Mwamba (dead).
7. Minister in charge of United Nations Affairs: Thomas Kanza (in exile).
8. Minister of Home Affairs: Christophe Gbenye (alive and in Zaire).
9. Minister of Finance: Pascal Nkayi (alive and in Zaire).
10. Minister for Economic Coordination and Planning: Aloys Kabangi (in Zaire).
11. Public Works: Alphonse Ilunga (alive and in Zaire).
12. Agriculture: Joseph Lutula (in Zaire).
13. Communications: Alphonse Songolo (murdered).
14. Economic Affairs: Joseph Yav (alive in Zaire).
15. Labour: Joseph Masena (assassinated).
16. Health: Grégoire Kamanga (alive in Zaire).
17. Mines and Power: Edmond Rudahindwa (in Zaire).
18. Social Affairs: Antoine Ngwenza (in Zaire).
19. Information: Anicet Kashamura (in exile).
20. Youth and Sport: Maurice Mpolo (murdered).
21. Local Trade and Industry: Joseph Mbuyi (murdered).
22. Education: Pierre Mulele (murdered).
23. Land: Alexandre Mabamba (murdered).

II. *Secretaries of State*

1. Joseph Mobutu (alive and in Zaire).
2. Jacques Lumbala (murdered).

3. Antoine Kiwewa (alive in Zaire).
4. André Tshibangu (alive in Zaire).
5. Maximilien Liongo (dead).
6. André Mandi (alive in Zaire).
7. Raphael Batshikama (alive in Zaire).
8. Albert Nyembo (alive in Zaire).
9. Antoine-Roger Bolamba (alive in Zaire).
10. Alphonse Nguvulu (alive in Zaire).

III. *Ministers of State*
1. Georges Grenfell (alive).
2. Charles Kisolokele (alive).
3. Paul Bolya (alive).
4. André Ngenge (dead).

None of the Ministers in Lumumba's government of 1960 holds any government office in Zaire today.

Index

Index

Index